The QUEST *for the*

ARK OF THE

COVENANT

As this book was going to press the Publishers received the sad news of the death of the author, Stuart Munro-Hay. It is their hope and expectation that this book will serve as a fitting tribute to his lifelong dedication to the study of Ethiopia and its people.

The QUEST *for the* ARK OF THE COVENANT

COVENANT

THE TRUE HISTORY
OF THE TABLETS OF MOSES

STUART MUNRO-HAY

I.B.TAURIS

LONDON · NEW YORK

Published in 2005 by I.B.Tauris & Co Ltd
6 Salem Road, London W2 4BU
175 Fifth Avenue, New York NY 10010
Website: http://www.ibtauris.com

In the United States and Canada distributed by Palgrave Macmillan,
a division of St. Martin's Press, 175 Fifth Avenue, New York NY 10010

ISBN 1-85043-668-1
EAN 978-185043-668-3

A full CIP record for this book is available from the British Library
A full CIP record for this book is available from the Library of Congress
Library of Congress catalog card: available

Typeset in Ehrhardt by Dexter Haven Associates Ltd, London
Printed and bound in Great Britain by TJ International Ltd, Padstow, Cornwall

Contents

Illustrations

Preface and Acknowledgements

The Quest for the Ark of the Covenant completes research I began in 1995 when writing *Ethiopia, the Unknown Land*, a guidebook to Ethiopia's historical sites (published by I.B. Tauris in 2002). To describe fittingly the church of Maryam Seyon at Aksum, and the adjacent chapel, supposed to house the Ark of the Covenant, it was crucial to investigate what allusions to the sacred relic existed in past literature. I summarised the available sources, and left it at that. I wondered, however, in passing why the object that supposedly arrived three thousand years ago in Ethiopia had so strangely obscure a recorded career.

Closer study was possible when I collaborated in writing *The Ark of the Covenant*, which Dr Roderick Grierson and I published in 1999. I concentrated on the Ethiopian material concerning the Ark, which swiftly outgrew the publisher's requirements. Information emerged not always narrowly related to the main theme of *The Ark of the Covenant* – the book's Ethiopian section focused chiefly on the Ark's contents, the tablets of Moses, and their transmutation over time into multiple 'Arks of the Covenant'. The most intriguing aspects of all, those directly associated with the Ark in Ethiopia, were left to this present book, *The Quest for the Ark of the Covenant*.

It is rare to find a theme so exotically attractive, so rich in the fields it covers, so challenging and intricate in analysis, that has received so little attention. For the benefit of my Ethiopianist colleagues, and others who require detailed references, I include a full apparatus of notes, citations of texts, and critical commentary. This was not (to my regret) part of the format proposed for *The Ark of the Covenant*.

I owe a substantial debt to friends and colleagues for their assistance, and express my thanks to them here. Three scholars contributed enormously, not just for this book, but for others in the past as well. My friend Dr Bent Juel-Jensen unstintingly helped with information drawn from his superb library, and many hours were passed in discussing certain problems and references. Dr W.L.G. Randles similarly shared not only his conversation, but also his library and his immense knowledge of important Portuguese sources, as well as translating the relevant documentation, for the first time in some cases, into English. Dr Greville Freeman-Grenville, with whom I have recently published *The Historical Atlas of Islam*, provided useful information about the topography of ancient Jerusalem, and the Holy Sepulchre, among other matters. Another good friend, Prince Asfa-Wossen Asserate, assisted with information on obscure points of Ethiopian literature.

During our collaboration on *The Ark of the Covenant*, Dr Roderick Grierson provided a useful supply of photocopies sent to me in Thailand, where the book was largely written. In Chiang Mai, Willis Bird several times saved my work by treating my computers for ailments induced by the tropical climate. Dr Pamela Taor and Dom James Leachman contributed with research into Catholic sources, while Murdo White kindly offered some comments on the completed typescript. The staff of the British Library and the Bibliothèque Nationale in Paris supplied information, or produced for my personal inspection manuscripts, incunabula and rare printed books of later times – one of the greatest pleasures when conducting research of this kind is studying such precious books as Caxton's *Golden Legend* or Foresti's works of the 1480s. More recently, as Visiting Professor at the Lepsius-Institut of the Humboldt-Universität zu Berlin, I received equal assistance from the staff of the Staatsbibliothek there.

Ethiopian, and in particular Aksumite, friends were of enormous assistance during my visits to Aksum and other places in Ethiopia. Without them, this book could not have taken the form it has. Because of the sensitivity of the issues discussed, touching on the deeply held faith of their own families and friends, their names cannot be included here. They will know who they are, and how greatly I have appreciated their help and advice, their hospitality and their many kindnesses.

I should also thank Graham Hancock, whom I have never met, but whose research assistant once approached me when I was lecturing at the British Museum for information on Aksum for *The Sign and the Seal*. At the time I thought that nothing useful could be said about the myth of the mysterious Ark, in whose aura I had lived for several months while working on the excavations at Aksum. I was wrong – in the end, it was Hancock's stimulating work that encouraged me to return once again to the presence of the Ark, and write this book.

Stuart Munro-Hay
Chiang Mai, Thailand

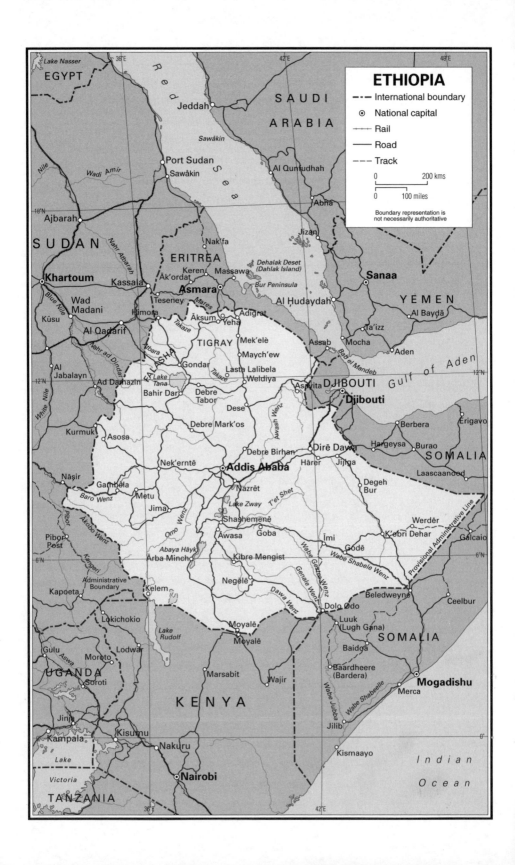

Introduction

N early two thousand years ago, a great African empire flourished in the highlands and torrid Red Sea coastlands of Ethiopia and Eritrea. It was ruled from a city in the province of Tigray, called Aksum.

Aksum is a realm of fable. The unusually rich traditions of this ancient, holy place range over many themes, unfolding a saga at once fascinating and elusive, in which kings and their wars, and monks and holy men with their miracle-filled lives, occupy a prime place. This is only to be expected for a city that once stood at the head of a mighty African realm, seat of a 'king of kings' and one of the first states in the world to adopt Christianity. For this reason, celebrated biblical figures, the queen of Sheba, and Candace, queen of Ethiopia, figure prominently in Aksum's myths, together with the apostles Matthew and Philip. The huge ancient stone monuments of the city – including some of the largest monoliths ever erected by man – are sufficiently imposing and enigmatic to have engendered a mythology of their own, focused around the major figures of Ethiopian legend or history. The wealth of the imperial centre was the stuff of later fantasy. The compilation called the *Book of Aksum* relates that once 'a rain of gold, pearls and silver fell at Aksum for eight days and nights…'

Central to Aksum, and its life both quotidian and mythological, is the old battlemented church of Maryam Seyon (Mary of Zion). Many tales about this superlatively sacred place are recorded in the antique Ethiopic parchment manuscript books, but one supreme mystery overshadows all else. In a chapel near the church there is kept, if we believe the Aksumite priests, the object that many regard as the most important religious relic of all time: the Ark of the Covenant. In the old Ethiopic or Ge'ez language it is called *tabota Seyon*, the Ark of Zion.

The Ark of the Covenant is a daunting subject, not least because it has so often been written about. Its significance, its mysterious powers and its even more mysterious disappearance and the 'conspiracy of silence' that seems to surround that disappearance in the Bible, have been the theme of endless conjecture. How could the central object of worship of a great religion, Judaism, the recognised source of two even greater world religions, Islam and Christianity, simply vanish without trace or even comment?

Naturally, this mystery has not remained unexplored. Generations of theories – more or less ingenious – are available to explain it. The 17th century Dutch Jewish philosopher Baruch Spinoza wrote in his *Tractatus Theologico-Politicus* that he found it 'strange that scripture tells us nothing of what became of the Ark of the Covenant; but there can be no doubt that it perished or was burnt along with the temple…' Others did not accept this simple explanation – the Ark lies under the Temple Mount in Jerusalem in a secret hiding place; High Priest Uzzi hid it in Mount Gerizim; it was taken to Arabia in the days of the Jurhum, lords of Mecca; the prophet Jeremiah concealed it in a cave in another mountain. Some say Jeremiah took it to Ireland, where it became the palladium of the High Kings of Tara…

Speculation today has grown increasingly extravagant. Several internet sites claim the Ark's 'discovery', always under circumstances that do not yet allow it to be revealed. Other tales describe Nazi searches for the Ark in the hope of utilising its terrible powers – this genre culminated in Steven Spielberg's film *Raiders of the Lost Ark*. Many web sites proclaim the real presence of the Ark in Aksum, with more or less ornate additions to the tale – Israeli plots to re-establish it in a restored Third Temple at Jerusalem, for example. Under the circumstances, it is not surprising if more sober scholars have been frightened off the subject.

The Ethiopian, particularly the Aksumite, situation, is a special case. There, the Ark retains an unusual prominence, being not merely a tantalising mystery of the past but a living daily presence. Aksum Seyon church is the only place in the world to claim actual possession of the ancient Ark of the

Covenant. Yet the Ark's story in this context has not been adequately told in any of the mass of literature available on Ethiopian religion or history. It is extraordinary that no Ethiopianist has yet tackled this subject, since the Ethiopians possess a book, called the *Kebra Nagast*, or 'Glory of Kings', directly relevant to the story of the Ark.

The book is of immense importance to Ethiopia's religious and political ideas – or at least to the official presentation of them at a certain period. The *Kebra Nagast* (henceforward *KN*) has been described as a national epic, the masterpiece of Ethiopian literature, a 'charter legend', even as an Oedipal myth. It has been published several times in modern European languages, and is cited frequently on Ras Tafarian and other internet web sites. It has even begun to assemble its own mythology. In one modern 'translation' (in which almost every word is copied directly from Sir E.A. Wallis Budge's 1922 version) the publishers state: 'lost for centuries, the *Kebra Nagast* is a truly majestic unveiling of ancient secrets. These pages were excised by royal decree from the authorised 1611 King James version of the Bible.' Even more recently, in the *Kebra Nagast. The Lost Bible of Rastafarian Wisdom and Faith*...the Budge translation was defined as something of quite exceptional rarity: 'the only extant copies...are at the British Museum and in some private collections'. Neither of these statements is true. They are part of the modern mythology of the *KN*, designed to add drama and an aura of the unattainable to the old Ethiopian epic. King James's translators had probably never even heard of the *KN*, while the Budge translation is often met with in booksellers' catalogues – it was not only reprinted but was issued in a second edition in 1932.

The *KN* states unequivocally that the Ark of the Covenant was transported to Ethiopia from Jerusalem during the reign of King Solomon of Israel, by a half-Ethiopian son of Solomon whose mother was no less a figure than the fabled queen of Sheba. His name was Ebna Lahakim or, a name apparently coined in more recent times, Menelik. Millions of Ethiopian Christians today, accepting the official position of their church on the matter, still believe that the Ark – the same object as that made on Moses' instructions in Sinai, brought to Jerusalem by King David, and later enshrined in King Solomon's temple in Jerusalem – returned with Ebna Lahakim to Ethiopia and now resides in a special shrine in the ancient imperial city of Aksum.

Because of the pre-eminence of the *KN* in Ethiopian literature, and because the imperial dynasty that fell with Emperor Haile Sellassie in 1974 claimed descent from Solomon and the queen of Sheba in accord with the

KN story, the subject crops up in passing in scholarly works on Ethiopia. Yet in every case – whether in the translations of the *KN* itself, or in books about Judaising tendencies, the Falasha (or Ethiopian 'black Jews') or Ethiopian Christianity – discussion about the Ark, a central element in the *KN*, remains brief and limited. This tremendous claim to possession of the world's most evocative religious talisman has never been thoroughly investigated in its Ethiopian context. Even in our recent book, *The Ark of the Covenant*, my colleague and I were able to offer only a brief summary of the story of the Ark at Aksum. What were for me the really intriguing elements – the search into the documentation relating to the Ark at Aksum and its history in Ethiopia, and the discovery of what it actually is – were left to this book.

'A RIDICULOUS FABLE'?

Even if millions of members of the Ethiopian Orthodox Church – the faithful are estimated at some 25 million strong, and church estimates are said to enlarge this to over 34 million – unquestioningly accept the *KN* story, there have been notable exceptions among prominent modern Ethiopian scholars. The Falasha historian Tamrat Amanuel, who died in 1963, rejected the relevance of the queen of Sheba to Ethiopian history. He denied it with vehemence, too, blaming the clergy and the rulers for keeping the people in ignorance of their real past in favour of a myth. Kidane Wald Kefle (d. 1944) considered that far from being a matter of pride, this history of the 'Solomonid travesty' Menelik merely discredited its author in the eyes of the learned.[1] Other distinguished Ethiopian historians of today also reject it, in common with many of their compatriots who have left the traditional church. A non-committal middle path, mentioning the Solomonic claim but not enlarging upon it, was evidently considered the safer path by certain non-Ethiopian writers during Emperor Haile Sellassie's lifetime. Their scholastic vested interests lay in Ethiopia. There was no point in upsetting the country's absolute ruler by questioning a story in which he apparently believed implicitly, to the extent of including it in the imperial Constitution.

A similar vagueness, almost avoidance, of the subject of the Ark, is typical of books on the Ethiopian church. This includes even those written by Ethiopians themselves under church auspices. But there are exceptions. Despite the hedging and uncertain phraseology conspicuous in interviews with priests on this subject, one Ethiopian cleric, Kefyalew Merahi, in a 1997 book, instead delivers a bombastic defence of the presence of the genuine Ark at Aksum. Behind him, as we shall see, is the significant support of Ethiopia's present patriarch, *Abuna* Pawlos.

The Ethiopian Orthodox Church has itself changed radically, becoming only relatively recently an Addis Ababa centred body under its own patriarch, after 1600 years of control from Alexandria. In mediaeval times, the Egyptian bishop appointed for Ethiopia led a peripatetic life, following the royal camp, with a more settled period later from the 1630s when Gondar became the semi-permanent capital. Some bishops who opposed the imperial will were sent back, or imprisoned, but in general they were kept close to the imperial person, and under strict control. It was the monasteries that were the centres of theological controversy in Ethiopia, and these it was harder for the kings to keep under their thumb. Flogging and savage punishments, or exile, did not always squash this powerful opposition party, which sometimes took on the monarchy itself. Their arguments were often debated before the king, ranging far and wide over the scriptural world. Such incidents were not remote sidelines to political life. They were considered important enough for citation in the royal chronicles, quoting pages of biblical text and discussion. Astonishingly, considering the Ethiopian claim to its possession, the Ark – supposedly the 'sign and seal' of God's mandate to the Ethiopian Christians as the New Israel – never figures in such debates, even though relevant to some of the themes. These at first mainly concerned Sabbath observance, the worship of Mary and the Holy Cross, and accusations against heretic Christians said to be 'like Jews': an intriguing indictment in a nation priding itself on its Israelite heritage. Later, after exposure to Jesuit argument in the 16th and 17th centuries, Ethiopian debate centred on elaborate distinctions in the nature of Christ.

Outright rejection of the story of Solomon and the queen of Sheba, and the Ark, has been the usual verdict of foreign writers not concerned with the vagaries of imperial favour. A. Murray's preface to the historical section of the 1805 edition of James Bruce's famous book about his search for the source of the Nile makes this quite clear: 'an ignorant monk' compiled 'a ridiculous fable, to please his countrymen'. For others, religious, racial or emotional attitudes have prevailed. The Ark as a great truth, vehicle of an identity with an African Zion or as the aim of a personal quest have characterised more recent writing.

Graham Hancock, the only writer to study the tradition of the Ark in Aksum at any length, perceived the Ark's presence there as a reality: it was 'the single ancient and recondite truth concealed beneath the layers of myth and magic' of the *KN*.[2] Ironically, despite Hancock's affirmation of the incredible legend of the Ark at Aksum, I have never met an Ethiopian who commends his book. Whether they are believer, agnostic or sceptic, the book's overburden of Templar knights, Freemasons and so on leaves them incredulous and irritated.

Ethiopian acceptance of the story – to the extent that it acted as a political manifesto for the claims of a ruling family – may have been far more limited than descriptions like 'national epic' would have one believe.[3] Ethiopia, however some writers may have represented it, has never been a monolithic society – far from it. The Solomonic monarchy ('Solomonic' is a common modern term for those Ethiopian rulers who claimed descent from the ancient king of Israel) even at its greatest strength always had its political and religious opponents, sometimes constituting important sections of the population, sometimes even entire provinces. Centrifugal tendencies were always active. The 'national epic', the *KN*, was not a common book in Ethiopian libraries. Although it is true that it enjoyed great prestige by the 17th century, this was primarily in clerical and ruling circles. Written in the Old Ethiopic language of Aksum, Ge'ez, the *KN* was only accessible to the learned, a tiny proportion of Ethiopian society.

The prominence of the book as we now interpret it may owe much to its connection with the so-called 'king of Seyon' (Zion), Emperor Yohannes IV of Ethiopia, 1872–89. He came from Tigray, where the old capital, Aksum, is situated. Certainly the *KN* was known and consulted earlier, in Emperor Iyasu I's reign (1682–1706) for example, but mention of it is very rare. Yohannes IV was a northerner, devoted to Aksum and its church of Maryam Seyon, where he was crowned in 1872 following a hallowed ritual that made him 'King of Zion of Ethiopia', as he expressed it on his official seal. Apparently he also felt a close interest in the epic work compiled there, the *KN*. To such an extent did he value it that he wrote to England – successfully – to retrieve from the British Museum a copy taken in 1868 by the British at the sacking of Maqdala. It is almost unheard of for the Museum to cede any object whatsoever: an Act of Parliament is required. It was a phrase in the emperor's letter, stating that his people would not obey him without it, that was at least partly responsible for the extraordinary reputation of the

KN today. But there is an anomaly here. Even if Budge and others cited it, this phrase does not appear in the original Amharic version of the imperial letter. The *Kebra Nagast* seems only to emerge in the guise of a 'true propaganda treatise' very late in Ethiopia's history, in the reign of Yohannes' successor, Emperor Menelik II (1889–1913).[4]

From what we know about the compilation of the *KN*, it derives from Aksum in the northern Ethiopian province of Tigray, though it was in the end employed to advance a claim to the universal throne by a dynasty from the more southerly province of Amhara. We should, perhaps, rather refer to it as the Tigray national epic. It was written there, by the chief of the clergy of Aksum, under the aegis of the local prince, and however much it might have been altered as time went on to fit it for another destiny – or for more than one – its origins lie firmly in Tigray. In Tigray and Eritrea there is still a rich fund of popular stories – regional rather than national – about a local queen, a serpent, and King Solomon as a great magician, strangely mixed with Christian elements like the Ark (or more than one Ark), Mary and local saints. Here, unlike anywhere else in Ethiopia, towns, villages, streams and other geographical settings are directly associated with the tale.

In addition, the *KN* story serves certain sections of the population as their myth of origin. They trace their descent, with some pride, from the companions of Menelik, son of Solomon and the queen of Sheba. This too is chiefly a northern phenomenon. The ancient Christianity of Aksum apparently did not penetrate deeply into the more southerly provinces of Amhara and Shewa until Solomonic times. When eventually it did reach these now central regions of Ethiopia, it brought with it the ingredients that developed into the Ark legend. Paradoxically perhaps, Amhara kings looked to Aksum in Tigray for legitimacy, to the epic work written there, the *KN*, for their ancestral charter, and – very occasionally – to Maryam Seyon church for confirmation of their rule through tonsuring and anointing ceremonies enacted there. Yet only in one single instance in the reign of Emperor Iyasu I was the Ark – the sacred object kept at Maryam Seyon church – singled out for detailed mention in the Ethiopian royal chronicles.

UNRAVELLING THE WEB

Now, at the dawn of the third millennium, the Ark is still supposed to remain in its chosen dwelling place, the church of Maryam Seyon in Aksum. More than that – whatever may be the final judgement of scholarship as to the precise nature of the sacred object concealed in the chapel of the Tablet of Moses at Aksum, the Ark, in a mystical, symbolic sense, *is* there: 'For those that can see them, the tents of Israel shine bright at Aksum.'[5] The belief of a large section of a Christian people reposes in the Ark, and in return it guards and protects them. Such belief may seem utterly irrational. Ethiopia is one of the world's poorest countries, living recently through decades of war and famine, yet an important section of a people that has suffered terribly from the worst that man and nature combined can inflict claims that the presence of God resides there and protects them. On such faith the arguments of scholars have about as much power of erosion as drops of water on rock. In the spiritual sense, there *is* an Ark of God at Aksum Seyon church. There, it holds a key position in the lives of many of the people. It is central to certain aspects of their faith, even of their identity. Its presence is a source of great pride among priests and laity alike, a pride reflecting first upon Aksum and its church of Maryam Seyon, then outwards, perhaps with rather diminishing fervour, to wherever Orthodox Christian Ethiopians are to be found. The Ark – with its contents, the tablets of Moses – is inextricably a part of Aksum, part of its history and that of Tigray and Eritrea, whatever might be the ultimate truth about its character or reality.

Retrospective or not, incredible or not, the Ark legend claims its connection with the city of Aksum over almost three thousand years. As an intimate and powerful part of Aksumite identity, the Ark calls for the same treatment that we have also given to Aksumite, religion, language, archaeology, architecture, chronology and other elements: serious study of its history. Yet until now it has not received it, being – presumably – either rejected as too obviously sensational a topic, or dismissed without serious consideration as a blatant piece of political mythmaking. The very mention of King Solomon of Israel, the queen of Sheba and the Ark of the Covenant in combination with an African country seems to smack more of the historical novel or alternative history. The sheer exoticism of the Ethiopian claim, perhaps, has discouraged scholars from pursuing this extraordinary subject. Otherwise – and with some reason – it may have been avoided as too sensitive a subject altogether. To question it seems to call into doubt a core belief of an entire ancient national church.

In the context of later Ethiopian history, regionalism, political thought and literature, too, there is much to be said, as the Ethiopian Christian matrix into which the Ark fits expanded further south over the centuries from imperial Aksum. The chronology of the development of the story of the Ark in Ethiopia is obscure and complex. There are great gaps. The Ark comes and goes. Elements of the story appear, disappear, revive, alter or die away according to the currents of the age, or the survival of documentation. Nothing is quite what it seems. Ethiopians recorded certain aspects of the story. Foreigners recorded others. Yet the material is there, to some degree, interwoven with other themes, with the rise and fall of dynasties, the identification with Israel, the history of the Ethiopian 'Jews' or of the 'Solomonic' dynasty of emperors. Part of the story concerns the Ethiopian *tabot*, the ubiquitous 'altar tablet' found in every church – this is a complex study in itself. Other elements are intermixed with the legends of saints and holy men compiled by Ethiopian literati, and the radical reinvention of Aksumite and later Ethiopian history. Finally, relevant to our own times, the Ark and the Solomonic dynastic legend culminating with Emperor Haile Sellassie, and the dream of the African Zion, receive significant attention as an intrinsic part of the Rasta belief.

What is really in the chapel of the Tablet of Moses at Aksum? By what authority is it claimed to be the Ark of the Covenant? Having set myself the challenge of resolving this enigma, it still required several years of research among the documents, and more visits to Aksum itself, before I could properly formulate my conclusions. The results were unexpected – divergent in almost all ways from those offered by the former journalist Graham Hancock. The exercise was not unlike preparing a legal brief. Readers will readily understand the cautious presentation of some of the material. At times, what seem like solid facts dissolve into a quicksand when analysed and interrogated. They offer no firm or reliable working basis. Much of what is said to be old – hoary customs or beliefs handed down from time immemorial – cannot actually be traced back more than a few centuries.

When, for example, I cite 13th or 14th century Ethiopian texts, they are in fact later copies. We may feel almost entirely confident that they have been properly copied, but there is always the possibility that some error has crept in, that in later transcription they have been tampered with. In some cases, we can actually document changes in an Ethiopian text, if older versions have survived. Newer versions simply claim the pedigree of the old, a palimpsest of ideas the latest of which is accepted as equal to the original. To us, this may seem odd, even unacceptable, but in the past the 'scientific', analytical mind-set was not typical. In other documents, the sheer ambiguity of the text counsels prudence in interpretation. I emphasise these uncertainties so that the reader can better judge the value of the evidence. Failing to consider the factual value or the original date of the material can result in major distortions of history – in fact, it already has.

In any research of this kind, where the date of composition of documents providing evidence is all-important, the discovery of indisputably dated information will modify gradually developing, tentative theories. This happened several times during my search. My ideas changed as research progressed. There were surprises. In the area where I most expected a shift as the study progressed from my earliest swift investigation – the chronology of the Ark's existence at Aksum – the evidence did not point in the direction I had foreseen.

For me, the important discovery was that the Ark at Aksum is not unattainable, a riddle that has no answer. By gradually unravelling the many strands of information – it is not a simple story, but a multi-layered conundrum – we can come to know it. New evidence or reassessment may well overturn aspects of this presentation; after all, one is limited by the data available, and this is always increasing. Or it may reaffirm it in unexpected ways. I offer here a survey of the diverse and fascinating story of Zion, the Ark of the Covenant in Ethiopia, from the days of King Solomon the Wise until the beginning of the third millennium.

1

Historical Outline

A first plunge into Ethiopia's past can leave a beginner stunned by the succession of unknown names and places, new customs and ideas. This summary of Ethiopian history introduces the main themes and names relevant to our story, embedded in a general chronological outline. In brief, and concentrating on the northern and central areas in which the events related in this book all occurred, we can describe Ethiopia's history in terms of the rise and fall of kingdoms or empires, separated by periods of extreme obscurity concerning which almost no documentation survives.

The monarchy named 'D'amat and Saba' on its own royal inscriptions consolidated its power in northern Tigray and Eritrea from perhaps 800 BC for a few hundred years. Its surviving monuments indicate strong associations with South Arabia, where similar material has been discovered. At Yeha in Tigray a large temple still stands in an area where a palace and tombs with rich grave goods have also been found. This may have been the central place of the polity. Particularly fascinating for our story is the name Saba, appearing so early in Ethiopian history. It gives an unexpected colour to Ethiopia's claim that the queen of Sheba came from there rather than from the kingdom of Saba in the Yemen.

As yet, archaeology has not properly explained the transition in northern Ethiopia and Eritrea from D'amat's authority to that of the next important local political manifestation: the kingdom of Aksum. Aksum, a town well to the west on the plateau, was the eponymous capital city of a large and prosperous empire from just before the beginning of our era until perhaps the 7th century AD. This was Ethiopia's first imperial power, constituted from a congeries of tribute-paying minor states dominated by a ruler who called himself the 'king of the Aksumites'. From inscriptions, coinage and archaeological investigation we have some idea, at least, about the institutions, culture, economy and social fabric of the Aksumite kingdom. Not only did Aksum occupy the Ethiopian and Eritrean highlands and Red Sea coast, but also by about 200 AD the title '*najashi* [the Ethiopian ruler] of Habashat and of Aksum' appears in Yemeni inscriptions. Habashat is the name from which the old European designation for present day Ethiopia, Abyssinia, is derived.

Aksum is today characterised by the great granite obelisks, called stelae, which stand or lie fallen in several groups around the ancient capital. These monuments and other remains of a developed civilisation reveal why Aksum, even long after its zenith, retained a certain aura of reverence and magnificence. Since it also contained the church of Maryam Seyon, apparently the oldest, and certainly the most revered, of all Ethiopia's thousands of churches, it is easy enough to see why it was later to be resurrected as a sacred city.

The chief events in the history of Aksum relative to our story here are its rise to power in the first centuries AD, its conversion to Christianity around 340 AD, and the 6th century war with the king of Himyar in the Yemen. The conversion of Ethiopia to Christianity is attributed by Ethiopian histories to two kings, Abreha and Asbeha. The Latin record of the historian Rufinus, and modern research, instead reveals King Ezana of Aksum as the monarch under whom Patriarch Athanasius of Alexandria consecrated the first bishop of Aksum, Frumentius of Tyre. This founded the tradition that the bishop of Ethiopia must always (until 1951) be a monk sent from Egypt.

The 6th century King Kaleb launched an invasion of Himyar in modern Yemen that resulted in the conquest of the country, and his own entry into the company of the saints. The war is supposed to have been fought because of the persecutions inflicted by the Jewish king of Himyar, Yusuf, on local Christians, and Kaleb's destruction of this last native king of Himyar was seen as a triumph of the faith. At this stage, Aksum was regarded internationally as an important regional power in the Red Sea area.

Kaleb installed a viceroy in the Yemen. He was soon overthrown by an Abyssinian called Abreha, who founded a more-or-less independent dynasty that ruled the Yemen for nearly half a century. Kaleb's reign saw the last of Aksum's overseas imperium. After the Persian invasion of the Yemen around

570, and the rise of Islam in Arabia in the mid-7th century, Aksum declined, and vanished from the record for centuries. Little is known about 'post-Aksumite' Ethiopia except that it still ruled substantial territories, received

1. The greatest of the granite stelae or obelisks at Aksum lying as it fell. Beyond is the dome of the modern cathedral of Maryam Seyon, built by Emperor Haile Sellassie. Photo Pamela Taor.

its bishops from the patriarchate of Alexandria and suffered, in the later 10th century, a major invasion by a foreign queen, remembered in Ethiopian tradition by the name Gudit.

From c. 1137–1270 a dynasty based on the local Agaw population of Bugna in the Lasta region, called the Zagwé dynasty, took power. Several Zagwé kings are commemorated as saints in the Ethiopian church, and to one, Lalibela, local legend attributes the remarkable churches carved from the solid rock at the place named after him, Lalibela. It is in his reign that we have the first claim for the presence of the Ark in Ethiopia.

Lalibela's dynasty was overthrown around 1270 by an Amhara based rebellion that set upon the throne a man called Yekuno Amlak. His successors came to represent themselves as descendants of King Solomon and the queen of Sheba: the 'Solomonic' dynasty. From the 1320s, under Amda Seyon, this dynasty began to rebuild a major empire in the region. With varying fortunes, the dynasty ruled over the Habash (Abyssinian) world for several hundred years. At this period we can observe a certain development of aspects relevant to the story of the Ark, such as the Solomonic legend of the *KN*, the worship of Mary and the use of the term Seyon or Zion.

Under Emperor Lebna Dengel (1508–40), a major blow to Christian Habash power came from the Muslim *amir* of Harar, Ahmad Grañ, who invaded the country in the 1530s. He destroyed Aksum Zion church, though not before the supremely sacred object it contained had been removed to safety. The Habash state was able to recover its authority, with Portuguese military assistance, but soon suffered substantial territorial losses through the arrival of the Oromo people, who began to infiltrate, more and more insistently, from the south.

In 1579 Emperor Sarsa Dengel was crowned at Aksum, in the presence of the '*tabot* of Seyon'. After a brief flirtation with Catholicism, accepted by two emperors (Za Dengel and Susneyos) but rejected by the mass of the population, the foreign missionaries, largely Jesuits, who had been introduced by the Portuguese, were expelled by Emperor Fasiladas in 1632. With their expulsion ended a century in which reports about Ethiopia, including speculations about the Ark, had been relatively voluminous. The Alexandrian faith was restored. Fasiladas began building a castle at Gondar. His successors Yohannes I and Iyasu I continued building there. The city became, to some extent, an imperial capital.

From the time of Iyasu I – the only emperor reported to have actually seen and 'spoken with' the Ark in Aksum – the power of the Gondar emperors declined slowly but irreversibly. There was a concomitant rise to power of local military leaders, often bearing the high title of *ras*, literally 'head', to inter-regional control. With their tutelage over the 'Solomonic' emperors in Gondar, fragmentation of authority and centrifugal tendencies grew stronger. One provincial kingdom, Shewa, maintained itself fairly well in virtual independence under a cadet branch of the old Solomonic dynasty. This period, called by the Ethiopians *zemana mesafint*, the 'era of the princes', terminated in 1855, when an interloper, Emperor Tewodros II, seized power. His reign ended with his suicide as British troops stormed his fortress at Maqdala in 1868.

A succession struggle brought Emperor Yohannes IV, formerly called Kassa, ruler of Tigray, to the imperial throne. A man of Tigray, he liked to call himself 'king of Seyon' (Zion). Yohannes IV eventually fell in battle with the Sudanese dervishes, leaving the way to the throne open to the king of Shewa, Menelik, who became Menelik II, emperor of Ethiopia. His name invokes the old Solomonic legend, Menelik I being the supposed son of King Solomon and the queen of Sheba, ruler of Ethiopia c. 2800 years before. Under Menelik and his successors, culminating with Haile Sellassie (1930–74), Ethiopia began to modernise, and to enter the contemporary community of nations. Only briefly, when Mussolini invaded the country, was Ethiopia forced to submit to European colonisation. Otherwise, it remained the only country in Africa to maintain its independence, becoming, indeed, a colonial power on its own account.

2

The Great Myth:
Solomon and Sheba

there is a book called Kivera Negust, which contains the Law of the whole
of Ethiopia

King of Kings Yohannes, King of Zion of Ethiopia

THE LEGEND OF THE HEAVENLY ZION

The path that leads to the Ark begins well over a thousand years before
the emperors of Aksum raised their mighty obelisks, and perhaps 1500
years before the first Christian king, Ezana, is reputed to have built the church
in which the supposed Ark was one day to reside. It began, the Bible story tells
us, at Sinai, when Moses obeyed the commands of Yahweh, relaying his
message about the construction of the Ark to his people (Exodus 25.1–21).
The divine message concluded with an extraordinary promise:

> And there I will meet with thee, and I will commune with thee from above the
> mercy seat, from between the two cherubims which are upon the ark of the
> testimony… (Exodus 25.22).

Leaving aside the complexities of biblical exegesis, already discussed in *The
Ark of the Covenant,* the Bible story as we have it reveals the Ark as the most
venerated thing in Israel. It remained the central element in Jewish religious
life as the brutal conquest of Canaan and the establishment of the Jewish

kingdom progressed. King David (2 Samuel 6.14–23) danced before the Ark as he brought it up to Jerusalem 'with shouting and with the sound of the trumpet'.

According to 1 Kings 6.1, it was 480 years after the Exodus that David's son Solomon began to build his temple on Mount Moriah. Seven years later the temple was ready to receive the Ark. It was brought 'out of the city of David, which is Zion' (1 Kings 8.1) with the tabernacle of the congregation and the holy vessels, and installed between two gold-covered statues of cherubim, each ten cubits high, set up in the Holy of Holies of the temple:

> And the priests brought in the ark of the covenant of the Lord unto his place, into the oracle of the house, to the most holy place, even under the wings of the cherubims. For the cherubims spread forth their two wings over the place of the ark, and the cherubims covered the ark and the staves thereof above. And they drew out the staves, that the ends of the staves were seen out in the holy place before the oracle, and they were not seen without: and they are there to this day. And there was nothing in the ark save the two tables of stone... (1 Kings 8.6–8).

This was the final marvel, the house of the Ark, the temple of stone and carved cedar wood, of olive wood and pure gold built by King Solomon of Israel. From afar, a woman heard about Solomon's glory and wisdom, and came 'to prove him with hard questions'. The Bible calls her the queen of Sheba. She set forth 'with a very great train, with camels that bare spices, and very much gold, and precious stones'. The queen was impressed by Solomon's wisdom and splendour. So dazzled was she that she admitted that 'the half was not told me'. The queen gave Solomon 120 talents of gold with her spices and precious stones. Somewhat wistfully, the biblical chronicler records that 'there came no more such abundance of spices as these which the queen of Sheba gave to King Solomon'.

So far, the story is clear enough – at least as the Bible presents it; we should not forget that among the rich documentation of Near Eastern sites, with all their archives and archaeological information, we still lack even one reliable mention of David, Solomon, or the splendours of early Jewish Jerusalem. Yet with the culminating glory, the installation of the Ark in the temple of Solomon at Jerusalem c. 950 BC, and the queen of Sheba's visit shortly afterwards, something altogether strange occurs. The Ark, centre of the ceremonial and the religious awe of all Israel, simply vanishes from the record. Nowhere is any further detail about it provided. The later books of the Bible virtually ignore it. It is at this moment that the quest for it must turn to the New Jerusalem, to the 'royal throne of the kings of Zion, mother of all cities, pride of the entire universe, jewel of kings'[1] – the holy city of Aksum in Ethiopia.

For the Ethiopians, there is no mystery here. They know exactly what happened. For, just as the first part of the story is set out in the biblical books of Chronicles and Kings, so the second part is revealed in Ethiopia's royal and national epic, the *Kebra Nagast* (*KN*). This book tells a relatively simple, but daring, tale. The queen of Sheba was called Makeda.[2] She ruled a kingdom in present-day Ethiopia from her capital city, Dabra Makeda. She went, as the Bible says, to Jerusalem to investigate the reputed wisdom of Solomon. There, duly impressed, she slept with him. Later, the queen gave birth to a son, Ebna Lahakim. His royal name was David, after his grandfather, the great king of Israel.[3] (In other later tales he is called Menelik, a name originating outside the *KN* cycle in local Ethiopian traditions.)[4] When he had grown up, Ebna Lahakim set out to visit his father in Jerusalem, bearing greetings from his mother with her request for 'the fringes of the covering of the holy heavenly Zion, the Tabernacle of the Law of God, which we would embrace' (*KN* 33). The young man reached Gaza, described as 'his mother's country' (*KN* 34) in recognition of Solomon having given it to Queen Makeda. The local people thought that Ebna Lahakim was Solomon himself, so close was the resemblance, but some were puzzled, sure that the king was in Jerusalem building his palace. Messengers soon ascertained that this was true, and told Solomon about the mysterious visitor. Ebna Lahakim's party stated that they came 'from the dominions of Hendake and Ethiopia' (*KN* 34).[5]

Ebna Lahakim was recognised joyfully by King Solomon as his first-born, and was offered kingship in Israel. Instead, the young man preferred to return to rule his mother's realm, Ethiopia. Zadok the high priest therefore anointed him in the Holy of Holies of the new temple, before the Ark, as king of Ethiopia, under the royal name David (*KN* 39). When he departed, his father appointed the eldest sons of some of the great men of Israel to accompany him back to his Ethiopian kingdom – the list of their offices is provided in *KN* 43. Further, King Solomon gave his son not just the fringes, but the whole covering of the Ark, replacing it with a new one. He also gave the golden mice and the emerods (mysterious objects, sometimes trans. 'tumour', placed in the Ark) that the Philistines had contributed (Samuel 6.4).

Solomon's generosity was not enough. Divine intervention was about to devastate Israel with the loss of its most precious asset. Urged on by angelic encouragement, Azarias (Azariah) son of Zadok and his colleagues, destined to go with Ebna Lahakim to Ethiopia, plotted together to acquire the greatest treasure of all (*KN* 45ff). By cunning they contrived to remove the Ark of the Covenant itself – with its acquiescence and with divine assistance – to take to Ethiopia. The Archangel Michael escorted and protected them on the way. When, in Egypt, the Israelites revealed to King David (Ebna Lahakim) what they had with them, he danced before the Ark in joy, as had his grandfather King David of Israel long before. The deities of Egypt, made in the shape of men, dogs, cats and birds, fell down and were shattered as Zion, shining like the sun, draped in purple, progressed on her airborne wagon towards her new home. In this way, the prince returned with his Jewish companions to Ethiopia, where he received the crown from his mother. The Jewish faith was established – the queen had already accepted it (*KN* 28) and abandoned the worship of the sun. The monarchy was settled in the male line through Ebna Lahakim. *KN* 87 describes how 'the kingdom was made anew', and the men of Ethiopia 'at the sight of Zion, the Tabernacle of the Law of God...forsook divination and magic...[and] forsook augury by means of birds and the use of omens...'[6]

This, in summary, is the tale supposedly presented to Ethiopia in the time of King Amda Seyon (1314–44) in the *KN*.[7] But nothing survives from that era to confirm it. In the oldest surviving versions that have a colophon or end note explaining how it came to be composed, the book's purported Arabic ancestry is recorded, stretching back at least to 1225 AD in the reign of King Lalibela, with a Coptic ancestry before that. But the earliest *dateable* versions of the complete story are much later, 17th–18th century. One manuscript alone, now in Paris, has a tentative claim to a 15th century date. Especially intriguing, there exists another version of the story taken by Francisco Alvares from a book at Aksum in the 1520s. It offers a different tale, with a different ancestry: Hebrew, to Greek, to Chaldean, and finally to Abyssinian.[8]

These chronological matters I will deal with closely later on. First, we need to explore a very basic point. Is the story of the queen of Sheba and Solomon, the very root and trunk of the *KN* story, and the chief support of the Ethiopian claim to the Ark, even credible?

MAKEDA, QUEEN OF SHEBA

The queen of Sheba is a figure of primary importance in Ethiopian myth, the country's legitimate ruler by descent, and the supposed progenitor of the Ethiopian imperial dynasty. Is this claim immediately to be dismissed?

The famous queen is usually regarded as monarch of the southern Arabian state of Saba, or at least a ruler attributed by the writers of the biblical books of Kings and Chronicles to Saba. Saba (in modern Yemen) became widely known in the eastern Mediterranean because of its rich trade in incense, some of which came to the port of Gaza by the desert routes from the south. But there was always some ambiguity in the attribution. A few ancient historians thought of the queen as an African monarch.

Josephus, for example, called her queen of Egypt and Ethiopia, though Ethiopia in his time referred to the kingdom of Meroë in present day Sudan.[9] The first surviving attribution to the Ethiopia of today is an Arabic account in the *History of the Patriarchs of Alexandria*. The chronicler of the Coptic patriarchs of Alexandria, Michael of Tinnis, wrote it during the patriarchate of Christodoulos of Alexandria (1047–77). He located Sheba in the country called al-Habasha (Abyssinia), the Christian kingdom in modern northern and central Ethiopia.[10] In the early 13th century, a writer called Abu Salih, probably an Armenian Christian living in Egypt, included a reference to Abyssinia in his book about the churches and monasteries of Egypt: 'Abyssinia is the kingdom of Sheba; from it the Queen of the Yemen came to Jerusalem to hear words of wisdom from Solomon.'[11] Clearly, he was himself confused about the attributions to the Yemen or to Ethiopia. In the 1520s the Portuguese royal chaplain, Francisco Alvares, travelling across Ethiopia, recorded references to the queen as an Ethiopian sovereign, Makeda. He was the first foreigner to publish an account of the story of the queen's visit to King Solomon as preserved in Ethiopian documentation. This earlier story, as we shall see, is rather different from the *KN* we now have.[12]

The prominence of Arabian Saba might seem to dismiss the Ethiopian claim. Yet we now know that there really was an Ethiopian Saba, part of an ancient polity that flourished in Tigray and Eritrea long before Aksum rose to power. The inscriptions of rulers of this pre-Aksumite kingdom refer to 'D'amat and Saba'. From the nature of the material found by archaeologists, it is evident that in language and material culture this Ethiopian polity was closely associated with the Yemen, but nevertheless it was an Ethiopian Saba.

The discoveries that revealed this kingdom's existence are relatively recent, unknown to earlier commentators. They even escaped Graham Hancock's more recent researchers as well. In his book Hancock still cites a remark of Budge written eighty years ago: that at the time of Solomon 'the natives of the country we now call Abyssinia were savages'. The people of D'amat and Saba were very far from that, as the traces of their civilisation clearly prove. The most splendid of D'amat's accomplishments, the temple of Yeha, has long been known, even if its significance as a monument much older than Aksum was not realised. It is now suggested that this temple rose on the ruins of an even older one, taking Yeha back perhaps to the 8th century BC.[13]

The discovery of the ancient inscriptions of the Ethiopian rulers of D'amat and Saba – often associated with their *'rkt*, queen – has created an interesting ambiguity around the significance of the name Saba. Even if we can tentatively date D'amat and Saba back to the 8th century BC, this is still later than Solomon and the queen of Sheba. But as it happens the Yemeni Saba itself can claim no much earlier origin. Evidence for the earliest written documents there may date to the 10th century BC, the time of Solomon and the queen of Sheba, but Ethiopia is not far behind. It is true that the vestiges of ancient Yemeni civilisation enormously outstrip what we have from Ethiopia. But an Ethiopian Saba need not be dismissed out of hand, however difficult it is to imagine that any memory of it might have percolated down the ages to inform Ethiopian historians.

The question of the queen's racial origins did not greatly preoccupy the author(s) of the *KN*, but to them she was clearly no foreigner. The book describes the queen of Sheba in most flattering terms. A sovereign for six years, she had remained a virgin. She was 'vigorous in strength and beautiful of form'. She possessed 'gracious attraction' and a 'splendid form' (*KN* 30). In the narrative, it is Makshara, the daughter of Pharaoh, the princess who led King Solomon into idolatry, who reveals to us the final vital characteristic of this paragon, when she exclaims to the king:

> Thy son hath carried away thy Lady Zion, thy son whom thou hast begotten, who springeth from an alien people into which God hath not commanded you to marry, that is to say, from an Ethiopian woman, who is not of thy colour, and is not akin to thy country, and who is, moreover, black (*KN* 64).

Later, Azarias (Azaryas) the chief priest touched delicately on this same point. After a short speech about the good things of Ethiopia, God's new chosen land, he adds (in Budge's translation):

there is one matter that we would mention: ye are black of face – I only state this [fact] because I can see [that ye are] – but if God illumineth (i.e., maketh white) your hearts, [as far as your colour is concerned] nothing can injure you (*KN* 90).

Doubtless the high ecclesiastical official Yeshaq and his team of collaborators who 'translated' the *KN* – black themselves – added these remarks to ensure that every possible aspect of Ethiopia was taken into consideration and accounted for. For the Ethiopians who read the *KN*, there was doubt. Makeda, queen of Sheba, was a black Ethiopian woman.

THE 'GLORY OF KINGS'

The *Kebra Nagast* is a truly extraordinary work. Profoundly permeated with the spirit and the letter of the Old Testament, it exhibits a substantial contribution from the New Testament and other sources as well. There are traces deriving from apocryphal works, patristic sources, Jewish rabbinical writings and others. The whole is woven into an irregular tale, with many interruptions and diversions. A word is enough to lead the train of thought off at a tangent. Original texts are quoted haphazardly, sometimes wrongly, sometimes with additions as the authors sought to enhance a theme. The citations are often incorrect, paraphrased, or anachronistic. King Solomon might cite a text from Isaiah, who lived centuries later. The same text might be used twice, attributed each time to different authors, or presented each time in a slightly different form. A text might be mistakenly attributed as well as wrongly cited. Certain texts are simply invented, not traceable to their supposed authors, conflations based on several different biblical texts. Some of this depends on the different sources, or derives from oral traditions or faulty memory. Some is due to the desire to render a good proof-text rather better than its biblical original, or to amplify it by using it again in another form. In general: '[Old Testament] words and phrases so permeated the thoughts of the authors of the *KN* that they could not help expressing themselves by means of OT material.'[14]

In addition, claims are made which supply impeccable antecedents for certain non-biblical themes. The episodes that make up the book represent the effort of the author(s) to distil from the available sources – Coptic, Arab, general Eastern (Oriental) Christians – the mixture that would redound best to

Ethiopia's glory.[15] The technique of endless citation is familiar in Ethiopia: the richer the bank of sources used, the more learned the writer seemed. For the *KN*, the highest authorities are shamelessly employed. In certain sections St. Gregory the Illuminator unveils his thoughts on the glory of kings to the Three Hundred and Eighteen Fathers of Nicaea in 325 AD, and expatiates on biblical symbolism. In others Dematiyos (Domitius), patriarch of Constantinople (c. 272–303), reveals how he found a manuscript at the church of St. Sophia, which demonstrated how world sovereignty was divided between the king of Ethiopia and the Roman emperor. It is from this mythical manuscript that the story of Solomon and Sheba in the *KN* is supposed to have derived. The miraculous discovery of a lost manuscript is a device employed in many similar tales. It retains its power even today, in speculations about the potential discovery of archives of fabulous lost wisdom secreted in chambers under the Sphinx, for example. Graham Hancock has propagated this sort of thing in *Keeper of Genesis*, and we can read other speculations of the same genre: 'could [a secret chamber under the Sphinx] contain the records of Horus, the wisdom of Thoth, and the secrets of alchemy?' asks Peter Marshall.[16]

The *KN* story exhibits another interesting characteristic. While some features – an airborne Ark, the shattering of idols in Egypt, the remarkable speed of the Ark's progress – test credulity, these are all of a piece with the magic and power indicated by the Ark's life in Israel as the biblical story recounts it. What is notable is that the rest of the tale is tame enough, and perfectly reasonable in contrast to the extravagances of the Jewish, Muslim and later local Ethiopian embroideries on this much loved theme. Whatever the *KN* version might owe to dramatised versions circulating in the Jewish–Muslim world, it has been carefully edited to make as much sense as possible – unless it sprang in part from another (Coptic?) tradition that had not absorbed these accretions. There are, of course, some embellishments. Solomon can converse with birds and beasts, and the demons obey him. These ideas are mentioned in an otherwise credible account (*KN* 25) of how King Solomon advised in the building work at the temple, showing how various tools were to be used, but not indulging, as in other versions, in magical means. Mention of the speech of birds and animals (see 1 Kings 4.33 for the biblical origin of this tradition) and the control of demons occurs probably because such ideas had by then, through tales in Greek, Coptic and other languages, thoroughly permeated almost any reference to King Solomon. He had become, like Alexander the Great, the hero of all sorts of quite incredible legends.

By and large the passage of events as narrated by the *KN* is fairly prosaic in comparison to other versions of the Solomon/Sheba legend. The meeting of the two sovereigns is not dependent on a winged messenger, a hoopoe, but on a simple merchant's report. Golden thrones are not whisked away by *jinn*, nor do shimmering glass-floored palaces appear. The queen is not cured of a deformed donkey-foot, nor is there any mention in the tale of magic wood. All these things occur in other recensions.

The revealing of the *KN* to the West, a major theme of this investigation because of the evidence recorded by European visitors concerning the Ark, came slowly. The first record of an early version of the *KN* was obtained by Alvares in the 1520s, and published in 1540 (see Chapter 4: Tales of Solomon and Sheba). João de Barros repeated a similar, but fuller, version. In the 17th century Péro Pais preserved a version of the story in its final form, including the Ark of the Covenant. James Bruce, too, reported on certain elements of the *KN* in 1790. It was he who brought back manuscripts of the text for European scholars to study at first hand.

Subsequently a number of scholars published sections of the *KN* in various European languages. Praetorius published part of the work in 1870. Le Roux produced a larger selection in 1907.[17] The first full translation by Bezold was published in 1909. Bezold's text was chiefly based on the manuscript sent to King Louis Philippe by Sahela Sellasie, king of Shewa. This, probably the oldest manuscript known that includes the complete story, is now in the Bibliothèque Nationale, Paris. The current English version is still that published by Budge in 1922, based on Bezold's text collated with a British Library ms, Oriental 818, brought from Ethiopia after the siege of Maqdala in 1868.[18]

In recent times we have an extraordinary plagiaristic work that claims to be the latest English translation of the *KN*, but in fact simply copies, word for word, the greater part of Budge's text.[19] Substantial sections of Budge's preface appear too, unaltered, or even dramatised.[20] Given this dependence on Budge, it is astonishing to read in the 'Note from the Editor':

> this complete, modern translation of the *Kebra Nagast* derives mainly from the Spanish version of this work which appeared in Toledo in 1528 and in Barcelona in 1547, with its French version published in Paris in 1558…This popular edition conforms to the classic literary style of Budge's Translation-Commentary…

It does – to the extent that scarcely a word differs in 169 pages, and every one of Budge's antique 'thees' and 'thous' remains intact. The book is a simple reprint of Budge, with a few missing sections. In a startling addition, the 'editor' explains that 'among the most complete, and least known, translations of the Kebra Nagast, is the exhaustive work of Enrique Cornelio Agrippa (1486–1535), *Historia de las cosas de Etiopia* (Toledo, 1528) – a greatly amplified account'. But Agrippa, the famous author of *De Occulta Philosophia* (1531) – philosopher, alchemist and magician, secretary to Emperor Maximilian I and professor of theology – is not known to have written a word on Ethiopia, though he was fascinated by Egypt. It was he who was commemorated by Christopher Marlowe in *Doctor Faustus*: '…as cunning as Agrippa was, Whose shadows made all Europe honour him'. If Agrippa had written about Ethiopia as early as 1528, it would have been among the earliest records available, pre-Alvares, and of immense importance. Why has no one ever noticed it?

The details already cited solve the dilemma. Agrippa stands for Alvares. Francisco Alvares' name is only once mentioned in the book, where his 1540 publication is noted (incorrectly dated 1533), even though Alvares was first to cite part of the queen of Sheba story – in a version neither complete, nor identical with the text of the *KN* as we know it. The date 1533 might refer to a news report published in Dresden that year about Alvares.[21] Alvares' book, first published as *Ho Preste João das Indias* in Lisbon in 1540, was translated into Spanish – with the same title as the supposed work attributed to Agrippa, *Historia de las cosas de Etiopía* – in 1557 (not 1547), in Antwerp (not Barcelona); another Spanish version appeared in Toledo in 1588 (not 1528). There was also a Zaragosa edition in 1561. The French version, *Historiale description de l'Ethiopie*, was published in Antwerp (not Paris), in 1558. All this is well known. But no one can identify any work by Henricus Cornelius Agrippa of Nettesheim entitled *Historia de las cosas de Etiopía*, published in Toledo in 1528. This copy of Budge's work derives from no Spanish antecedent. The purported Spanish publications by Agrippa never existed. Citing Agrippa is a monumental blunder, a major distortion of African historiography.

A book called *The Kebra Nagast*, subtitled 'The Lost Bible of Rastafarian Wisdom…' also includes modernised abbreviated sections from the Budge translation, while citing the pirated work as an authority. The *KN* is important to Rastafarians, who regard the late Emperor Haile Sellassie as a deity or messiah, descendant of Solomon and Sheba. By and large, the book, introduced by Ziggy Marley, avoids profound discussion of the *KN*. It is, instead, a work of Rasta philosophy interwoven with citations from Budge. There is only a thin thread of connection with the matter of the Ge'ez *KN*, and the Ark appears only in the context of the John Canoe celebration.[22] On the internet, too, Rasta web pages devoted to the Ark and its African setting are largely filled with citations from the *KN*.

3

The Tabot *and the* Ark: The Mysterious Altars of Ethiopia

The *tabot* itself is a mystery

C.H. Walker, *The Abyssinian at Home*, 1933: 95,
citing an Amhara informant

TABOTAT, *ARK AND TABLETS*

In searching for the true identity of the sacred object kept at Aksum, we need to understand something inextricably bound up with it: the convoluted role of the mysterious *tabot* of Ethiopia. This is the word used in the Ethiopic texts for the Ark itself, *tabota Seyon*, the Ark of Zion.

The *tabot* (plural: *tabotat*) or altar tablet is one of the most exotic elements of Ethiopian ecclesiastical custom – a phenomenon exclusive to Ethiopia, a unique ritual object central to all church services. Its origins, purpose, symbolical meaning and use have often aroused confusion among foreign commentators on the Ethiopian church. Similar confusion exists even among Ethiopians as well.

When Emperor Iyasu I of Ethiopia dedicated a *tabot* at the church of Dabra Berhan Sellassie in the capital, Gondar, the chronicler Hawarya Krestos sang a paean to the Ark of the Covenant, which he identified with the *tabot*. Another chronicler, Sinoda, writing of one of Iyasu's last expeditions, saw nothing strange in closely comparing a biblical story with the Ethiopia

27

of 1704. Joshua is Emperor Iyasu of Ethiopia; the Jordan river is Ethiopia's great river, the Abbay or Blue Nile; the Israelites are the soldiers of Iyasu. The Ark of the Covenant is not here paralleled with the relic at Aksum, but with two *tabotat* that accompanied the emperor, Gimjabet (the *tabot* of the church of Mary of the Gimja Bet, Gondar) and Iyasus (the *tabot* of Jesus, a church of the camp), and with another great relic of Gondarine times, the *kwerata resu*, an icon of Christ wearing the crown of thorns.

When Iyasu's father, Emperor Yohannes I, departed on an expedition, 'before him went the *tabot* of Our Lady Maryam Seyon of Gimja Bet, and the image of Our Lord Jesus Christ called Kwe'erta Re'esu...' Later, too, in Emperor Iyasu II's time, a chronicle mentions the clergy of '*tabota seyon* (the *tabot* of Zion), which is Gimja Bet'. The royal chronicles of the Gondarine emperors allow us to glimpse a fascinating process taking place as late as the 18th century at Gondar – as at Aksum, a *tabot* of Mary was gradually transformed into an Ark of Zion.[1] Clearly, to learn more about the Ark at Aksum we must study these Ethiopian *tabotat* as well.

The *tabot*, identified with the Ark, is hedged about in the same way with mystery, hidden in the holiest part of the churches, always wrapped in concealing veils, never seen by a layman's eye. Should profane persons approach it, it must be reconsecrated. Yet it is a simple enough thing, a flat oblong or square tablet, made of wood, stone or even precious metal, inscribed with a dedication in the form 'this is the *tabot* of...' – with the name of a saint or other holy figure, or several. A cross is usually engraved on it, sometimes with carved decoration, often geometric or floral borders. It is the sole consecrated object in the church, having been anointed with the holy oil, *meron*, by the patriarch or a bishop.

A *tabot* – alternatively referred to as a *sellat*, a tablet representing the *sellata hegg*, the tablet(s) of the Law of Moses – is kept in the altar table or stand called the *manbara tabot*, in the *maqdas*, the sanctuary or Holy of Holies of every Ethiopian church. The *tabot* is stored, always wrapped in cloth, in the *manbara tabot*, but when the liturgy is to be celebrated it is unwrapped and placed on top of it. The paten and chalice for the bread and wine are in turn set out on the consecrated tablet. By this means the bread and the wine that represent Christ's flesh and blood are directly connected to Christ, the consecrated *tabot* being linked through the anointing by the bishop or patriarch with the apostle Mark, founder of the patriarchate of Alexandria, and disciple of Christ himself. The ceremony takes place veiled from the view of the people, only the priests and serving deacons being present in the sanctuary.

The *tabot* is popularly envisaged nowadays as a replica or representation of the Ark of the Covenant – or, perhaps, more strictly, of the tablets of the Law – at Aksum. This sort of symbolism means that there are many thousands of 'Arks of the Covenant' in Ethiopia today, since every church has at least one *tabot*. The supreme model of the *tabot* remains the mysterious relic at Aksum, somehow supposed to be both the Ark and the tablets of the Law. All others are considered to be replicas of this one.

Very likely, the *tabot* developed out of the Coptic church's use of the altar board called a *maqta'*, probably in the period of increasing isolation even from Egypt after the consolidation of Islamic states largely cut Ethiopia off from the Christian world. In Egypt, this consecrated board is set into the altar and serves the same purpose as the *tabot*: the chalice and paten for the wine and bread of the eucharist are placed upon it. The use of the altar board must have been perfectly acceptable to the Egyptian bishops who succeeded as heads of the church in Ethiopia over the centuries, since they consecrated the *tabotat*. This suggests that the rich symbolism that came to surround the *tabot* – its identification with the Ark in particular – was to some extent unofficial, a popular Ethiopian contribution to its significance.

In the Coptic church, the *maqta'* has not adopted the Ark symbolism. For the Copts the 'ark' is the wooden container for the chalice that contains the wine mixed with water during the liturgy. It occupies the centre place on the altar, and is regarded as embodying

> various symbolic analogies. It is sometimes called a throne in reference to the majesty of the crucified Christ. Like the ark that was the instrument of salvation to Noah and his family, the altar ark holds the chalice carrying the life-giving Blood of Jesus Christ. It is also analogous to the Old Testament ark of the covenant. But, whereas the old ark was used to hold the tables of the law, the new ark holds the chalice of Christ's Blood, God's new testament with man...and while the old ark included Aaron's rod which budded (Heb. 9: 4), the new ark symbolises the Virgin Mary who gave birth to God...Finally the old ark contained the golden pot of manna (Ex. 16: 32–34), whereas the new ark holds the true heavenly Manna which gives life everlasting (Jn. 6: 57, 58).[2]

These symbolic characteristics of the Coptic 'ark' for the chalice are almost exactly the same as those attributed to the Ark of the Covenant in the *KN*.

The *KN* directly identifies the Virgin Mary with the Ark of the Covenant in several places, and similar comparisons occur in Ethiopian sacred poetry.

2. A splendid silver cross from Aksum. The bottom section shows a *manbara tabot*
   above the flat plaque often conjectured to represent the *tabot*. From the
   author's collection. Photo David Henley.

In the *KN*, for example, in a speech attributed to the Three Hundred and Eighteen Orthodox Fathers (*KN* 11), we read:

> the testimony (or proof) is the similitude; the heavenly Zion is to be regarded as the similitude of the Mother of the Redeemer, Mary. For in the Zion which is builded there are deposited the Ten Words of the Law which were written by His hands, and He himself, the Creator, dwelt in the womb of Mary, and through him everything came into being.

It is often repeated that the *tabot* is an ancient feature of the Ethiopian church, but this is mere surmise. No document refers to a *tabot* in Aksumite times. There is no reason to suppose that the Aksumite church used them. Even in later times, under 12th-13th century Zagwé kings, the word *tabot* is only known from some box-like carved wooden altars, inscribed with dedications beginning: 'This *tabot*...' Sometimes they name King Lalibela, who ruled around 1200 AD. They may be genuine relics of Lalibela's time. What is intriguing about these *tabotat* is that they are legged cubic or box-like objects, very different from flat tablets like the *tabotat* that are in use today.

We can distinguish two distinct types of altar (*manbara tabot*) today. The first is this Lalibela type, clearly defined on inscribed examples as *tabotat*. They are small enough to be easily portable. These small, low, cubic, carved wooden *manbara tabotat* with legs are quite rare.[3] Possibly these 'cube altars' were specifically designed as portable altars, or perhaps they were placed on a larger altar, either as the consecrated *tabot* on which the paten and chalice stood, or to receive a *sellat* for this purpose. Nowadays they have lost their function as altars, and are used as miscellaneous church furniture.

These *manbara tabotat* are the earliest we know of, if we credit the attribution to Lalibela's reign. The second type, the usual *manbara tabotat* in use today, are much taller and bigger, a sort of stand or cupboard with shelves for storing the *tabot* and various liturgical books and instruments, with pillared and domed canopies on top, and coverings of drapery. This type was usual by Alvares' time, in the 1520s, and is still in use.

TABOT: *CONFUSED DEFINITIONS*

The word *tabot* strictly implies a container for something, a chest or coffer. The word therefore describes the Ark of the Covenant, as well as the Ark of Noah, in the Ethiopian Bible. Abu Salih uses the same term, *tabutu*, but

3. Entrance to the sanctuary in the church of Abba Pantelewon, near Aksum. Inside is a *manbara tabot* with a pillared and domed top, in which the *tabot* is kept. Photo Pamela Taor.

enlarges it to *tabutu al-'ahdi*, 'Ark of the Covenant' in Arabic, when describing the Ark of Lalibela (see below). But the term *tabot* has come to apply normally in Ethiopia today to the *sellat*, or altar tablet, supposed to represent (one of) the tablets of the Law contained in the Ark. This is why the 'ark'-like or 'altar'-like canopied stand that serves as an altar in the sanctuary of Ethiopian churches is today not commonly called a *tabot*, but a *manbara tabot*, throne or seat of the *tabot*.

Bewilderment results from enquiry into the meaning of the different terms used for Ethiopian altars and altar tablets: 'the word *tabot* may mean according to the context: – the Ark in the Sanctuary, the Sanctuary, the church, the Saint to which the church is dedicated, the sacred objects of mystery carried in procession'.[4] Ethiopians who understand English use the term 'Ark of the Covenant' casually to refer to any *tabot*, wherever it might be. I have been told, at two churches near Gondar, that 'the Ark of the Covenant' has been stolen, or that an attempt has been made to steal it. The priests referred not to the Aksum 'Ark', but to those of their own relatively unimportant churches. Nevertheless, even if in the modern post-Haile Sellassie period there has been a definite loss of respect for traditional religion, the theft of a *tabot* is still regarded as a horrible crime. The form of an excommunication launched by the Egyptian bishop *Abuna* Salama against Emperor Tewodros II makes the point: 'Chi segue questo re, è come se rimovesse un *Tabot*.'[5]

Similar confusion is apparent in books about the Ethiopians. David Kessler, writing about the *tabot*, recounts the famous *KN* story of the coming of the 'original Ark containing the tablets of the Ten Commandments'. He adds that 'reproductions are kept in every church', and notes the *tabot*'s appearance for the Epiphany (*Timqat*) ceremony.[6] For those who are aware of the size and shape of *tabotat*, even veiled as they are on ceremonial appearances, it is obvious that it is *not* a replica or reproduction of the substantial box-like Ark from Jerusalem that is taken out for *Timqat* or other festival processions. Nor is it on a box-like object that the paten and cup for the eucharist are placed during the liturgy. Patently, different concepts are at work here.

Kefyalew Merahi, an Ethiopian priest writing in 1997, confirmed that

> the *tabot* is the most holy object of the Ethiopian church. Its sanctity, function
> and centrality in the ritual of the Ethiopian church is the same as that of the
> Ark in ancient Israel. But, whereas the Ark was carried on the shoulders at
> ceremonies in ancient Israel…in Ethiopia it is carried in religious processions
> on the heads of officiating priests.[7]

As so often, there is immediate and automatic confusion between the Ark of the Covenant in Israel and the Ethiopian *tabot*. An illustration enhances this with its caption: 'The Ark is carried on the heads of officiating priests'. We are shown a line of priests carrying many *tabotat* covered in veils of cloth. All of them are evidently far too slender to represent the chest or box-like form of the Ark – yet all of them are 'Arks of the Covenant'.

The official publications of the church do nothing to dispel the confusion. In the 1970 booklet entitled *The Ethiopian Orthodox Church*, the '*Tabot*, or Ark' is mentioned as the 'chief feature of the ceremony' of consecration of a church, the object that bestows sanctity upon the church in which it is installed. This is, evidently, the altar tablet anointed and blessed by the patriarch or a bishop. The glossary, typically, defines the *tabot* as 'Ark of the Covenant'.[8]

The confusion between *tabot* = Ark of the Covenant, and *tabot* = stone or wooden altar tablet, has been discussed by many prominent writers on Ethiopian religious affairs, Ludolf, Dillmann and Guidi, for example. The most widely cited modern explanation for this confusion suggests that the original meaning of the word was indeed 'ark', in the sense of box-like container, but the term was transferred, *pars pro toto*, to the contents of the Ark of the Covenant, the tablets of Moses bearing the Decalogue or Ten Commandments.[9] It is these that are replicated by the *tabotat* in every church.

Maxime Rodinson considered that this idea that 'the contents were designated by the name of the container, or a part by the whole' was very dubious. He also disagreed that the way *tabotat* are carried in procession round churches is 'strongly reminiscent of the way Torah scrolls (the scrolls of the Law, called '*aron*, or *tebuta*) are carried in Jewish synagogues'.[10] Instead, he stated:

> no object of the Jewish cult is analogous to this sacred tablet. On the contrary…the Ethiopian object is strictly analogous to the Christian altar table. This takes forms in the East which, in the Coptic church in particular, are very close to that of the Ethiopian *tabot*.[11]

We might ask why, if it were merely the name of the whole designating a part, was the word *tabot*, referring to a box, applied to a slab of wood and not to the more box-like container in which it was placed? A more sophisticated explanation derives from the *tabot*'s ritual use:

> the point here seems to be that the word *tabot* was used in the Ge'ez Old Testament, and in the Old Testament the Ark is a box. When the symbolism of the Ark was finally applied to the altar-boards in Ethiopia, which were

already in use, it did not matter that the pieces of wood were not boxes. They were already involved in ritual activities that were ark-like. The question was therefore one of ritual function, and not of physical resemblance…It may be that the Ark's attributes were assigned to the *tabot* by the understanding that both were involved in sacrifice. The first received the blood scattered over it by the high priest, the second was the locus for the sacrifice embodied in the eucharist.[12]

LINKED IDENTITIES

For our theme here, the important aspect of the *tabot* is its eventual identification with the Ark of the Covenant. However this came about, it has obviously been contributory to the idea that the original Ark itself is preserved at Aksum. I will demonstrate later how the Ark gradually emerges in the literature, and how the *tabot* is in time identified with it – an identification that gave rise to the idea that in Ethiopia 'the concept and function of the *tabot* represent one of the most remarkable areas of agreement with Old Testament forms of worship'.[13]

But is this true? The Ethiopian priest I have just cited agrees with it, and one can easily see the reason behind the idea – the claim in the *KN* that the Ark itself is in Ethiopia, and that the *tabotat* of the country represent this holy relic. Yet in reality both the concept and the function of the Ethiopian *tabotat* – a Christian altar board – are very far removed from those of the Jewish Ark, even if the Ethiopians themselves have endeavoured to link the two conceptually.

At what period in this history of the *tabot* did it acquire, not just its central place in the church ritual, but its symbolic identification with the Ark or the tablet(s) of Moses? When, by the theory of the Ark's infinite replication in the *tabotat*, did the Ark become universal, symbolically entering the centre stage of every celebration of the eucharist throughout Ethiopia? Is it true that 'by the fifteenth century, the sanctuary of every Ethiopian church edifice had come to be regarded as a copy of the Holy of Holies [in Solomon's temple at Jerusalem] and the *tabot* a copy of the Ark of the Covenant'?[14] Studying the evidence, we find that identification of the *tabot* with the Ark is confirmed only much later.

Around 1200, Abu Salih described an Ark in Ethiopia. It was carried in procession in the same way as *tabotat* today are carried during church festivals. But this early claim by a foreign author who never went to Ethiopia remains the only direct reference to the Ark for many hundreds of years, and there is good reason to be wary of Abu Salih's interpretation (see Chapter 4: The Ark of Lalibela).

When, then, did this symbolical link emerge? King Zara Yaqob (1434–68) identified the Ark ('the golden *tabot*') with Mary, and the tablet of the Law as the likeness of her womb, but the stage whereby the altar tablet itself became identified with the Ark had not yet arrived. Francisco Alvares, the first foreigner to write about the *tabot*, in the first half of the 16th century, apparently learned nothing about any Ark-related symbolism in six or so years of discussion about Ethiopian religious matters. Even when he describes a revered altar stone from Mount Zion in Aksum, Alvares merely mentions that churches are designated by their altar stones.[15] He makes no allusion to further ramifications. The tablets of the Law are mentioned in a note in Archbishop Beccadelli of Ragusa's copy of Alvares' work, but in connection with one of the church tents accompanying the royal camp rather than with Aksum. The note, interestingly, derives directly from Ethiopians living in Rome around 1542, not from Alvares himself (see Chapter 4: *Ho Preste João das Indias*). Beccadelli remarked himself in a letter to Pietro Danes in 1542 that he had 'ordered and divided and reduced to greater clarity' Alvares' work. He made certain additions whenever 'our Ethiopians of Rome' (who included the famous scholar Tasfa Seyon) were not in accord with what was written.[16] The note clearly indicates that in the mid-16th century Ethiopians themselves identified what was probably a *tabot* in the royal milieu with the tablet(s) of the Law – but not with the Ark.

Earlier, in the 15th century, there is a vague hint of a link between the *tabot* and the tablet(s) of the Ten Commandments in King Zara Yaqob's words: 'every *tabot* with the Ten Commandments is exalted'.[17] The chronicle of Zara Yaqob mentions an ordinance on the subject of the *tabot*: 'one must not put only one *tabot* into the churches, but two or several, and that among them must be one consecrated to Mary'.[18] Zara Yaqob's devotion placed Mary, in the form of her *tabot*, in the sanctuary of every church – and Mary, of course, in whose womb once dwelt the New Law, Christ, was identified with the Ark of the Covenant that had contained the Old (Mosaic) Law in the form of the Ten Commandments.

The actual identification of the *tabot*, the altar tablet, with the Ark was a much later phase. The *KN* itself neither implicitly nor explicitly makes the parallel between *tabot* and Ark. On the other hand, the claim that the tablet(s) of the Law from Jerusalem were in Ethiopia, not necessarily implicit in Zara Yaqob's comment about the Ten Commandments, is made explicit by the ambassador Saga Za-Ab in the early 1530s, and a little later by João de Barros, in their versions of the Ethiopian story of Solomon and the queen of Sheba. They do not mention the Ark, however, nor do they identify the tablet(s) with the *tabot*, though the Ethiopian note in the Beccadelli manuscript seems to imply that this idea was already current.

After Abu Salih, the idea of the Ark of the Covenant in Ethiopia does not appear again until the 15th century at the earliest, a date depending exclusively on the uncertain dating of the Paris *KN* manuscript. Apart from that, as my exploration of the documents will reveal, its presence is next implied in the late 16th century in the chronicle of Emperor Sarsa Dengel, soon to be confirmed by Pais' translation of the *KN* early in the 17th century. Anticipation reaches new heights when Manoel de Almeida, around 1627, provides the first explicit reference to an association of the word *tabot* with a material object proclaimed to be the Ark itself: 'a casket they call *Tabot* of Zion, that is to say Ark of the Covenant brought from Mount Zion...' (see Chapter 5: The Ark of the Covenant at Aksum).

'IT IS HERE...'

Whatever the processes that led to the identification of *tabot* and Ark, most rural Ethiopians today, worshipping in minor parish churches, believe that the *tabot* is somehow both the Ark of the Covenant and the tablets of Moses, an unquestioned mystical merging of three powerfully numinous objects, one very substantial in size, into a single smaller object. An Aksumite friend described it to me as 'virtually God himself'.

Among the population of the Ethiopian countryside, the fact of the 'real' Ark of the Covenant's presence in the church of Maryam Seyon (Mary of Zion) at Aksum, and its presence universally throughout Christian Ethiopia by its immanence in every other *tabot*, is not in doubt. Among the more learned priests and the cantors or *dabtarat* there are more or less sophisticated explanations about *tabotat*, their meaning, function and relationship with the Ark or the tablets of the Law, but no precise definition seems to have been laid down.

The *nebura'ed*, administrator of the church at Aksum – Belai Marasa was in office when I conducted my research, but has recently been removed, and has not yet been replaced as far as I know – confirmed to me in October 1997 that a committee of enquiry was to attempt to define these matters properly. Such issues are unique to Ethiopia's church, not arising even in the Coptic mother church. The Ethiopian ecclesiastical establishment – thrown unexpectedly into the limelight over the Ark as a result of Graham Hancock's best-seller *The Sign and the Seal* – perceived that a vital and unique characteristic of their church was, and is, ill-explained and ill-understood. Although, with the concept of the *tabot* as an image of the Ark, the Ark or one of the two tablets of Moses that it contained is fully integrated into Ethiopian orthodox observance in this symbolic or 'replica' form, much remains unclear to the laity and to foreign enquirers. In particular, this lack of clarity surrounds everything to do with the claim to possession of the 'real' Ark itself, at Aksum. Among Ethiopian ecclesiastics there is today a visible confusion and hesitancy. They are reluctant to respond to questions that involve difficult definitions of the *tabot*, Ark or tablet(s) of Moses, and their complex symbolic inter-relationships.

Unfortunately for the ill-prepared clerics of Aksum, skilled in the ancient rites and deeply learned in the Bible, the liturgy and the hagiographies though they are, Hancock's book and subsequent film and internet publicity introduced something quite new. It removed discussion of the Ark from Ethiopia and from the small group of generally sympathetic savants who interested themselves in it as an aspect of Ethiopian – and, particularly, Aksumite – Christianity and culture, catapulting it into a much larger arena, and into the colder light of day where proof is demanded. The clergy of Aksum have to some extent lived outside the world, the old church of Maryam Seyon functioning more or less as a monastic establishment. The years after the 1974 Revolution, though profoundly unhappy ones for Tigray as well as for other parts of Ethiopia, assisted this isolation by cutting the province off from most communication with the outside world. Hancock's own stay at Aksum was both brief and difficult to arrange.

Now matters have altered. Since Hancock's visit, the entire world can interest itself in Aksum's affairs, with pages posted on the world wide web and other international publicity inconceivable, and as yet largely unknown, to the priests at Aksum. None of them possesses a computer, and hardly anyone can speak English. Few if any Aksumite priests read and understand the latest studies on church matters written by either European scholars or Ethiopian scholars, much of whose important work is published in English. The glare of Hancock's publicity has reshaped things. An abstruse and rather mystifying Ethiopian claim has been transformed into the bold statement, internationally read and discussed, that the original Ark of the Covenant is at Aksum, kept concealed there by the priests. The Ethiopian Orthodox Church itself, beyond just Aksum Seyon church and its enclaved ecclesiastics, must present coherent answers to persistent questions about the Ark and the *tabotat*.

Even among Ethiopians the matter has become serious. If the Ethiopian Orthodox Tewahedo Church, held in such tremendous reverence by so many millions of Ethiopians, claims that a conspicuous aspect of its worship is based on its actual possession of the Ark of the Covenant from Jerusalem, the faithful – and other Christians – are justified in requiring that so monumental a claim be confirmed by the church leaders in no uncertain terms.

An 'official' point of view was expressed publicly in 1999 by *Abuna* Pawlos, Patriarch of Ethiopia, in the BBC 2 film *Holy Land*. In an interview with Prof. J.H. Gates, the patriarch was asked if some dating analysis might be undertaken on the Ark 'to prove to all these sceptics that it is actually here'. The patriarch replied:

> No, faith does not go well with scientific proof. We don't doubt it, that it is here, in our place. We don't have to prove it to anyone. You want to believe, it's your privilege. If you don't want to believe, it's your own privilege again… It is here and we believe it.

In the same film the archbishop of Canterbury was asked for his opinion. His response was precisely what we might expect. He did 'not accept the reality of that (the Ark's real presence)…but we have to pay attention to the seriousness with which they hold that theology…we come at things in too cerebral a manner'.

The situation has parallels with the Shroud of Turin. As with that equally enigmatic artefact, the presence or absence of the Ark, deeply rooted though it might be in the popular mind, does not really impinge upon the Ethiopian Orthodox Church's fundamental beliefs. It merely reflects to a certain extent upon the way that worship in the churches is conceived by the faithful. The Ethiopian church itself is firmly associated doctrinally with the rest of the Orthodox communion, and the Ark stands apart from that connection. It is an aspect in which the other churches do not share. For despite this special

4. A deacon exhibits a lavishly decorated and interlaced brass processional cross from the treasury of Aksum Seyon church. Directly above the treasury, on the second level of the building, is the small domed chapel of the Tablet of Moses. Photo Pamela Taor.

claim to possession of the Ark, and its prominence in Hancock's book, the Ark of the Covenant scarcely enters the theology of the Ethiopian church at all. It is an exotic, its only literary offshoot the *KN*, or the occasional allusion to it during the installation of a *tabot* or in a royal chronicle. It has never entered into doctrinal disputes or theological questions, and has largely been avoided in official works presenting the Ethiopian church. In the 1936 book *The Teaching of the Abyssinian Church*...publishing the responses to doctrinal questions of a number of Ethiopian theologians under *Abuna* Mattewos' supervision, and signed by Ras Tafari, regent of Ethiopia, the Ark is not mentioned – and neither are the *tabot* nor the *KN* except in a rather dismissive aside in the preface.[19]

The Ark's most vital role is in the semi-official symbolism associating it with the altar board or the *tabot*. This is, of course, important, but not fundamental. The consecrated altar board, as a perfectly legitimate descendant of the Coptic *maqta'*, would still serve in precisely the same way whether it was popularly identified with a 'real' Ark of the Covenant at Aksum or not. As we have seen, similar associations form part of the Coptic church's beliefs, but are regarded as symbolic analogies rather than claims for the actual possession of the Ark.

If the sacred relic concealed in the chapel of the Tablet of Moses at Aksum were revealed as simply an altar stone, a long-hallowed *representation* of the Ark and/or the tablets of Moses, what would the effect be? The most profound impact would surely be upon certain elements of Ethiopian Christian exclusivity: the concepts of a chosen people, the *daqıqa Esrael*, or Children of Israel, and of a chosen city, Aksum, and its church of Maryam Seyon, seat of the Ark. Certain Ethiopians are proud of their claim to be descendants of Queen Makeda and her maidservant, of Menelik and his company of Jewish officials. They assert a descent from the tribes of Benjamin, Levi, Judah, Reuben and Simeon, and the Aaronic origin of the priests of Aksum.[20] These beliefs, still current though perhaps not quite so widespread as they once were, would all be brought into question. The concept of the semi-divine origin (in the sense of derivation from a family related to Christ) of the imperial dynasty, which would also be undermined, is now largely irrelevant, except perhaps to Rastafarians and traditionalists. Without the Ark, the religion of the Orthodox church would not alter, nor would the church of Maryam Seyon lose its claim to be the oldest and most revered church in the land by virtue of its reputed ancient foundation. Whether the 'real' Ark of the Covenant is there or not, Aksum remains the seat of Ethiopia's first church and the centre of a more than 1600-year-old ecclesiastical history (see Chapter 6).

The need for clarity is recognised by the church, as the creation of the committee mentioned above indicates. The matter is easier to resolve now in some ways, having shed its political ramifications. There is now no reigning absolute ruler, claiming Solomonic descent for his dynasty according to the same book that grants Ethiopia the Ark, fear of offending whom could impede proper investigation. Solomonic descent, stated as a fact in the 1955 Ethiopian Constitution, is no longer part of the national image. If ever one of the Ethiopian imperial family were restored as a constitutional monarch, the lineal descent from the more than 700-year-old line of Yekuno Amlak constitutes as good a claim as the myth of Solomonic blood. The church, too, no longer depends on the state for finance. It is an independent entity, religion in Ethiopia having become a private matter between individual and church. This of course makes the church dependent on its flock for its survival. The issue of the Ark and the *tabotat*, the conceptual centre of Ethiopian popular worship, if not of Orthodox theology, cannot be unimportant in such a relationship.

There remains a certain dichotomy in ideas within the church. The Ethiopian Orthodox Church, modernising in its ideas a little under the present patriarch (Pawlos, a man with a degree in theology from Princeton University, and originating from Adwa), is one thing. The exclusive, proud and anciently established priesthood of Aksum, largely dependent on heredity and locality, guardian of so much of the traditional aspect of the church, is another. Aksum tends to think of itself as the centre, not the periphery, and it is in Aksum that the 'Ark' is concealed. Patriarchs and emperors have been successfully defied in the past, and Aksum's individuality – primacy, almost – within the church is as strong as ever: at least in Aksumite eyes.

A CHAPEL AND ITS GUARDIAN

The *tabot*, for Ethiopians as well as others, is sometimes one thing, sometimes another. A *dabtara* (lay canon) in Aksum might say that the *tabot* is the object whereon the *sellat* rests, implying that it is the altar, *manbara tabot*, with the *sellat* on top. This is perfectly correct linguistically; but it is not nowadays the normal way of referring to these objects. The same person might also say that the *sellat* is unique, which implies that the *sellat* in question is the *sellata Muse*, the sacred relic kept in its special chapel at Aksum. It might also imply that other *sellat* are to be called *tabotat*.

This is, of course, the case in Aksum alone, where reposes the *sellat* 'par excellence', the *sellata Muse*. The *sellata Muse* or tablet of Moses at Aksum is kept in a chapel known as the *enda sellat*, the House or Dwelling of the Tablet. The *sellata Muse* is also called *tabota Seyon*, the *tabot* of Zion, which is translated to mean Ark of Zion, or Ark of the Covenant.[21]

A *dabtara* of Aksum explained to me the special significance of the *sellata Muse* or tablet of Moses. God is in it, and no one can make another one. He added, apparently because there is only one such object in the *enda sellat* at Aksum, although two are mentioned in the Bible, that it is composed of two elements – the actual tablet prepared by Moses to replace the original tablets he broke in anger at Sinai when he saw the people worshipping the Golden Calf, and the Word written on it.[22] Such conceits are very much part of the *dabtara* tradition, in which the composition of the poetry known as *qene* embraces a double meaning. This is defined as *samenna warq*, 'wax and gold', where the wording conceals behind the apparent banal significance of the 'wax' or surface meaning, another esoteric or 'gold' content. Despite the identification of *sellata Muse* and *tabota Seyon* (the Ark of Zion), in my recent discussions at Aksum about the *sellata Muse*, the Ark of the Covenant itself was never mentioned. As with the name of the shrine, the *enda sellat* or Dwelling of the Tablet, the reference was always to the tablet alone. Is this evidence of the nervousness any mention of the Ark of the Covenant now arouses? – of new doubts? – or simply of identities so intertwined that the Ark need not be mentioned?

A modern Ethiopian priest states:

> From the time of its arrival in 4570 B.C. (*sic*) until now the Ark of the Covenant has remained in the most famous and revered church in Ethiopia, Mary Zion in Axum...Guarded by a monk who devotes his life to the task, it is off-limits to all persons, including kings and bishops. Its replicas, however, are found in all Ethiopian churches and monasteries. No one is supposed to see or touch even these replicas, let alone the original Ark.[23]

According to my conversations with Aksumite ecclesiastics and members of ecclesiastical families, and with the guardian of the chapel himself, this charge is given to one man alone, appointed for life. He is usually nominated by his predecessor, and appointed by the elders of the church under the presidency of the *qese gabaz* or provost. The guardian (*aqabet*) is a virgin and a monk, not a priest. The task of the guardian is not solely devoted to the Ark. He is the church treasurer, as is common to all other churches, and his title is no different from theirs, though he has the extra prestige bestowed by his guardianship of the sacred object. This relic is considered as among the *newaye qiddisat*, the holy treasures of the church. On the day before special feast days like the festival of Zion, Hedar Seyon, the *aqabet* at Aksum can be seen at his task, distributing the church treasures, robes, crowns, crosses and so forth to the deacons and priests who will wear or carry them on the feast day itself.

No special guardian of the Ark is mentioned in the Old Testament apart from the normal Levite guards – except during a period of twenty (or more) years, when the Ark was kept in the house of Abinadab, and his son Eleazar was appointed to guard it (1 Samuel 7.1–2). But *KN* 87 supplies one in 'Almeyas, 'the mouth of God, keeper ('*aqabe*) of the Law, that is to say, keeper of Zion'. Pétridès defines the *nebura'ed* (dean) of Aksum as 'guardian of the Book of the Law at Aksum...successor of Azarias', son of Zadok the high priest.[24] Presumably, by analogy, the guardian of the Ark should be considered as the successor to 'Almeyas. Aksumite priestly families still today pride themselves on descent from Levites who accompanied Ebna Lahakim to Ethiopia from Jerusalem.

Perhaps in earlier times the *nebura'ed* himself was envisaged as the guardian of the mysterious talisman of Aksum. This was the opinion of James Bruce, who wrote that with Menelik and the Jews

> came also Azarias, the son of Zadok the priest, and brought with him a Hebrew transcript of the law, which was delivered into his custody, as he bore the title of Nebrit, or High Priest; and this charge, though the book itself was burnt with the church of Axum in the Moorish war of Adel, is still continued, it is said, in the lineage of Azarias, who are Nebrits, or keepers of the church of Axum, at this day...[25]

The *dabtarat* say that the guardian or *aqabet* is there to do honour to the tablet, for respect only. It needs no guardian. Even the *aqabet* apparently never sets eyes on the tablet, which is always veiled. This is what one is told, but as we will see, people have occasionally viewed it, or claim to have done so. The *aqabet*, of course, must have some idea of its size and shape, but in the prevailing atmosphere of secrecy, this is almost never revealed to the enquiring foreigner. It is said, by one *dabtara* among my informants, that the tablet shines, and inspires fear. The guardian at certain times offers it incense, but there are no other services, though he will chant the psalms of David before it. There is no idea that there should be an equivalent of the high priest of Israel to make incense offerings, though Bruce's theory came near this.

The *dabtara* I spoke to claimed that the tablet was never in the church, having its own chapel. This is true nowadays, and the existence of this chapel is confirmed in the late 19th and early 20th centuries. The *dabtara* who supplied this information could go only so far back, and knew nothing of the time when there was no such chapel. However, in the sole Ethiopian text referring to an imperial encounter with the Ark, the chronicle of Emperor Iyasu I, the 'Ark' was kept in the *maqdas* or sanctuary of the main church.

After *Itege* Menen, wife of Emperor Haile Sellassie, built the new chapel in the mid-1960s, there was a three-day feast when the tablet of Moses was moved to the new building and installed in its special chamber. There it still lies, covered with a costly green jewel-encrusted cloth (as a former guardian imparted to his relatives). I was told that local people experienced miraculous or wonderful events at that time.

Nowadays few people have access to the inner area around the chapel of the Tablet of Moses, though a few years ago Christian Ethiopian males could approach to kiss the doorpost before the curtain suspended there. The chapel and its mysterious contents gained a new publicity worldwide through Graham Hancock's book, and the church authorities, always relatively closed – if not actually blinkered – in their relations with the outside world, tightened even their earlier rules. As one result of this, the *sebel*, blessed water, is now dispensed outside the chapel through the railings. Such holy water is brought to a church and blessed by priests, and then distributed, just as in the Catholic church. There are stories about the *sebel* of the *sellata Muse*. The *aqabet*, the present guardian monk, confirmed that a cross kept inside the chapel drips the water from its arms. The water, supposed to have the flavour of incense, is administered into the hand from a bottle by a boy assigned to the task. It is said to have been blessed by the guardian, and perhaps even has been placed over the *sellata Muse* to add to its efficacy.

A caution, perhaps even paranoia, has developed about the sacred area. Tales abound that the Israelis want to recover the Ark, or that others might try to steal it (despite the supposed divine force which would never permit such a removal unless God himself decreed it, and which is supposed to have brought it there from unworthy Israel in the first place). There are alarming precedents that have already fanned such fears into more vigorous flame, not difficult among a people whose history has led them to regard the activities of foreigners, and even their own compatriots, with a generally untrusting eye. David Mathew appositely commented how in past times even the *abun* himself, the Egyptian bishop of the Ethiopian church, was 'an object of reverence, anxiety and an unfatigued suspicion'.[26] In Ethiopia, the beautiful cross of Lalibela was not long since stolen by a priest from Medhane Alem church in Lalibela. (It was later traced in Belgium, and returned.) Even priests of Aksum itself have been found guilty of the theft of objects from the church, and jailed. In this sort of atmosphere, in a book published as recently as October 1997, an Ethiopian priest expresses the opinion and the hopes of at least some members of the Ethiopian Orthodox Church:

> any Anti-Ethiopian forces who ever provoked her [Ethiopia] and the Ethiopian Orthodox Tewahedo Church have hurried their own downfall, and will do so in the future. For instance organized forces from within and without, expecting to find the Ark of the Covenant…, through their intelligence elements, are looting the Sacred Tablets and Relics\ of the Ethiopian Orthodox Tewahedo Church…But because of the Tablets of the Law of the Covenant between our Blessed Lady the Virgin Mary and Ethiopia it will remain firm forever. And the trial of those bad elements would be futile. Those who guard this church are no human soldiers but are St. Mary's m(u)ltitude of invisible saints.[27]

The statement might be illogical – few 'intelligence elements' are really likely to be pursuing 'sacred tablets', presumably *tabotat*, if they are hunting for the substantial chest-like Ark from Jerusalem, and if there is a genuine belief in efficacious divine guardianship, why the exclusion and secrecy surrounding the sacred relic at Aksum? The citation indicates how the Old Covenant and the tablets of the Law have merged with the New Covenant, the Virgin Mary and nationalistic pride. It indicates too, clearly enough, the 'unfatigued suspicion', even belligerence, that the whole question of the Ark arouses now in the Ethiopian priesthood.

There is nothing new in this suspicion. There existed in 1906 a 'small Zion church', oddly oriented (north–south), situated to the north of the main church, in line with the two western bell-towers. Enno Littmann wrote that the local people held it in particular veneration, and guarded it suspiciously from his German team, because usually the Ark of the Covenant and the tablets of the Law were housed there.[28] This was the 'Chapel of the Tablet of Moses' seen by Jean Doresse in the 1950s, who provides photographs of some of its internal decoration.[29] It must have been demolished not long after the 1958 excavations of Henri de Contenson at Aksum – it still appears on his plan of 1957, to the west of the site of the new chapel, and can be seen in some of the photographs.[30] The still open excavations of de Contenson now occupy the whole area directly north of the cathedral terrace, where in 1906 stood the church of Mary Magdalene, a treasury, and this little church of Zion. Only the treasury of Yohannes, which lay behind this little church of Zion, survives today.

ZION AT AKSUM

The reason that only the Ethiopian church employs the *tabot* is, for Aksumite priests and *dabtarat*, very simple, and absolutely exclusive – only they possess its original, the *sellat*, the tablet of Moses. It is the only one extant. It is Zion. The Law comes out of Zion for the entire world (this derives from Isaiah 2.3: 'for out of Zion shall go forth the law'), and Zion is now at Aksum, in the chapel of the Tablet of Moses. The *tabotat* in all the churches of Ethiopia are merely images of this single tablet, with the difference that *tabotat* are New Testament versions, created with Christian symbolism.

Zion represents many things, according to the *dabtarat* and priests of Aksum – St. Mary, shelter, the land of Ethiopia, the land of King David. Similarly, the *KN* provides a whole list of epithets for the Tabernacle of the Law (*tabota hegg*). It is the mercy-seat, a place of refuge, the altar (*meswa'*), a place for forgiveness of sins, salvation, the gate of life, glorification, a city of refuge, a ship, the haven of salvation, the house of prayer and the place of forgiveness of sins for whoever prays in purity in it (*KN* 104). The former *nebura'ed* of Aksum defined Zion to me as representing, in the Old Testament, Jerusalem, while in New Testament times it stands for all Christians, as well as, of course, St. Mary herself. This interpretation is certainly as old as the time of Amda Seyon's chronicle, which mentions 'Sion the spouse of heaven'.[31] On a 19th century protective parchment roll in the British Library, in a very unusual set of pictures, a certain *abeto* Walda Dengel is illustrated standing with his gun and sword below an image of Mary labelled simply '*Seyon*', with, to her left, what may be the depiction of a church with the label '*tabot*'.[32]

Kesis Kefyalew Merahi defines Zion in much the same terms: 'Zion means the house of God. In the Old Testament, Zion was the city of King David, which was mount Zion. And it was the symbol of Our Lady Mary and its second meaning is the house of God (church)...' He adds, linking the sacred city of the Ethiopians and its mysterious talisman firmly into the equation: 'The Ark of the Covenant of the Old Testament and the Ark of the Tabernacle of the New Testament whose throne is in Axum Zion are our Patron.'[33]

The festival of Hedar Seyon (the feast of Mary) or Dabra Seyon (the 'Mountain of Zion'), is held annually on 21 Hedar (30 November). It celebrates the arrival in Aksum of the Ark of the Covenant (or the arrival of the *tabota Seyon*, the tablet of the Law)[34] as well as the dedication of the church of Maryam Seyon by Frumentius. Yet the *sellata Muse* or *tabota Seyon* itself is never taken out of its chapel at this time – or indeed at any other time, whatever might have happened in the distant past.[35] The *KN* offers a variant date for the coming of the Ark: 'now Zion came into the country of Ethiopia... in [the] Ge'ez [month of] Miyazya, on the sixth (or seventh) day'. Local people in Aksum say that the feast was once celebrated on 21 Ter (29 January) – it is still commemorated monthly on the 21st of each Ethiopian month. The 21 Ter was an auspicious day, associated with Mary. The chronicle of Zara Yaqob reports that his coronation was celebrated at Aksum on 21 Ter, 'the day of the death of Our Holy Virgin Mary'.

According to one author the *tabot* at Maryam Seyon church is designated, 'Our Mother Zion': *emmena Seyon*,

> *Emmena Seyon* means 'Our Mother Zion', the epithet of the ark of the church of Aksum. The name is presumably biblical, taken from Ps. 86 (87), 5, where the Ge'ez *emena Seyon* is misunderstood as *emmena Seyon*; both are written [with the same Ge'ez letters, without gemination].[36]

This presumably is the *tabot* of Mary currently in the church, not the *sellata Muse* or *tabota Seyon*, which, kept concealed, cannot participate in the eucharist – even if perhaps once Alvares' altar stone from Zion, or de Almeida's '*tabot* of Sion', performed this function.

Emmena Seyon certainly exists as a phrase in the *Book of Aksum* and in Ge'ez prayers, or even as a personal name, as for example the mother of the Ethiopian saint Yohannes Mesraqawi, and also the wife of Mattewos of Wagda and Katata who later married Tasfa Iyasus, by whom she became mother of Emperor Yekuno Amlak. It is supposed to derive from a psalm of David, which (interpreted) represents Zion as our mother: (Psalm 87.5).

'And of Zion it shall be said, This and that man was born in her…' The *KN* cites this psalm (*KN* 50) in a slightly different form derived from the Greek Septuagint: 'The Law shall be given unto them, and they shall say unto Zion, "our mother because of a man who shall be born"' (in *KN* 106 the verse is cited again but, typically, in another version without any mention of the word 'mother'). The Ark, too, is regarded as 'our Lady, our Mother and our salvation' (*KN* 53).

When *ras* Alula in the 1890s endowed the church of Dabra Seyon of Aksum and other churches, his chronicler remarked how he gave 'most of all, for our mother of Zion'.[37]

But *emmena Seyon* is not – according to members of priestly families in Aksum – the dedication of a *tabot*. The *tabot* of the church of Mary of Zion, they suggest, is simply designated '*tabot* of Maryam' or perhaps '*tabot* of Maryam Seyon'. The last *nebura'ed* of Aksum defined *emmena Seyon* as Jerusalem in Old Testament times and, logically enough, says that it represents all Christians in our New Testament times; an answer based perhaps on Hebrews 9, where the Ark, the Holy of Holies and the blood offerings prefigure the New Covenant sanctified by Jesus' blood.

TABOT *AND GRAIL*

The concept of the *tabot* as a sacred stone has had further ramifications, in the unlikely setting of the Grail legend. Helen Adolf, in a study of Oriental sources of Wolfram von Eschenbach's *Parzifal* and other Grail legends, provides a new facet to the story of the *tabot* and the Ark.[38] She presents Maryam Seyon church at Aksum in an unusual context.

Because the stone tablet of Moses is supposed to be kept at Aksum in the *enda sellat*, and a large sacred stone is noted at Aksum by various records at least from the 16th century, Adolf considered that Ethiopia might have been a source for certain details in the *Parzifal*, in which the Holy Grail becomes a stone fallen from heaven rather than the cup in which Christ's blood was collected. According to Adolf:

> three features of the Parzifal, all missing in Chrétien [de Troyes' late twelfth century romance *Perceval* or *Le Conte du Graal*] force our eyes to look towards far-off Abyssinia: first, India and the Prester John; second, the Grail as a stone; third, Feirefiz, son of Belakane.

The first of these features in the *Parzifal* legend is easily comprehensible. The name India was often applied to Ethiopia, and Prester John was a common European designation for Ethiopian emperors at a certain period. The second element associating Grail legends and Ethiopia concerns the *tabot* as a representation of the tablet(s) of the Law, which were of stone. Adolf, assembling information from Abu Salih, Eldad Ha-Dani, Rufinus, the *Kebra Nagast*, copies of the 1165 letter from 'Prester John' which circulated in many languages in Europe, and other works, suggests that 'rumours about this land of India with its Priest Kings, its sacred stone and Quest connected with it (a quest pursued by the fatherless son of a Queen), may therefore have reached the West'. The Ethiopian quest concerned alludes to Menelik's journey to meet his father Solomon, and his gaining the Ark thereby. This introduces Adolf's third element, the piebald black-and-white prince Feirefiz. He is for various reasons likened to Menelik of Ethiopia – the son of a white Jewish father and a black Ethiopian mother – while Belakane, the lovely black queen of Zazamanc, is identified with Bilqis, queen of Sheba.

Adolf accepts Ethiopia's contribution to the Grail story as indirect. She proposes that von Eschenbach 'found [the Ethiopian elements] in his source, liked their Oriental flavour, used them in the composition of the work, but was never able to locate them accurately'. She adds that there are a number of similarities between Grail and *tabot*:

> to ensure sexual purity, the *tabot* is carried only by young deacons eleven to
> fifteen years of age; the *tabot* bears an inscription (the name of a saint is
> written upon it); it is placed on trestles; light emanates from its Aksum
> prototype, which came down from heaven, can wander through the air, and
> will ultimately return to Jerusalem.

The first of these is completely untrue, priests usually carrying the *tabotat*, while the last four derive from *KN* 17, 55, 114.

From the point of view of Ethiopian history and literature, relatively little can be added to Adolf's study. So far, there is no evidence for the existence of the *KN* early enough for it to have been a source for von Eschenbach (c. 1170–1210: a contemporary of Abu Salih and King Lalibela – and Pope Alexander III, who is said to have written in 1177 to a certain 'John, the illustrious and magnificent king of the Indies'). The statement in the *KN* colophon dating the translation from Coptic into Arabic to 1225 in the reign of Lalibela Gabra Masqal could allude to an early Coptic story about Solomon and the queen of Sheba, or to one of the Coptic apocalypses that prophesied the destruction of Egypt by Ethiopians. We have no reason to assume that it included any mention of the Ark at that date.

On the other hand, Abu Salih believed that the Ark was supposed to be in Ethiopia by the early 13th century, and that Ethiopian kings were priests (Prester = presbyter, priest). *Tabotat* in the form of tablets are not known from this period, but *tabotat* in the form of cubic altars from Lalibela may date from the late 12th–early 13th century. Their existence implies that altar tablets, perhaps made of stone, might have existed as well: Abu Salih mentions 'tables of stone'. The Coptic versions were usually of wood, though Ethiopian ones are sometimes of stone. It is only later that we have evidence (again, apart from assertion in the *KN* colophon that the book existed already in Lalibela's reign) for the Ethiopian monarchy's claim to descent from the House of David. There is certainly no evidence for it before 1270, and nothing until – we presume, though without actual contemporary documents – the edition of the *KN* produced by Yeshaq and his associates just before 1322. Abu Salih attributes to Lalibela another descent, from Moses' and Aaron's family, although he states that descendants of the House of David were in attendance upon the Ark (this, presumably, at Lalibela's capital, Adefa, not Aksum). Davidic descent was a requirement also in later versions of the Grail story for the winner of the Grail. All we can say is that perhaps stories about Ethiopia could have reached the authors of early Grail legends, in more or less garbled form.[39]

4

The Ark and the Tablets: From King Solomon to Queen Gudit

un peuple ne se défend pas seulement avec ses armes, mais avec ses livres

Menelik II, Emperor of Ethiopia

MANUSCRIPT TREASURES

On the arch of Titus, erected in 81 AD at the entrance of the Roman Forum, are some remarkable carvings. They depict the holy objects brought in 70 AD from the sacking of the temple of Jerusalem, most conspicuously the *menorah*, the great seven-branched golden candlestick. In an amusing account of a trip to Rome, A. Mallinson observes:

> Among these objects [looted from the Holy of Holies], on the arch the Ark is not represented. When the profane Romans entered the sacred place the Ark was missing! It is said that at the moment when Christ was crucified and the veil of the Temple was rent in twain, the omnipotent hands of Yahweh twitched it away. It is said that He hid it away in Egypt as once He had hidden His Son. It is now in one of those remarkable, mysterious, Coptic churches in Ethiopia carved in the solid rock. I do not know which; neither for that matter does anyone else. I have a number of mystical Ethiopian manuscripts… Perhaps if they were studied they might tell where the Ark was…[1]

He was evidently unaware that, as far as the Ethiopians and their manuscripts are concerned, the fate of the Ark, and its present dwelling place, were already well known.

A treasure of ancient manuscripts lies concealed in Ethiopia's innumerable churches and monasteries. Such manuscripts, written in the ancient Ethiopic language, Ge'ez, on parchment, sometimes adorned with paintings, and bound in heavy leather-covered wooden boards impressed with decorative designs, were the object of continuous recopying and editing as the originals, much handled, wore out. Many of the old monastic foundations and churches that lie scattered in the most inaccessible recesses of the mountains of Tigray and Eritrea, the monasteries supposedly founded by the Nine Saints or by other distinguished ecclesiastics, and the church of Maryam Seyon (Mary of Zion) at Aksum itself, possess or possessed in the past substantial libraries.

Major programmes of research and recording are currently in progress on this mass of literature. Two of my colleagues, Jacques Mercier and Girma Elias, explored many sites in Tigray and other places, even if, in a film that described their efforts, Mercier was heard to mutter in exasperation: 'on est toujours embêté à chaque moment'. Other colleagues, Stanislaw Chojnacki and Paul Henze, have investigated countryside churches, often extremely difficult of access. A great deal has been done, and previously unknown manuscripts or paintings revealed. Even so, many Ethiopian texts still remain unpublished, and there may yet be unknown works to discover.

The process has been almost continuous since the days when Ethiopian manuscripts first came to the attention of an eager foreign observer, the Portuguese priest Francisco Alvares. He was the first foreigner to publish such documentation in any detail, though two of his contemporaries, early 16th century Ethiopian ambassadors to Portugal, Matthew the Armenian and Saga Za-Ab, had both left hints that Ethiopia was the repository of literary works of some importance. The latter specifically referred to a book containing the story of King Solomon and the queen of Sheba. Alvares' Spanish successor a century later, Péro Pais, was another important recorder of Ethiopian literature, the earliest to tell the *KN* story in the form we now know it. Pais' work long remained unpublished, though it was available in manuscript form. Job Ludolf, the German scholar who became the first important European historian of Ethiopia with his books published in the 1680s and 1690s, added more information, based to some extent on the 1660 compilation by the Portuguese ecclesiastic Balthasar Telles. He in turn drew on then unpublished manuscripts by other Iberian ecclesiastics who worked in Ethiopia: Manoel de Almeida, Péro Pais, Afonso Mendes and Jerónimo Lobo. Also, very importantly, Ludolf could rely on discussions with a learned Ethiopian monk,

Gorgoreyos, who resided for a time at the monastery of St. Stefano dei Mori in Rome.

Nearly a century later, in the 1770s, a large collection of *Aethiopica* was assembled by the Scots traveller, James Bruce. This was the first time that copies of the *KN* actually reached Europe, as far as we know.[2] Bruce also added considerably to knowledge about Ethiopia with his famous multi-volume *Travels to Discover the Source of the Nile* published in 1790, in the third volume of which he included an account of the *KN*. Other manuscript collections were assembled by travellers or residents in Ethiopia like the d'Abbadie brothers, Arnaud and Antoine. Many manuscripts ended up in the Bibliothèque Nationale in Paris, or in the Vatican Library. A very large number of volumes, gathered from the churches of Gondar by the Emperor Tewodros II and lodged at his mountain fortress of Maqdala before 1868, were in that year captured as war booty and transported to England. Most still remain there, protected and secure in the royal collection at Windsor Castle or in the British Library.

The Ethiopian manuscript volumes in Europe have usually been catalogued,[3] and studied. Now, microfilming and photography are opening an ever widening access to those sources still guarded in Ethiopian libraries – though, unfortunately, in the last few decades of civil strife and starvation, many manuscripts have been broken up, stolen, sold or destroyed. Nevertheless, gradually, a solid core of information has been assembled, increasing regularly through the literary studies of such scholars as Sergew Hable Sellassie and Getatchew Haile, among others.

A SEARCH BEGINS

There is only one way to solve the mystery of the Ethiopian Ark of the Covenant, since it will probably never be openly shown to the world – intensive study of the documentation about it in many languages and over many centuries. This fascinating study occupied me for several years. When I began to trace the saga of the Ark for a brief note in my guide to Ethiopian historical sites, *Ethiopia, the Unknown Land*, I had no idea that the search could branch into so many different directions, indeed into a maze of diverging paths. I assumed that I would study Ethiopian, Portuguese and other texts, trace those mentioning the Ark, and arrive at the date when it was first mentioned.

I was already fairly sure that the story would not go back to the time of King Solomon in Israel, but I hardly expected that the evidence for the Ark would prove so elusive and ambiguous. The Ethiopian Ark can be several things, in several places, at different times. The *KN* too exists in several versions. These facts, together with a vocabulary that was often equivocal or opaque, posed a stimulating challenge.

I had taken on a massive, if exhilarating, task. Whatever seemed likely to refer to the holy object had to be hunted out and studied. I needed to contact scholars with specialist expertise in dating specific types of old texts: Ethiopic has its own specialists, and others have devoted years to studying Arabic or Coptic, for example. When possible, I looked at manuscripts and other works in person – I have studied all these languages myself, at least to some degree – despite the difficulties of access. Ancient and precious manuscripts apart, even some printed books are rare and very valuable. Incunabula and some of the early printed books are treasures to be protected, and are not readily available. Special permission must be obtained to leaf through something as remarkable as Caxton's *The Golden Legend*, for example, one of England's earliest printed books. London, Oxford, Paris, Berlin, the Italian libraries, private collections, all required investigation. In addition, hundreds of articles from learned journals to newspaper cuttings had to be collected, read and analysed. Under circumstances like these, the real value of email for speeding up the process of enquiry and answer is deeply appreciated.

I had worked at Aksum in 1973–74 with the British Institute in Eastern Africa team, when we discovered and partly excavated the royal tombs of the kings of Aksum – while Emperor Haile Sellassie, last 'Lion of the Tribe of Judah', and reputed 225th descendant of King Solomon of Israel, was still on his throne. But even though I had returned several times since for research purposes, new visits were called for, both to look into matters related to the Ark, and for other research reasons. The terrain of Maryam Seyon church, and the remains of its more ancient predecessors, required closer study. I needed to talk to the church treasurer, the guardian of the sacred object at the church and the *nebura'ed*, in charge of church administration, as well as with some of the local clergy, infinitely learned in the practices and secrets of their religion. Essential, too, was investigation into the mysteries of another subject that proved both elusive and obscure, the Ethiopian altar tablet or *tabot*: with the results just described. Luckily, I had made Aksumite friends in the past, and matters could be arranged.

Collecting the evidence was an intriguing task. Gradually building up an account of what had been said about the Ark in Ethiopia over the centuries became as thrilling as any whodunit. There were – and are – some who revered and worshipped the Ark, and some who scorned and laughed at it. Many simply do not know what to think. Most amazing was the richness of the material that had to be investigated, and its labyrinthine complexity. The simplest thing opens doorway after doorway of enquiry. A name like Maryam Seyon, for instance, seems easily enough defined: a church at Aksum in Ethiopia dedicated to Mary of Zion. Everyone from the Ethiopian authors of religious books via distinguished Ethiopianist professors to Graham Hancock says it is very old, and guards or is supposed to guard the Ark. Such matters are taken for granted. But when you study the documents, and actually begin to look at Maryam Seyon in history, the questions come leaping to the eye. When is the dedication to Mary first attested? When, even more vital, does the word Seyon appear, linking it with the Ark? Why this pairing of the mother of Jesus and the name of a mountain in Jerusalem? When does any document first actually state that the Ark is at Maryam Seyon church? What do archaeology and the records of foreign visitors say about the church? The answers, as they emerge from the mass of evidence, result in something very different from 'what everyone says'.

The search for the truth about the Ark at Aksum begins with this exploration through Ethiopian history as the documents reveal it. The Ark has not over the centuries behaved as it once did in Israel. It does not advertise its presence with the drama of destruction and punishment that once, we are told by the Old Testament books, followed it wherever it went. It has changed utterly, becoming a secret thing, a holy mystery, its story attainable only through studying obscure writings of the past. To appreciate the nature of the mysterious talisman that the Ethiopians call *tabota Seyon*, the Ark of Zion, we need to establish exactly what, century by century, is recorded about it in these old records. Equally important, we must register how the story alters and shifts perspective as time passes.

NINE SAINTS

In the infinitely tempting setting of the traditional stories about the conversion of Ethiopia by Feremnatos/Frumentius and Abreha and Asbeha in the 4th century, and the building of the church at Aksum, a strange fact is immediately noticeable: the Ark is never mentioned (see Chapter 4 *The Book of Aksum*). It does appear in a 1943 story of the life of Abba Salama, as the Ethiopians call Frumentius, but that work is filled with anachronisms: Schneider called it a 'feuilleton hagiographique de la pire espèce'.[4] It describes the converter of Ethiopia in the 4th century, the first bishop of Aksum, meeting Minas bishop of Aksum (!) and travelling in Gojjam and other far-flung spots that never belonged to Aksum's empire. Frumentius invites the governors of Gojjam, Gondar and Harar (regions historically quite beyond Aksum's pale) to venerate the Ark in Aksum.

The Ark is also completely ignored in documents that allude to a slightly later period, when the stories are told of the lives of a group of holy men who lived and died in the ambience of the kings, bishops and church of ancient Aksum.

The life stories of the Nine Saints, and other missionaries or local holy men, the *sadqan*, are detailed in a cycle of hagiographical tales set in the Aksumite Ethiopia of the 5th-6th centuries AD. None of these revered ecclesiastics are ever in any way associated with Aksum's great palladium, the Ark of the Covenant, nor did the 15th or 16th century compilers of their *gadlat* (literally, 'struggles' – meaning life stories) feel much impulsion to add this sort of material to whatever legends they had access to, or to what they invented. The Ark seems not to have entered into the Ethiopians' own religious mythology for that period, as it is represented by these hagiographies. This is natural enough if at the time of writing of the stories no one claimed that the Ark was in Ethiopia. Virtually every other imaginable ingredient is present in the *gadlat*, factual or marvellous, anachronistic or plausible. Aksumite kings, metropolitan bishops, churchmen both local and foreign, rural hermitages and monasteries, even the church of Aksum itself, are all intimately involved in the stories of the lives of the Nine Saints and other holy men. So are miracles of all sorts, giant serpents, tame lions, tunnels to impossibly distant spots, and saints divinely transported floating on clouds, among other paranormal phenomena – but not the Ark.

The 'Israelite' monarchy may be alluded to, as in the *Gadla Aregawi*, where King Gabra Masqal is addressed: 'may God bless your kingdom, as he blessed the kingdom of David and Solomon, and as he blessed the kingdom of Kaleb your father'.[5] This might indicate that the writer of this late *gadl* knew the story related in the *KN* – it is difficult to imagine that he did not –

and meant to refer to it. But in fact no claim is made suggesting Kaleb's royal descent from King Solomon and the queen of Sheba. In the *Life of Garima*, however, another unhistorical late 15th century homily, it is specified that as a consequence of the anarchy in the country after the death of a serpent-king Arwe, the Nine Saints begged for a king of the line of David, and God gave them King Kaleb.[6]

Interestingly, the *KN* makes no reference at all to the Nine Saints or indeed to any other of the holy men of Ethiopia, even those who were supposed to have moved in King Gabra Masqal's circle. Nor does it refer to those revered figures Iyasus Mo'a and Takla Haymanot, who, in later *gadlat*, were assigned a major part in the 'Solomonic restoration', justified in Ethiopian history as re-establishing 'the House of Israel' on the throne it had lost to the Zagwé. The omission of the Nine Saints is extraordinary for an Aksumite *nebura'ed* like Yeshaq – supposedly the chief of the compilers/translators who prepared the first version of the *KN*. He was a churchman whose city and its environs were thronged with places associated with saints like Pantalewon, Liqanos and the famous sacred musician Yared. We might expect him and his fellow writers to be steeped in the tales of the lives of these saints, as are modern Aksumites. But perhaps the majority of the tales that became so well known later were not extant at the time the *KN* was written? Evidence for most of the '5th-6th century' Ethiopian saints is not of very ancient date, and indeed there is no mention of any of them before the date of the redaction of the *KN*, except perhaps for Libanos, the 'Apostle of Eritrea' (sometimes included as one of the Nine Saints, but usually not). If there *were* certain tales circulating about them in early 14th century Ethiopia, they were perhaps not deemed relevant to the theme pursued by the *KN*. Or perhaps during the editing process we suppose the book to have undergone over the centuries, certain specifically 'Aksumite' or northern elements were eliminated?

The *Life* of Yared, on the other hand, does make oblique allusion to something derived from the story of Solomon and the queen of Sheba's son, in citing the place near Aksum where Ebna Lahakim (Menelik) was buried. It also refers to *daqiqa Seyon gabaza Aksum*, 'the children of Zion the Cathedral (lit. guard/guardian, protector) of Aksum' in several places.[7] The *gadl* situates the events of Yared's life in the reign of Gabra Masqal, son of Kaleb, in the 6th century. Like all the rest of these hagiographies of 5th-6th century ecclesiastical figures in Aksum, the *Life* of Yared dates from much later. Conti Rossini did not attribute a date to the sole manuscript known to him, though Guidi attributed its original composition to the late 15th century.[8] This may be so, but the sole surviving copy dated to the 19th century and may have been edited one or more times. Now another text is known, dated to the 17th century.[9]

The *gadl* mentions the Nine Saints, the mythical (?) Degnayzan, 'Israelite' king of Aksum, the Zagwé Merara who took the empire from the Israelites, Yekuno Amlak and Amda Seyon, 'from the tribe of Judah and from the house of David...' By the time the surviving texts were written, these matters were part of accepted history, after centuries steeped in the legends of the *KN*. In the manuscripts, *malke'a*, a genre of poetic expression praising each part of the saint's body, follow the life and miracles of the saint. Like the *Synaxarium*, the *malke'a* mention how Yared was raised a cubit above the earth before the *tabot* (altar tablet) of the Lord of Zion.[10] The author of the *Life* of Pantalewon, too, may have derived some ideas from the *KN* (or from Coptic apocalypses which contain very similar material), in such statements as 'our king Christ strengthened the empire of Rome and the empire of Ethiopia', and in a note that superiority was bestowed on the Roman and Ethiopian kings.[11]

WAR IN HIMYAR

The absence of the Ark is also remarkable in the accounts of the best known of all Aksum's foreign ventures, the conquest of Jewish-ruled Yemen in the 6th century. A vast literature was inspired by this campaign.[12] Nevertheless, despite the multitude of records about King Kaleb and Yemen preserved in Ethiopic, Coptic, Arabic, and especially Syriac versions, the Ark, supposedly residing in Aksum – or, at least, in 'Dabra Makeda' – since the queen of Sheba's time, is never mentioned in the Ethiopian context, however obliquely.

If there were a moment when the passing of the Ark, with all its symbolic power, and the immanent presence of God, from Israel to Ethiopia, should have been emphasised, surely this was it. The king of Aksum, Kaleb, was departing from his African capital to lead his armies overseas to the conquest of a Jewish Arab ruler who had dared to persecute Christians in his own land. It would have been an inspired moment to triumph – as the *KN* does so ostentatiously (in *KN* 87 for example) – in the possession of what had been the glory of Israel and Jerusalem, and was now the glory of Ethiopia and the Second Jerusalem, Aksum.

At the time of this war, c. 520 AD, King Kaleb, according to the hagiographies, consulted Abba Pantalewon, one of the Nine Saints, about his plans. He later even sent his crown to be hung above the Holy Sepulchre in Jerusalem itself (or so it was later claimed).[13] The *Book of the Himyarites*, a genuine contemporary document, relates how the emperor conferred with Euprepios, bishop of Aksum, about such questions as the readmission of apostates to the faith. Yet never, at this time when the glamour of the Christian kingdom of Ethiopia was at its apogee, and the name of Kaleb, the 'God-loving king of Ethiopia' was on the lips of the entire eastern Christian world, does any contemporary source allude to the existence of what would have been the greatest of all the treasures of Christian Aksum: the Ark of Zion. Unlike his distant successor Iyasu I, Kaleb is not recorded visiting and consulting the Ark. Nor is it ever described functioning as a battle standard as in the days of the Israelite conquests, or in Ebna Lahakim's time if we credit the *KN*. Only *KN* 117, in a curious and interesting apocalyptic passage, associates Kaleb, dead nearly eight hundred years before it was written, with the Ark.

Intriguingly, the Ark, with the tablets of the Law, *is* mentioned by a contemporary writer but on the other, Jewish, side of the Himyarite conflict. In the *Letter* attributed to Simeon, bishop of Beth Arsham, dated in July of the year 830 of Alexander, 518 AD,[14] the Jewish king Yusuf of Himyar is said to have sworn an oath to the Christian people of Najran that if they surrendered he would send them safely to the king of the Kushites (Kaleb). This message was borne by 'Jewish priests from (Tiberias)', who came carrying

> the Torah of Moses and a letter of oaths with the seal of this Jewish king; and
> he swore to them by the Torah, the Tablets of Moses, the Ark, and by the
> God of Abraham, Isaac, and Israel that no harm would befall them if they
> surrendered the city willingly...

They did so, and were executed. Later, when Harith ibn Ka'b, a Najranite leader, was similarly promised freedom if he denied Christ, he replied: 'Do (remember) the oaths (you swore) to us by the God of Abraham, Isaac and Israel, and by your Torah and the Tablets and the Ark.' Similarly, in the *Book of the Himyarites*, the Jewish priests from Tiberias and others are said to have delivered a letter to arrange the surrender of Abyssinians in Zafar. The Himyarite ruler, named disparagingly as 'this tyrant Masruq', swore this time by 'Adonai, and by the Ark, and by the Thora' to send them back to their own country and king. They too surrendered, with the same result.

These citations, though contemporary with the events, are still from second-hand reports asserting repetitions of a formal oath based on Jewish themes. This was an age when rhetoric was a valued part of education, and when certain prerequisites went into 'historical' accounts. If a king about to go into battle, say, failed to give a stirring speech, or no proper account of what he had really said could be obtained, something suitable was invented. Yusuf, king of Himyar, may never have actually uttered these words. Yet it

5. King Kaleb's victory over Yusuf Dhu Nuwas, king of Himyar. Manuscript painting. Photo courtesy of Dr B. Juel-Jensen.

seems strange that if Aksum was by then known universally to be in possession of the tablets of the Law and the Ark of the Covenant, the Syrian ecclesiastic who wrote the *Book* and probably the *Letter* as well – a man who was in contact with Euprepios, bishop of the Kushites, and with Kaleb the king of Aksum himself – would not have added some comment about the singular inappropriateness of the oath. It was addressed to persons whom the Jewish king was promising to send back to that same Kushite king whose dynasty – supposedly – had already possessed the most important sacred Jewish relics on which he based his oath for over fourteen hundred years.

In the port-city of Adulis and in the capital, Aksum, just before the war with Himyar, the traveller whose work is known under the name of 'Kosmas Indikopleustes' was recording some facts about the Ethiopian kingdom. He would later present them in his book, *The Christian Topography*, a work 'still very much worth consulting as a wholesome tonic for any who believe there may be limits to human credulity'.[15] Kosmas, with his companion Menas, was commissioned by the Aksumite governor of Adulis, Asbas, to copy a Greek inscription, which Kaleb of Aksum required to justify his invasion of the Yemen. This inscription Kosmas published later, preserving the details of a now-lost Aksumite document. Kosmas recorded numerous interesting details about what he observed in Ethiopia, though as incidentals, not attempting to offer a complete description of the Ethiopians and their way of life.

Instead, his great theme, the key to his book, was his attempt to fit the design of the known world in parallel with the construction of the tabernacle of Moses. As he wandered about Aksum, noting the four-towered royal palace, the bronze statues of unicorns, the stuffed unicorn (rhinoceros) in the palace, and other such details, is it possible that he would have heard no whisper that in Aksum's chief church (which tradition claims had been long in existence by then) reposed the Ark of the Covenant – that very object which had once been enclosed in the tabernacle, the model of the universe, that so fascinated him? In addition, when Kosmas refers to the queen of Sheba, she is described as 'the Queen of Sheba, that is to say of the country of the Himyarites' – Himyar, Yusuf's kingdom in what is today the Yemen. Kosmas accepted that the queen collected some of her valuable gifts from Ethiopia, but that was all.

DATING THE KEBRA NAGAST

Irfan Shahid twenty years ago revived the old notion of a 6th century date for the original composition of the *KN*, which Budge too had considered.[16] Shahid particularly emphasised that Kaleb and his (legendary?) sons Gabra Masqal and Israel were the Ethiopian 'heroes' of the book – though they only appear in the short final chapter, *KN* 117 – while there is no mention of vital later elements in Ethiopian history: Islam, Gudit, the Solomonic rulers and so on. Shahid suggested that if the *KN* were a legend composed to glorify the 14th century monarchy, silence on these subjects would be, to say the least, strange. The idea is an interesting one, and the apocalyptic image of Kaleb and his sons certainly bestows prominence on these three royal figures. The *KN* selects them alone from all the kings after Ebna Lahakim as worthy of mention in this treatise supposed to have been written to glorify the ancestry of the Solomonic kings. The passage in *KN* 117 (in which a rather mysterious date, 'at the end of this cycle, twelve cycles' is inserted)[17] reads as follows:

> And thus after they [Kaleb and Justin] had become united in a common bond, and had established the right faith they were to determine that the Jews were no longer to live, and each of them was to leave his son there; and the King of Ethiopia was to leave there his firstborn son whose name was Israel, and was to return to his own country in joy. And when he came to his royal house, he was to give abundant thanks to God, and to offer up his body as an offering of praise to his God. And God shall accept him gladly, for he shall not defile his body after he hath returned, but he shall go into a monastery in purity of heart. And he shall make king his youngest son, whose name is Gabra Maskal, and he himself shall shut himself up [in a monastery]. And when one hath told this to the King of Nagran, the son of Kaleb, he shall come in order to reign over Zion, and Gabra Maskal shall make his armies to rise up, and he shall journey in a chariot, and they shall meet together at the narrow end of the Sea of Liba, and shall fight together...And God will say to Gabra Maskal, 'Choose thou between the chariot and Zion,' and He will cause him to take Zion, and he shall reign openly upon the throne of his father. And God will make Israel to choose the chariot, and he shall reign secretly and he shall not be visible, and He will send him to all those who have transgressed the commandment of God...

KN 117 is introduced by the mention in *KN* 116 of Najran, naturally associated with Kaleb's Himyar war, and the 'chariot of Ethiopia'. The chariot is also mentioned in *KN* 113, where the supposed testimony of Gregory the Illuminator is cited. Gregory is made to say: 'Now this hath God showed me in the pit' (where he had been consigned during the persecution of Christians by the king of Armenia).

> And as concerning the King of Ethiopia, and Zion, the Bride of heaven, and her chariot whereby they move, I will declare unto you that which my God hath revealed unto me and hath made me understand. Ethiopia shall continue in the orthodox faith until the coming of our Lord, and she shall in no way turn aside from the word of the Apostles, and it shall be so even as we have ordered until the end of the world.

The chariot vanquishes the enemy of the king of Ethiopia, and also contains Zion – perhaps it is a derivation of the chariot of 1 Chronicles 28.18, 'the chariot of the cherubims, that spread out [their wings] and covered the ark of the covenant of the Lord'. *KN* 113 prophecies how, even though the 'kings of Rome also have become great because of the nails [of the Cross] that Helena (Emperor Constantine's mother, discoverer of the True Cross) made into a bridle', Rome would lose its glory through a corrupt emperor (Marcian, 450–57, is cited by name) and 'a certain archbishop'.[18]

More confusion follows with the description of the *dénouement*. Through a king of Persia, Harenewos (Irenaeus), Marcian would be defeated, and the horse bearing the bridle with the nails would flee into the sea and perish. This, interestingly in terms of the interweaving of Kaleb-associated legend, was the fate met by Kaleb's opponent, Yusuf of Himyar. He rode his horse into the sea and vanished, according to later Arab historians. The king of Ethiopia, however – it was revealed to Gregory in the pit – with 'Zion, the Bride of heaven, and her chariot whereby they move', would continue orthodox until the end of the world. Ethiopia would survive the coming of Antichrist (*KN* 114), until Christ himself returned to Mount Zion, with Zion (the Ark) sealed with three seals. The Jews, 'the crucifiers', would be judged and punished.

This emphasis on Kaleb and his (mythical?) sons, with allusions to the Himyar war, is extraordinary in a book whose aim, it is usually thought, was to glorify the Solomonic dynasty, particularly the reigning Amhara emperor, Amda Seyon. Yet if the *KN*, the great storehouse of Judaising features connected with the royal and national legend of Ethiopia, had really been compiled in the 6th century, it is astonishing that no hint of this legend seems to have seeped into other Ethiopian, or even foreign, records. There is no sign of this for a very long time. The first record of even the simple unadorned statement that the queen of Sheba came from Ethiopia occurs over five centuries after Kaleb, with Michael of Tinnis.

Allusions or anachronisms in the *KN* do in fact hint at a later setting than the 6th century. Shahid and others have noted them, but those who favour a 6th century date explain the anachronisms away as later accretions. Among them is the mention of Cairo, so named in 973–74, as the city of the king of Egypt in King Solomon's time. Another is the account of David laying waste 'the district of Zawa with Hadeya, for enmity had existed between them from olden time' (*KN* 94). This should allude to the defeat of the Muslim kingdom of Hadya, extremely topical at the time of Yeshaq's 'translation' of the *KN* because in 1316–17 Amda Seyon had fought a successful war there. Yeshaq's name (assuming him to be the *nebura'ed* of Aksum of the time: see below) is cited the very next year in a land grant. A third allusion is the reference, not just in the colophon, but also in *KN* 34, to the rule in Ethiopia of non-Israelites, transgressors of the Law; that is, the 12th-13th century Zagwé dynasty. Finally, the mention of Shewa in *KN* 39 as part of the kingdom is certainly not appropriate to Kaleb's time. Instead, it reflects the exact situation in the time of the early Solomonic rulers, whose base territory was in that province.

If these details were additions to some older core, one wonders why Yeshaq and others who might have added these accretions were so restrained, and did not add much more. An out-and-out declaration that the reigning king of Ethiopia was the legitimate heir to this dynastic saga would certainly have earned them favour – unless they had some ulterior design, and supported another candidate?

There appear be two possible interpretations. Yeshaq and his helpers may have translated, as the colophon indicates, from an older text extant already in Lalibela's time. We do not know how much of what later became the *KN* might have been contained in this text, but they could have expanded the original at will, including amendments such as the 'anachronisms' cited above. Or they may have composed the book (not excluding the use of older texts for sections of it, partially justifying the colophon's claims) with another, specific intention. They limited it to the Solomon and queen of Sheba story, but added the Kaleb apocalypse, basing it on already extant Coptic apocalypses that designate Ethiopia as the ultimate destroyer of Muslim dominance in Egypt. They cleverly insert Ethiopia's great Christian hero king, Kaleb, adding emphasis to the paramount position of the Ethiopian ruler. The *KN* story made the Ethiopian monarch a holy king, possessor of the tablets of the Law most precious of the relics of ancient Israel.[19] Yet, in the versions that have reached us, at least, it did not specify who that ruler was.[20]

Very probably, the book was created by Yeshaq and his assistants with a specific agenda in mind, at the order of, or to win the favour of, an ambitious regional governor: Ya'ibika Egzi (see Chapter 4: The *nebura'ed* Yeshaq). If this is so, the usual interpretation would be completely wrong. Far from being written to justify the Amhara Solomonic monarchs, it was designed at the behest of a northern ruler whose ultimate aim was to remove the southern dynasty from the scene. In the apocalyptic passage, it is northerners, kings of Aksum, who are lauded. It is not Muslims, as in the Coptic apocalypses, who are the enemy, but Jews, whose place these Aksumite rulers will take as kings of Zion.

AFTER KALEB

Kaleb's sons appear also in the late king lists and hagiographies. They are known only from such late Ge'ez works. We have seen how in *KN* 117 their succession to their father after the accord between the emperors of 'Rome' and Ethiopia is described, with the pursuit of the war in Himyar. Yet Gabra Masqal and Israel, sons of Kaleb, remain obscure to historians of Aksum.

Gabra Masqal was to become a very popular figure in the *gadlat* or *Lives* of the Nine Saints and in other hagiographies of the 14th-15th centuries. Local legends often cite him as the founder figure for a church. Whether he actually existed or not remains an open question. Certainly he does not appear, as yet, in any primary Aksumite documentation.

Gabra Masqal, 'Servant of the Cross', it is an authentic Zagwé and Solomonic name – though it was unknown, as far as we are yet aware, in Aksum, where the nearest epithet to it so far, found in inscriptions of Kaleb and his son Wa'zeb, was Gabra Krestos, slave or servant of Christ. It is striking that both Lalibela, the king mentioned in the *KN* colophon, and Amda Seyon, emperor of Ethiopia (1314–44) when that colophon was written, as well as Amda Seyon's father and predecessor Widim Ra'ad (1299–1314), all used the throne name Gabra Masqal. In the next century Emperor Yeshaq (1414–29) adopted it, and it was also one of the names offered to, but not selected by, Baeda Maryam, at his accession. If a compiler of the 13th-14th centuries were seeking a plausible royal name to introduce for a son of Aksum's most famed ruler, Gabra Masqal could most readily leap to mind.[21]

One small tantalising fact associates the Aksum of the post-Kaleb period with a King Israel, and with the *KN*. The name 'Israel, king of the Aksumites', an otherwise unknown ruler, is stamped on very rare bronze coins, and on 33 golden coins contained in a sort of money-box of pottery discovered at the ancient Aksumite port of Adulis.[22] A few other examples of King Israel's gold have also been found elsewhere. From study of Aksumite coinage, this king can be dated after Kaleb's reign. He does not seem to have been a direct successor, though his precise position in the coinage sequence still remains uncertain. The *KN* is at pains to point out that after the civil war between the sons of Kaleb, the firstborn, Israel, formerly established in Arabia as 'King of Nagran' (an allusion to King Kaleb's Himyar war and its aftermath), inherited a mystical spiritual kingdom, while it was Gabra Masqal who continued to reign as earthly king. We should, then, rather expect coins of Gabra Masqal, king of the Aksumites, than of Israel. Nevertheless, the coinage does authenticate the Aksumite royal name Israel, whether or not Israel was truly a son of Kaleb, brother to another king called Gabra Masqal, as the *KN* claims.[23]

The apocalypse of Zion in *KN* 117 gives great prominence to these two mysterious sons of the hero king Kaleb, neatly using them to encompass the Ethiopian sphere. Gabra Masqal, the 'Servant of the Cross', by his name evokes Christianity. He reigns openly over Zion. Israel, redolent of vengeance and the punishment of transgressors, represents the Jewish world of the Old Testament. Together they hold the reins of power in the real world and in the hidden realm of the spirit, each with his celestial implement of power, Zion or the chariot.[24] The *KN* apocalypse presents the two kings as symbols, like the Ethiopian Zion itself, of Ethiopia triumphant under a God-given order. But there is no proof for the existence of these two sons of Kaleb in reality. Like the Ethiopian Zion, too, they may be nothing more than the creation of the fertile minds that compiled Ethiopia's great myth, the *KN*.

If it is strange that the Ark, supposedly at Aksum for over a millennium, does not appear amid the high drama of the Jewish-Christian war between Himyar and Aksum, except in King Yusuf's treacherous oath, it is just as perplexing to observe its absence during other crucial moments in later Ethiopian history. Ethiopian tradition preserves accounts about later, vital events in the history of the monarchy that was supposedly invested in the 'Israelite' dynasty of Ebna Lahakim or Menelik. Yet in the dramatic tales concerning the decline and fall of the Aksumite dynasty, the establishment around 1137 AD of the Zagwé, and the 're-establishment' of the Solomonic dynasty by Yekuno Amlak with the help of the holy men Iyasus Mo'a or Takla Haymanot around 1268–70, we can trace only one reference to the Ark (see Chapter 4: The Ark of Lalibela).[25]

It was during the 'dark age' in Ethiopian history, in the second half of the 11th century, that Michael of Tinnis recorded in the biography of patriarch Kosmas III (923–34) that: 'al-Habasha...is a vast country, namely the kingdom of Saba from which the queen of the South came to Solomon, the son of David the king'.[26] Rodinson envisages that this theme of the queen crossed the sea from Arabia, where a *midrash* (explanation of Biblical text) had been developed on the story by local Jews.[27] The appearance of the tale in the Qur'an attests to this. The midrashic story of the queen of Sheba as found in the *Targum Sheni of the Book of Esther* is the most developed version.[28] Apparently the first mention in Jewish writings of the birth of a son to King Solomon and the queen of Sheba occurs in the *Alphabet of Ben Sira* – 9th or 10th century? There, with a fine disregard for mere chronology, the son is identified as Nebuchadnezzar, the king of Babylon who destroyed the first temple at Jerusalem![29] At this period the tale makes no reference to Ethiopian dynastic origins.

QUEEN GUDIT

Queen Gudit (Yodit) holds pride of place with the 16th century Muslim invader Ahmad Grañ as one of the monsters of Ethiopian history. She is said to have swept across Ethiopia with her army, pillaging and destroying. Belai Giday attributes some information about the Ark at this time to the *KN*:

> It is written in the Kibre Negest...that during the war waged by Yodit on Christian Ethiopia, in order to save the Ark of the Covenant from destruction, it was brought from Aksum to an island of Zuai [Lake Zway] in Shewa by the priests...Some of the Aksumites remained on the island of Zuai and to this day the majority of the present-day population who live in Zuai, Debre Zion, claim to be the descendants of Aksumites and they speak Tigrigna.[30]

In fact the *KN* never once cites Gudit, or indeed any other historical events in Ethiopia – the very reason why Irfan Shahid found it so difficult to believe that it could be dated later than the 6th century. The tale of Gudit is told in other traditional Ge'ez manuscripts, chronicles and the like, where it appears in a variety of forms, and with some confusion of dates, names and events. There is an Ethiopian legend that the Ark was hidden on an island in Lake Zway, but not in the *KN*, nor even in the short compilation known as the '*Kebra Nagast* of Lake Zway'.[31] Instead, it appears among the chronicles assembled and amalgamated not long ago by the *qese gabaz* (provost of the church) Takla Haymanot of Aksum. The compilation offers an account of Gudit's actions, and the flight of the Ark to Zway in response (see Chapter 6: Wanderings of the Ark).

Queen Gudit, clearly, was modelled on an historical character, who really did conquer part of Ethiopia, including perhaps the Aksum region. Her existence is confirmed in Arabic records around the 960s. She may have destroyed a church at Aksum, but it is only a very late – mid-20th century – document that links her invasion with the Ark.

The Tigray population of Lake Zway add a mysterious element. Why should northerners dwell so far south, over four hundred miles from their homeland? Zway is not in Shewa, but even further south. It makes a good tale to claim that Tigray people have lived there since the 10th century because of the Ark, retaining their language, but we have clear confirmation otherwise. In one document the 14th century missionary monks Filipos and Anorewos visit Zway, and find, on one of the islands, 'pagans who did not have any religion and who ate the flesh of both properly slain and dead animals'. They converted the local people, and a monastery probably flourished there by the end of the century. Tigrayans of four hundred year old stock are not mentioned in these traditions. Even the later monastery does not seem to have flourished. Francisco Alvares mentions 'a big lake like a sea' (Lake Zway) in Hadya. Emperor Lebna Dengel (1508–40) once journeyed to Hadya with his army and several Portuguese and Genoese, who later told Alvares:

> the monks of [the island monastery built by a former 'Prester John'] nearly all died of fevers, and some few remained in another small monastery not on the island, and near the lake...And that this time the Prester John ordered many monasteries and churches to be built, and left there many priests and monks, and many laymen to inhabit and dwell in that kingdom.[32]

Perhaps some of the replacement monks originated from Tigray. Celibate monks would not reproduce, or were not supposed to, but the text does emphasise that laymen came too. Later the emperor sent many books to Zway to be preserved there from Ahmad Grañ's raids.

COPTIC MEMORIES

Even the most fragmentary parchment scraps, a few lines fortuitously preserved, can help trace the origins of the *KN*. David Hubbard remarked that one component of the *KN* story, the clever way that Solomon seduced Makeda, 'seems to occur only in the Ethiopian and Coptic account and is found in similar form in virtually all Ethiopian legends dealing with the Queen of Sheba'. If it is true that there is 'no parallel to this tale elsewhere',[33] it could constitute a telling point in favour of a Coptic origin for a part, an important part, of the *KN* story – explaining why the colophon or end note cites a Coptic original translated into Arabic in 1225.

A Coptic document apparently relevant to the Solomon and Sheba story, a 10th or 11th century fragment published by Erman in 1897, includes a fair amount of magical embroidery. If such a Coptic original were used, it would have been drastically pruned when Yeshaq and his companions undertook the redaction of the *KN*. In the surviving brief and battered extract from this otherwise lost text, a queen, who is unnamed, is found in discussion with Solomon:

> Then he [took?] a cup of wine and gave it to her [and placed?] his ring in it…
> [She] said to him: 'If I drink a cup of wine, which is in your hand, thus I shall humble myself before you. 'I shall…and I speak with [you?], O Solomon, you [lord] of kings. If…a queen…This cup [of wine]…[I] humble myself before you.
>
> [There is a] pillar in my country, O Solomon, you lord of kings. If you send there and bring it here, thus it is useful (?) in (?) your palace'.
>
> Gather to me all your spirits that are under your authority…the pillar'…the first made haste and said: '…until evening'. The second…: '…likewise'. The spirithalf (?) made haste…and said: 'From breath…to breath [I] bring you the pillar.
>
> Then, as the word was still in Solomon's mouth, look, there came the spirithalf and the pillar was on its wings, and it turned in this way and that as the…and the…
>
> All wisdom, that is [on the] earth, stands written on the pillar, and the…the sun and the [moon] stand on it. It is a marvel to see it.[34]

For Erman, this scene involved King Solomon and the queen of Sheba, probable enough in terms of the context: Solomon, magic, and a foreign queen drinking wine with Solomon in his palace. The queen has come to see Solomon, and as usual in these tales magic is involved. The marvellous pillar collected by the 'spirithalf' was apparently not acquired quickly enough by the first two demons, but the 'spirithalf' (a translation deriving from Coptic words whose meaning is not clear) was able to fulfil the task in the space of a single breath. Hubbard remarks that the form of the story is unknown in Islamic sources (though the bringing of the pillar is reminiscent of the demons bringing the queen's splendid throne to Solomon, a scene that occurs in other versions).

Might a text of this sort concerning Solomon and the queen of Sheba have circulated in the Coptic (and general Eastern?) Christian world even before the time when Michael of Tinnis was writing? The queen of the Coptic text, combined with the Ethiopian identification of Sheba by Michael of Tinnis, could imply Coptic antecedents for the later Ethiopian version of the story.

We might recall that when Alvares cited the languages from which the version of the *KN* story he knew of at Aksum derived, they were not Coptic and Arabic as in the colophon of the 'official' version of the *KN* we have today, but Hebrew, Greek and Chaldean (which usually meant Ge'ez at this time, but could mean Aramaic).[35] Alvares' record could have genuine relevance to the history of the Coptic fragment cited above. It may derive in part from a much earlier text in Greek, dated to around 200 AD, that links Solomon and the queen of the South – the *Testament of Solomon*.

This pseudepigraphic text seems to be the earliest to present the king of Israel in what became his classic role as a mighty magician, lord of demons and the spirit world. The *Testament* relates (Appendix, 5) how Solomon built the temple, and how the witch-queen of the South (the queen of Sheba) came to him. She was stunned by the magnificence of the temple, and by the king's wisdom and wealth. At this time, Solomon received a letter from the king of Arabia, beseeching him to capture Ephippas, a spirit who caused a terrible destructive wind to blow in his country. Solomon sent a servant of his with his seal-ring to capture the Arabian spirit, whom he brought back to Jerusalem in a flask. The king questioned the spirit, to find what he could do. He could move mountains, and 'break the oaths of kings'. More, he was mighty enough to raise a certain stone to position on the pinnacle of the temple. Together with a demon of the Red Sea, he fetched a pillar and set it up in the temple.[36]

The story soon spread to other areas and languages: 'This legend of the heavy cornerstone and of the spirits supporting a column in the Temple reappears in the Georgian Acts of Nouna in the 4th century. There it is a huge wooden column that is lifted by spirit-agency, when the king and workmen had failed to move it into place. The spirits support it in the air before letting it sink into its place.'[37]

It seems that stories told in the *Testament of Solomon* survived, one way or another, perhaps via the Coptic language, to be included in the *KN* in adapted form. There is another intriguing trace of the *Testament* in the *KN*'s story about the way Solomon was induced to worship false gods. Makshara, daughter of Pharaoh, lured the king to come to her, avoiding a thread tied across the doorway. He then killed three locusts before her gods. In the *Testament of Solomon* the woman is not Makshara, and the details vary, but Solomon cites the strange use of insects for the same purpose:

> And when I answered that I would on no account worship strange gods, they told the maiden not to sleep with me until I complied and sacrificed to the gods. I then was moved, but crafty Eros brought and laid by her for me five grasshoppers, saying: 'Take these grasshoppers, and crush them together in the name of the god Moloch; and then will I sleep with you.' And this I actually did. And at once the Spirit of God departed from me, and I became weak as well as foolish in my words. And after that I was obliged by her to build a temple of idols to Baal, and to Rapha, and to Moloch, and to the other idols (TS129).

KHAZAR INTERLUDE

The Ark crops up, too, in a rather obscure way, in an utterly unexpected place: the Jewish kingdom of Khazaria, beyond the Caucasus north of the Caspian and Black Seas. Here the Ark was a new creation, made like the old one as the result of a covenant with God. The Khazar Ark does not intrude on the story of the Ethiopian Ark, but is of interest here as part of the story of Judaism in the only other country apart from South Arabia (Himyar) to convert to the Jewish faith as its state religion.

The Khazars' *kagan* or king converted around 740, Judaism remaining the state religion for several centuries afterwards. They did not claim to be Jews by blood, but a very significant consequence of their conversion has been suggested by several writers, Arthur Koestler among them (in *The Thirteenth Tribe*). Was it Khazar 'Jews' who later contributed heavily to the origin of the Jews of Eastern Europe? There were diaspora Jews in Khazaria prior to the conversion of the Khazar elite, and these would naturally have been included

6. A priest exhibits a magnificent processional cross in one of the churches of Lalibela. Photo Pamela Taor.

among Khazar Jewry, but otherwise the majority of the Ashkenazi of later times in Poland, Russia and other lands would be descendants of Turkic convert Khazars, not true Israelite exiles.

In a Hebrew letter dictated c. 960 by Hasadi ibn Shaprut, minister of the Cordoban caliph Abd al-Rahman III (d. 961), to Joseph son of Aaron, *kagan* of the Khazars, the Jewish statesman asked for details about the Jewish state. King Joseph himself replied. The *kagan* related how an angel came to his ancestor Bulan, offering him blessings and conquests in return for worship of the one true God. He was to build a dwelling place for the Lord. This he did after a victorious expedition in Transcaucasia. Bulan constructed 'a holy tabernacle equipped with a sacred coffer [the "Ark of the Covenant"], a candelabrum, an altar and holy implements which have been preserved to this day and are still in my [King Joseph's] possession'. Far to the north in Khazaria, at a time when in Ethiopia the foreign queen known as Gudit was ruling conquered Ethiopia, another Ark was created.

THE ARK AND THE ZAGWÉ KINGS

From the earliest records of Christianity in Ethiopia until the watershed of the rise to power of the Zagwé, we have explored the documentation that might lead to the Ark. The result is surprising. Despite the claim that the Ark story is an ancient one, in all this material we find nothing convincing that suggests that the Ark, or indeed any other especially sacred talisman, lay hidden in the church at Aksum. No document supports the *KN*'s claim that the Ark came to Ethiopia in antiquity. It is only in the middle period of Zagwé rule in Ethiopia that a new twist to the story emerges. At first sight it seems to be definitive – and was accepted as such by Graham Hancock. For, at last, the Ark appears in the Habash empire.

The mystery, however, is not so easily solved – the search is far from over. The evidence turns out to be equivocal, even though we have uncovered a document of the 12th-13th century that on the face of it seems to clearly state that the Ark resides in Ethiopia. With the analysis of the *tabotat* of Ethiopia that we have already undertaken, the real identity of this 'Ark' can be established.

THE USURPERS

Ethiopia recovered from the disaster of Gudit's invasion, but the dynasty that ruled afterwards did not last long. Around 1137, the founder of a new dynasty was able to seize the throne. The Ge'ez legends hint that the usurper was assisted by a woman of the old royal family. It has even been suggested that this female treachery led the compilers of the *KN* to their harsh attitude towards women.[38]

The Zagwé were of Agaw ethnic origin, Cushitic speakers, the original inhabitants of extensive regions south of Aksum. As the colophon of the *KN* emphasises, they were not 'Israelites'. We read in *KN* 34:

> He gave him one on the earth who should become king over the Tabernacle of the Law of the holy, heavenly Zion, that is to say, the King of Ethiopia. And as for those who reigned, who were not [of] Israel, that was due to the transgression of the law and the commandment, whereat God was not pleased.

This divine displeasure took a long time, nevertheless, to manifest itself, the monarchy continuing for around 130 years in the Zagwé royal family, some of whom were recognised by the Ethiopian church as saints.

If the Ark were truly the palladium of Ebna Lahakim's two thousand year old 'Israelite' dynasty, and had survived Gudit's fury, surely the advent of the Zagwé would have been the moment for it to figure in some way in the course of events. But none of the Ethiopian stories relating how a princess of the royal line transferred the sovereign power from the 'Israelite' to the Zagwé dynasty, when we might expect to learn of the Ark's transference in triumph to the new dynasty, even mention it.[39] If, alternatively, we imagine that the Ark was spirited away to a place of safety with the old dynasty's fall, to figure later in the glorious 'restoration' with the deposition of the Zagwé usurpers in 1270 by the rightful 'Israelite' king, Yekuno Amlak, we are still to be disappointed. During these momentous events for the Ethiopian kingship, the Ark remains shrouded in silence. An obscure episode in the *gadl* of King Na'akuto-La'ab, relating how the king was deprived of his *tabota Seyon* (see below), is the sole event in the Zagwé hagiographies (compiled in the 15th century) that might evoke the Ark.

Surprisingly, however, it is during the tenure of this 'non-Israelite' dynasty (to employ the *KN*'s term) that the Ark is for the first time said to be in Ethiopia – ignoring here the claim for its age-long presence asserted by the final version of the *KN*. It does not appear in early Zagwé times but around 1200, in the reign of King Lalibela. We owe this record to Abu Salih, the author who, unlike the *KN*, assigned to Lalibela a thoroughly Israelite ancestry derived from the house of Moses and Aaron. At any rate, he reported this with the caveat: 'it is said'. Abu Salih al-Armani is the first person to state clearly that the Ark of the Covenant was in Ethiopia. He adds, however, that it was lodged in the Ethiopian royal city, which was then Adefa (Lalibela) in Lasta, not Aksum in Tigray.[40] In addition, his description of this 'Ark' raises important questions.

THE ARK OF LALIBELA

What Abu Salih tells us raises a vital question. What, exactly, is the relationship of this early 'Ark' to the wooden altars called *tabotat* found at Lalibela and a few other places? [41]

Abu Salih resided in Egypt in the late 12th to early 13th century. He therefore probably lived during the latter part of the reign of the saintly Zagwé king Yimrehana Krestos, and the reign of Harbay. It is absolutely certain that he was a contemporary of the most famous Zagwé king, another saint, Lalibela. Abu Salih's record is fascinating, but it is certainly not the 'eye-witness account of the Ark' that Graham Hancock affirms: very far from it.[42] Abu Salih's comments on Ethiopia amount to repetition of things he was told in Egypt, though his description of the 'Ark' is evidently based on some genuine information. This probably came from Ethiopians or Egyptians involved in a *cause célèbre* of the time, the deposition in Cairo of Mikael, bishop of Ethiopia, for 'misuse of his stewardship'.[43] Abu Salih's report is very valuable, all we have concerning Ethiopian sacred paraphernalia at so early a period.[44]

According to Abu Salih, the Ark of the Covenant, which he referred to, in Arabic, as *tabutu al-'ahdi*, contained 'the two tables of stone, inscribed by the finger of God with the commandments which he ordained for the children of Israel':

> The Ark of the Covenant is placed upon the altar, but is not so wide as the altar; it is as high as the knee of a man, and is overlaid with gold; and upon its lid there are crosses of gold; and there are five precious stones upon it, one at each of the four corners, and one in the middle. The liturgy is celebrated

upon the Ark four times in the year, within the palace of the king; and a canopy is spread over it when it is taken out from [its own] church to the church which is in the palace of the king...

No such remarkable talisman appears in the *Zena Lalibela*, the life story of the king-saint, neither in reference to the Heavenly Jerusalem, where the king was transported while lying in a coma, nor when he constructs an earthly New Jerusalem at Lalibela. Whatever it was, Abu Salih's 'Ark' had apparently been forgotten by the time the king's story was written down in the 15th century. Nor is there any hint about it in the Egyptian records referring to the Zagwé metropolitan bishops of Ethiopia.

Clearly, with its Christian crosses, the Lalibela Ark was a Christian artefact, not resembling the biblical Ark. We can immediately see that there is a distinct relationship, in its function as an altar, with the modern Ethiopian *tabot* or altar tablet. We are not informed how this 'Ark' was carried. There is no mention of the carrying poles that were so important an element of the Old Testament Ark. The Lalibela Ark might have been carried, like the present *tabotat* today, on the head of a priest. Abu Salih alludes to 'a large number of Israelites descended from the family of the prophet David', attendants of the Ark, which might suggest that it was carried on a litter on the shoulders of several men, being too large or heavy for one man. Or it might imply that it was carried in relay by a number of different people. In later times, from Alvares, we read that some of the royal *tabotat* were carried on litters by several priests (see below, *Ho Preste João das Indias*).

Some writers, as we have seen, maintain that the Ethiopian Ark, or *tabot*, functioned in a way identical to the Israelite Ark. But Abu Salih tells us that the liturgy was celebrated 'upon' the Ark, an unheard of suggestion for the Old Testament Ark, an untouchable thing from which, 'between the cherubim' above the throne, or mercy-seat, God communicated with Moses. On the other hand, the liturgy of the Ethiopian church is celebrated – and presumably was similarly celebrated in Lalibela's time – exactly in this way; *on a tabot* placed upon a *manbara tabot* or altar. The *tabot* is used for every service of mass in an Ethiopian church. It generally remains in the church, except on a few special occasions when it is carried out with some ceremony. The Lalibela Ark therefore functioned in the same way as a *tabot* of today, with lavish ceremony in its four annual processions from its own church to the royal church.

What Abu Salih had heard about in current use in the royal city, Adefa, in the reign of Lalibela was a gold-covered (wooden?) box, perhaps two feet high, with exclusively Christian decoration, functioning like a *manbara tabot*. Abu Salih wrote that the Ark was placed upon the altar, being narrower than the altar. Evidently it was not a *manbara tabot* of the modern type, a tall cupboard-like structure enclosing the *tabot* and other liturgical instruments, functioning as an altar for the *tabot/sellat* or altar tablet. Abu Salih's 'Ark' resembled the other, much rarer, type of *manbara tabot*, known, appropriately enough for our comparison, from Lalibela and a very few other places – a low, cube-like chest standing about two feet high on legs.

The object Abu Salih described had a lid, upper cover or perhaps top shelf, but no solid gold 'mercy seat', and no cherubim. It contained the two tablets of the Law. It may be that Abu Salih, when gathering information from his informants, combined two elements, *manbara tabot* and *tabot* or *sellat*, the reference to a lid or cover actually referring to the *tabot*, which would have borne the decoration of crosses, and on which the liturgy would have been celebrated. When not in use, it would have been kept inside. Indeed, if the ritual was then the same as it is now, the 'lid' or 'upper cover' must have functioned as a *tabot*, or for the emplacement of a *tabot*, the consecrated object essential to the celebration of the liturgy. Abu Salih's description includes the contents of the 'Ark': 'two tables of stone', which could hint that stone *tabotat* were in use. On the other hand, the Lalibela cube-altars are inscribed with dedications, implying that they themselves were consecrated objects that could serve for the eucharist without an altar tablet placed on top. The cube-altars were certainly portable, and could easily have been placed on a larger altar as described by Abu Salih. An example now in the Institute of Ethiopian Studies, Addis Ababa, just under two feet high, is decorated with carved cross designs on sides and top, as are others from Lalibela as well.

In brief, the Lalibela 'Ark' described by Abu Salih was probably nothing more than a small cube-form *manbara tabot*. Such objects, perhaps not coincidentally, are known from Lalibela. Their inscriptions specifically attribute them to *negus* (king) Lalibela, the reigning monarch when Abu Salih wrote his book.

Why was such an object named as the Ark of the Covenant, at least by the person or persons reporting to Abu Salih? The explanation may be very simple, an early example of a frequent confusion in terminology. The word *tabot* in Ethiopian, meaning at this stage a cube-altar, was understood quite naturally as signifying 'the Ark of the Covenant', *tabutu al-'ahdi*, in Arabic.

There is strongly suggestive evidence for this idea. We have seen that Lalibela himself (accepting him as responsible for the altars found at several Lalibela churches) refers to these altars, in the inscriptions carved upon them, by the term *tabot*: the correct term, deriving from the root *tbt* in Semitic languages, for box or chest-like objects.

So the Ark once again recedes from our view in Ethiopia. The mysterious 'Ark of the Covenant' described to Abu Salih by his informant – himself perhaps merely repeating hearsay – turns out to be one of Lalibela's portable *tabotat*, or an amalgam between this and a *sellat* or altar tablet decorated with crosses. If there were an altar tablet, perhaps it was of stone, and inscribed with the Ten Commandments, a feature later mentioned by Emperor Zara Yaqob. The five jewels on the lid (if not simply imagined) might be special adornment to enrich the *tabot* used for celebration of festivals in the royal church.

Could there already have been a tendency in Ethiopia to identify the *tabot*, the cubic-form altar, with the Ark? Was a particular *tabot* at Lalibela's capital considered as symbolising the 'Ark of the Covenant' itself? A *tabot* dedicated to Seyon seems quite plausible at this stage, consistent with the rest of the Israelite paraphernalia that Abu Salih attributes to Ethiopia: the throne of David, the descent from Moses and Aaron's family and so on. The difficulty about the Lalibela Ark lies in knowing how to interpret Abu Salih's information. His descriptions and attributions can be confused. With as much confidence as he places the Ark in Ethiopia, he claims that the 'Abyssinian' king of al-Muqurra, a Nubian Christian kingdom, possessed the Ark of Noah, an embarrassing blow to his credibility. Tellingly, the idea of the portable *manbar* symbolising the Ark, if it ever existed outside Abu Salih's record – the product of a simple misunderstanding – does not occur again in Ethiopia. Instead, the *tabot*, or altar tablet deriving from the Coptic *maqta'*, adopts this symbolism, together with the designation *tabot*. As the use of the altar tablet develops, we find a correlation with the tablets of the Law. In time, this is upgraded to eventual identification with the Ark of the Covenant itself.

The Ark of Lalibela is a red herring in the story of the Ark in Ethiopia. The Lalibela *tabot*'s irrelevance to the story of the sacred relic at Aksum is confirmed by the clear fact that this 'Ark' at Lalibela bore no resemblance to the hallowed stone altar tablet of Zion that was later – many centuries later – revealed, in the time of the succeeding Solomonic dynasty.

A COLOPHON

The author of the colophon or end note preserved in several copies of the
KN refers directly to King Lalibela Gabra Masqal and the Zagwé dynasty,
claiming that the book was translated into Arabic from a Coptic manuscript

> in the four hundred and ninth year of Mercy in the country of Ethiopia, in
> the days of Gabra Masqal the king, who is called Lalibala, in the days of
> Abba George, the good bishop. And God neglected to have it translated and
> interpreted into the speech of Abyssinia. And when I had pondered this –
> Why did not 'Abal'ez and Abal-Farog who edited (or, copied) the book
> translate it? I said this: It went out in the days of Zagua, and they did not
> translate it because this book says: Those who reign not being Israelites are
> transgressors of the Law. Had they been of the kingdom of Israel they would
> have edited (or, translated) it. And it was found in Nazret.[45]

The Years of Mercy were calculated in two systems, one dating from the
creation in BC 5500, the other from the Era of the Martyrs beginning in 284
AD with the reign of Diocletian. They were calculated in cycles of 532 years,
this constituting the Great Lunar Cycle. The year 809 EC (Ethiopian
Calendar)/815–6 AD was calculated as the beginning of the second such
cycle in the Era of Martyrs. Year 409 in this cycle is 1225 AD. The exact dates
of Lalibela's reign are not known, but traditional lists note a forty-year reign
– the same as King Solomon and, according to some lists, the same as seven
other Zagwé kings. This ludicrous assertion effectively means that the total
of the regnal years of Lalibela remains uncertain. The *History of the
Patriarchs* confirms that Lalibela was king of Ethiopia around 1205–10. In a
16th century copy of a land-grant dated also to 1225 AD, in the reign of
Lalibela, a Bishop Giyorgis is again named – the land-grant is recorded in
the *Golden Gospel* of the monastery of Dabra Libanos in Eritrea.[46] Nazret in
southern Tigray was for a long period a seat of the Ethiopian bishops, several
of whom were buried there. The episcopal seat could easily have contained a
library containing Coptic or Arabic texts as well as Ge'ez ones.

Only a few decades after the claimed translation of the *KN*, under the
impetus of a remarkable man a good deal of work was done with the translation
of Arabic works to Ge'ez. Abba Salama 'the Translator' was metropolitan of
Ethiopia c. 1348–88, one of the few Egyptian bishops who made any mark in
Ethiopia (except for scandals). He is commemorated annually in the
Ethiopian church with a reading from the *Synaxarium*: 'From your lips
sweeter than the scent of myrrh…came forth books from Arabic into Ge'ez'.

The colophon of the *KN* therefore expresses a process, translation from Arabic to Ge'ez, entirely right for the times. The colophon adds that Yeshaq (Isaac), the translator into Ge'ez of the *KN* in Amda Seyon's time, had

> toiled much for the glory of the country of Ethiopia, and for the going forth of the heavenly Zion, and for the glory of the King of Ethiopia. And I consulted the upright and God-loving governor Yâ'ebîka 'Egzî'e, and he approved and said unto me 'Work'. And I worked...And pray ye for your servant Isaac, and for those who toiled with me in the going out (i.e. production) of this book, for we were in sore tribulation, I, and Yamharana-'Ab, and Hezba-Krestos, and Andrew, and Philip, and Mahari-'Ab...

This 'tribulation' may have come upon them with the Amhara emperor Amda Seyon's military victory over Ya'ibika Egzi, the 'governor of Intarta' in Tigray – scion of a house that had long governed the northern region, and the translators' patron.

Is the colophon a forged addition to the book, penned simply to give the work a spurious ancient origin? If so, the presence of the name of Ya'ibika Egzi would be extraordinary. It is hard enough even to understand why it was allowed to survive in the copies we have – the name of a defeated Tigray 'rebel' cited with praise and respect in a book supposedly glorifying the Amhara Solomonic kings of Ethiopia, not one of whom is mentioned by name. There seems no reason to doubt that the mention of Ya'ibika Egzi, Yeshaq and his companions, and Abu al-Faraj and Abu al-'Izz, are genuine, and that they had their part to play in the earliest origins of what became the *KN*. Yet despite containing genuine information from c. 1320, the colophon in its present form may be a more recent innovation, the result of the changes through which the book has passed from edition to edition. In the early version of the story recited by Alvares, he cites the details about the translating in a completely different form, at the *beginning* of the book. The information may have been removed to its present position at the end during subsequent recopying and editing.

The colophon sets the scene of the translation of the *KN* into Arabic from Coptic during the reign of Lalibela, while George was bishop. It would imply that the story told in the *KN*, or part of it, perhaps the Solomon and Sheba episode, existed already at the time when Lalibela's 'Ark' was described by Abu Salih. If there really was a Zagwé 'Ark' and 'tablets', perhaps a portable altar, with or without a *sellat*, called something like *tabota Seyon*, at Adefa, could it have inspired the *nebura'ed* Yeshaq and the other anti-Zagwé translators/compilers of the version of the *KN* produced just before 1322 to present a rival tale concerning its ownership? It is not likely. Apart from one *KN* for which a tentative 15th century date has been proposed, other versions of the story in the mid-16th century still claim that only the tablets of the Law, not the Ark, came to Ethiopia.

TABOT *OF SEYON*

Lalibela's 'Ark of the Covenant' is not again mentioned. The records of the fallen dynasty are meagre, largely suppressed, one supposes, by the succeeding kings, but as the downfall of the Zagwé approaches we do have an intriguing – if thoroughly obscure – reference to a *tabot* of Seyon.[47]

It is far from a contemporary record, but comes from the 15th century *Gadla Na'akuto-La'ab*, the miracle-filled story of a Zagwé king, apparently the son of King Harbay, who had been deposed by Lalibela. It may be that on Lalibela's death there was a succession struggle. Na'akuto-La'ab son of Harbay was at first successful, but was later forced to cede the throne to Yitbarak, Lalibela's son, the last Zagwé king. Na'akuto-La'ab was the last of the crowned saints produced by this 'non-Israelite' and 'usurping' dynasty. The hagiographer alludes to the king's final defeat in the following passage:

> There was a man in the land of Ambagé. He went and entered the king's encampment. He met the king and accused our blessed father [Na'akuto-La'ab] saying, 'He took your kingdom before, and now he is hiding in a cave with your *tabot* of Siyon. Command your soldiers to come with me, and I will lead them to where he is, so that they can bring your *tabot* back to you…'

The 'cave' apparently denotes the cave church of Qohqinna, near Lalibela, still dedicated to Na'akuto-La'ab. What was the *tabot* of Seyon (Siyon)? Was it created entirely from the 15th century chronicler's imagination as a suitable royal attribute? Can we connect it with the 'Ark of the Covenant' described by Abu Salih – a portable altar table? Or was it another *tabot* consecrated in the name of Seyon? This is possible. A royal church begun by Lalibela and completed by Na'akuto-La'ab, as described in the latter's *gadl*, was named Dabra Seyon, Mount Zion. It was situated near Na'akuto-La'ab's new foundation at Wagra Sehin, not far from Qohqinna. In addition, officials bearing the evocative title *qaysa gabaz Seyon* (provosts of Zion) are known from this period as well.[48]

Finally, in our survey of the Ark in Zagwé times, we should cite another document, the history written by the encyclopaedist Bar Hebraeus (1226–86). In his political history of the world, this *maphrian* (patriarch) of the Syrian church, of Jewish descent, had naturally turned his attention to Israel, and to the history of the Hebrew kings. Describing the end of the kingdom of Judah, when Nebuchadnezzar's army destroyed and plundered the Jerusalem temple, Bar Hebraeus states that 'when Jeremiah knew of the burning of the Temple, he hid in a cave the Tabernacle of Witness, and the Ark, and no man knoweth the place'.[49] This indicates, conclusively enough, that one of the great scholars of the age did not know about, or did not credit, Abu Salih's story that the Ark was at Adefa, the Zagwé capital. He believed that the Ark had been hidden forever at the time of the destruction of the temple.

Bar Hebraeus had another name, Abu al-Faraj, the same as one of the supposed 'translators' of the *KN*: a parallel that raises interesting possibilities, that I have dealt with elsewhere. But, particularly interesting for our theme here, Gregory Bar Hebraeus was not just a foreign prelate ignorant of Ethiopian church affairs, writing from his own provincial perspective. His matter-of-fact 'no man knoweth the place' is actually a significant piece of information, because Bar Hebraeus was very familiar with current Ethiopian ecclesiastical and royal affairs. He records, and discusses, a very unusual occurrence in 1237, when Ignatius II, patriarch of Antioch, consecrated an Ethiopian called Thomas to be Ethiopia's bishop. It was an illegal act, undertaken to avenge the Coptic patriarch of Alexandria's illegal consecration of a bishop for Jerusalem. It may, too, have had a strange sequel, since in the early reigns of the Solomonic dynasty – and Bar Hebraeus was alive during the whole of Yekuno Amlak's reign – we read of Syrian metropolitans, not Egyptians, at the head of the Ethiopian church. The Syrian *maphrian* cannot have been ignorant of both generalities and particularities concerning the Ethiopian church.

HEIRS OF SOLOMON

With the rise of the early Solomonic rulers the search for the Ark gains coherence. For this is the age of the emperors who called themselves kings of Zion, who attributed to themselves a glorious descent from King Solomon and the queen of Sheba, and whose Christian kingdom in the mountains of East Africa was conceived to be the New Israel. For such rulers, the throne of David, the ring of Solomon, even the tablets of Moses, were to become symbols of the mystic power God had bestowed on the dynasty. The Ethiopian documents reveal a preoccupation with Zion, the New Israel and biblical themes, and news of these developments percolates through to Europe as well. Ethiopia, we can see from hindsight, is moving towards the Ark. But still (outside the *KN*, and its claim for 14th century authorship), the documents breathe no word about the holy relic.

THE NEBURA'ED *YESHAQ*

Yeshaq, 'translator' of the *KN* into Ge'ez, lived in stirring times. He identifies himself with monastic humility in the colophon of the book: 'your servant Yeshaq, the poor man'. Yet Yeshaq is probably to be identified as the *nebura'ed* (dean) of Aksum, holder of the city's highest office.[50] According to the colophon, the Yeshaq of the *KN* lived at the time when Ya'ibika-Egzi, representative of an important and powerful local family, ruled as the virtually independent governor of Intarta, in northern Tigray. Aksum, too, was under his control.

A document written in a 16th century hand in the *Golden Gospel* of Dabra Libanos, but supposedly a copy of an older land grant of Ya'ibika Egzi dated to 1318/19, includes Yeshaq's name in the customary list of officials in office: *Yeshaq, nebura'ed of Aksum*.[51] He is the prime candidate for identification with Yeshaq, chief compiler of the *KN*. This Yeshaq, *nebura'ed zaAksum*, is cited together with a number of other distinguished ecclesiastics. That he should be named in a document emanating from Ya'ibika Egzi implies a close relationship, that of a great official to his local prince.

The identity seems doubly likely if we consider the kind of man portrayed by the *KN*'s colophon. Yeshaq, chief compiler of the book, was evidently a man of education. He worked under the orders of Governor Ya'ibika Egzi. His concerns were with high, even celestial, matters – 'the country of Ethiopia, and for the going forth of the heavenly Zion, and for the glory of the King of Ethiopia'. Such characteristics might well have distinguished the incumbent of Aksum's highest ecclesiastical post.

Ya'ibika Egzi was ambitious. He gambled for independence from the Solomonic ruler further south, perhaps even for the highest office of all, but against the newly strengthened power of the Amhara emperor, Amda Seyon, he had no chance. By 1322 he had failed, and Amda Seyon seized control of the territory of the old governing family, significantly, 'as far as the cathedral of Aksum'. We do not know what happened to *nebura'ed* Yeshaq, but the colophon may imply, without too imaginative interpretation, that his companions in writing the great work may have perished: 'Yamharana-'Ab, and Hezba-Krestos, and Andrew, and Philip, and Mahari-'Ab. May God have mercy upon them, and may He write their names in the Book of Life in the kingdom of heaven, with those of all the saints and martyrs for ever and ever! Amen.' Perhaps Yeshaq too was a casualty in the political maelstrom of the time, leaving only his great literary work as his memorial. Perhaps he was compelled to re-edit an original work, removing certain Tigray-weighted elements from it, trimming it for another destiny. Although it might be tempting to imagine the ex-*nebura'ed*, imprisoned in his house, toiling at the task of writing under command of his new master such chapters as *KN* 44, 'How it is not a seemly thing to revile the King', this scenario is perhaps rather unlikely. One would have expected overt glorification of the reigning dynasty, mention of some ancestral names and excision of the name of Yeshaq's erstwhile master from the colophon. For now Yeshaq's work was destined to serve the Solomonic dynasty, the conquerors of his patron Ya'ibika Egzi.

The usual reason offered for the writing of the *KN* envisages Solomonic propaganda:

> There is virtually unanimous agreement among scholars as to the political motive. The KN was written to justify the claims of the so-called Solomonid dynasty founded by Yekuno Amlak over against those of the Zagwé family who had held sway for well over a century.[52]

Another and more complex view suggests that after the decline of Aksumite political power, monks inherited the mantle of Aksum's prestige. Amhara kings could accept their 'moral authority and ideological formulations because Tigray was no longer a serious political competitor'. This theory, whose thrust emphasises Tigray and Amhara interdependence, proposed that Yekuno Amlak's usurpation

> was as much a vindication of the centrality of Aksumite traditions concerning Makeda and Solomon as a source of cultural legitimation for the monarchy. Tigreans and Amhara leaned on one another in a particularly effective way at that juncture...[53]

To me, this conclusion, though presented by a skilled analyst, does not ring quite true. The book certainly did disapprove of the non-Israelite Zagwé, but mention of them is incidental, to say the least. Their reign was fifty years gone when Yeshaq was working. What were *nebura'ed* Yeshaq's motives? For whom did he, an official under the authority of Ya'ibika Egzi – ruler of a strong and divergent Tigray, rather than a politically unimportant monkish group – undertake his task of editing the *KN*? To glorify the theoretical masters of his master, those distant and rather feeble early Solomonic rulers, who were, unfortunately for Ya'ibika Egzi, soon to produce a descendant of great capacity in Amda Seyon? Or had he another aim in mind, inflating the Ethiopian monarchy in support of the aspirations of Ya'ibika Egzi himself?

The Russian scholar Servir Chernetsov suggests that the Intarta dynasty derived from old Aksumite origins, that they possessed the 'Ark', and that the *KN* was destined to be the literary vehicle of their revolt.[54] Could this be the real explanation for the writing of the *KN*? Leaving aside the question of an Aksumite 'tabernacle of Zion', for which there is still no reliable evidence at this period, it is notable that the reigning king, Amda Seyon, is not mentioned in Yeshaq's colophon. To suggest that the name Gabra Masqal in *KN* 117 is intended to evoke Amda Seyon's own throne name as well seems far too subtle to be likely in a politically motivated document, despite the Ethiopian penchant for 'wax and gold' poetical imagery. On the other hand, Governor Ya'ibika Egzi is singled out, described as 'upright and God-loving', and treated as the motive force behind the work. A reasonable interpretation would be that Yeshaq worked in his service before the governor's failed rebellion. Somehow, relegated to the colophon, Ya'ibika Egzi's name survived excision. Did this local Tigrayan ruler, successor to his ancestors in an area never firmly reduced to the new Amhara dynasty's control, derive from some former Ethiopian royal house? Did he have plans – implemented in his eventual revolt – aiming at the reassertion of an 'Aksumite' or Tigray-based monarchy rather than an Amhara one? Evidently, as his rebellion proves, this was not really a time of Tigray and Amhara accord. Under these circumstances, the *KN* – which only became 'the Amharic "national epic"' by adoption[55] – would have served Ya'ibika Egzi quite as well as it would later serve Amda Seyon or his successors.

The royal names of Solomon Yigba Seyon and Amda Seyon, as well as Tasfa Seyon, *'aqabe sa'at* (a high ecclesiastical court title signifying 'guardian of the hour') of Dabra Zayt, confirm Ethiopian reverence at this period for Zion, and hint at imitation of Israel. Do they suggest a Davidic dynastic claim on the part of the kings of the Amhara family? David as a model was a classic piece of imperial rhetoric in 7th century and later Byzantium. Even earlier, in the Ge'ez inscriptions found in Yemen (Marib) and attributed to the 6th century King Kaleb of Aksum, there are citations from the psalms of David.[56] To claim actual physical descent from the second king of Israel was to go a step further. Perhaps, together with memories of the Zagwé, and their moves towards judaisation of the monarchy, as suggested by Abu Salih, this current emphasis on Israel by the Amhara kings contributed to setting the mood for Yeshaq's work. Because Amda Seyon was the eventual victor in the combat between the Intarta and Amhara polities, it was his dynasty that could exploit the results of the labours of Yeshaq and his companions. The *KN* would be harnessed to enhance the prestige of the victorious Amda Seyon, and of his kingdom, the Ethiopian Zion.

Perhaps we can observe the influence of the *KN* in the famous 'glorious victories of Amda Seyon', the chronicle of his 1329 war – though this record may date rather later, perhaps to his great-grandson Zara Yaqob's reign. In an apocalyptic passage citing a prophecy that the kingdom of the Muslims would in its proper time be extinguished, while the kingdom of the Christians would continue until the Second Coming, the chronicler adds: 'and above all (we know) that the kingdom of Ethiopia shall endure till the coming of Christ, of which David prophesied saying: "Ethiopia shall stretch her hands unto God."'[57] Could this derive from a passage in *KN* 93, mentioning that Ethiopia would endure in the faith until the coming of Christ? Even closer is *KN* 113: '[Ethiopia] shall continue in the orthodox faith until the coming of our Lord...(followed by a question – will Ethiopia's faith be destroyed with the coming of the Antichrist?): and Gregory answered and said, "Assuredly not. Hath not David prophesied saying, 'Ethiopia shall make her hands come to God'?"'

After the victory of Amda Seyon, the linking of Tigray and Amhara ideologies becomes far more credible. By the next century, from Zara Yaqob's reign onwards, priestly Aksum was glorified as the seat of royalty, then firmly in the hands of the Amhara dynasty. The kings, apart from occasional visits to Aksum on northern campaigns, and exceptionally rare sacring ('coronations') in the holy city, remained mostly in the south. Levine noted that later kings sometimes sent their high multi-tiered crowns, covered with gilt and dangling silver tassels, to Aksum, as an act of veneration.[58] One can see them there today, in the treasury of Zion. But it was not an exclusive act signalling unique reverence for Aksum. The emperors sent similar crowns to venerated places in the south, particularly to churches of Lake Tana and the Zagé peninsula.

KING YESHAQ, LION OF DAVID

We are now at the threshold of the time when Ethiopia begins to become known in Europe. Fantastic legends slowly give way before an equally fantastic reality. Prester John moves from Asia to Ethiopia, and all sorts of dreams come to preoccupy those Europeans – popes, kings and the crusader-minded – who earnestly desire to motivate new endeavours to crush Islam, whose heart and centre, the two towns of Mecca and Medina, lay so temptingly between them. Intriguingly, elements of the *KN* legend are evoked in certain mediaeval documents preserved in Catalonia, in the royal archives of the kingdom of Aragon. The documents date to the reign of Yeshaq in Ethiopia (1414–29).

In the reply to a letter he had sent to King Alfonso V of Aragon in 1427, and in another letter from the Spanish ruler confirming the arrival of five Ethiopian ambassadors, the Ethiopian king is addressed by some unusual titles: 'Yeshaq, son of Dawit, possessor of the Tablets of the Law and of the Throne of David…'[59] The original text of the letter from King Yeshaq does not survive. We have – astonishing enough in itself – only the copies of the correspondence of Alfonso V preserved in the archives of Aragon at Barcelona. The reply to Yeshaq's letter is dated from Valencia, 15 May 1428. The Latin document carries the titulature twice, once at the beginning of the letter, and again below in another hand, as if for clarification:

> Most eminent and most invincible monarch Lord Ysach (Yeshaq) son of David by the Grace of God Prester John of the Indies lord of the tablets of Mount Sinai and the throne of David and king of kings of Ethiopia.

We might expect the Aragonese chancellery, in preparing a reply, to have copied Yeshaq's own style and title from the original, but part of this titulary is evidently not what an Ethiopian king would have written. 'Prester John of the Indies' reflects Europe's ideas, not Ethiopia's. On the other hand, 'Yeshaq, son of Dawit…king of kings of Ethiopia' is precisely what one would expect. The details about the tablets and throne may also be part of the legendary attributes added by European scribes following reported legend. Perhaps the information was gleaned from Ethiopian visitors or pilgrims, or from the ambassadors who brought Yeshaq's letter, or from gossip relayed by Alfonso's subjects who had encountered Ethiopians in Jerusalem. Can we imagine that, if they had heard that Yeshaq possessed the Ark of the Covenant itself, the Aragonese chancellery clerks would refer only to its contents when composing their inflated titulary for the Ethiopian sovereign? To Yeshaq are attributed only two of the three treasures that Abu Salih claimed for King Lalibela, the tablets of the Law, and the throne of David – but not the Ark.

What did the Ethiopic text of King Yeshaq's original letter actually say? If it actually mentioned his possession of these talismans, and the text read *sellata hegg*, tablet of the Law, one could be fairly sure that the tablet of Moses only was meant. On the other hand, it could have used the expression *tabota hegg*, the *tabot* of the Law, which could mean either the tablet or the Ark. This in fact is the usual form for 'Ark of the Covenant' in the *KN*, where there is often a divine name appended to it, usually *egziabeher*, God.

The evidence from Yeshaq's reign remains equivocal. It confirms no more than that 15th century Europeans for one reason or another attributed the possession of the tablets of the Law and the throne of David to the Ethiopian sovereign. Later the same two attributes, with a ring of Solomon, are attributed to Lebna Dengel, but by two different sources. Andrea Corsali mentions the throne and the ring, and Ethiopians in Italy around 1542 add the tablets of the Law. As usual, the Ark is not even mentioned.

Yeshaq, son of Dawit (David), was also entitled, in one of the praise songs that soldiers would sing to commemorate their emperor's great deeds, 'lion of David'.[60] This doubtless alludes to Revelation 5.5: 'the lion of the tribe of Judah, the offspring of David, has conquered'. The motto 'the lion of the tribe of Judah has conquered' was to become a favourite one with the kings of Ethiopia, still familiar to anyone who remembers the last for whom it was employed, the late Emperor Haile Sellassie.

CORONATION AT AKSUM

The old city of Aksum, apparently, was ignored by the Zagwé rulers, who developed their capital at Adefa or Roha, the Lalibela of today. But in post–Zagwé times Aksum may have experienced a renaissance, favoured by the governors of Intarta and even the more distant Amhara kings, followed by the affirmation of Solomonic power in the region around 1322. The office of *nebura'ed* had already appeared at Aksum at the beginning of the dynasty, and the city's clerics, exploiting their residence in the old imperial and ecclesiastic centre, were perhaps able to win back some of the prestige Aksum had lost. After centuries of silence, Aksum's name begins to appear again in the documents. As a venerated ecclesiastical centre, Aksum was to regain some vestiges at least of its aura of imperial power and consequence. This renaissance Zara Yaqob's 'coronation' in 1436 and his three years' subsequent residence in the city must have consolidated, making Aksum for a brief moment once again an imperial capital.

Crowning was not in fact part of the ritual, which was instead an induction ceremony involving tonsuring, anointing and other procedures – among them killing a lion and a buffalo, and presenting milk, water, wine and mead – that confirmed kingship over Ethiopia.[61] Combined with this, though only equivocally attested as early as Zara Yaqob, were potent allusions to the concept of rule over the Ethiopian Zion. From this time, Zion enters ever more significantly into the imperial vocabulary. Among the innovations – doubtless entirely Solomonic in inspiration – are the 'daughters of Zion', the women of Aksum who questioned the uncrowned king to ascertain his true kingship of 'Zion'. They are first attested at the coronation of Emperor Sarsa Dengel in 1580.

In *KN* 39 and 92 brief and imaginary anointing ceremonies are described for Ebna Lahakim, the half-Jewish, half-Ethiopian son of Solomon and the queen of Sheba. The first of these is supposed to have taken place in Jerusalem, before the Ark in the Holy of Holies of the temple of Solomon, and the second in Ethiopia, at the capital Dabra Makeda, presided over by Azarias, son of high priest Zadok of Jerusalem. The origin of these mythical ceremonies is clearly the ritual used for Solomon himself, at Gihon, by Zadok, as described in 1 Kings 1. 33–40.

Aksumite coronation rituals remain completely unknown. Abu Salih claims that the Zagwé kings were crowned in the churches of the Archangel Michael and Giyorgis. As he describes it, these were actual crownings with the royal crown, followed by robing. No overtones relating to Zion are recorded.[62] Perhaps we can see a reflection of the *KN* in an incident mentioned in Yimrehana Krestos' *Life* just before the account of his enthronement.[63] Yimrehana Krestos had solved a dispute between two brothers. The people said: 'As for us, we learned from our fathers that in the reign of Yemreha the faith would be orthodox, and the people of Rome would submit to those of Ethiopia, under him.' This might echo the theory of the primacy of Ethiopia, and the discomfiture of Rome, of *KN* 113 and 117. Naturally enough, the 15th century compiler of the 12th century Zagwé king's *gadl* was familiar with the current version of the *KN* and the theories expressed in it.

The *gadl* of King Na'akuto-La'ab, a purely hagiographical work, is replete with citations from the Psalms of David or the Song of Solomon, with references to Mount Zion, to Solomon, to the Law of Moses, to Aaron, to Levite blood sacrifices in the sanctuary of the Law, or to 'Our Lady Mary Mother of God, Ark of the Divinity, from whom came forth the Sun of justice'.[64] There is no suggestion either of royal Solomonic descent or of contact with the Ark of the Covenant. Na'akuto-La'ab, the 'plectrum of the harp of David', sent to chastise Sara-Qemes, ruler of Gojjam, is even directly compared to David and his defeat of Goliath. Yet there is no hint that Na'akuto-La'ab was an actual lineal descendant of David. Nor, for that matter, is descent from Moses or Aaron suggested when they are mentioned, as one might perhaps expect from Abu Salih's claims. Na'akuto-La'ab's enthronement was similar to the ceremony for Lalibela described in the *Zena Lalibela*.[65] It was Lalibela who, following divine instructions, set his 'son' on the throne, and anointed him.

Solomonic coronations at Aksum perhaps became possible when, early in the reign of Amda Seyon (1314–44), Ya'ibika-Egzi of Intarta rebelled and was defeated. 'God delivered into my hands the ruler of Intarta with all his army, his followers, his relatives, and all his country as far as the Cathedral of Aksum (*gabaza Aksum*)', the king declares.[66] The *nebura'ed* of Aksum – supposed translator of the *KN* into Ge'ez – was one of Ya'ibika Egzi's court. I have already mentioned, and rejected from lack of evidence, Chernetsov's idea, emerging from the common assumption that the claim for the Ark at Aksum is very ancient, that it might have appeared in the propaganda of this time.[67]

By 1400, in the reign of Dawit I, Aksum is mentioned as a coronation place. The document known as *Iter de Venetiis ad Indiam* states that at 'Chaxum' the kings subject to 'Prester John' were crowned. It may refer to the memory of ceremonies performed for Ya'ibika Egzi's family, the local rulers before 1322, or to the investment ceremonies for the Solomonic governors of the region under Amda Seyon and his immediate successors. The deposed family of Ya'ibika Egzi were succeeded by persons of the very highest rank in the Amhara dynasty, at first the queen, Belen Saba, followed later by one of the Amhara princes, the emperor's son Bahra Asgad. There is every possibility that considerable ceremony was used for their investiture, and that it took place at Aksum. At any rate the *Iter* suggests that coronation ceremonies of rulers inferior to the emperor himself took place at Aksum antecedent to the coronation of Zara Yaqob in 1436.

The records of the royal ceremonies at Aksum from Zara Yaqob's time are recounted in chronicles and other records. In Zara Yaqob's case, the first since 'the throne of the kings of Aksum had been abandoned', as the *Book of Aksum* puts it,[68] we cannot be sure that elements relevant to Aksum as the new Zion were actually in place. The text does not mention any such details. Only after Zara Yaqob had scattered gold to the people does the chronicle state: 'The king did this for the greatness of Zion, and made largesse like the kings his predecessors.'[69] It is a pity that the description – written over seventy years later in Lebna Dengel's reign – with its claim for the antiquity of the ceremony, its evident knowledge of the topography of Aksum and its passing mention of Zion, did not go into more detail. As we shall see, the later records of the coronation ceremonies refer to rituals directly invoking the Solomonic legend.

Some modern writers assume that Zara Yaqob instituted exactly the same ritual that was described later in Sarsa Dengel's chronicle. Jean Doresse even replaces the words of Sarsa Dengel's responses with his own imaginary description of the ritual for Zara Yaqob. 'I am the son of Amda Seyon, son of Sayfa Arad, son of David', Doresse puts into the mouth of Zara Yaqob, 'I am the king of Sion, Constantine'.[70] But we cannot be so sure. The entire ritual of the 'daughters of Zion' may have been a product of the development of the Aksumite myth during the intervening century and a half before Sarsa Dengel came to Aksum to undergo his tonsuring. It could, specifically, have been written into the ceremonies for Sarsa Dengel's coronation. Two French writers in recent times have considered Zara Yaqob's relationship with Aksum in rather different terms from an orientation towards an Ethiopian Zion. Hirsch and Fauvelle-Aymar interpret Zara Yaqob's interest in the old city as an attempt to institute a code of royalty based on continuity with the old Aksumite kings. This is the usual interpretation but, for them, the accent is placed on the fundamental Christian aura of Aksum, rather than on any attachment, via the Ark of the Covenant, to the Old Testament. The king, a descendant of David – rather than Solomon – is to be regarded as a representative, even an equivalent, of the messiah.[71]

The book of 'the Laws and Institutions of the Kingdom' was supposed to have arrived 'with Ebna Lahakim, son of Solomon, that is, Menelik, and the twelve high judges who came with him'.[72] These judges officiated at the later Aksum coronations, bearing the necessary implements. The *saraj masare* (official who supervises aspects of the royal court), like Azarias in the ceremony for Ebna Lahakim, carried a horn of oil. Anointing was the important element in the ceremonies. Other officials took charge of the royal horses, mules and the like. An official entitled '*best egre*, with *dabana beta hays* (tent of the house of mice)' is rather mysteriously recorded as bringing 'the vessels of Seyon'. However, this 'Seyon' probably does not refer to Aksum. The officer concerned had the duty of spreading carpets before the king, but also guarded the 'furniture of the chapel royal'. The designation probably indicates the tent church of Gimja Bet or Mary of Zion that accompanied the royal camp.[73]

The first 'coronation' at Aksum offering explicit reference to kingship of Zion and to the Ark is recorded in the chronicle of Sarsa Dengel. When the king sent to Aksum to announce his arrival, he stated that he was coming to 'celebrate the ceremonies of royalty before my mother Seyon, tabernacle of the God of Israel (*tabota amlaka Israel*), as did my fathers David and Solomon...' On the day of the ceremony, while priests chanted 'May you be blessed, O king of Israel!', the king, entering the city, encountered the 'daughters of Seyon'. The term is taken from the Song of Solomon 3.11: 'Go forth, O ye daughters of Zion, and behold King Solomon with the crown wherewith his mother crowned him in the day of his espousals, and in the day of his gladness.' The women waited at the place where an inscription of King Ezana of Aksum still stood. It was here, at *Mebtaka Fatl* ('cutting the cord'), that Sarsa Dengel enacted the important part of the ritual. The chronicle tells us what happened:

> The maidens were standing to the right and to the left, holding a long cord. There were also two old women, standing, with a sword, beside these maidens, one to the right and one to the left. When this powerful and victorious king arrived, mounted on his horse, the old women raised their voices, asking in an arrogant and insolent way: 'Who are you? Of what tribe and of what family?' The king replied saying 'I am the son of David, son of Solomon, son of Ebna Lahakim'. A second time they questioned him insolently, and he replied 'I am the son of Zara Yaqob, son of Baeda Maryam, son of Naod'. At their third demand, the king raised his hand saying 'I am Malak Sagad, son of King Wanag Sagad, son of Atsnaf Sagad, son of Admas Sagad!' Speaking thus, he cut with his sword the cord that the maidens held; and the old women cried aloud saying 'Truly, truly, you are the king of Seyon, the son of David, son of Solomon!' Then the priests of Aksum began to chant on one side, and the maidens of Seyon to rejoice on the other: he was thus received until his entry into the court of the house of the heavenly Seyon (*Seyon sama'wit*).[74]

A similar ritual was recorded by Péro Pais for the next Aksumite coronation, that of Emperor Susneyos (1607–32).[75] The emperor approached the same place by the Ezana inscription, where two girls held a twisted rope. One of the girls demanded of the emperor: 'Who are you?' He replied that he was the king, but she answered: 'No you are not.' A second time Susneyos approached, and she asked: 'Of what are you king?' This time he responded that he was the king of Israel, but she said again, 'No you are not our king.' The last time, the king simply cut the cord, saying: 'I am the king of Zion,' and everyone cried out: 'Long live the king of Zion.' After that, the bishop performed the tonsuring and anointing, and mass was said in the church.

Iyasu I's coronation is only very briefly described. He had previously wished to go to Aksum

> to accomplish the law of the kingdom (*hegga mangest*) according to the custom of the kings his fathers who previously accomplished the law of the kingdom there. For Aksum is the sanctuary of Seyon (*makana Seyon*) whence comes the law, as it is said 'For the law shall come forth from Seyon and the word of God out of Jerusalem.[76]

But urgent affairs at Gondar constrained Iyasu to delay his visit. It was only in 1691, when he paid a visit to the holy city, that we are told the strange story of how he opened and 'conversed' with the sacred relic kept in the church. At that time, he still did not undergo the tonsuring and anointing ritual. It is said that the Ark itself invited him to return to do so. At last, in 1693, he came to complete the ceremonies. At Aksum, he was received by

> all the clergy of Aksum and by the daughters of Seyon, with joy, to the sound of the drum, the psaltery, stringed instruments and flutes, with cries of joy and canticles, as the law of the kings his fathers requires. He remained there for the day, giving commands relative to the Ark of Seyon (*tabota Seyon*), with all the clergy and the liq, who were with him on that day. They conversed about the Ark (*Seyon*), which had spent such long years since King Ebna Lahakim until our days. They spoke of peace for her, and asked the happiness of this house of the Lord our God...[77]

A possible allusion to another coronation occurs in the chronicle of Iyasu II, but if so it is very vaguely worded. Iyasu II visited, in 1750, 'the celestial Seyon, the Ark of the Law of the Lord'. His 'accomplishment of everything that he intended to do' is recorded, but there is no description of any ceremony.

These ceremonies at Aksum were to be repeated only once more, with the coronation of a Tigray prince, Kassa, as Yohannes IV, emperor of Ethiopia, in 1872. Yohannes IV, who also claimed Solomonic ancestry,[78] was crowned at Maryam Seyon church in Aksum with all the ceremonial of the kingship of Zion. This ceremony is too late to have relevance to our subject here, the quest for the Ark at Aksum. Yohannes' successor Menelik II, though named after the son of Solomon and the queen of Sheba, did not claim the kingship of Zion. Menelik II's chronicle was the first to include the *KN* story, abbreviated and with minor variations.[79] The last coronation of an Ethiopian emperor, that of Haile Sellassie at Addis Ababa in 1930, evoked none of these old rituals of Zion. Nevertheless, the emperor's descent 'from the line of Menelik, son of King Solomon and Queen Makeda…' was proclaimed by the *abun* (patriarch), and a 'sword of Solomon' was presented to him during the ceremonies.

QUEST FOR A LEGEND

Up to this point, my scrutiny of Ethiopian and European literary works to the mid-15th century has still unearthed no reasonably acceptable evidence for the Ark's presence in Ethiopia – except where I have anticipated a little to describe 16th and 17th century coronation ceremonies. By and large, the evidence, or rather the complete lack of evidence, seems to point rather in the opposite direction. From the 15th century, we possess certain Ethiopian ecclesiastical writings that do mention the Ark and the tablets of Moses, but their significance to our quest is that they make no claim that these things are in Ethiopia. As with *maphrian* Bar Hebraeus, there is no hint that the authors or translators considered the 'real' Ark or the 'real' tablets of Moses to be treasures of the Ethiopian state and church laid up in Aksum.

SOME LITERARY FRAGMENTS

A 15th century Ge'ez note about the Ark, for example, provides food for thought. The *Gadla Yohannes Mesraqawi*[80] describes the birth in Palestine of the saint, son of Dilasor, a man of royal birth (inevitably), and his wife, who bore the evocative name of *Emmena Seyon*, 'our mother Zion'. It is not certain in what period the events are supposed to be set. In the long introductory preamble, filled with citations about the sins of the Israelites, how they drank wine and mead, how they worshipped idols, how their daughters were perfumed, and their songs changed into the songs of Babylon, comes the remark:

> But the Lord's song departed from Zion, the Lord's song became the song of prostitutes, until the destruction of the city of Zion. The lamp was extinguished and the Ark of the Law (*tabota hegg*) plundered…

The cleric who wrote the *gadl* of Yohannes in the 15th century accepted that the Ark was plundered from Jerusalem, probably by the Babylonians, given the apparent allusion to a verse in Psalm 137, 'How shall we sing the Lord's song in a strange land'. He apparently had no thought that it might be in Ethiopia, in Maryam Seyon church at Aksum.

Similarly, in other Ethiopic texts Zion and the Ark are evoked without any attempt to introduce an Ethiopian slant, or to add a gloss explaining that the Ark was now in Aksum.[81] A book translated into Ge'ez before 1379, the *Gadla Hawaryat*, published by Budge as the *Contendings of the Apostles* – apocryphal tales detailing the lives and deaths of the twelve apostles of Christ – relates how St. Clement of Rome, a follower of the apostle Peter, assembled documentation concerning the mysteries of the faith.[82] Peter instructs Clement to compile an account of everything he has seen in Rome (including magic contests with Simon Magus), and to place it in 'the treasury of books in Rome'. Clement does so, and Peter seals the account. Other apostles contribute other books, and Clement places them 'in the Cave of the Treasures of Rome, which I have called the "Cave of Life"…' Clement receives still other books from disciples in remote lands, and adds these to his collection. Then follows the interesting passage:

> Now I Clement called that ark (*or* chest) wherein I had placed the mysteries, 'The Ark of the Covenant', and I rolled all the books up in the napkin wherewith my Lord and God Jesus Christ, girded Himself about when He washed the feet of His disciples, and I covered them over with the face-cloth which was upon His head when He was in the grave. And I, and many of the disciples, placed what remained of His burial wrappings therein; and the garments which had been woven without seam, and which was that in which our Lord was arrayed on the day of His crucifixion, and for which the soldiers cast lots; and the crown of thorns which the Jews plaited for our Lord; and the apparel and tunic of purple in which they dressed Him; and the sponge, and the vinegar, and the wormwood; and the spear wherewith our Lord was pierced; and the rope wherewith they bound Him upon the wood; and the rods wherewith they scourged Him – all these, I say, we laid up in the 'Ark of the Covenant', wherein we had placed the books of mysteries, where they shall be preserved until the time of the Second Coming of our Lord Christ…

The Ark of the Covenant and the Shroud of Turin appear together in this Ethiopic manuscript translated from Arabic about half a century after the composition of the *KN*. No alteration or comment was deemed necessary – naturally enough, for at that time, following my thesis here, the Ark was not included in the *KN* story, which anyway may not by this time have much circulated in Ethiopia. Although Budge in his translation supplies quotation marks around 'Ark of the Covenant', in the Ge'ez text there is no such distinction. Apparently the author is not claiming that he has placed everything in the Ark of the Covenant that Moses constructed on Mount Sinai. He has created another 'Ark of the Covenant' himself, something that was to become normal in Ethiopia with each newly consecrated *tabot*. Clement's Ark is placed in Rome, with no mention of an Ark at Aksum or anywhere else in Ethiopia. Another intriguing passage occurs in the following chapter:

> And it came to pass that when I had heard these things from my master Peter, concerning these mysteries, their honour was greatly added to in my sight, and I asked him to inform me concerning the history of the bodies of the fathers, Abraham, Isaac, and Jacob, and the story of the Tables of the Law which Moses, the chosen one, received from the hand of God, (Whose Names are holy!) and broke in pieces. Then my master Peter said unto me, 'Know, O my son, that a certain pure woman shall rule in the last days over the Christian people; and all the bodies of the believing Patriarchs shall be transferred unto the holy city of Rome, and the holy tables of Moses which were among the treasures laid up shall be sought for, and people shall bring them into the city of Rome.'

The text does not mention the second set of unbroken tablets placed in the Ark, nor their supposed presence since Ebna Hakim's time in Ethiopia. The translators from the Arabic appear to have accepted a text that ignores significant associated claims put forward in their own supposed 'national epic': the epic that has been compared to the Old Testament and the *Qur'an* as a 'repository of Ethiopian national and religious feelings'.[83]

EUROPEAN RUMOURS

To Europe, Ethiopia remained for centuries a country of profound mystery. A further layer of obscurity and confusion was added when it became commonplace to situate the mighty Prester John there instead of in his former supposed habitats in Asia or India. Ethiopia became a dream kingdom of infinite potential in the struggle with Islam because it was Christian, and neighboured Egypt and the holy places of Islam. Prophecies were remembered, or coined. Anecdotes spread concerning the Solomonic ancestry of the emperors of Ethiopia.

On 18 September 1517, the Florentine Andrea Corsali wrote to the 'the Most Illustrious Prince, Duke Lorenzo dei Medici, concerning the navigation of the Red Sea and the Persian Gulf, to the town of Cochin in the country of India'. He related how the power of the Portuguese 'augments from day to day in the Indies', where he was serving under Captain-Major Lopes Soares. On the way to Ethiopia from Portuguese India, with 'Matthew, ambassador of King David' (Dawit, Lebna Dengel, emperor of Ethiopia), he described the island of Socotra and its Christians: 'Christians by nature like the Christians of King David'. He was enchanted by a chameleon he saw there. He mentioned the treasures of the sultans of Aden, so great that – like Alvares when he wrote of the glory of the churches of Lalibela – he feared to describe them in anticipation of being called a liar. He described the islands of Dahlak and their king.

There he heard news about the 'state of King David, whom we call Prester John'. His kingdom, it was said, comprised all Ethiopia Interior and Lower Egypt. Some said it extended to Congo. The monarch was then at Chaxumo, once called Auxuma (this king was one of the successors of Zara Yaqob who occasionally visited Aksum but did not undergo ritual tonsuring there). The emperor was eighteen years old, of olive complexion, handsome; he was always veiled, appearing only once a year to his subjects. Conversation with him was conducted by intermediaries, sometimes passing through up to four messengers. All the people were marked with fire, something already remarked upon with the Ethiopians in Rome. This was not, as some said, their form of baptism, since they baptised in fact with water, but

> to observe the customs of Solomon, who marked his slaves thus; from whose line it was said that this king of Ethiopia came, because a queen, passing by there, became pregnant, and gave birth to a son, from whom came this line, who observe the old and new law, as coming forth from the house of Israel... Others say there is there a ring of Solomon, with a crown, and a throne of King David, held in great reverence.[84]

Among the treasures of the Solomonic rulers, and the oblique reference to the queen of Sheba, no mention of the Ark is made. Alessandro Zorzi, at Venice, spent years, 1519–24, collecting itineraries concerning Ethiopia.[85] The documents he has left us are accounts of journeys gathered directly from Ethiopians who were living in Italy at exactly the same time as the first Portuguese embassy was in Ethiopia. In some cases they are more than simple itineraries, but enlarge a little. The tendency for exaggeration, unless

Zorzi misunderstood on occasion, might emerge at times, but by and large the notes about Aksum, and the status of the ruler, are recognisable. The Ark is never mentioned. The king, as usual at this period, is referred to as Prester John, and there is confirmation, not really surprising by now, that he was of the family of David and Solomon. When exactly the story of Solomonic descent gained currency still remains unclear. Perhaps it was adopted as early as Yigba Seyon's (1285–94) reign, if his throne name Solomon is significant in this context, or perhaps it emerged in Amda Seyon's time (1314–44) under the influence of the *KN* as edited by *nebura'ed* Yeshaq. Or perhaps it was Emperor Zara Yaqob (1434–68), that eager and compelling reformer of the beliefs of his people, who adopted the claim. His name, significantly in this context, means 'Seed of Jacob'.

One itinerary, collected from 'Brother Thomas (of Ganget in Anguot province) of the Order of St Francis who came from Jerusalem and from the lands of Presta Davit, most mighty Lord of Aethiopia Tragloditica', was collected on 7 April 1523, at Venice. From Thomas, Zorzi heard the legend of the Solomonic descent of the emperor (then Dawit, Wanag Sagad or Lebna Dengel): 'Presta Davit, which means Emperor, King and Lord; Davit is not his proper name. They say he is of the line of Davit.'

THREE BOOKS

The search for 'Zion' in Ethiopia – even if at this stage the Ark itself is still barely visible – at last begins to yield some concrete results with documents of the 1520s–30s. A new puzzle enters the story with a venerated but still mysterious object, apparently a large altar tablet associated with Zion. The Ark itself remains shrouded in the same silence as before, but that is only one strand in a skein of developing complexity. There are signs of the Ark's imminent arrival. Outside Ethiopia, as we shall see, it has almost certainly already been mentioned in an Arabic story from Egypt, a successor to Abu Salih's tale. In Ethiopia, a newly augmented version of the *KN*, not yet circulating widely, has perhaps by this time included it – if we accept the proposed dating of the manuscript of the *KN* in the Bibliothèque Nationale, Paris – even if all other documents tell a different tale.

We have now to delve into three books, of very different origins, but all important for the history of Aksum. One is written in Ge'ez, one in Portuguese, and one in Arabic. Part at least of the Ge'ez text, the so-called *Book of Aksum*, is often said to have been written before the destruction of the old Maryam Seyon church at Aksum in 1535, perhaps in the later 15th century, but many documents in surviving copies are much later. The earliest provable date for a tiny part of it (the description of the church) comes from the early 17th century, when Péro Pais translated it. The second book, the otherwise rich description of the land of 'Prester John' by Francisco Alvares, introduces a revered stone from Zion at Aksum, but makes no reference to the Ark. This is really astonishing, because one can safely say that Alvares left out virtually nothing else, especially anything to do with religion, including matters of no such intrinsic importance. Alvares' book describes Aksum and its church as he saw them during a stay of several months during the 1520s. Could anyone have remained there for so long, with the Ark close at hand, and not have heard tell of it? The third book, in Arabic, is the *Futuh al-Habasha*, a chronicle of Ahmad Grañ's virtual conquest of Abyssinia. It dates to around 1535 (see above), and it too records a stone, greatly venerated, and encrusted with gold, that was taken in panic from Aksum into safety in the mountains as the Muslim armies advanced.

The Book of Aksum

In the Ge'ez treatise known as the *Book of Aksum*, a short section recounts the wonders of the sacred city. The book, sometimes found as a supplement attached to copies of the *KN*, is arranged in three parts: 1, a description of the city with details about the church; 2, copies of land grants to the church and certain other places; and 3, a number of supplementary historical and legal documents.[86]

Conspicuous among the personalities and objects of Aksum noted in section 1 are Abreha and Asbeha, the monuments, wells and sources, mysterious underground structures in the stele field area – the reality of these was discovered during our excavations in 1974[87] – and other remarkable buildings (accompanied by the usual tales of treasures of gold and pearls). The book also describes wonders like the round stone called *berot* (*berota eben*), divine footprints, or the outline of Frumentius' cross left in the rock, as well as the churches of Aksum, including, of course, '*gabaza Aksum*', the church of Maryam Seyon.

Several paragraphs in section 1 are devoted to the church. Among the officers designated *'aqabta gabaz*, 'guardians of the cathedral' of Mary of Zion in the *Book of Aksum*, a title equivalent to the title of the modern guardian of the Ark, the *aqabet*, is listed: *bet tabaqi* (guardian of the house).[88] The office of *bet tabaqi*, like *aqabet*, refers to a steward or treasurer, and can be traced at Aksum back to the reign of Lebna Dengel. It appears in many land grants, listed among the most important titles of the Aksumite clergy, with the *nebura'ed*, the *qese gabaz*, and the chief of deacons. But this is not in itself enough to postulate the presence of the Ark – every church has its treasurer, *aqabet* or *bet tabaqi*.

Surprisingly, if the Ark of Zion were really present at Aksum, it is not referred to even obliquely in any of the numerous land grants made in favour of Maryam Seyon church, copies of which are included in the *Book of Aksum*. Some of these grants purport to date from the reigns of the kings Abreha and Asbeha, and Anbasa Wudem, mythical sovereigns attributed to a period many centuries earlier than the surviving copies of the grants.[89] The 'Abreha and Asbeha' grants merely designate the church by the term *gabaza Aksum*, 'cathedral (lit. guardian) of Aksum'. The term may allude to Mary herself as guardian of Aksum.[90] Only the grants issued by Anbasa Wudem, a supposed predecessor of the formidable Queen Gudit, employ the designation Seyon (Zion): *Seyon gabaza Aksum*, 'Zion, cathedral of Aksum', or *emmena Seyon*, *gabaza Aksum*, 'our mother Zion, the cathedral (guardian) of Aksum'. This ambiguous term may refer to the Ark of the Covenant, in which the older Law, the tablets of Moses, were kept. Or it may mean Mary, the 'ark' in whose womb the Word, Christ, was carried, and by extension the Zion church of Aksum.

These grants in the *Book of Aksum* are 17th century or later 'copies'. For the earliest period, they are probably pure invention, and do not mean that the terms used in them applied in the 4th or 10th century. The rulers named are known exclusively from such suspect grants, late Ethiopian king lists or other late Ge'ez documents, usually hagiographies. None are known to history from reliable documentation. Two of the grants, written using precisely the formulae of more recent grants, name 'Ella Abreha and Asbeha' as the donors. One refers to the 'throne of David'. Had they been written in the name of King Ezana, the real name of the first Christian Aksumite king, and resembled the formulae known from Ezana's inscriptions, the case would be very different but, as it is, they look like monkish forgeries of a later era. The aim in creating them was to glorify the church by asserting an old and distinguished pedigree, harking back to the legendary founders of the Christian faith in Ethiopia, and more practically to confirm claims to certain landholdings.

Land grants from later reigns in the *Book of Aksum* are attributed to the kings Sayfa Arad (1344–72) and Zara Yaqob (1434–68). These may be genuine. One of Sayfa Arad's grants (in two redactions) refers to fiefs bestowed upon *gabaza Aksum*, the cathedral of Aksum: 'for the commemoration of my Lady Mary'. It does not add the designation *Seyon*. A grant of Emperor Zara Yaqob finally unites all the elements: 'Our Mother Seyon the Cathedral of Aksum… for the commemoration of my Lady Mary'. It will be remembered that Zara Yaqob's chronicle (written, however, in Lebna Dengel's time) attributes to him the distribution of largesse at Aksum for 'the greatness of Zion'.

But what does Seyon mean here? Does the term imply the presence of a holy object, possibly the altar stone of Zion soon to appear in other descriptions? No indisputably dated Ethiopian or foreign source – discounting the uncertainly dated *KN* manuscript kept at the Bibliothèque Nationale in Paris, which I will deal with later, and Abu Salih – suggests that the Ark was in Ethiopia at this time, but the revered 'altar stone of Zion' might have been installed by Zara Yaqob's reign. Perhaps, given the description of it over half a century later by Alvares as a stone from Mount Zion, it was already called Seyon, and like any *tabot* gave its name to the church. If Zara Yaqob's chronicler is really using a phrase current in the king's own time when he refers to him as scattering pieces of gold 'for the greatness of Zion', it may be that he alluded to this Zion stone. The name referred to Mount Zion, the stone's place of origin – it was not yet identified as (or confused with) the Ark of the Covenant.

After my investigation into Ethiopian hagiographical literature, as it is known to date, it was not very surprising to find no trace of the Ark's presence – or for that matter of the tablet(s) of Moses – in the first two sections of the *Book of Aksum*, even though the book could be bound in as an appendix to the *KN* itself. Despite its detailed description of Aksum, its 'cathedral' and other churches, and many other remarkable features in the town, the book reveals nothing of the Ark. The Ark is absent from the sections describing Abreha and Asbeha's foundation of the church. Nor does it emerge in the minute descriptions of all sorts of details about the church's fabric, administration, functionaries, maintenance, possessions, income and so on. In the parts of the book dedicated to the marvels of Aksum, the city's greatest claim, by far, to heavenly glory is ignored, just as it is in the land grants.

We should consider the nature of this book, and why it was written. First, simply enough, it affirmed and justified, in the section containing the copies of land grants, the possession of large tracts of land and subject villages. But Hirsch and Fauvelle-Aymar have pointed out that there could be much more to it than that. Zara Yaqob may have celebrated his coronation there, but even in the *Book of Aksum* itself it is emphasised that after him no king was crowned there until Sarsa Dengel. The Holy City, the New Jerusalem, in reality seems to have lain rather outside the central concerns of the monarchy and church, for the next 144 years at least. The *nebura'ed* was a prominent official, yes, but not the greatest of the ecclesiastics at court. Baeda Maryam, Eskender, Naod, Lebna Dengel, Galawdewos, Minas: emperor after emperor built their great churches in the south, specifically designed as mausolea for themselves and their families. These places held their treasures, and participated significantly in the endless round of imperial travels. Aksum was sometimes visited, of course but as a marginal element, far from the chief centres of affairs. The primary function of the *Book of Aksum*, then, was to rescue Aksum from obscurity: 'l'oubli d'Aksoum par les rois'.[91] If the original compilation was designed as a response to this requirement, and the Ark, chief glory of Maryam Seyon church, and supposed palladium of the entire 'Solomonic' state, was resident, is it conceivable that it would not even be mentioned?

Logic suggests that when these parts of the *Book of Aksum* were originally compiled the Ark of the Covenant was not yet associated with the city, nor were the tablets of Moses associated with the altar tablet of its church. Only in the descriptions of the flight of the Ark to Bur in section 3 of the *Book of Aksum*, written well after the expulsion of the Catholics in 1632–33, does the Ark appear. This story will be told in its place below.

But even if the Ark and the tablets of Moses do not appear among the descriptions of Aksum in the *Book of Aksum*, there was a sacred stone connected to Jerusalem in the city, and this receives the attention that one might expect for the Ark if it has really been there. The strange object called the *berot* stone or *berota eben* was apparently so celebrated that it was considered as an identifying feature of the town:

> Also, there is the berota eben, near the throne, of which the name is invoked at Jerusalem (or: which bears the name of Jerusalem); it is round like a shield; in the centre, it is red and round like a cup. When someone travels, they ask him 'What is your country?' He answers: 'Aksum'. He is asked: 'Do you know the berota eben?' If he says: 'I don't know it', they reply: 'You are not an Aksumite'.

The throne mentioned must mean one of the thrones in the church compound, described two paragraphs previously in the *Book of Aksum*, perhaps the most conspicuous one called 'the king's seat'. It is possible that this mysterious stone might be identified with a large round stone now placed at the top of the western steps of the church, but the rest of the description, 'red and round like a cup', implying a hollowed area, hardly fits. The stone seems to have had nothing to do with a *tabot*, nor with an 'Ark', and its identity remains a mystery. It is, however, intriguing that a stone already existed at Aksum that was intimately associated both with the city and with Jerusalem.[92]

The land grants preserved in the *Book of Aksum* do confirm one thing: the church of Aksum was greatly revered. Its reputed age, its situation in the old capital city, and its association with the holy kings Abreha and Asbeha and bishop Frumentius were quite enough to earn it this veneration. The city and the church must have experienced a resurgence of prestige under Zara Yaqob, with his coronation there, and his three years' residence in the town.[93] Soon the veneration accorded the altar stone from Mount Zion would raise the city's status even higher.

Ho Preste João das Indias

Francisco Alvares saw the church of Maryam Seyon at Aksum in its prime. When describing 'Aquaxumo' in *Ho Preste João das Indias*, Alvares actually discusses the name of the church, and the attribution to Zion. The Portuguese chaplain's information dates to about a decade and a half before the attack by the forces of Ahmad ibn Ibrahim, called Grañ, and the utter destruction of an edifice never again equalled among Abyssinia's churches.

Alvares says nothing about the 'Ark'. He merely relates the tale of St. Philip and the eunuch of Queen Candace from the *Acts of the Apostles*, adding that the church was built by Candace, 'the first Christian that there was in this country':

> In this town of Aquaxumo, where she became Christian, she built a very noble church, the first there was in Ethiopia: it is named St. Mary of Syon... because its altar stone came from Sion. In this country (as they say) they have the custom always to name the churches by the altar stone, because on it is written the name of the patron saint. This stone which they have in this church, they say that the Apostles sent it from Mount Sion.[94]

This describes an ordinary Ethiopian *tabot* (though with a splendid legendary pedigree) with the name of the patron saint carved on it, from which the church is named. The altar stone of Zion at Aksum, though, seems to have been something rather exceptional among *tabotat*. Only a few years later, to avoid the menace of *imam* Ahmad Grañ's army, Emperor Lebna Dengel ordered the hasty removal from Aksum to Tabr of a very large gold-encrusted stone (see below).

The name 'Zion' in Alvares' description approaches as closely as it is possible to come to Zion, the Ethiopian Ark of the Covenant that we are searching for. But, disconcertingly for any claim that the Ark had long been at Aksum, there is no mention of it anywhere in Alvares' very detailed book. Alvares offers no hint even of the existence of a legend about the Ark in Ethiopia – nor is the simple designation Seyon or Zion, already employed in the dedications of several other churches in Ethiopia, enough to suggest it.

In one of the surviving versions of Alvares' work, a copy by Ludovico Beccadelli, archbishop of Ragusa, some supplementary notes obtained c. 1542 from Ethiopian priests residing in Rome are cited. When Alvares describes how 13 tent-churches travelled with the mobile imperial camp-capital, one of these notes enlarges: 'The Ethiopians say that the churches are twelve, as also are the tribes, and besides there is the church of the king, which contains the tablets of the law given to Moses'.[95] The information is curious, to say the least. The supposed contents of the Ark are described, but with no relationship to Aksum, and there is no mention by these 16th century Ethiopians of the Ark itself.

The Conquest of Abyssinia

The literary glorification of the Muslim 'conquest of Abyssinia', the Arabic text called the *Futuh al-Habasha*,[96] offers us a solid clue, and one moreover completely divorced from Ethiopian ecclesiastical propaganda. It confirms that a sacred object was removed with some effort from the church at Aksum before its destruction. The book is a contemporary Arabic account of Ahmad Grañ's expedition, richly descriptive. In 1535 – the year of the church's destruction[97] – its author, Shihab al-Din (nicknamed Arab-Faqih), recorded that *imam* Ahmad fought against Raqat, *shum* (local chief) of Agame, near the tomb of Ahmad al-Nagashi. He next intended to move on Aksum.[98] Emperor

Lebna Dengel marched with his nobles and his troops to Aksum. There the emperor made special arrangements to protect a mysterious 'idol' from the church:

> They gathered there in great numbers, and (the king of Abyssinia) brought forth from the church of Aksum the great idol that was there. This was a white stone with encrustations in gold; this idol was so large that it could not go out of the door of the church; a hole the size of the idol had to be pierced in the church because of its size, and so they got it out; it was necessary to employ four hundred men to carry it. They took it to a fortress of the country of Siri (Shire); the name of this idol was Tabor, and it was in this fort that they left it.

Different translations do not interpret Tabor (which one might otherwise assume to stand for *tabot*) as the name of the idol, but suggests that it was rather the name of a stronghold, Tabr.[99] This place Tabr is Medebai Tabr, a village in Shire set amid mountains and gorges, where recently the Tigray fighters also found a haven from their enemies. It was a logical choice. Emperor Lebna Dengel himself was to find shelter there, in this 'high and elevated amba of Siré',[100] in the 31st, and penultimate, year of his reign, 1539. Perhaps the presence of the 'Ark' brought some comfort to this tragic emperor as he surveyed the ruin of his shattered country.

The story of the flight of the idol receives some circumstantial confirmation from the *Book of Aksum* in the shape of an inventory listing the 'objects from Aksum, which our king Lebna Dengel entrusted to the chiefs, while he was in the land of Zobel' (on the eastern escarpment of the Ethiopian highlands).[101] Evidently it was decided to remove everything possible from the church, for safety. A good deal of gold, some silks and other garments, and church ornaments of all types, are listed. A total of 1705 golden objects were distributed in one day. The mysterious white stone is not mentioned. Separate arrangements must have been made for its disposal.

If Shihab al Din's description is correct – and although he was not an eyewitness to the events, as far as we know, his story chimes extraordinarily well with that of Alvares a few years earlier – this venerated 'idol' is likely to have been an unusually big stone *tabot* or altar tablet. The description bears no resemblance to the far more easily portable wooden Ark of the Covenant. Possibly the story reached Shihab al-Din in a slightly garbled form, since it is almost unimaginable that the stone could really be of the immense size that he suggests. If it could not be taken out, it could not have been taken in either without great effort and the demolition of part of the wall, unless when it was introduced some more developed handling techniques had been used.

Perhaps the stone was large, but not as enormous as Shihab al-Din implies. Panic, and the need for urgent haste, may have encouraged the simple brutal solution of breaking a hole in the wall to remove the stone as quickly as possible on a substantial litter with carrying poles. The *tabotat* of the royal camp were carried this way – among them, perhaps, the so-called tablets of the Law noted in the Beccadelli version of Alvares, clearly something different from the altar stone of Zion at Maryam Seyon church. If the stone were sufficiently heavy to require a litter with cross-poles and bearers on all sides, it might have been for that reason that the hole had to be pierced. One would assume that the stone was too weighty to have been brought out by standing it on its side, and anyway there was no time for preparation. However large the stone was, it seems exaggerated to claim that four hundred men were needed to carry it. Anything with this requirement could not anyway have progressed along Ethiopia's tracks and mountainous reaches, nor could the technology of the time have encompassed such a task, whatever the Aksumites might have been able to do a thousand years or more before. The number, if it has any relevance beyond just imagination or hearsay, may include not just the bearers but also a corps of guards assigned to oversee its transport.

TALES OF SOLOMON AND SHEBA

When I began to read the Portuguese records concerning Ethiopia from the first half of the 16th century, I found that several referred to Ethiopian tales about Solomon, the queen of Sheba and the prince their son. They confirm the existence of a work similar in content to the *KN*, and they cite from it. From the general acceptance that the story of the Ark was an old legend of Ethiopia, I expected that these excerpts would mention or even describe it. To my surprise, they did not. None of the earlier Portuguese records affirm that the Ark of the Covenant itself was brought to Ethiopia. Instead, they cite a less extreme version of the story, in which only the tablets of the Law figure.

This immensely important point seems to have been overlooked. The discussion of what these books reveal is vital, the key to our search for the truth about the Aksum Ark of Zion. The Ark is visible to us only through literary records over several centuries. Paraphrases are insufficient to present the precise meaning of the authors concerned, in the first period chiefly Jesuits living in Ethiopia as missionaries. They were eyewitnesses and even direct participants in one phase at least of the life of the holy talisman. Later, other foreigners came, and one or two of them also came close to the holy relic at Aksum. The immediacy of their testimony, and its value in following the path of the Ark in Ethiopia, necessitates citing in full the information they have left us.

FRANCISCO ALVARES

In reports about the interminable conversations by messenger, or in person, conducted on almost every conceivable subject of religious debate between the Ethiopian emperor, Lebna Dengel, the *abun*, Marqos, and the Iberian priests in Ethiopia, the Ark, incredibly, is never mentioned. Francisco Alvares, for example, was constantly bombarded with questions on a wide variety of ecclesiastical subjects, for hours on end, day after day. Wryly as Alvares describes it, it must have been a strain for a man not trained in theology in the stamp of his Jesuit successors. In addition, the Ethiopians had a penchant for summonings late at night, when the unfortunate priest was not at his best. Even the three queens, Lebna Dengel's step-grandmother, mother and wife, helped, adding their own queries to the rest. The questions went on and on. On one occasion, Alvares writes that he at last sent to 'ask His Highness to have pity on an old man, who had neither eaten nor drunk since yesterday at midday, nor had slept, and could not stand for weakness'. But never once, under this intense scrutiny of religious issues in Ethiopia, does Alvares refer to the Ark in his book. Nor does the Ark figure in the account of the close examination of Alvares by Diogo de Sousa, archbishop of Braga and primate of Portugal, after his return from his travels in Ethiopia in 1529.[102] The questions, and his replies, were all carefully recorded, and published subsequently in Alvares' book.

Francisco Alvares was well aware of the story of the putative origins of the Ethiopian dynasty. But the version he knew was significantly different from the *KN* story in its final form. Alvares found it in 'a very long chronicle' kept in the church of Maryam Seyon at Aksum. He explained that it was

> written in the language of the country, and it stated at the beginning that it had been written first in Hebrew, and afterwards put into Greek, and from Greek into Chaldean, and from Chaldean into Abyssinian, in which it is now, and it begins thus. How the Queen Saba hearing related the great and rich

buildings which Solomon had begun in Jerusalem, determined to go and see them; and she loaded camels with gold to give for these buildings. And on arriving near the city, and being about to cross a lake, which they passed by a bridge of boats, [possessed by the Spirit,] she dismounted [knelt] and worshipped the beams [of the bridge] and said: 'Please God my feet shall not touch the timber on which the Saviour of the world has to hang'. And she went round the lake and begged him to take away those beams from there…[103]

The queen inspected the buildings, finding them richer than she had supposed. Apologising for her meagre gift, she promised to send more gold and 'black wood to inlay'. She slept with Solomon, gave birth to a son, and then departed to her country. Seventeen years later, all Israel and Judea were irritated by the pride of the son of Solomon and Sheba. They approached the king, saying, 'We are not able to maintain so many Kings as you have got, for all your sons are Kings, especially this one of Queen Saba; she is a greater lady than you, send him to his mother…' So the son departed, with a train of officers.[104] Solomon also gave him the city of Gaza. The son became a great ruler: 'the chronicle says that he ruled from sea to sea, and that he had sixty ships in the Indian sea'. Alvares concludes: 'This book of chronicles is very large, and I copied only the beginning.'

In the part he copied, there is no reference to the Ark or the tablets of Moses at all. Although this story was an Aksum recension of the Solomon and Sheba story, and although in another context Alvares describes Aksum as 'the city, court and residence of the Queen Saba, whose own name was Makeda', echoing the name of the queen in the *KN*, the content of the tale as Alvares recounts it is quite different from the version in the *KN*.

What book was it that Alvares partly copied at Maryam Seyon church? Alvares' editors proposed that it might be either a long version of the royal chronicles, or the *KN*, which is often bound with royal chronicles or king lists.[105] But its contents show that it was not the same version of the *KN* that Péro Pais was to translate later (see below), also from a document in the church at Aksum – the current version as now accepted in Ethiopia. On the other hand, the preamble that Alvares cites resembles the colophon of certain versions of the *KN*, providing details about several translations. The implied pedigree, right back to Hebrew, is different, and was inserted, apparently, at the beginning and not in a colophon at the end.

The *Golden Legend*

Especially intriguing is the story of the wooden bridge. This is no Ethiopian invention, but an old tale very popular in Europe long ago. We can read it in the *Golden Legend*, a compendium of tales of the lives of the saints, apostles, Mary and Jesus, translated and printed by William Caxton at Westmestre (Westminster) in England as early as 1483, very soon after he had introduced the secrets of the early printers of Germany and Italy into England in 1476. When Caxton printed the book, the story was already old.

The *Legenda Aurea* was compiled by Jacobus de Voragine, the monk who in 1292 was elected, because of his exemplary life, archbishop of Genoa – an office he had already refused once. The book was a reflection of the times, when credulity for the most ridiculous of Christian legends was at its height; later it was to be held up to scorn and condemnation. The episode involving the queen appears in the section of the *Golden Legend* dealing with the Invention (Discovery) of the Holy Cross. It tells the tale of the tree growing from a branch broken off the Tree of Paradise by the Archangel Michael and given to Seth, who had come to the gates of Eden. It was planted on Adam's grave, and eventually was cut down by Solomon. In Caxton's version we read:

> Than Salomon sawe this tree so faire (he) commaundid to smyte him down, and putte him safe in the house of Saux…And as John Belet saith, that Tree wolde neu(er) be mete to no manere of werke; for other hit was to large, other to shorte; and therefore the werkemen…leide hit ou(er) a water as a brigge men for to passe ou(er)e. And than the Quene of Saba whan she came to hure the wisdome of Salomon, and than as she sholde passe ou(er)e that water she sawe in spirite how that the saviour of al the worlde sholde deie on that same Tree; and therefore she wolde not passe there-ouere, but worship that tree.

> And hit is read in the maistre of stories [Belet: see below] that the Quene of Saba saughe that tree in the hous of Saux. And whan she was go home agen to her owne cuntre, she sent Salomon worde, that a man sholde be hangid in that Tree bi whos dethe the kingdome of Jewes sholde be distroied. And than Salomon take awaie that tree, and hidde hit deep in the earth…

Later, the wood was to resurface, floated up by water that appeared at the spot, to become the cross of Christ.[106]

Archbishop Jacobus was not entirely sure about this legend, and remarked that 'it is left to the judgement of the reader whether this be true or not, as these things are not to be found in any chronicle or authentic history'. He had found the story in a source of a century earlier, the *Rationale*

Divinorum Officiorum of Johannes Belethus, 'John Belet' in the English version. Belethus was a rector in Paris. He is known to have been active between 1182 (when he is mentioned in the *Chronicon* of Albericus Trium Fontium) and 1190. His work was not published until 1553, in Antwerp, but would have circulated long before in manuscript. Of this tale of the wood of the Cross, Johannes Belethus has this to say: a branch was given by an angel to Seth, when he was sent to Paradise; it became a large tree; it proved of no use in building the temple, and was placed over a ditch of the city to assist access; and, when the queen of Sheba saw it, she did not wish to cross it, but instead worshipped it.[107]

It is not surprising that a popular story of mediaeval times should have circulated in Ethiopia. *The Miracles of Mary* offers just one example of a set of popular stories that passed from European books via Arabic into Ethiopia, where they were augmented at will. However suspicious we might be of changes and alterations to manuscripts, we have no reason to suspect that the story was added by Alvares, or that the editors of his book, preparing it for publication, inserted it. João de Barros, too, knew of the story, as we shall see, probably from Alvares' draft work that circulated in India.

In addition, vestigial relics of the story of the wood of the Cross may still be detected in the *KN*, even if the version as told by Alvares has vanished. In *KN* 100 and 104 allusions to wood are preserved. These, which seem to lack any relevant antecedent, perhaps once referred back to the tale, later suppressed, of the queen of Sheba's prophecy about the wood of the Cross. In *KN* 100, God ordains that Noah can be saved from the water by wood, and commands Noah to build the ark: 'God was well pleased that by means of wood which had been sanctified the salvation of His creation should take place, that is to say, the ark (*tabot*) and the wood of the Cross.' In *KN* 104, the text deals with wood in several different settings, including 'salvation through the wood of His Cross, in the Tabernacle of the Law (*tabota heggu*)...' This almost seems to imply that the wood of the Cross was represented by the wood of a *tabot* in its identification as the '*tabot* of the Law', even though the tablets of the Law themselves in the original story were of stone. The text continues: 'Salvation came unto Adam through the wood. For Adam's first transgression came through the wood, and from the beginning God ordained salvation for him through the wood.' Adam's transgression was the eating of the fruit of the tree of the knowledge of good and evil: his salvation came through the Cross of Christ.

There is another corollary, deriving from a further tale about the queen of Sheba that circulated in Ethiopia. The Amharic text the *Hemamata Krestos* or *Hemamata Masqal*, the 'Passion of Christ', is a treatise relating the thirteen sufferings of Christ during Passion Week.[108] One text published in 1972 without any citation of sources includes in the *Hemamata Masqal* a version of the popular Ethiopian tale about the wood of the Cross. It brings in, as usual, some favourite heroes: Alexander the Great, the queen of Sheba and King Solomon. Alexander had visited Paradise presumptuously, and attached his mount to a branch of the tree of Paradise. He was expelled by a seraph. Leaving in a panic on his mount, the branch was torn from the tree and fell to earth, to Jerusalem. Solomon (never mind that he lived long before Alexander!), building the temple, wanted to use this wood, but it was useless. It burned his demon helpers, and would not behave properly as pillar or lintel even with human builders. The queen of Sheba had in the past slain a terrible serpent that had subjected her people. Its blood had caused a deformity on her leg. But when she came to Jerusalem, her leg touched this piece of wood, and she was miraculously cured. King Solomon placed the wood, destined to become the wood of the Cross, in the temple, and both sovereigns decorated it with silver, laying a curse on any who might steal the silver. Solomon's successors also did the same, and thus the thirty pieces of silver given to Judas were assembled (see Chapter 5: An Arabic Tale). Alvares' story thus survived in Ethiopia, but not as part of the *KN*.

SAGA ZA-AB

Most decisive of all is another variant of the *KN* story, more or less contemporary with Alvares' version. This time it is not based on a European's interpretation, about which, however careful or well informed he might be, some doubt might still remain. Instead, it was written in Lisbon by Emperor Lebna Dengel's ambassador, Saga Za-Ab, who arrived there in 1527. A translation of it was published by Damião de Góis (1502–74), the great Portuguese humanist, and English versions have appeared in works by Geddes and Ludolf.[109]

Ambassador Saga Za-Ab assigns himself the titles '*ras* (head) of Bugna, *liqa kahenat, qal hase* to Jan Belul, *hase* Lebna Dengel'. In short, he was a nobleman and court priest of consequence.[110] Saga Za-Ab summarises the story of the *KN* in a few pages. He describes the book – I cite the English translation of Ludolf – as 'the history of the said King David, which is a book about the bigness of St. Paul's Epistles, and very pleasant to read'. Saga Za-Ab's version – described contemptuously by Geddes as 'a blind story of the Queen of Sheba and her Son' – refers to the Ark in Jerusalem, and other details as they occur in the *KN*. Yet Saga Za-Ab specifically states that only the tablets of the Covenant were taken from the temple of Solomon:

> Azarias after having with great speed and secrecy got Tables made in imitation of the Tables of the Covenant of the Lord, did whilst he was offering sacrifice, with great dexterity steal the True Tables of the Ark of the Covenant, and put his new ones in the place of them, none but God and himself being conscious to what he had done...

Azarias eventually revealed to King David that 'he had brought the Tables of the Covenant of the Lord along with him', and the king went 'to the place where those Tables were kept,' and danced in joy before them. The Ark's place in these passages is solely that of the original repository of the tablets in the temple of Jerusalem. With Saga Za-Ab we find an Ethiopian cleric who believed, and recorded, around 1534, in a document specifically about Ethiopian religious belief, that only the tablets of Moses had reached Ethiopia.[111]

What are we to make of this? At a stage when the *KN* is supposed to have for long been the official account of the national and dynastic saga, the strange silence about the Ark in Ethiopia continues, even in documents that discuss the theft of sacred objects from the temple of Jerusalem. Neither the intensely interested Portuguese priest, Alvares, nor the Ethiopian ecclesiastic who had been sent as ambassador to Portugal, so much as hint at the presence in Ethiopia of the Ark. Only if we credit the 15th century date tentatively assigned to the *KN* manuscript in the Bibliothèque Nationale, Paris, do we have an Ethiopian rival to this story in which the Ark is actually present.

To be sure, Saga Za-Ab's confession of his faith was not received without criticism. Abba Gorgoreyos, the Ethiopian monk who assisted the famous 17th century historian of Ethiopia, Job Ludolf, regarded it balefully enough. After hearing how some doctrinal points were delivered by Saga Za-Ab, Gorgoreyos exclaimed: 'That they were Fictions, Dreams, nay meer Lyes... If he said that, he was a beast of the field!' Ludolf himself found the information from both the Ethiopian ambassadors to Portugal, Matthew the Armenian and Saga Za-Ab, sadly wanting. The first contained 'many things ambiguous and many other things altogether false', while the second 'did not much excel him either for truth or probability'. Ludolf evidently enjoyed the riposte of his Ethiopian friend and mentor Gorgoreyos, and scrupulously inserted the Ethiopic text of it into his book.[112] Nevertheless, if Saga Za-Ab had really believed that the Ark of the Covenant was taken to Ethiopia, as well as the tablets of Moses, surely he would have included this absolutely vital element of the story.

The explanation is of course that even by the 1530s, the presence of the Ark of the Covenant in Ethiopia was not yet a universally accepted fact there. One of the many monastic scriptoria *may* by this time have begun to include it in an updated version of the *KN*, but elsewhere, even close to the court or using information from holy books at Aksum, the claim was still limited to the tablets of Moses. The Solomonic origins of the dynasty, of course, had long since become standard belief.[113]

JOÃO DE BARROS

In the third part of his celebrated *Decadas da Ásia*, in which the Portuguese writer João de Barros recounted the Portuguese discoveries in their great age of maritime expansion, he touched also on Ethiopian matters. His book, completed in draft by 1539, and first published in 1552, also included the story of Solomon and Sheba. It was very similar to the versions of Saga Za-Ab and Alvares. He probably had the opportunity to read the latter before Alvares' death and the book's posthumous publication in an edited form. Gaspar Correa certainly saw a copy of Alvares' book, apparently an early version with more information in it than the final published version. Alvares lent it to him in India in 1526. It is cited in places in Correa's *Lendas da India*.

Barros' version of the Solomon and Sheba tale, the fullest we have so far, is very different from the tale of the *KN* in its final version. Like Alvares, from whom he probably got his information, Barros includes the story about the wood of the Cross (Appendix, 2). But when he reports the theft from the temple in Jerusalem he merely states that the tablets of the Law were taken by Azarias, and others put in their place.[114]

The versions of Alvares and de Barros, incidentally – to return to a remark I made in the Introduction of this book – were all that were available in Europe at the time when the King James translation of the Bible was being produced.

NICOLAO GODINHO

The work of the Jesuit Nicolao Godinho or Codigni is relatively rarely cited in books about Ethiopia.[115] Born in Lisbon, he was received into the Jesuit order at Coimbra in 1573 at the age of 14. He died at Rome in 1616. In his *De Abassinorum rebus...*(first published at Lyon in 1615 as a counterblast to a book of nonsense published in Valencia in 1610 by Luis de Urreta, about vast Dominican convents, superb libraries, magnificent jewels and the like in Ethiopia), the Ark still did not appear in the Ethiopian part of the story. Nor did the tablets. The Ark was mentioned only in its proper place, Solomon's Jerusalem. Godinho cited the story of the claimed royal descent from Solomon and the queen of the South or queen of Sheba. The Abyssinians, he wrote, 'derive the descent of their emperors from Solomon king of the Jews'.

Godinho's version of the story of the queen differs in some details from the *KN* as we have it from the manuscripts translated by Bezold and Budge. The queen departed from Meroë, then capital of Ethiopia – this sounds like some rationalising of the story by Godinho himself – via Mazua (Massawa), the Erythraean Sea and the Arabian Gulf, whence she reached Jerusalem in eight days.[116] After her visit, she gave birth to a son, Melich or Melilech. When he grew up, he was sent to his father in Jerusalem and crowned as emperor of Ethiopia before the Ark of the Covenant, taking the name of David. From this Melilech, Godinho states, the Ethiopians derive their royal descent, claiming that the dynasty belongs to the House of David. He also notes that before the queen of Sheba the Ethiopians were sun and moon worshippers, and that after Queen Candace they were Christians.[117]

Godinho cites the use of the imperial insignia of the lion and cross, the motto 'The Lion of the Tribe of Judah has Conquered, Ethiopia shall stretch out her hands to God' and the designation 'son of David and Solomon'. The claim to Solomonic descent, he notes, is recorded in the Ethiopian archives, in the book inscribed *Historia Davidis, qui Melilechum aliter dictus est* ('History of David, who is also called Melilek') – evidently a book very similar to, but not identical with, the *KN*, which does not mention the name Menelik.

Godinho was not impressed. He summed the story up as an extremely inept fable, worthy neither to be believed nor to be listened to. This is a judgement that applies equally well to Urreta's fanciful legend of 'la Reyna Saba', whose fabulous jewels, he claimed, were still guarded in the city of Saba in the church of the Holy Spirit, where she was buried.[118]

5

The Ark of Zion: The Coming of the Ark

For out of Zion shall go forth the law…

Isaiah 2.3

THE ARK OF THE COVENANT AT AKSUM

From Alvares' time, during several decades of vehement religious discussion between Ethiopians and Iberians, and Iberian commentary on Ethiopian belief and ritual, the Ark never figures in the colloquy. There was something important at Aksum, an altar table or the like consecrated in the name of Seyon, and this is noted in the documents. The sacred object, however, is not identified with the Ark of the Covenant from Jerusalem.

But the Ark was by now on the threshold of its revelation in Ethiopia. Nearly a century after Alvares, much had altered. The hiatus in the Portuguese missionary efforts in Ethiopia, brought about largely by the enmity or indifference of the emperors after Galawdewos (1540–59), lasted for many years. Emperor Sarsa Dengel (1563–97), succeeding his father Minas, found the Portuguese who remained in his country useful for building and gunsmiths' work, but remained entirely impervious to their ecclesiastical influence.

During this interval something happened that altered the status of the great gold-covered altar stone from Mount Zion in Maryam Seyon church at Aksum. Unless we assume that the sacred stone or *tabota Seyon* was abandoned or forgotten at Tabr, to be replaced by another holy relic symbolically imbued with the same virtues, it must have returned to Aksum. We can legitimately suppose that the relic was brought back from Tabr sometime after Grañ's defeat to be installed in the modest rebuilt church of Sarsa Dengel's time, for two reasons. First, Sarsa Dengel, going to Aksum for his tonsuring ceremony in January 1579, states that the ceremony will take place before his mother Zion the *tabot* (or Ark) of the Lord of Israel: *Seyon tabota amlaka Esrael*. He seems to evoke the same object that Alvares cites, the *tabota Seyon*...even if its rank has by this time augmented. (A year afterwards, in an extraordinary gesture to honour Aksum, he proclaimed himself *nebura'ed* of 'the cathedral of Aksum, Glory of Zion, tabernacle of the God of Israel'.) Second, it was from Aksum that the sacred talisman was to flee again around 1620 in the face of Catholic ascendancy. But it was not the same hallowed object that fled the second time. It had become the Ark of the Covenant.

Péro Pais

The Spanish Jesuit missionary Péro Pais, who died in Ethiopia in 1622 after 19 years' laborious work there, could consult more up-to-date sources than Godinho. He knew the story of the removal of the Ark of the Covenant itself, and not just the tablets, from Jerusalem. The story was related in a copy of the *KN* kept in the church at Aksum when Pais was there around 1620 – the '*livro de Agçum*', or *Book of Aksum*, as he called it. Pais translated much of the book into Portuguese, and his version is more or less the same as that Bezold and Budge were later to present to Europe. Pais' own work long remained unpublished. The translation here (Appendix, 1) is the first in English.[1]

Pais' translation is of primary importance. This Portuguese translation of an Ethiopian holy book of the early 17th century can be compared with the Ge'ez versions we know of the final form of the book, and especially with the supposed 15th century manuscript in Paris. The order of events, the turns of phrase, characters and chief episodes are the same, though Pais' version is considerably abbreviated. Doubtless Pais merely sketched the basic theme of the story, leaving major sections out as irrelevant. But Pais' version derives without question from the same original as the oldest surviving Ge'ez manuscript of the *KN*.

With Pais, at last the full story is attested with an undoubted date – over 2500 years after the alleged events. The text of the legend is substantially different from that of the 1520s–30s that Alvares, Saga Za-Ab and de Barros recorded. The new version – which *might* date from the 15th century if we accept that date for the oldest manuscript we know, in the Bibliothèque Nationale de France in Paris, a point which I will discuss in detail later – was now definitively set to prevail over the other versions. When, as regularly happened with the parchment codices of Ethiopia, a new copy of the work in Aksum had to be prepared, this newer version would be substituted. In this case there was very good reason for the recopying of old texts. A terrible disaster had intervened. The books seen by Alvares must have been destroyed with the old church of Maryam Seyon in 1535, or been scattered to other havens, or lost. Today, no surviving Ge'ez version of the *KN* – though perhaps one may yet be found in some obscure library at Lake Tana or a similar out-of-the-way spot – preserves the old story, with the wood of the Cross (though this occurs in the *Hemamata Masqal* and some local queen of Sheba tales) and the absence of the Ark, as Saga Za-Ab, Alvares and de Barros related it. The new version, the *KN* we have today, featuring the Ark itself, has become the standard text.

What is more, after 1535 the sacred stone, *tabota Seyon*, had gone from Aksum. When we next hear of the sacred relic of Aksum in 1579 at Sarsa Dengel's coronation it is named *Seyon tabota amlak Esrael*; the same words used by the *KN* and *Gadla Marqorewos* (see below) to describe the Ark. By the end of the century the object at Aksum seems to have definitely crystallised for the Ethiopians as the Ark of the Covenant. Further, by the 1620s a 'casket' existed at Aksum to support the upgraded legend.

Manoel de Almeida

It is now, for the first time, that the Jesuits begin specifically to cite the Ethiopian claim for material possession of the Ark of the Covenant. Manoel de Almeida recorded its existence, just before the end of the period of Jesuit influence in Ethiopia, in the annual letter written from Ethiopia for the period March 1626–27. He remarked that instead of a consecrated altar stone the Ethiopians possessed something altogether more fascinating:

> ...a casket that they call *Tabot* of Sion, that is to say Ark of the Covenant brought from Mount Sion; and they are so devoted to this that all the altar stones they call *Tabot*. And in the principal churches the altars were as all the churches had in ancient times, made in the form of boxes.[2]

Here for the first time (leaving aside Abu Salih's red herring) we have a description of an object that can plausibly be applied to the Ark of the Covenant. It was now not just an altar stone from Zion. It was a casket or chest called *tabota Seyon*, and it was identified directly as the Ark of the Covenant from Jerusalem.

The mysterious casket, *tabota Seyon*, the 'Ark of the Covenant', was, in Almeida's opinion, the thing from which all other *tabotat* derived their name. Almeida provides an early explanation for the fact that although a *tabot* is plainly only a tablet, all *tabotat* are for the Ethiopians the 'Ark of the Covenant'. The box-like 'altars' that Almeida mentions are the *manbara tabotat*. The important difference is the reference to a casket. The great relic is still supposed to originate from Mount Zion, as in Alvares' day, but now it has developed from an altar stone into a (presumably wooden) casket.

Manoel de Almeida also offers a most bizarre account about the *tabot* of Zion, one that sounds utterly improbable:

> And in the principal churches the altars were, as the whole Church had them in the past, in the manner of boxes. On the *Tabot*, that is on the altar of this church I heard it said by the Emperor that it was a regular tradition and held to be most certain by the most expert in the country, that there was contained within it a *pagode* (shrine?) or an idol which had the figure of a woman with a large bosom. Led by this tradition, the Emperor, when some years ago he came to this church to be crowned, greatly insisted with the Deptèras that they open the said box and show him what was inside it. This they never wanted to do.

Emperor Susneyos never got the chance to prove what was really inside the sanctuary at Aksum, and we hear no more of this strange statuette. Statuary was rare, even exceptional, in the Ethiopian church, though perhaps it is not totally to be excluded that at some time in or around the rich archaeological site that is Maryam Seyon precinct, an old statue of pre-Aksumite times had been found and kept. Intriguingly, it was at the excavations there conducted by de Contenson, on the site of the future chapel of the Tablet of Moses, that a single small basalt fragment of the head of an ancient D'amat female statue was found. Elsewhere, at Hawelti, Matara and Adulis, rather more primitive pottery 'earth-mother' figurines have also been excavated, indicating that they were once common in Ethiopia. As for the presence of a preserved statuette within a Christian altar in the sanctuary, that seems on the face of it more than doubtful. Almeida admits that it was an unconfirmed rumour. But, just possibly, considering how little we really know of how the Ethiopian church sometimes expressed its individuality, we should not forget what the *History of Hanna* says: 'And inside the Holy of Holies, at the place where the holy Tabernacle rested, was a figure of Mary, the daughter of Joachim.'[3]

Manoel Barradas

On 11 December 1625, at Danqaz, an emperor of Ethiopia, Susneyos, knelt before a Catholic patriarch to offer obedience to the Roman pontiff, Urban VII. In February 1627, as the emperor faced up to the mounting troubles his religious convictions were causing him, the pope, according to Geddes, wrote blandly adjuring Susneyos to 'assume a courage...worthy of the Race of David, in whom the house of Ethiopia glories as in their Ancestor...' He added no word of the soldiers the emperor had pleaded for.

Ethiopians reacted with horror as the new patriarch, Afonso Mendes, pursued his religious reforms, riding roughshod over Ethiopian susceptibilities and raising up a storm of fury that was soon to wipe out all chance of a Catholic Ethiopia. After the debacle, the embittered Mendes, exiled from his patriarchate immediately on the accession of Susneyos' son Fasiladas, passed his time writing despairingly from Goa, trying unsuccessfully to persuade the Portuguese government to obtain by military force what had not come from preaching and example. Mistreatment of the ecclesiastical furniture was one of the crimes the Ethiopian priests held bitterly against the Catholics. Later, in a reply to one of the patriarch's letters, Emperor Fasiladas roundly accused them of vandalism, burning the wooden *tabotat* and replacing them with their newly consecrated stone altars.[4]

Father Manoel Barradas was one of those driven out with the patriarch. He occupied himself in Aden in 1633–34 writing the history of the Catholic experiences in Ethiopia – an intelligent and measured description of the country. But he achieves a complete *volte-face* with his history of the Ark and the tablets, in which he also refutes certain references that Luis de Urreta had made a short time earlier in his 1610 book published at Valencia. Barradas writes that the story of the Ark, Zion of Aksum, was deeply embedded in Ethiopian legend. But – oddly enough considering the literature available to him – he insisted that there was no trace of the tablet(s) of Moses in Ethiopian memory:[5]

> They say also and affirm most tenaciously, believing it to be a most infallible claim, that the son of Solomon, Milelec, brought with him, or better said his

father sent with him, a priest by the name of Azarias, to accompany him and bring with him the Ark of the Covenant, stealing it and leaving another similar in its place. It is this which the *Deptorâs* of Acçum believe to be their *tabot*, which is the same as an altar stone, which they call Sion of Acçum, because it came from Sion, so revered by them and known by all. Not at all as Father Frej Luis [Urreta], Book 2, chapter 4, says: that when the Virgin Our Lady was still alive, the Apostles sent the altar stone of Sion to the church of Acçum. I never heard the Abexins say that this church was built during the lifetime of the Virgin, as I heard that the one in Asmarâ was built in honour of Our Lady before she was even born; nor did I hear that this *Tabot* or Sion of Acçum was sent by the Apostles, only that it was brought by Milelec...This rigmarole of the theft of the Ark of the Covenant is covered by the Reverend Brother Luis in Book 1, chapter 5, and he refutes and disputes it very well. In the same way should he refute another fable, one to which he gives much prominence, concerning the existence of a piece of the tablets of the Commandments, broken by Moses, about which there was never any tradition, nor recollection in Ethiopia that it might ever have been spoken of here, as there is of the Ark of the Covenant having been brought to Ethiopia, stolen by Milelec and to exist even today in Acçum. Nor is it such a small matter that its fame would not have been known, and if it had been here then it would not have been lost.

Did Barradas not know that Saga Za-Ab's memoir and other documents of the period, including the Beccadelli copy of Alvares, and João de Barros' book, claimed that the tablets – though not those broken, which receive no further mention in the Bible, but those which replaced them in the Ark – were in Ethiopia? Was he unaware of the claim put forward in Abu Salih's time, and reiterated in Alfonso of Aragon's letter to King Yeshaq? Or was he in fact differentiating between the first, broken, set and the complete tablets that were put in the Ark? Barradas, apparently, believed there had never been any reference to any tablets at all in Ethiopia. He concludes:

> Nor is there any memory of Mount Amarâ, where (Urreta) says it is located, ever being entered, destroyed or assaulted by enemies who carried it away or who lost it; and just as the Ark of the Covenant never came to Ethiopia neither did the relic of the broken tablet of the Commandments.

The business of the mountain and the broken tablets evidently both intrigued and irritated Barradas. He continued to assert that there never had been such a claim in Ethiopia.[6] He airs some more of Urreta's incorrect claims. The monastery of Alleluia, in Tigray, was supposed by Urreta to be a place to which Jewish traders made pilgrimage; they came 'from Africa, Asia, Persia, Meca and Arabia and travel on to Libya, Nubia and Borno, prostrating themselves on the earth and throwing their caps on the ground'. At Alleluia they would bow with great devotion before a relic of the tablets of the law that were broken by Moses that is kept on Mount Amara [Amba Geshen, far to the south, but, according to Urreta, visible from Alleluia]. The reverend Father was persuaded to write this because Dom João Balthazar [the man from Fatagar in Ethiopia whom Urreta cited as his informant] swore to him that said relic was indeed there, and that not only had he seen it but what is more several times had held it in his hand. All of which is pure fiction and nonsense: for not only is there no memory of any such relic having been in Ethiopia formerly but neither is it spoken of today: for if such a relic were being kept there, there would be no way to hide the fact or deny it; and had it ever been there, even though it may have been lost some memory of it's having once been there and of the devotion, reverence and respect it received, would persist... (see also Appendix, 6).

Afonso Mendes and Balthasar Telles

This was not the end of the Jesuit confusion about what was at Aksum. Another Jesuit, Balthasar Telles, wrote a history of Ethiopia, *Historia geral de Ethiopia a alta*, published in 1660. An English edition followed in 1710. Telles cited a note, differing from all previous accounts, written about 1655 by Patriarch Mendes on the theme of the mysterious tablet at Aksum. For Mendes, the sacred relic is not of stone as Alvares and Shihab al-Din had suggested. Nor did the patriarch agree with the accounts of two of his own Jesuit colleagues who had been with him in Ethiopia. The sacred object was not supposed to be the Ark as Almeida recorded. Instead, it is said to be one of the tablets of the Law as Barradas had denied:

> A similar tale, which the Ethiopian historians recount and which is widely believed among them, is that one of the Tablets of the Law is the altar stone of the Church of Aksum, which was in the past the capital of Ethiopia and the seat of the Patriarchate; they say that even today this persists; and further, that it is a tablet and of a very precious wood. However, if it were one of the Tablets of the Law, which were in the Ark of the Covenant, it could not be of wood, because the Tablets which God gave to Moses, whether the first or the second, were of stone. Hence it is obviously a complete fiction to assert that there were tablets of wood in the Ark and that one of them is in Aksum.[7]

Mendes has reverted to the older story of the tablets, but altered their material. The casket called *tabota seyon* has again vanished. How did these different, but contemporary, ideas about tablets or Ark, stone or wood, develop? Inevitably, the Jesuits must have derived their 'knowledge' from Ethiopian informants, perhaps Catholic converts, perhaps orthodox Ethiopians. Part of the confusion may have come from people who actually knew nothing but unconfirmed reports about Aksum and what was kept there. General hearsay, misinformation or miscomprehension supplied the rest.

THE FLIGHT OF THE ARK

As the Catholic faith grew stronger, with the conversion of *ras* Sela Krestos, the emperor's half-brother, and finally of the emperor himself, certain Aksumite priests realised that previously inconceivable transformations were in progress, to their detriment. In the face of active imposition of changes to bring worship into line with the Roman way, *tabotat* and *manbara tabotat* were directly endangered. Concealment of their religious treasures was likely to be their only protection. In a dramatic and successful effort to preserve their most sacred relic, some priests fled with the holy *tabot* of Aksum, keeping it safe under guard until the storm was over. The Catholics were able to seize the *manbara tabot*, the tabernacle of the *tabot* of Aksum. It was taken to their centre near Adwa at Maigwagwa or Fremona, while an altar suitable for the Roman rite was installed at Maryam Seyon church:

> ...only a few months ago, a few zealous priests, obstinate in their error and seeing that the Roman Faith was growing in the area and suspecting that the Emperor and the Viceroy might play some trick, seized the *Tabot* with other precious furnishings and fled with them. And it is said that they hid this superstitious relic in a harsh desert, until, as they said, the fury of the persecution of their ancient faith passed. Now at this time, since the Emperor was desirous that all superstition be eliminated, the Viceroy one day sent the Priest [this was Thomé Barneto] accompanied by a guard for all that might be necessary. But as all of the most obstinate ones were away, the Priest opened the church without hindrance and pushing aside the veils with his hand, reached the Holy of Holies and stole (*ruppe*) a tabernacle where the Ark of Zion was [= had been] and sent it to Maigoga so that it might not be put back in it again. He then immediately ordered that an altar be put up according to our custom, maintaining the dedication of the church, and he said the first mass there on the day of the birth of the Blessed Virgin Mary, to which came a great many people and above all women who had not previously been allowed to enter there.[8]

We even have, in a letter from Father Thomé Barneto from 'Maygoga' written to Stefano da Cruz on 15 March 1627, the report of the man who actually performed the sacrilege. Barneto had been sent to Aksum on 18 August 1626, by Takla Giyorgis, the *Tigray makwennen* ('the Viceroy') and son-in-law of Susneyos, who was a Catholic – at least for the moment. Barneto's mission is quite candidly described: 'to destroy the Holy of Holies of the schismatics'. Reaching Aksum, he reports that he 'dismantled the ark of the testament', meaning, in this context, the *manbara tabot*, the 'ark' having already vanished towards Bur. Barneto confirms this too, though he does not mention the sacred relic: the 'frati eretici' had fled to Bur from Aksum. In the sanctuary at Aksum – and this is the sole description we have of it as it appeared in the restored church of Sarsa Dengel – he found an old crucifix, painted, with two nails at the feet, between the Virgin Mary and St. John, and some holy objects including a metal cross with sculpture. 'I reduced this church', he goes on, 'alla romano': to the Roman way. He thought to dedicate it to Mary on the day of her birth.[9] The Tigray governor, Takla Giyorgis, incidentally, seems to have repented. He rebelled in 1628, smashing the sacred ornaments of the Catholics and killing his own Catholic priest Yaqob. His rebellion failed, and he was hanged with his sister despite the pleas of a court horrified that such a punishment could be meted out to so great a noble.

In the midst of his account about the removal of the Ark cited above, Manoel Barradas included a note about the flight of the Ark c. 1620. He added an update with the latest information he had heard in 1633-4, and incidentally confirmed Emperor Fasiladas' accusations:

> And with this *tabot* some *Deptorâs*, namely the literate of the church, who work there as canons, being zealous of their Alexandrine faith, fled to Bur taking the stolen *tabot* with them, at the time the faith of Rome was received in this kingdom, in order to prevent its being taken as others were.[10] And even at the time of my departure from that kingdom [1633] it was still there despite the many demands of the old King [Susneyos] before his death that it be restored there; and the present one [Fasiladas], once he assumed command, ordered its return as they had returned to the old faith, but they never wanted to return it. Later, however, as we were departing, we heard the news that it had been restored.

Balthasar Telles too learned something about the hiding place of the Ark, or *tabot*, of Zion during the Catholic's brief period of triumph. Telles remarked that the Abyssinians

> thought they added much Reputation to their Church of Auxum or Aczum, by saying their Chest or *Tabot*, was the very Ark of the Old Testament that was in Solomon's Temple, and that God brought it so miraculously to Ethiopia...The Abyssines to gain more respect to this little Chest of theirs, always kept it so close and conceal'd, that they would not show it even to

their Emperors. They call it by way of excellency Sion, or Seon, as they pronounce it, and for the same Reason the Church, where they kept this to them so precious a Relick, being dedicated to the Virgin May, had the name S. Mary of Seon. Not many years since, perceiving that the Catholick Faith began to spread abroad, and fearing lest this little Chest of theirs should be taken away, or disregarded, the most Zealous of their Monks remov'd it thence, and very privately convey'd it to the Territory of Bur, near the Red Sea, where they hid it among close Thickets and vast high Mountains, in order at a convenient Time to restore it to its ancient Place, in the Church of Auxum or Aczum...[11]

He added – correctly, if Barradas' remarks cited above were true – that 'in all likelyhood' it was now back there, restored by the Ethiopians after what he blithely termed 'their Revolt' against the Catholic church.

By great good fortune, we do not depend on Jesuit accounts for all this. We can also read Ethiopian accounts of events. The *Book of Aksum* confirms the flight of the 'Ark' to Bur, northeast of Aksum. The Ge'ez record preserves the 'sure and certain memory' of those terrible times of 'the great persecution'. Then, 'in the likeness of sheep, ravening wolves and deadly serpents, the (Jesuit) Fathers, disciples of Leo, the seducer, vessel of crime and perfidy', came to Ethiopia. After a description of their dreadful heresies, the chronicler relates what occurred in Year 271 of Mercy (1619–20 AD): 'Syon, the tabernacle of the law, was expelled'. At this, the ultimate horror, the very doors of the churches wept, and the crosses bearing the image of St. Mary and Jesus streamed with tears:

> When the Ark of the Law fled, its people went towards Sarawe; they were guided by a young man who knew the most hidden places of the region called Marab. He took them to a place where he knew there was formerly a water source; but they found it dry. They went on, tormented by thirst. In the evening, they prepared to pass the night in this land; suddenly, a spring gushed out for them by the help of this Ark, of holy power...Finally, the Ark reached the territory of one of the towns of the frontier of Bur, called Degsa; it stayed there for eleven years and six months.[12]

A second version of this text, after qualifying Pope Leo in rather different but still trenchant terms as 'the uncircumcised, full of fraud and impurity', adds that 'even Syon, the Ark of the Law, was driven away...' noting the same place of exile:

> The day when it was driven out and fled from Aksum, was in Year 7111 of the creation of the world (1611 EC/1618–19 AD), 1614 of Christ (1621–2 AD), on 6 Hedar, a Saturday. The Daqq Degna [the people of the Digsa region] received it with the highest honours, keeping it under the strictest

guard for twelve years. When the Alexandrian faith was restored, it returned to the city with great honour, on 27 Hedar, a Sunday, during the first year of the reign of our king Fasiladas, the orthodox (i.e. from September 1632–September 1633).

In gratitude for their guardianship of the Ark, the Daqq Degna, by royal command and with the consent of the *dabtarat* (lay canons), were enrolled among the people of the House of Seyon. It was probably because of the events related here that Digsa, in the eastern highlands of Eritrea between Segeneiti and Addi Qayih, came to be considered in local legend as one of the places where the Ark rested on its original journey from Jerusalem. The *KN* names Bur as a stage on the route taken by Ebna Hakim when he brought the Ark into Ethiopia.

These accounts in the *Book of Aksum*, with additional confirmation from Barradas and Telles, and a further note in the annals of Addi Neamin in Eritrea under Year 274 of Mercy (1622–23 AD) that 'Seyon was carried away from Aksum' in that year, illuminate one of the most dangerous episodes the holy Zion of Aksum had lived through. We learn that for the second time in a century the 'Ark' had been forced to flee from its shrine at Aksum Seyon church – once in the form of a gold-encrusted stone from the Muslims in 1535, and once more as a *tabot* or (presumably wooden?) chest or 'ark' from the Catholics around 1620. In our pursuit of an Ark at Aksum, we may discount Abu Salih's portable altar at Adefa/Lalibela, and set to one side the stone slabs described by Shihab al-Din and Alvares. This done, we find that the first appearance in literature of an object at Aksum that could really be an Ark, outside the uncertain 15th century dating for the *KN* of the Bibliothèque Nationale in Paris, seems to be the late 16th century 'Ark' mentioned – without any details of its appearance – in Sarsa Dengel's chronicle. This was soon followed by the early 17th century Arks of the Iberian reports, some of which actually describe it as a 'casket'.[13]

GADLA MARQOREWOS

Among the many Lives of the saints composed by Ethiopian clerics, one, Gadla Marqorewos, the life story of a monk who died in 1419/20, is particularly interesting because it actually names and cites the KN. The sole known manuscript (though another is reported at Dabra Demah monastery in Eritrea) was largely destroyed in a fire in Asmara in 1902. Carlo Conti Rossini had fortunately prepared a résumé with the aid of an Ethiopian priest, publishing in 1904 an account of this and what was left of the book after the fire.[14] The *gadl* cites, with various elaborations, the tale related in the *KN* about Solomon, the queen of Azeb, Makeda, and her son Ebna Hakim, Menelik (adding that local name for the prince, which does not appear in the *KN*).

The text, discussing the mutation of names of cities, notes that Barantya became Questentenya, which in turn became Estenbul (Byzantium, Constantinople and Istanbul). The last did not become current until after the fall of Constantinople to the Turks in 1453. Guidi was unsure about the date of the manuscript, writing that 'perhaps' it dated from the 15th century. Bezold came to the same conclusion.[15] But the version seen and recorded by Conti Rossini was apparently a 17th or even 18th century manuscript: Lusini suggests that it was composed in the reign of Yohannes I (1667–82), who is mentioned in it. The story – even if it distils much of its information about the queen of Azeb from the *KN*, with some direct citations – employs Tigray language expressions and is much embroidered with odd, manifestly late, features. In the tale of Solomon and the queen, the merchant, Tamrin, like so many merchants in Ethiopia, was a Muslim; many exotic products are listed as his stock in trade; the additional complication in the seduction scene, that Solomon slept with his eyes open, and shut them on waking, is present; the queen's return journey, too, involves Muslims; and Meswa' (Massawa) is mentioned, a place first described in 1520 by the Portuguese.

The *Gadla Marqorewos*, if the surviving text as we have it really dates to the late 17th century (this was Huntingford's date for it as well), is one of the earliest preserved Ethiopian texts to cite the *KN* by name. Other more or less contemporary works also cite it. Gorgoreyos, Ludolf's mentor, mentioned the book by this title, before 1681, and in 1689, according to the chronicle of Iyasu I, it was consulted during a debate about court precedence in Gondar. In *Gadla Marqorewos* we read:

> ...this history is written in the *Kebra Nagast* which Abba Gorgoreyos, bishop of Armenia...edited concerning the glory of Seyon the *tabot* of the Lord of Israel (*laseyon tabota amlaka Esrael*), and concerning the glory of the kings of Ethiopia (*Ityopya*) who were born of the loins of Menyelek son of Solomon son of David.

If the *gadl* dates before the end of the 17th century, its designation *laseyon tabota amlaka Esrael* may be one of the earliest surviving citations of the terminology used by the *KN* to describe the Ark. Alvares of course implies the designation *tabota Seyon* already in the 16th century. The first use of the phrase *Seyon tabota amlaka Esrael* that I have found is in the chronicle of Sarsa Dengel. At the time of his coronation in 1579, the king speaks of 'my mother Seyon, *tabot* of the God of Israel'. We cannot be absolutely sure what is implied by the phrase. It could still allude simply to the church of Mary at Aksum with its *tabot* or altar tablet of Zion. But it is more likely that at this stage the Ark is meant. The chronicle was completed c. 1590, and we might expect the sacred relic to have been brought back from exile at Tabr and installed at the church by the 1580s. Its new mythology we would also expect to have been enshrined by this time in the revised version of the *KN* that we suppose had been spreading for some time, replacing the older version cited by Alvares and others. Manoel de Almeida confirms the phrase. Pais translates: 'the celestial Zion, the Ark of the God of Israel' from the Ge'ez text of the *KN* in the early 17th century. *Gadla Marqorewos* and the final version of the *KN* as we have it in surviving copies share the phrase used by Sarsa Dengel's chronicler.[16]

AN ARABIC TALE

The story of the Ethiopian Ark is not exclusive to Ethiopia. Indeed, part of its mystery is that it may not have emerged there at all, but in a neighbouring land, once at the head of the Christian world for its religious zeal, the austerity of its monks, and the widespread influence of its patriarchs, but now for over 1300 years subject to Muslim political control. From Egypt comes a rather different Ark story, a much-embroidered Christian Arabic tale entitled: '*The explanation of the reason for the transfer of the kingdom of David from his son Solomon, King of Israel, to the country of the negus, that is to say, to Abyssinia*'.

This story – which *does* include the Ark (*tabut 'ahdi illah*) – contains many fabulous additions. It was a tale made to entertain and delight, and naturally should contain magic and mystery. As in Alvares' and de Barros' versions, a piece of wood figures also in this tale. This wood, as in Belethus' and Voragine's accounts, derived from Paradise. Solomon obtained it by a stratagem from the *rukh* bird, and employed it to cut great stones required for the temple. The wood remained at the entrance of the temple, where it later cured the queen of Abyssinia's goat foot, obtained through her mother's contemplating 'with greedy desire' a particularly handsome goat. (This part of the story, describing the queen's hair-covered legs, or goat's foot, does not appear in the earlier Arabic version of the story in Sura XXVII of the *Qur'an*, and no marriage and no half-Abyssinian son are there included; later commentators amplified the tale, also naming the queen Bilqis.) Solomon had flooded the court of the temple with water, a ruse to see the queen's feet. Dismounting at the threshold of the temple, and entering the holy place supported by her attendants, her goat foot touched the wood and became normal. As in the story preserved in Ethiopia in the *Hemamata Masqal*, the grateful queen decorated the wood with a collar of silver, and Solomon and his successors all did the same. In this way the decorated piece of wood, which was kept in the temple, furnished the thirty pieces of silver paid to Judas, serving also to provide the wood for the Cross for the crucifixion of Jesus.

Both in the *KN*, and in this Arabic version, the queen was seduced by means of spicy thirst-inducing dishes. But the story is not exactly the same. In *KN* 30 the queen swears not to take anything by force from Solomon's house but, sleeping in the king's chamber, she is overcome by thirst, drinks, and so breaks her oath. In the Arabic version Solomon swears that he will not molest the queen, but if she comes to his bed at night while he is there, she will become his wife. Solomon ensures that she does come by arranging that after eating the pungent dishes, water is to be found nowhere in the palace except the king's room.

The section concerning the Ark in this version also varies, leaving David, son of Solomon and the queen of Abyssinia, far from guiltless in the theft of the Ark. In fact, the whole story is one of scheming, coercion and outright murder. The queen's son, David (Daud ibn Suleiman ibn Daud), returning from Abyssinia to meet his father, asks directly for the Ark. Solomon finally agrees: 'if it be the will of God'. The king tells his son not to let him know about it, because he will be required to swear his own innocence when its absence is detected.[17] Tacit permission for the theft being granted by this subterfuge, a copy of the Ark was made, and covered with gold plates. David then killed the workmen involved. The prince next kidnapped and chained four Levite priests, whom he forced to make the exchange under the guard of soldiers armed with swords. King Solomon had already remarked that no one but Levites could touch the Ark. In this way David of Ethiopia carried the Ark away secretly by night.

Such a version of the Ark story, representing David as a thief with his hands stained with the blood of several victims – even if by 'the will of God'

– would evidently lack, in the eyes of the Ethiopian royal family, the appeal of the tamer *KN* version. In the 'authorised' Ethiopian version of the tale, the innocence of David/Ebna Hakim even in the plotting of the theft of the Ark is emphasised.

This Arabic tale, attributed by Guidi to the late 16th century because the manuscript in which it appears is dated to 1594, appears to be an early version of the story including the Ark itself. Yet the Arabic story, though evidently connected with the final *KN* version in many respects, differs radically in others. It contains features from the version recorded by Alvares and de Barros, but there is no doubt from the description of the forging of a wooden gold-covered case that it is the Ark of the Covenant that is concerned, not just the tablets, which in any case were made of stone.

Like the *KN*, this version claims a Coptic origin. It was certainly written by a Christian Arab, in Egyptian-style script, on oriental paper. A Copt seems the most likely author. Not surprisingly, he was familiar with popular Arabic tales relating to Solomon and the queen of Sheba, and Solomon's magical reputation. He also seems to have had respect for Abyssinia, which he calls a 'blessed' country.

When he includes the Ark, the author of this Arabic manuscript incorporates an aspect of the story that was not the generally favoured one in Ethiopia, as far as the evidence to date indicates, when Alvares was in Aksum in the early 16th century. The Ark story may have existed in Ethiopia by this time, if the date of the Bibliothèque Nationale manuscript of the *KN* is accepted, but it was not the most widespread version. It had achieved general acceptance, however, by 1579, when Sarsa Dengel was crowned, and it was shortly afterwards recorded by Pais and de Almeida as well. If we follow Guidi's date, 1594, this Arabic manuscript belongs late in the reign of Sarsa Dengel.

Evidently, the Arabic manuscript constitutes an important piece in the puzzle. I went to see it at the Bibliothèque Nationale in Paris in December 2001, and consulted with the curators and experts about its possible date. I found that revision was not only possible, but was imperative. Ms. Arabe 264 is not a single work. It is a combination of three manuscripts bound together. Only the first section is dated to year 1310, Era of Martyrs: 1594 AD. The other two, including the account of the Ark, are undated, but the type of paper and the style of writing seem, according to the experts, to date earlier. They belong not to the end of the 16th century, but to the 15th century, more specifically to the second half of the century.[18]

The nature of the enquiry had changed. Now it seemed that the earliest account we possess involving the Ark in Ethiopia derived from a Christian Arabic source. A Coptic ancestry is alleged, from '*the Histories of the ancient fathers of the Coptic Church*', just as in the final version of the *KN*. This version of the story, different as it is from that of the *KN* in certain respects, would have been circulating in Egypt for some time while the Ethiopian sources – with one enigmatic exception, manuscript no 5 (94) in the Bibliothèque Nationale – still continued to mention only the tablets.

EXOTIC EMBROIDERIES

In Ethiopia, too, there are a number of local variants of the *KN* story that show fertile imagination and local colour augmenting the basic themes. Kolmodin collected a tale of indeterminate – but not very great – age in Hamasen in Eritrea. It is similar to other modern legends cited by Conti Rossini, Littmann and Budge,[19] in versions current in Eritrea and in Ethiopia, particularly in Tigray. Such tales open the account of many of the abbreviated chronicles of Ethiopia, and foreign visitors to the country – especially Conti Rossini, who commented on a number of them, and discussed the variants[20] – also collected localised versions.

These local legends, still very much alive today, hark back to the reign of a mythical serpent in the land, a serpent that may embody older pagan strata in Ethiopian religion and history. Often some local landscape feature or conspicuous monument around Aksum, a mountain, stele, ancient stone fruit-press or the like is somehow associated with this mythical creature of the past. These associations are not esoteric; one hears them casually from the local people of the region. Walking once with Aksumite friends in the countryside some distance from Aksum, we stopped to converse with an old woman sitting under a tree. She related how in ancient times a nearby hill had been the lair of the great serpent that had once ruled the land.

Similar serpent stories are not uncommon in other cultures, and often, as in the Ethiopian version, they explain the original institution of human monarchy.[21] The serpent, or dragon, in Ethiopia is often called *arwe*, or *zando* in Amharic. The person, usually an outsider, who kills the serpent becomes ruler, by rescuing a local ruler's daughter from sacrifice to the monster. A Christian overlay permeates some of the tales, the serpent representing rejected pre-Christian practices. In these versions, the Nine Saints or others destroy the serpent/dragon, while the queen of Sheba, Makeda, or the queen of Azeb, 'queen of the South', is identified as the heroine of the tale.

In the version related by Kolmodin, the reign of the serpent in the region was terminated by the (Nine?) Saints. There are seven in Littmann's and Budge's versions, and four *sadqan* ('just ones', a common name for local holy men) in Conti Rossini's, but in all cases only three persons are named, Sts. Garima, Sehma and Pantalewon. But Macheda, queen of Azeb, killed them in a fit of fury. She was therefore accursed, and one of her feet was changed to a donkey foot. In the Conti Rossini, Littmann and Budge versions, Eteye Azeb, the queen of the South, did not kill the saints. It was the serpent's blood spilling out that caused the deformation. This blemish damaged her matrimonial prospects. In time, she learned that just by setting foot on the threshold of the house of Solomon, she could count on a cure. It was for this reason that she went to Jerusalem. The ploy was successful. Macheda became desirable, and Solomon then set in motion his plot to seduce her, employing a very hot sauce. (This is the same story as in *KN* 29–30, though the Littmann and Budge versions now add a second woman, the queen's chief officer. Disguised as men, they met Solomon. They ate so little that Solomon suspected the truth, which he soon proved by setting a trap baited with honey. He then slept with both of them.) Macheda returned, pregnant, and reached Eritrea, where at the river between Addi Kontsi and Weche Debba, at Azhit Bela, she gave birth. The midwives' constant cries of *mai bela*, 'bring water', gave the name Mai Bela to the river.

When Melilec (Menyelek in Budge's version) was grown, he became tired of the mockery of his companions, who called him 'son of a woman'. His mother revealed his father's name, and he set off for Jerusalem. He was welcomed, and in due course returned to govern his mother's land, with some sons of Reuben, Simeon, Mosef, Minab and Judah, and some Levite clergy. Solomon also gave him a holy ark to guide him, the Ark of St. Michael. The Levites, who knew the temple secrets, exchanged this secretly, taking the Ark of Our Lady instead: the tale has incorporated the quintessentially Ethiopian concept of 'arks' or *tabotat* dedicated to Our Lady or the saints. After their departure Solomon learned that they had taken Zion, but could not pursue them effectively because they had been able to cross the Red Sea like Moses.

The party arrived in Eritrea. The children of Judah journeyed on to Shewa with the royal family. Zagua, a brother of Melilec's, by a servant girl of the queen of Azeb, stopped in Lasta (this version, where Menelik has a half-brother who becomes the ancestor of the Zagwé, appears in some modern 'comic-strip' paintings of the Sheba legend).[22] Some Levites remained in Temben, but most accompanied Melilec to Shewa. The other Israelites dispersed to different parts of the country. The legend adds that the Israelite tribes of Dan, Nephthali, Gad and Aser were also represented in Ethiopia. The Gallas and Somalis were descended from a slave of Rachel, and the Barya and the people of Wolqayt from a slave of Leah. Further ramifications, spreading the 'Israelite' blood far and wide, came with attributions to various groups. An Irob genealogy recorded in a document inserted into the *KN* of Gunda Gunde derives from 'those who came with Holy Zion from the land of Israel to Ethiopia'.[23] David, son of Jesse, was the father of Solomon. Helen, Solomon's sister, married the king of Rome (called Simeon in another text). Helen gave birth to Endreyas, who went to Ethiopia with Zion and Ebna Hakim, his cousin. The descent of three peoples of the Saho region of coastal Eritrea is then traced from Endreyas.

In the Littmann, Budge and Conti Rossini versions, different variants enhance the story. The Ark of Mary refuses to depart from Qayeh Kor because of the improper burial of the deacon, Gabra Heywat, one of its porters – or it refuses to leave when the bearer of its cross, Kebra Ab, dies at Digsa. He was carried to Aksum, and buried there, the Ark of Mary also remaining there with the officiating Levites. In the Littmann and Budge version, when they reached Aksum, Satan was constructing a house there to war against God. He cast this down when he learned what had arrived in the city, and Menyelek used the stones to build a church for the Ark. The devil dropped one very large stone, and it still stands there today – presumably the decorated standing stele at Aksum.

Littmann considered that these modern tales contained some old features which had 'been handed down by oral tradition and must have been known in Abyssinia even at the time when the literary rationalistic version [the *KN*] was composed'. These tales, he suggested, were only influenced to a small extent by the Arabic legends of which Queen Bilqis is the heroine.[24] In the absence of any ancient records, it seems to me just as likely that these tales are not of early, pre-*KN* date, but are later local embroideries on the basic theme of the *KN*. The serpent ingredient grafted on might, perhaps, represent a remnant of older origin, but it is a tale still in full vigour even today.

Another, probably 18th century, version of the story was recorded by Antoine d'Abbadie from the recitation of an old blind *dabtara*, Atqu, who recalled it from frequent readings. The original document from which it came, belonging to *echege* (head of the monks) Filpos, was kept at Mahdara Maryam church in Begemder. To summarise this adaptation of the tale, the dragon-killer is Ityopis (Ethiopis). His successors are Atrayn, Sarayn, and then the queen of Sheba, Makeda.[25] A condition for her continuing to rule was that she must remain virgin. Makeda journeyed to see Solomon, and the wood of the threshold at his door cured her goat foot. The seduction story is more or less like that in the *KN* except for the addition that Solomon slept with his eyes open, and closed them when he woke up. The rest of the story, including the theft of the Ark by Azarias, is also similar to the *KN* version, as one might expect.[26]

A fable also recorded by Kolmodin from a chronicle kept at the church of St. Mercurius at Dabra Dima renders the story of Makeda thoroughly regional, shifting the scene from Tigray to Eritrea. A woman of Madabay gave birth to a snake and a woman. The snake was called Agabos. Gabgab of Hamasen agreed to kill the snake in return for tribute. He constructed seven enclosures, snared with knives, and when the snake emerged it was cut into pieces. *Teff*, the staple Ethiopian grain, emerged from its blood. After seven generations, Makeda, daughter of Agabos (II), should have succeeded, but the people refused to pay tribute to a woman. Makeda went to the spot where the serpent was buried, and prayed there, and a new serpent was born. It grew rapidly, but was killed by Makeda when the terrified people consented to her rule.[27]

In the Staatsbibliothek at Berlin there is a 20th century manuscript in Ge'ez and Amharic in which, together with a charming set of pictures, the story of the queen of Sheba is told in its modern popular version.[28] In this tale, the *zando* or dragon is killed and the victor becomes king. Later on, in the time of the queen of the South (*negasta azeb*), we see the merchant (Tamrin) paddling his canoe-like boat on the Nile past the pyramids, which also feature in the journeys of the queen and her escort, and of Menelik and his half-brother Zage. Several pictures illustrate the tale of the queen and the wood of the cross – an episode not lost in Ethiopia even if suppressed in the current 'authorised' version of the *KN* – and its decoration with circular silver ornaments by the queen and Solomon. Three racial types are included in the illustrations. Solomon, coloured pink, sleeps (it seems first) with the black servant who accompanies the queen, then with the queen (yellow in colour) when they try to take water from his chamber. Afterwards, Solomon gives two rings to the queen. After the two women give birth, and the children have grown, they go to Solomon, but only Menelik sees through the ruse when the king disguises himself. Menelik eventually returns with the Ark, and builds a 'Beta Kristiyan' (a Christian church, nine hundred years before Christ!) to house it.

EMPEROR IYASU I AND THE ARK

From the silence of the chronicles, we might assume that Ethiopian emperors largely ignored their country's greatest religious talisman, the holy relic at Aksum. Fortunately, other sources elaborate that impression, and show that it was actually an object of interest, devotion and care, at least intermittently, from the 16th century. We know for example that Lebna Dengel organised the flight of the stone 'idol' from Grañ (*Futuh al-Habasha*), that Susneyos is supposed to have been interested in the story of the Ark and a female image (after de Almeida), and that after the flight of the Ark to Bur, first Susneyos and then Fasiladas tried to get it back (Barradas, the *Book of Aksum*, and Telles). Among the chronicles, only Sarsa Dengel's seems to allude to it earlier. But a unique event occurred in the reign of Emperor Iyasu I (1682–1706). The Ark, as in ancient Israel, is at last accorded an active role by a royal chronicle.

A link between Iyasu and the Ark was introduced right at the beginning of his chronicle, when the author stated that King Iyasu Adyam Sagad had been named for Joshua, who had received the Ark from Moses, crossed the Jordan, and destroyed the walls of Jericho. Even Queen Walatta Seyon, 'daughter of Zion', was associated with the Ark in a roundabout way by the chronicler. She came from Hamasen, and when she travelled south she took the Aksum route. There, 'she received the benediction of the priests of Zion, the Ark of the Law, about which it was said: "For the law will come forth from Zion and the word of the Lord from Jerusalem"' (Isaiah 2.3).[29]

Emperor Iyasu, according to his chronicle, exploited a power over the priests that his great-grandfather Susneyos evidently lacked, entering the sanctuary in 1691 to see the Ark – *tabota Seyon* – itself. Iyasu had also previously granted favours to the church in 1687, according to a land charter.[30]

The events of 1691 bear repeating in full – the sole material appearance of the Ark of the Covenant in an Ethiopian royal chronicle. The text states that Iyasu was received honourably by all the clergy who were at Aksum, with canticles and psalms. The king mounted his horse, and all those in his suite mounted horses also, and they came with the king up to the main gate (*dage salam*) which is the gate of the Ark of Seyon (*tabota Seyon*). The king, having entered the sanctuary of the Ark of Seyon (*maqdas zatabota Seyon*) kissed it and seated himself on the throne, according to the custom of the kings his fathers, who seated themselves formerly on this throne seat; he was clad in a brocade robe of unknown and wonderful colours, which was the glorious royal vestment which anciently clad David his father, when he received the Ark of Seyon (*tabota Seyon*) at the house of Abidara [Obededom]...The priests brought the book of the history of the kings his fathers, and read it to him, in his presence, until the time for Mass. At the time of Mass the king entered the holy of holies (*qeddesta qeddusan*) and received communion from the hands of the priests...After the king had received communion, on Sunday 7th Yakatit, he went to the chamber close to the *beta maqdas* [church, or sanctuary]; he offered a feast to the clergy, and there was great joy. On Monday 8th Yakatit, when the fast of Nineveh begins, the king entered the *beta maqdas*, and ordered the priests to bring the Ark of Seyon (*tabota Seyon*) and show it to him. They brought it to him, enclosed within a coffer with seven locks; each lock had its own key, whose form was in no way alike one to the other; on the contrary, the method of opening them was in each case different. They brought the keys, and the priests began to open each lock with its own key; they opened these locks...beginning by opening the first and the second, the third, the fourth, the fifth and the sixth. They came to the seventh lock, and they made great efforts to open it, but they did not succeed and could not open it. When it was impossible for them to do it, they took it to the king and the lock opened of itself; all who saw this miracle were astonished and amazed. This occurred by the will of the God of the Ark of Seyon, which dwelt upon it, when it saw the purity of spirit of the king and the excellence of his orthodox faith, as He himself said: 'If you have faith like a grain of mustard, say to that mountain: Arise, and it will arise; and if you say to this sycomore; Be uprooted and transplanted in the sea, it will come to pass as you have said'. Then the king beheld and looked upon the Ark of Seyon, and spoke to it face to face, as formerly Esdras saw and spoke to it. Then the Ark spoke and gave counsel to the king giving him wisdom and wise counsel to govern the earthly world and to inherit the heavenly world. The king, having been invited, arranged a time to return to her on the appropriate day, to accomplish in her presence the law of the kingdom [the coronation] with all the troops and the magistrates, according to the custom of the kings his fathers. He commended to her his soul and his body, that she might guard him from all evil, and took farewell of her...[31]

A shortened version of the Ethiopian chronicles edited by R. Basset confirms the events of 1691 as Iyasu's main chronicle describes them – the sole occasion, in the entire history of the Ethiopian monarchy from Adam to Emperor Bakaffa as related in this chronicle, in which the Ark is actively associated with an

Ethiopian emperor.[32] In other chronicles (Sarsa Dengel's, Iyasu II's), the Ark Zion of Aksum is merely mentioned in passing, although Iyasu I's chronicle does mention a special throne, apparently used by the emperors in the sanctuary (*maqdas*) itself. The abbreviated chronicle limits itself to describing Iyasu's arrival at Aksum, and his receiving of communion on a Sunday. The next day 'he penetrated into the sanctuary and opened with his own hand the Ark of Zion, something which the priests could only do with numerous keys'.

Iyasu may have viewed the 'Ark' exactly as described. There is no need to doubt that he went to the church, and even entered the sanctuary and surveyed the holy object called the Ark of the Covenant. But the special details of this account clearly owe something to a literary conceit of the chronicler, Hawarya Krestos. Ethiopian chronicles customarily contain unbridled praise for even the most feeble and incompetent rulers, though Iyasu was certainly not on that level; he was sometimes surnamed 'the Great'. In Iyasu's case the chronicler seized his chance to introduce a flattering comparison between the emperor and a dramatic event narrated in the Bible: Revelation 5.1–5.

In the vision of John the Divine, a scroll was held in the right hand of 'Him who was seated on the throne'. It was sealed with seven seals, and an angel called out to summon whoever was worthy to open the scroll and break the seals. No one, in heaven, in earth, or under the earth, could open the scroll and look inside it. While John lamented this, one of the 24 elders surrounding the throne bade him not to weep: 'behold, the Lion of the Tribe of Judah, the Root of David, hath prevailed to open the book and to loose the seven seals thereof'. This designation of the Saviour, 'Lion of the Tribe of Judah', was a motto borne by the Ethiopian emperors. It is supposed to be of comparatively recent origin[33] – although already alluded to indirectly in King Yeshaq's time (see Chapter 4: King Yeshaq, Lion of David), and possibly even earlier if Huntingford is correct in referring certain soldiers' songs to Amda Seyon's time.[34]

The motto, also attributed to Iyasu by the author of the last part of his chronicle, Sinoda, priest of Dabra Berhan, was also well known in Europe. Job Ludolf, an exact contemporary of Iyasu I (reigning 1682–1706), included in his book a map bearing an illustration of the imperial insignia, a lion holding a cross with the motto: 'The Lion of the Tribe of Judah has Conquered', demonstrating that the emperor was of the tribe of Judah, and the house of David. Even before this, perhaps owing to Portuguese influence, the lion was becoming the heraldic symbol of the emperors, as we can see from Ortelius' map printed in Antwerp in 1570, purporting to represent the 'titles and insignia of Prester John'. The lion is shown with the name of 'David…of the tribe of Judah, son of David, son of Solomon…', that is, attributed to Emperor Lebna Dengel, Dawit (1508–40), using the titles taken from his letters to Clement VII and the Portuguese kings D. Manuel and D. João. The ridiculous fairy tale of Frey Luis de Urreta, published in 1610 with a few facts from Damião de Góis fleshed out with far more that was totally imaginary, invents a completely fictitious coinage of Ethiopia:

> engraved on one part the image of the glorious Apostle and Evangelist St. Matthew, Patron of Ethiopia, and on the reverse of the coin the image of a Lion with a Cross in its hands, which are the arms of the Emperors; the legend which is around is, on the lion's side, Vicit Leo de Tribu Iuda (the Lion of the tribe of Judah has conquered), and where the figure of St. Matthew is, Aethiopia preavenit manu eius Deo…(Ethiopia has stretched out its hands to God).[35]

Nicolao Godinho, too, mentioned the lion, cross and motto.[36] According to Iyasu I's contemporary, the French visitor Charles-Jacques Poncet, the emperor sent headbands of taffeta inscribed with the motto 'Jesus, Emperor of Aethiopia, of the tribe of Judah, who has always vanquish'd his enemies', when he endowed his vassals with their fiefs.[37]

With the Ethiopian usage of the title in mind, *azaj* (court judge) Hawarya Krestos, the sycophantic – as we might see it: he was a man of his time, utterly dependent on the favour of the emperor – chronicler of Iyasu I, was able to portray the emperor in magnificent guise: the Lion of the Tribe of Judah, who alone could open the seventh seal and penetrate to the mysteries beyond. Hawarya Krestos was not the first royal chronicler to allude to the verse from Revelation. Some hundred and fifty years earlier the chronicler of Galawdewos explained the defeat of the sons of Tubal (the Portuguese) and the death of Cristovão da Gama as occurring because: 'they did not fight under the orders of Mar Galawdewos, to whom alone was the victory; who was powerful, and was entitled to open the sealed book of the future: to undo the seal and be hailed victor'.[38] Royal chroniclers had every reason to applaud the emperors for whom they wrote, if a story about *azaj* Sinoda was typical – he was ordered to read out his work publicly to the court at Aringo, and later in the *warq saqala*, one of the imperial reception halls at Gondar, by no less a figure than the formidable reigning emperor, Bakaffa, 'the Inexorable', Iyasu's son.

Charles-Jacques Poncet

In 1700, C.J. Poncet, physician (for a time) to Iyasu I, passed through Aksum in transit for Gondar. He described the church of Maryam Seyon briefly, but provided no useful information about it.[39] That he did not even mention the Ark is hardly surprising in so very abbreviated an account. Poncet never discovered the real dedication of the church or even the correct name of the town. Mystifyingly, he wrote: 'it is dedicated to St. Helena, and it is apparently from this church that the town took its name Heleni'.

Poncet's eulogies of his king, Louis XIV, greatly impressed Emperor Iyasu I. Inspired by his visitor, the emperor wrote a long and rather tedious letter on religious subjects to 'Lerons', apparently his secretary's interpretation of the name of the French monarch. The letter now in the Bibliothèque Nationale, Paris, is in the form of a small book of good clean vellum, of 41 pages, bound in boards enclosed in a rather beautiful fine silk floral cover.[40] In the first portion of the text, the emperor is expansive on the theme of the Trinity as the ultimate Sanctuary, and devotes a considerable section to the story of the Jewish temple. This passage is doubly fascinating as an account from the pen of the amanuensis of the emperor who in 1691 had himself entered the holy sanctuary at Aksum and, according to his biographer, spoken there with the Ark. Basing himself on the *Yosippon*, a history of the Jews written by Joseph ben Gorion, and translated into Ge'ez as the *Zena Ayhud* perhaps in the 15th century, the emperor describes the history of the Jerusalem temple at length, until its final destruction by Titus. He adds that 'since that time the Jews have had neither temple nor sanctuary'. He makes no claim that there was a new sanctuary of the Ark at Aksum, merely referring to another heavenly protector: 'our sanctuary, which is the most holy Trinity...' (I transcribe the text, not otherwise relevant to the story of the Ark, from the original French handwritten copy, in Appendix, 4).

Abba Gorgoreyos and Job Ludolf

Job Ludolf, writing in the 1680s, and following the counsels of his mentor in Ethiopian matters, Abba Gorgoreyos, naturally included the Ark as part of the *KN* story. It is mentioned in the text of Ludolf's book when the Solomon and Sheba tale and the supposed Jewish pedigrees of the Ethiopian nobility are introduced. Gorgoreyos had informed Ludolf of the existence of the book called 'Glory of the Kings' (*Kebra Nagast* – with *Gadla Marqorewos*, Gorgoreyos makes one of the earliest references to the book by this title), emphasising its importance to the Ethiopians. It was 'of great authority among them' and 'no person in Ethiopia doubted of the Truth thereof'. Ludolf repeats this later in his book, adding even higher praise: 'as it were a Second Gospel, and preserv'd in the Pallace of Axuma'.

Gorgoreyos' remarks are interesting, indicating that by the late 17th century the *KN* had attained a certain importance in educated circles in Ethiopia. This cultivated Ethiopian of Iyasu I's time considered the book authoritative – and we gain exactly the same impression from the contemporary chronicle of Iyasu I, which tells how the *KN* was consulted when a question of court precedence was at issue.[41] Ludolf was rather disapproving of the book's content, remarking that the story about the removal of the Ark was a

> Tale no less insipid, then (sic) misbecoming the new King. That these noble Jews, nefariously and Sacrilegiously took away with them the Ark of the Covenant, together with the Tables of the Ten Commandments, the Temple being carelessly lookt after, and the Gates being left open as it were by the Providence of God.[42]

The theme of the Ark, however, is not enlarged, or emphasised, even during Ludolf's long discussion on the meaning of the *tabot*.[43]

EMPEROR IYASU II AND REMEDIUS PRUTKY

A rare glimpse of Ethiopia, and the decadent court at Gondar in the mid-18th century, is furnished by Remedius Prutky. This irascible and disapproving man was a Bohemian, a Franciscan and a medical doctor, trained in Prague. Emperor Iyasu II, fond of novelties, invited the Franciscans to his court, and Prutky and his companions arrived in Gondar via Massawa in 1752. Prutky promptly noticed some 'Jewish' customs, like the slaughtering of an ox 'according to the Jewish rite'. In the report that he was eventually to write, Prutky several times indulges himself with long lists of the Ethiopians' faults.[44]

The visitors found Iyasu II at Kaha, his residence near Gondar. They were admitted to his presence, and conversation began. The emperor's questions came, very different from those of Lebna Dengel some 230 years before. The Ark was not mentioned, but: 'Where are the tablets of Moses?'

the imperial translator, the Greek treasurer Draco of Nios, enquired. 'Sheba, queen and ruler of the kingdom of Abyssinia?' was another question. Whatever it was that the Franciscans replied, apparently the emperor 'was much encouraged' and said that he was 'mightily satisfied with your answers'.[45]

This is intriguing. They can hardly have been expected to accept that the tablets were at Aksum, yet whatever they did say pleased the emperor, or so Prutky says. Did they suggest that the tablets had been lost at the time Nebuchadnezzar took Jerusalem? Did the emperor agree, not himself believing that they were at Aksum? Or did their reply merely indicate that they did not know, allowing him to assume that they had indeed vanished from Jerusalem, but were now in Ethiopia? If so, he evidently did not reveal his thoughts to Prutky and his companions at the audience. As for the second question, Prutky later informs us that the emperor kept his genealogy, claiming descent from Solomon, written in Greek, Arabic and Abyssinian on a document that hung from his neck in a golden locket.[46]

FOREIGN COMMENTARIES, 1764–1881

Was Emperor Iyasu I the only person ever to see the sacred object at Aksum? Strange tales occasionally emerge that allude to actual encounters with the mysterious object at Aksum Seyon church, or to rumours about it. A new transformation is about to take place in this ever-shifting landscape. After the long delayed entry of the Ark into the records, and what seems to be the end of our search for an Ark with its manifestation in the form of a revered casket at Aksum, suddenly it vanishes again. The sightings of the holy object that I describe here once again treat of a stone tablet, by now of very modest dimensions, while one man, James Bruce, denies that it had ever existed.

An Armenian Visitor

Yohannes Tovmacean was an Armenian merchant who brought jewels to Ethiopia to sell to the imperial family. He was discouraged to find that in return for his gifts to the Empress Mentewab and her grandson Iyoas, he got nothing more than some animals and chickens, and a house in the palace compound bare of anything save one small carpet. He nevertheless stayed on to supervise the (extremely meagre) Ethiopian state treasury, the contents of which he details in his record.

Tovmacean is that rarest of figures – a man who claimed that he actually saw part of a stone slab purporting to be (one of?) the tablets with the Ten Commandments kept in the church at Aksum. This occurred in 1764, at the town he calls 'Saba'. Here is what Tovmacean has to say:

> There was also a large and ancient Abyssinian church where they said a piece of the stone tablet of the Ten Commandments carried by Moses had been preserved, and they took T'ovmacean and Bijo (his companion) into the church, and showed him a closed altar said to contain this tablet of the Ten Commandments, but they refrained from opening it. However, on the insistence of Bijo, who claimed that he was a relative of the King, they very hesitatingly obliged. They took out a parcel wrapped in cloth, and began ceremoniously to unwrap it. There was a packet wrapped in another parcel of velvet, and it was not until they had removed a hundred such wrappings that they at last took out a piece of stone with a few incomplete letters on it, and, kneeling, they made the sign of the Cross, and kissed the stone, after which the object was again wrapped up, and put back into the altar which was then closed. This was a great relic – if it was indeed a piece of the tablet of the Ten Commandments which God gave to Moses.[47]

This anecdote moves away from a casket-like Ark of the Covenant, reverting once again to a (small) stone tablet. Nothing Ark-like is concerned unless the 'closed altar' was not a *manbara tabot*, as one might expect, but some sort of chest. Nothing is even mentioned about an Ark. The stone Tovmacean saw could have been a fragment of an old inscription, or possibly an old (broken?) *tabot*, still treated with reverence. If the 'closed altar' were in the sanctuary, as is likely, the stone may have been one of the current *tabotat* in use in the church. In any event, it is improbable that Tovmacean and his companion would have been shown the real relic, concealed before even from emperors. Tovmacean and Bijo were doubtless fobbed off with some handy stone *tabot*, though even that would be deserving of veneration in the eyes of Ethiopian priests. It was perhaps the same one that reappeared later when the Reverend Father Dimotheos also came to Aksum, and succeeded in gaining permission to view it (see below).

James Bruce and the *Kebra Nagast*

'You are come from Jerusalem, through vile Turkish governments, and hot, unwholesome climates to see a river and a bog.' In these uninspiring terms,

James Bruce himself informs us, Empress Mentewab – herself dreaming hopelessly of one day seeing the earthly paradise of Jerusalem – summed up the Scotsman's dream of finding the source of the Nile. Bruce did discover it, or at least he saw what others had long since discovered. He wrote about it. The emperor even made him 'lord of Geesh', the district of Gish Abbai where lay the little bubbling 'bog' that represented the source of the (Blue) Nile. Yet, though he denied it vehemently, someone had been there before. Worst of all, that somebody was a Jesuit: Péro Pais. In fact, his achievements had already been notified to the world in Latin by Athanasius Kircher as early as 1645.[48]

James Bruce of Kinnaird was a remarkable man. His great claim to fame is his life in Ethiopia in the early 1770s, and the resulting book, *Travels to Discover the Source of the Nile*, published in 1790. It was a much-needed update on events in that distant, closed empire. It was not long after Tovmacean's visit that James Bruce arrived in Ethiopia. His contribution to Ethiopian studies was enormous. He became an intimate – a respected servant is the impression he himself gives – of the imperial family, a collector of manuscripts and a compiler of history.[49] Bruce supplies an exceptional glimpse of life in Ethiopia during a few years of the reign of Emperor Takla Haymanot II.

Graham Hancock awards Bruce a significant place in the history of the Ethiopian Ark, or rather in the esoteric pseudo-history of its concealment. But his bizarre conclusions about Bruce fail to take into account the Scotsman's extraordinary character: his obstinacy, his strong dislikes, and his wilful blindness on certain points. Instead of a mission to seek out the source of the Nile – the reality of which shines out in his narrative – and to collect information about Ethiopia, Hancock suggests that the whole of this was no more than a masquerade. It concealed a far more important quest. As a Freemason, and therefore member of a body that possessed some of the secrets of the Templar Knights of old, Bruce's real aim in coming to Ethiopia was to seek out the Ark that the Templars had discovered there in Lalibela's time.

Hancock claims that Bruce credited the story of the queen of Sheba as an Ethiopian sovereign. He notes that Bruce did not completely exclude the idea that the queen had a child, first emperor of Ethiopia, by Solomon, without adding Bruce's full, rather more equivocal, conclusion. Bruce wrote: 'the annals of the Abyssinians, being very full upon this point, have taken a middle opinion, and by no means an improbable one…' But he also added that 'however dangerous it would be to doubt it in Abyssinia, I will not here aver it for truth, no much less will I positively contradict it, as Scripture says nothing about it'.[50]

Following Hancock's interpretation, Bruce did not mention the Ark in these passages because he 'knowingly misled his readers about the Ark'. Assertions like this are very difficult to counter. They are also impossible to prove. There is nothing but inference built on inference to support them. Yet Miles Bredin, too, in a recent book about Bruce, *The Pale Abyssinian*, reiterates this mysterious 'other agenda' of Bruce, though in a curiously desultory way, without pursuing what would, if true, have been a most remarkable fact about Bruce's life. Bruce, he writes, 'makes almost no mention of the Ark of the Covenant when one of the few things then known about Abyssinia was that it claimed to be guarding the Ark'. The people that had reported this claim, though, were Jesuits. This may have been quite enough, even apart from an 18th century rationalist approach that would surely have rendered such a story ridiculous to Bruce, to ensure his disparagement of the tale. The Jesuits did not believe it either. Later Bredin asserts that Bruce ascertained swiftly that the Ark, or the object claimed to be the Ark, was still at Aksum, and then, 'assured of its safety' (something he could reassure the Masons at home about) he could continue elsewhere, using the excuse of the Nile discovery. Bredin also suggests that Bruce returned through Sinnar because that had been the route of the Ark. These few phrases concerning the Ark, derived from Hancock's story, are supposed to sum up the main driving force of Bruce's extraordinary journeys through Syria, Ethiopia and the Sudan.[51] All in all, the evidence presented to suggest that Bruce was in Ethiopia primarily to observe the Ark is strikingly feeble.

I have written elsewhere (in *Ethiopia Unveiled*) about the books available to Bruce that confirmed Pais' earlier visit to the sources of the Nile in 1618, and a subsequent visit by Lobo. These existed, and provided a full and convincing report, but Bruce was capable of actually acknowledging them while simply sweeping them to one side in the face of his own superior claim. It is hard to credit that a man of Bruce's pride could publish statements about the Nile many years after he came back from Abyssinia that would make him seem a charlatan and a laughing stock, just to conceal a recondite purpose – the search for the Ark. It was quite unnecessary for him to behave like this, nearly two decades after his travels ended. There were many other reasons that a well-known traveller of his calibre could have coined for going into Ethiopia. The search for antiquities and historical material, which he had pursued in other countries as well, would have richly answered this requirement. But publish it he did – and was roundly chastised in the third (1791) edition of Lobo's 1669 book *A Short Relation of the River Nile* for not acknowledging his predecessors.

When Bruce comes to describe the Ark of the Covenant, it is with disappointing brevity and total dismissiveness. Even if he does not exclude the possibility that the queen of Sheba, an Ethiopian, gave birth to a son who was the progenitor of the royal house, and brought Judaism to the country, he does not accept the Ark story. Bruce refers to the 'fabulous legends' about the Ark, still believed by Ethiopians to be in Aksum. I see no compelling reason not to accept that this was exactly his opinion of the story, rather than a deliberate deception to hide a quest for the Ark, as Hancock and Bredin assert.

Bruce cites an occasion when the reigning king, Takla Haymanot II, talked to him about the Ark. The young ruler claimed that 'whatever this might be it was destroyed, with the church itself, by Mahomet Gragn, though pretended falsely to subsist there still'. The king may well have told Bruce this – it would be very interesting to know if he really believed it. But bearing in mind Shihab al-Din's testimony about the withdrawal of the great 'idol'

7. The treasury of Yohannes IV at Maryam Seyon church, Aksum. Next to it once stood the small Zion church, in which the Ark was kept. Photo Pamela Taor.

to Shire, it is unlikely to have been true. If it had been, would Grañ's biographer, who wrote with such relish about the mass destruction of the churches of Ethiopia and the burning or pillaging of their contents, have failed to make propaganda out of so major a moral disaster to the Christian state as the obliteration of the country's greatest religious talisman? True, the account of the destruction of the church at Aksum is missing in the *Futuh al-Habasha*, but Shihab al-Din had already told the tale of the withdrawal of the great gold-encrusted stone from the church, so soon to burn. The Muslim writer accepted that the great talisman, whatever it was, was saved. Bruce himself was prepared to accept only this: 'some ancient copy of the Old Testament, I do believe, was deposited here, probably that from which the first version (translation) was made'. In another passage he noted that 'Azarias, the son of Zadok the priest…brought with him a Hebrew transcript of the law…' to Ethiopia. The sacred object at Aksum, for Bruce, was no more than a book or scroll. To him, as to his editor and early biographer Murray, the tale of an Ethiopian Ark was simply nonsense.

James Bruce's contribution to the story of the Ark did not end with his observations or with his tremendous tomes of history and social study. For it was he who, at last, brought into Europe copies of the text of the *KN* itself, in addition to publishing an account of the epic in his own book.[52]

Father Dimotheos, Gerhard Rohlfs

Another record of a sighting of the holy relic at Aksum – again not in the form of an Ark but as a tablet – was by a churchman of an associated Orthodox community, the Armenian father Dimotheos Sapritchian. The *vartabet* or archimandrite came to Ethiopia in the reign of Emperor Tewodros II (1855–68) on a mission led by Archbishop Sehak de Kharpert of Jerusalem. The Armenian patriarch of Jerusalem had charged them with the task of trying to liberate British prisoners who were held by the emperor at the fortress mountain of Maqdala. Dimotheos had no delicacy when it came to expressing his opinion of the Ethiopian claim. He roundly denounces it as a revolting lie.

Dimotheos recorded that in May 1869 they reached Aksum, where they viewed the church of Maryam Seyon:

> This church, much celebrated throughout Abyssinia, is formed of an
> enclosure of stones set one upon the other without cement: it is surrounded

by a cemetery. One climbs up to this church by four or five steps in marble, which occupy the whole width of the façade on the west side; the door, made of wood, is quite high and of imposing construction; the vault constructed according to Greek architecture, is supported by four large columns; the main altar is equally of Greek form. Outside the enclosure one can see here and there several funerary monuments of pyramidal form, on which are illegible inscriptions: most are ruined or half buried in the earth.[53]

Father Dimotheos had heard that there was supposed to be a holy relic of importance in the church, but he adds a new twist. The stone was supposed to be the tablet of the Ten Commandments, brought by Menelik (the bringing of the Ark itself is not mentioned in this story) but it had also been taken back to Jerusalem to be authenticated by Jesus himself:

> In Abyssinia they have very great veneration for a certain tablet in stone, which is called the Tablet of the Ten Commandments, and which the people of the land believe to be the same that the Lord gave to the prophet Moses, which, according to them, was brought there from Jerusalem during the reign of Minilik, first king of Ethiopia. At the time of Jesus Christ, they say, a certain individual called Ezekiel, a pious and inspired man, took this Tablet with him to Jerusalem, and presenting himself to Jesus Christ, said to him: 'What is your advice about the divine commandments written on this tablet? Should they be accepted or not?' Then Jesus, without opening his mouth, took the tablet in his hands, and wrote on the other side in letters of gold. 'Accept everything which is written here.' Since then this tablet has been regarded as having been written by God himself.

> The Abyssinians affirm that this legend is found in their ancient books; but as it is contrary to the Holy Scriptures, in which it is expressly stated that the said tablet was placed in the Ark of the Covenant, I was indignant and outraged to see so revolting a lie accepted as truth in the whole kingdom of Abyssinia. Naturally we wished greatly to see this stone, so as to let the people know, if possible, about such a lie and such a deception. They told us that it was in the Church of Aksum, placed in a precious coffer, and that one could neither see nor touch it without being immediately struck by punishment. King Theodore, it is said, had wished to see it, but God did not judge him worthy.

The Aksumite priests did what they could to prevent Dimotheos and his party seeing the stone when they went to the church. They claimed that ancient tradition forbade anyone from touching the tablet. Even just to look at it required the permission of the metropolitan. This must have seemed the perfect way out for the priests, since *Abuna* Salama was dead, and his successor had not yet arrived. Dimotheos was impatient with the secrecy, and was not afraid of causing embarrassment. Christians were prevented from honouring a sacred object, he declared. After questioning the priests about the relative

merits of the tablet in comparison with the Holy Cross, in which the Cross
was accorded the superiority, he demanded why, if the Cross was not
concealed, should the tablet be hedged about with such secrecy? The mystery
surrounding the sacred object merely encouraged suspicions about it – a
comment that still applies today. In Dimotheos' view: 'it would be better,
then, that all were free to come and venerate it publicly, for then belief in its
authenticity would be better affirmed, and it would attract greater respect'.

It became impossible for the priests to keep on refusing these
distinguished ecclesiastical visitors, whose church was of their own Orthodox
persuasion. Dimotheos reports that the matter was raised with *Dejazmatch*
(general) Kassa, who was to become Emperor Yohannes IV a few years later.
He told the priests (according to Dimotheos): 'Did I not tell you that you
would be covered with shame and mockery; the tablet of the *tabot* of Moses
has just lost its reputation by this, and it is a great blow for it, until now
regarded among us as an object more worthy of respect than the Holy Cross
itself, and to which, I dare to say, we render honours due only to the Divinity…'
It was at last concluded that the foreign dignitaries might go to the church
with the governor and see the relic:

> When we arrived at the church everyone went into the vestibule, and we alone
> were taken by several of the clergy into the sacristy,[54] built outside the church
> to the left, at the end of a row of other rooms. Inside this sacristy on the ground
> floor, was a sort of wooden attic, which one went up to by a movable ladder.
> One of the priests who accompanied us went up, and having entered, took
> up two planks of the ceiling to give room for two other priests who followed
> him there; then a deacon with a censer in his hand approached a coffer,
> which he censed, and presented us the censer to do the same. The coffer was
> a casket of Indian work; when it was opened we saw revealed the Tablet of
> the ten commandments. We removed it to look at it more closely. The stone
> was a pinkish marble of the type found ordinarily in Egypt. It was quadrangular,
> 24cm long by 22cm wide, and only 3cm thick. On the edges it was
> surrounded by engraved flowers about half an inch wide; in the centre was a
> second quadrangular line in the form of a fine chain of which the interior
> space was empty, while the space between the two frames contained the ten
> Commandments, five on one side, five on the other, written obliquely in
> Turkish fashion; at the base of the tablet, between the two frames, were three
> letters…

Father Dimotheos described the letters. One was a figure that did not exist
in the Abyssinian alphabet, although he states that the stone was inscribed in
'Abyssinian'. It indicated 'ten' (ten in the Ethiopic language is indicated by a
letter resembling an I with a short line above and below it). The remaining

letters, he wrote, indicated the sounds '*tsa*' and the unvoiced French 'e'. Dimotheos considered that the three letters together constituted an unreadable date. On the reverse of the tablet more flowers were carved in a different style. Dimotheos' final opinion of this great relic was that 'this stone was near entirely intact, and showed no sign of age; at the most it might go back to the thirteenth or fourteenth century of the common era' – though how he came to that fairly precise estimate he does not reveal.

In *Dejazmatch* Kassa's presence, they were asked what they had seen: 'were not the ancient laws inscribed on the two sides of the mosaic Tablet, just as they are on the Tablet you have just seen?' (This alludes to Exodus 32.15: 'Moses…went down from the mountain, with the two tablets of the Testimony in his hand, both tablets written on both sides.' The same is not stated of the second tablets, but God promised Moses [Exodus 34.1] that he would write on them 'the words that were on the former tablets, which you broke', so one can assume they were the same as the first set.) The Armenian party replied that they were inscribed on both sides:

> The conversation went no further on this subject, because the Clergy feared that the truth would be discovered. Seeing that we triumphed by our affirmative response, the great prince was glad and said: 'The suspicions which have occupied the spirits of some are now dissipated; they believed that the Ten Commandments were inscribed in the middle, see now that this Tablet is regarded by them as apocryphal'.

Dimotheos was certain that 'the stone which they guarded with them, in such great veneration, was not the true original, but those who know the Holy Scriptures need no proof to admit it'. In his opinion, the Ten Commandments had been inscribed on two tablets, in Hebrew writing, without a date. They had been kept in the Ark of the Covenant, and were now lost. The stone they had seen was a forgery, and the priests were well aware of this. Dimotheos again presses his point about the suspicions raised by the secrecy. In his opinion, deception of the faithful was maintained by the 'traditional defence' in such cases – concealing it where no one could see it.[55]

As with Tovmacean a century earlier, the story does not refer to an 'Ark', but to a tablet, although a container, in this case an 'Indian' coffer, was involved as well. Dimotheos may have seen a stone *tabot*, or altar tablet. The sketch that he provides is intriguing, showing the three letters as IXS, the X in the form of a waisted H – strongly reminiscent of the IHS of Catholic symbolism, standing for Jesus. Could the stone have been some forgotten relic deriving from the brief period of Roman Catholic ascendancy in Ethiopia, not understood by the priests for what it really was? Some of the known (wooden) examples of *tabotat* in collections outside Ethiopia are of very similar decorative type to the tablet described by Dimotheos (particularly the *tabot* in the collection of the Department of Ethnography, British Museum, no. 1868–10–1–21). It has a similar style of decoration, including a fairly long inscription (though not with the angled lines of writing in 'Turkish' style).

Finally, in this history of the Ark in literature over the ages, in 1881 the German envoy Gerhard Rohlfs also records his conversation with the incumbent *nebura'ed* about the relic.[56] Rohlfs asked whether the Ark had survived the Muslim onslaught by the soldiers of Ahmad Grañ of Harar, when the old Maryam Seyon church was burnt in the 1530s. The answer was positive; the relic had not only survived, but was still there, concealed in the walls of the church, accessible only by a secret door. What was in the Holy of Holies was nothing but an ordinary copy (i.e. a *tabot* of Mary of Zion?). No one was permitted to see the Ark save its guardian – neither clergy, emperor, *echege* nor even the *abun* himself could bear the sight of the relic: 'so it as thousands of years ago', declared the *nebura'ed*, 'and so will it be until the last days'.

EPILOGUE

A last claim to a sighting of the 'Ark' might be that of an American, Theodore Vestal, working in Ethiopia in 1965.[57] While in Aksum, he paid a visit to the church of Maryam Seyon. Without any request from him, he was brought, while standing outside the church itself, a fair-sized (estimated c. 60cm. long x 45 wide x 35 tall), dark-coloured, wooden chest. A priest carried it out from the church. The chest was lidded, and it remained shut. This chest, it was said (in translation from the priest's words), was the Ark of the Covenant. Having no special interest in the object or in its splendid claim, and no belief in the claim's veracity either, Vestal did not study it as closely as perhaps a member of the clergy or a historian might have done. He recalls some sort of decoration on the sides, though nothing in any way splendid or even particularly interesting. Gold, evidently, did not glitter from every surface, or from the wings of two cherubim.

What was this 'Ark'? There may be an answer this time. Very probably it was the box that is still carried out from the church on the heads of priests at various ceremonies, and which, on these occasions, contains one or other of the *tabotat* of the church. It – or a predecessor or companion – was photographed early last century[58] in processions in Aksum, covered with a cloth ornamented with silver appliqué designs. It is nowadays usually covered with a cloth embroidered with a dove at the front. Much bulkier than the majority of *tabotat* borne on these occasions on the heads of priests, it seems, beneath its draperies, to be a box of similar dimensions to the one Vestal saw.

The Ark of the Covenant has, of course, been the subject of many books of varying value since the last accounts I cite above. Some were serious biblical studies, others extravaganzas not far from the script of the film *Raiders of the Lost Ark* in content. None give much attention to the Ark in Ethiopia. The Ark is of course mentioned more or less discréetly in most serious books on Ethiopia, simply as a reflection of the place it holds in Ethiopian Christian belief. Kirsten Stoffregen-Pedersen, for example, is a model of discretion in *Les Ethiopiens*, which concerns Ethiopian religion and religious practice.[59] She simply remarks at the end of her account about the *KN* that: 'in our times, many Ethiopian Christians believe still that it is really the Ark of the Covenant which is kept in the church of Sion at Aksum'. She is also extremely restrained in approaching the question of the *tabot*. It is only once mentioned, as a mere aside, in a book which otherwise enters into close detail about the church, its rituals and symbolism. In a note about the burial of the leg of St. Takla Haymanot under the 'Ark', she explains the word *tabot* as referring to 'the tablet of wood, symbolising the ark of the covenant, which is placed on the altar of Ethiopian churches'.

On quite another plane is the work of Graham Hancock. There, the Ark is accompanied by every sort of speculative association, including those permanent stars in popular writing: Freemasonry, the Knights Templar, the Order of Christ, the Holy Grail, Atlantis, the Great Pyramid, secrets of ancient Egypt and mystic energy sources. This is, of course, the version that has had the greatest popular impact, creating a bestseller. It offers exciting reading, even if some of the evidence presented is more than suspect. When, for example, Hancock found crosses of a characteristic form cut in the stone near the carved figure of a lioness at Gobedra, and in the 'tomb of Kaleb', both near Aksum, he enthused: 'I now felt certain in my own heart that the Templars had indeed been here.' Proof, at last, for a far-fetched theory? Had he been familiar with the ancient coinage of Ethiopia, he would have known that the coins issued by the Christian kings of Aksum over several centuries bear a rich variety of cross forms, including precisely the 'Crusader' and 'Templar' crosses that he describes. They preceded the European usage of the same form by many centuries, and can be seen carved on Egyptian temples by Coptic Christians as well.

Hancock's interpretation of Ethiopian history suffers from major lacunae. He fails to include information from more recent publications. His main arguments, leading to his sensational but mistaken conclusion, depend more on drama and ingenuity than fact. But nevertheless there is value in *The Sign and the Seal*. It is stimulating to follow an argument in which questions are asked from a perspective entirely different from more scholarly approaches. Hancock sees incisively through the lapses of logic in some presentations of Ethiopian history. In addition, there are some very entertaining passages, particularly those describing the various attempts to find the Ark in relatively recent times.

6

Mary of Zion: The Dwelling Place of the Ark

For wheresoever God is pleased for her to dwell, there is her habitation, and where he is not pleased that she should dwell she dwelleth not

Kebra Negast 8

MARYAM SEYON, AKSUM

The *KN* tells us of the splendours of the heavenly Zion, whose image on earth the Ark was. The text clearly evokes the Ethiopian concept that a sacred object might be a replica, but is nevertheless imbued, provided the circumstances of its creation are pristine, with the same sanctity as the original. The Ark (*Seyon tabota hegg* – Zion the Ark of the Law) was created 'at the very beginning, as soon as God had stablished the heavens'. It was 'ordained that it should become the habitation of his glory upon the earth', for which reason it was brought down so that Moses could make 'a likeness of it':

Now the heavenly and spiritual [original] within it is of divers colours, and the work thereof is marvellous, and it resembleth jasper, and the sparkling stone, and the topaz, and the hyacinthine stone (?), and the crystal, and the light, and it catcheth the eye by force, and it astonisheth the mind and stupefieth it with wonder; it was made by the mind of God and not by the hand of the artificer, man, but He Himself created it for the habitation of His glory. And it is a spiritual thing and full of compassion; it is a heavenly thing and is full of light; it is a thing of freedom and a habitation of the Godhead, Whose habitation is in Heaven, and Whose place of movement is on the earth, and it dwelleth with men and with the angels, a city of salvation for men, and for the Holy Spirit a habitation (*KN* 17).

The original Ark, even for the compilers and editors of the *KN*, is not the Ark of Moses, David and Solomon, but an ineffable heavenly presence called forth at the very beginning of time. It is the copy, the replica, of this glorious celestial abode, made at Moses' order under specific divine authorisation, that rests today, the Ethiopian church tells us, in the chapel of the Tablet of Moses at Maryam Seyon church, Aksum. By the transfer of this object from Jerusalem to Aksum, the transfer of royalty from Israel to Ethiopia, instituted by God, was affirmed, and by the Ark's physical presence at Aksum the primacy of the Ethiopian sovereign over the other kings of the earth was established for all to understand.[1]

The present church of Mary of Zion – Maryam Seyon or Enda Seyon (Place/Dwelling of Zion) – at Aksum is the very late descendant of a number of other structures built successively on the same spot. Despite the tendency to refer to it as the 'great' or 'cathedral' church of Maryam Seyon, the present building is a relatively modest stone-built edifice little larger than ordinary parish churches in small villages in other Christian lands. Although tradition places it at the centre of antique-seeming traditions, it is a mid-17th century

8. The western terrace and steps at Maryam Seyon church, Aksum, surmounted by the façade of Christian Ethiopia's holiest shrine. Photo Pamela Taor.

structure with even later restorations. It was reconstructed on part of the ruins of a much larger church through the generosity of Emperor Fasiladas and the empress-mother, Wald Sa'ala, and consecrated in 1655 in the presence of Princess Yodit, Fasiladas' daughter. Later, and perhaps resulting in the classical Gondarine form we see today, Iyasu II, visiting Aksum in 1750, ordered restoration work on the church.

This church replaced a number of predecessors. Some of these, clearly, were great and splendid enough in their time. The designation 'cathedral' tends to be used to magnify its importance and, since Frumentius, the earliest bishop we know of, was entitled 'bishop of the Aksumites', and his successors were called 'metropolitan of Aksum', we might expect that their episcopal seat would indeed have been at the chief church there. Maryam Seyon church is regarded as the first church of Ethiopia, again perfectly plausible since it was built at the royal capital. It seems to have lost its place as the episcopal seat in later times, when the bishops were far away from Aksum, in Adefa/Lalibela, or wearily dragging their way round the land in the wake of capricious monarchs dwelling in tents. Yet even with the rise of Gondar with its reputed 44 churches, when the bishops dwelt in the *Abuna* Bet suburb of the capital or at their country fiefs like Janda, or after the building of Addis Ababa and the Holy Trinity Cathedral, Aksum's chief church has remained in the eyes of most Ethiopians, whether Aksumite citizen or Amhara emperor like Sarsa Dengel, the most revered in the land.

Inside, the dignified battlemented stone rectangle of the present 'old' church of Maryam Seyon – so-called to distinguish it from the round modern one built by the last emperor of Ethiopia – is disappointing. It is neither remarkable for its architecture, nor well kept, nor well decorated. Poverty and neglect have reduced to nothing whatever splendours it may once have possessed. Dr. Poncet, rather astonishingly for a Frenchman of the time of Louis XIV and Versailles, described it in 1700 (under the name Heleni rather than Aksum) as a 'magnificent church. 'Tis the fairest and largest I have seen in Ethiopia...'[2] James Bruce, some seventy years later – after whatever restorations Iyasu II might have made – regarded Maryam Seyon church with disdain: 'a small, mean building, very ill kept and full of pigeons' dung'.[3] Henry Salt, who often criticised Bruce's opinions, attempted to rehabilitate the place, which he had seen on his 1805 visit. He declared that Bruce had 'most unjustly depreciated it, since...compared with all others in Tigré it has no rival (except Chelicut) with respect to size, richness, nor sanctity'.[4] To no avail: Combes and Tamisier saw the church in 1835, and although they did agree that it was the most notable in Abyssinia, they concluded that Salt had overdone the praise and that Bruce had more nearly described the truth – it was a building 'inférieure à...nos greniers ordinaires'.[5] Nevertheless, because of its reputed original foundation by the famous, if historically elusive, Aksumite kings Abreha and Asbeha, and because of its supposed possession of the Ark of the Covenant and the tablet(s) of Moses, it is for most Ethiopian Orthodox Christians the holiest place of all in this land filled with churches.

The peculiar holiness of the church in the eyes of Ethiopians, as the dwelling place of 'our Lady, the heavenly Zion, the habitation of the glory of God' (*KN* 88) has not inspired a desire among the Aksumite priests to search deeper for their church's origins. Rather – as with the Temple Mount in Jerusalem, though problems there are enhanced by the need to maintain a delicate balance between religions – it has engendered exclusiveness, effectively preventing any archaeological exploration in the immediate environs of the church itself. In both these holy places, where the science of archaeology alone can be expected to really clarify matters, religious biases and sensitivities conspire to impede progress. At Aksum, restrictions were briefly set aside when the new chapel of the Tablet of Moses was constructed. Henri de Contenson and Francis Anfray were permitted to excavate in an area – still open and visible to visitors – just to the north of the position of the chapel. The work was revelatory, providing some real information about the history of the site. It was diametrically opposed, as one might perhaps expect, to the late Ge'ez documents' own explanation recorded in the *Book of Aksum*:

> A third time it [the city of Aksum] was built by Abreha and Asbeha (at the place) where is (now) this sanctuary of the cathedral of Aksum. Now the foundation was performed by means of a miracle, for previously there was (there) a great lake; and the holy kings Abreha and Asbeha climbed a great mountain called Mekyada Egziena and prayed that (God) might reveal to them where they should build a cathedral for the dwelling-place of His name. And Our Lord descended and stood between them, and took earth, and cast it where it is now; and above (the place) there stood a column of light; and there they built the sanctuary; and behold it is there to this day...[6]

Reminiscent though this last phrase is of the passage in 1 Kings 8.8, where the writer interjects the same words after the description of the installation of the Ark in the sanctuary, the author of the Ge'ez book, in the section devoted to the church, makes no claim at all about the Ark.

The church of Mary of Zion today, despite the attractiveness of its old stones and its tree-filled enclosures, can be a rather daunting spot for visitors. A generally unwelcoming attitude prevails, though the church urgently needs the money that foreign tourists bring it. Graham Hancock's popularisation of Aksum and its church has encouraged more visitors, some specifically intent on asking awkward questions about the Ark of the Covenant. Foreigners are now kept away from the area of the chapel of the Tablet of Moses, and security is tighter.

Women are not allowed inside the inner enclosure anyway, except to view from behind an iron grille some votive crowns laid out on a sort of stall. This sexual exclusivity prevails because the older church is regarded as a monastery, forbidden to women, though women worshippers may enter the newer round church nearby. In fact, if Francisco Alvares is to be believed, in the 1520s entrance was even more restricted than today: 'neither women nor laymen go into the enclosure of this church, and they do not go in to receive the communion'.[7] The church has only once been briefly open to women, as Manoel de Almeida tells us, during the period of Portuguese Catholic influence.

Maryam Seyon church possessed an important privilege in the past, that of sanctuary. This is alluded to in various documents. One example, a document in the *Book of Aksum*, written by 'the priests of Seyon', is filled with eulogy for the man who was then master of Tigray:

> the prince of princes *dajazmach* Walda Sellase, powerful of the powerful, master of masters, mighty over all the governors, who tramples everything beneath the feet of his power. If anyone does not prostrate himself before him, his house will be destroyed, his possessions plundered. Amen!

The scribe describes a campaign, and, mentioning the region of Waldebba, cites it as being the same as 'the first town of refuge, Seyon' (that is, Maryam Seyon church). It is specified that 'those who come to seek asylum here are not obliged to leave, for it is a place of refuge like Seyon'. This document, incidentally, later makes clear the reason for the adulation of this powerful prince, Walda Sellassie (d. 1816). He had come to Aksum, spent the night at prayer in the sanctuary on the eve of the Feast of Our Lady, and then declared before all his governors and officials: 'I renew the fiefs formerly under its control, which the former kings gave and which I had suppressed.'[8]

THE FOUNDATION OF MARYAM SEYON CHURCH

How long has there been a church of Maryam Seyon at Aksum? The notion that Aksum's 'cathedral' church, dedicated to Mary of Zion, is of very ancient foundation is almost unchallenged, both in Ge'ez histories and in modern writings. It is what we would expect of the Ge'ez histories, anxious to emphasise tradition – but it may not be true. In the next few sections I traverse the minefield of potential inaccuracies about the history of this famous church, sown through the bland assertions of both ancient ecclesiastic writers and their modern followers.

Certainly no reliable evidence about Maryam Seyon church is available from Aksumite times. Yet many modern scholars unhesitatingly accept the very late legends at face value, asserting, for example, that 'the most famous rectangular sanctuary is that of St. Mary of Zion at Aksum which has been known since the sixth century'.[9] In reality, apart from much later Ge'ez legends purporting to hark back to the time of its founders, Maryam Seyon church is not attested until many centuries after that. Similar unquestioning belief in legends which are not even unanimous among themselves encouraged Graham Hancock to state that

> [his informant] dated the start of construction works on the first Saint Mary's at AD 372 – which meant that this was quite possibly the earliest Christian church in sub-Saharan Africa. A great five-aisled basilica, it was regarded from its inauguration as the most sacred place in Ethiopia. This was so because it was built to house the Ark of the Covenant...[10]

This citation expresses the commonly accepted view of the church; its date of origin (one among several supplied by the Ge'ez documents) was early, it was dedicated to Mary, it was very large, it was five-aisled (nave and double flanking aisles), and it sheltered the Ark of Zion. Yet for no single detail cited here is there any real evidence.

Maryam Seyon church has been associated with the 6th century church of the Apostles on Mount Sion:

> Traditions recorded in the *Book of Aksum* credit...king Kaleb Ella Asbeha with building the great metropolitan cathedral at Aksum, whose altar was dedicated to 'Our Mother Zion'. In its size, plan, and its dedication, the cathedral followed the Church of Zion in Jerusalem, which had been built in 340 on Mount Zion, the traditional site of the Last Supper. A pilgrim to Jerusalem in 518 described the church as 'Holy Zion, the Mother of All Churches', and the cathedral at Aksum was intended to create a new version

of this holy site. Ella Asbeha was also known as Kaleb, a name referring to the Israelite leader who followed the Lord 'with his whole heart' (Numbers 14:24–5), and while another Ethiopian tradition states that it was Ezana who built the Cathedral of Aksum, it is unlikely that either Ezana or Frumentius could have conceived of building a cathedral that was in plan or dedication a deliberate copy of the Church of Zion. It was their contemporary, Cyril of Jerusalem (351–86), who first taught that the earthly city of Jerusalem was the Holy City, and thereby created a foundation for the development of Christian pilgrimage to Jerusalem and the cult of the holy sites there.

> …According to Ethiopian tradition, Kaleb retired around 540 to the monastery of Abba Pantalewon, one of the Nine Saints, near Aksum. When he entered monastic life, he sent a delegation to Jerusalem with a crown to be hung before the door of the tomb in the church of the Holy Sepulchre. His donation of this crown reveals the continuity of his devotion to the Holy City, already displayed in the dedication of the cathedral at Aksum to Mary of Zion.[11]

Does this furnish a reliable outline of the origins and dedication of Maryam Seyon church? Probably not. The Ethiopian information cited here derives from late traditions. The attribution of an early dedication to Zion is highly suspect. It follows traditions recorded long after the spread and acceptance as historically valid of the *KN* story and similar tales, with their strong Zion emphasis. This question of early dedication I will deal with in the next section.

In citing information from the *Book of Aksum*, we should keep in mind that the document is a compilation written, where it deals with the foundation and structure of Maryam Seyon church, over a millennium after the events it purports to relate. Archaeological evidence confirms that it is quite wrong in the details it supplies about the foundation of the church, and the rest must be treated with equal caution. The *Book of Aksum* survives today only in very late versions (which include fragments from a presumed original composition), attached to manuscripts of the *KN*.[12] Surviving copies are augmented with much more recent additional material up to the 19th century – updates of older grants, alterations by later kings to previous decrees, new land grants and the like. Péro Pais cited a very small section from an early version of the book that he saw. Happily, this is enough to be certain that the description of the church existed already in the early 17th century, before Emperor Fasiladas' new work at the site – but several decades after Sarsa Dengel had built a new church there among the ruins of the one destroyed by Grañ. This event appears to be commemorated in a chronological list in the *Book of Aksum*, under year 236 of Mercy (1577 EC/1584–5 AD): 'la construction d'Aksoum fut restaurée'.

Considering the evidence from the *Book of Aksum* in detail, we find that Kaleb Ella Asbeha is not described as the founder of the church. The text names the legendary kings called Abreha and Asbeha as the founders. In the Ge'ez documents, these are the rulers who were converted to Christianity by Frumentius, which places them in the 4th, not the 6th, century. Scholars usually identify them not with Kaleb Ella Asbeha, but with his by two centuries' predecessor King Ezana and his brother Sazana. There is solid primary evidence, provided by contemporary inscriptions, coins, and a record by Patriarch Athanasius of Alexandria which names Ezana, Sazana and Frumentius together, that Ezana converted to Christianity around 340 AD.[13]

Most probably, a church was built at the Aksumite capital after the conversion of King Ezana. The church chronicler Rufinus suggests that as a result of Bishop Frumentius' labours, 'Christian peoples and churches have been created in the parts of India [Ethiopia], and the priesthood has begun'. We can easily accept that at Aksum the first church could have been built on the site of the one now called Maryam Seyon. Marilyn Heldman's reluctance to accept the idea that Ezana built the first church is based on a strange assumption – that Christianity did not become the official religion of Aksum until the reign of Kaleb. This is quite ruled out by an element she has not utilised in her analysis, the powerful Christian imagery of the coinage of all the kings of Aksum from Ezana onwards, without exception. Heldman appears to accept that 'Abreha and Asbeha' in the *Book of Aksum* represent Kaleb Ella Asbeha, while they represent Ezana in 'another Ethiopian tradition'. This is merely the same tradition, differently interpreted. In reality, no Ethiopian tradition mentions Ezana. The great event of his reign, the conversion, is always attributed in Ethiopic documents to Abreha and Asbeha, who appear in the king lists and other manuscripts, preceding Kaleb by several reigns. The name Ezana was entirely forgotten in the Ge'ez tradition, and does not re-enter Aksumite historiography until the early 19th century, when the Englishman Henry Salt first read his name on a Greek inscription at Aksum.

Comparison of the measurements of the destroyed church of Zion in Jerusalem with those of the destroyed church of Maryam Seyon in Aksum offers little convincing evidence. For the church of Zion in Jerusalem, we have the report of a 19th century excavation with meagre results, and 'an Armenian Guide-Book, the core of which dates to the seventh century'.[14] For Maryam Seyon church we have measurements assumed from a survey of the present platform or terrace, without excavation, and some equivocal notes in the *Book of Aksum* (Appendix, 3). Patently, this is not enough. Survey and archaeological work are necessary before the dimensions of the different churches that have stood on the Aksum Seyon site can be reliably affirmed. The measurements supplied in the *Book of Aksum* may not even refer to the original church, but to one that had been radically altered since the time of Kaleb a thousand years before, or was even in ruins and partly restored.

Although we lack any pre-17th century examples of the text, when the *Book of Aksum* describes the Maryam Seyon church structure, it is usually assumed that it refers to the larger, older edifice destroyed by the Muslim incursion led by *imam* Ahmad Grañ around 1535.[15] At first, this attribution seems logical enough. Its many columns, and especially its 'monkey-heads', the protruding round beam ends characteristic of Ethiopian architecture, call to mind a substantial building of the typical Aksumite stone-and-wood style of architecture, very different from the much smaller Gondarine-style church that stands on (and partly incorporates) its ruins today. If a section of the *Book of Aksum* describes this early church, the origins of this section must surely date before 1535.

But in this part of the book, section 1, commemorations and decrees of kings are included taking the text to a much later time. One chapter dates to 1824. Though we know that the description of the church dates at least to the early 17th century, when Pais copied it, it contains details that, on reflection, seem highly suspect. True, an old-style Aksumite building seems to be described, but what a building…461 cedar doors, 168 windows, 780 *mankuarakuer* ('wheels', perhaps arches, although there are also 10 'rainbows' as well), apart from the 3815 'monkey heads'? These seem to suggest exaggeration, or even more or less unrestrained imagination at play. Buxton and Mathew tried to explain how some of these elements might have been included in the structure, but not very convincingly.[16] A glance at Beta Emanuel or Beta Medhane Alem at Lalibela, the most impressive surviving structures illustrating Ethiopian ecclesiastical architecture in the Aksumite tradition, shows that the figures for doors, windows and so on for the Aksum church exceed these other churches several times over. The number of doors in particular seems simply impossible in any imaginable form of church architecture. Most Ethiopian churches have three.

How can we explain these improbable figures? Rationally, we cannot expect to apply them to a real building, however splendid, in Ethiopia. There is, as in so much at Aksum, a mythical element to account for as well. Perhaps the text does not date from before 1535, and the description is an amalgam, with some make-believe as well. It might describe the restored, rather modest building of Sarsa Dengel, mingled with some details from old memories of the former church. Some fact there might be as well concerning the style ('monkey-heads', arches etc.), since the ruined walls of the older church, as we know from Portuguese descriptions, still stood long after it was burned. Sarsa Dengel's church was built within the still-standing skeleton of the much vaster old church. For some decades the ruins must have remained impressive symbols of former glories. From the miracles and wonders we read about in other parts of the *Book of Aksum*, we might expect equally unrestrained exaggeration when the old men of the city gathered to remember the vanished splendour of the former House of Zion.

We have to accept that the description of the church, though not entirely uninformative, hardly represents to our understanding a dependable summary of the church's dimensions, let alone indicating which stage of the building's history it describes. Bizarrely, two different widths are provided, 92 ells for the 'north-south' measurement, or 53 ells for the 'width'. Could these two measurements for the width indicate that the writer was not recording the pre-1535 church, but was actually describing the width of the two churches that occupied the plinth in Sarsa Dengel's time? One measurement may have derived from that emperor's own restored smaller building, standing amid the ruined walls of the larger older edifice destroyed by Grañ. This situation is described clearly by Almeida.[17]

In some ways, perhaps, Buxton and Mathews' restoration of the church on paper was unfortunate. It gave too much solid reality to what was, after all, mere theory. In their plans and elevations based on known Aksumite architectural forms combined with a contemporary but incompetent architectural description (Alvares), an exaggerated dream of the past (*Book of Aksum*), and a shaky theoretical comparison (church of the Redeemer, Lalibela), they created a wonderful composite structure that never existed. The reality is still buried there at Aksum, in the foundations that can be revealed, one day, by archaeology.

Although Marilyn Heldman cannot envisage that the Jerusalem church of Zion built in 340 could have been the inspiration for a church built by Ezana and Frumentius, she does suggest, in another place in the same book, that 'the original church, with its five aisles, may have been modelled on the Church of the Holy Sepulcher or one of the other great five-aisled Constantinian churches'.[18] All of these were built earlier than the church of Zion. But the need to search for a five-aisled precedent derives from an assumption: that the five-aisled church whose description we have from 1520 was the 'original', whether built by King Ezana or King Kaleb. The Ethiopians themselves, at Aksum, tell how the 10th century Queen Gudit destroyed the ancient church, and how King Anbasa Wudem restored it. They show the excavated remains of a structure below the podium of the present church as evidence. These ruins actually belong to earlier Aksumite buildings, but it is interesting that a local legend claims that an older church was destroyed well over half a millennium prior to the damage meted out by Ahmad G100 Grañ in 1535.

Even if the original church did have five aisles, and was built by Ezana, local architecture should not be dismissed as a possible precedent. At Yeha not far away, within the heartlands of the Aksumite domains, there still stands the great temple of Ilmuqah. Once, as modern excavations have only just shown us, a portico of six columns led by an entranceway into a *cella*, or square main chamber, in which a wider nave was flanked by two aisles on each side, the whole divided by four rows of three pillars each, with a sanctuary at the end. The structure, which seems to be modelled on the old temples of Ma'in in Arabia, was therefore five-aisled.[19] At a later date, a baptistery was constructed in the temple, and we suppose that it became, in effect, a five-aisled church. Even later, a smaller church dedicated to one of the Nine Saints, Abba Afse, was built inside the ancient walls. We have no idea when the pillars were removed and the temple disaffected from the old faith. Might it have been in the reign of Ezana, first Christian king of Aksum? It was perhaps a thousand years old by that time, and we do not know if it was maintained as a cult centre for the later gods of Aksum, or simply abandoned to other uses. In any event, we cannot exclude that the pillars still stood in Ezana's time, and that when he sought to build a house for his new deity he took the example from his own land. Even closer to Ezana's time, though we do not have a reliable date, the substantial 28 pillared halls of the Aksumite palace dubbed 'Enda Sem'on' by the German Aksum-Expedition were also five-aisled, with four rows of seven pillars each.

Aksumite architecture, very individual and local in spirit, was already well developed by Ezana's time. No monarch of Aksum was compelled to look elsewhere for architectural inspiration. Some, of course, did, as we know from other churches built in the apsidal basilica fashion, but this should not predispose us to assume that even from the very first they used this model unadapted to local forms. In fact, we can see from the excavated examples that when they did use it, they did so in structures whose exterior was of the Aksumite form, and even the basic internal arrangement of rows of pillars forming aisles is typical of Aksumite 'palace' buildings. The apses alone, gradually becoming important for the practise, might have necessitated innovation. What survives of the exterior of the early buildings on the Maryam Seyon site, including the base of the present podium itself, is Aksumite. Why should not the inspiration for the interior have derived from this same source too?

The truth is that we lack any genuine information whatsoever about the church of Mary of Zion during the whole of its existence until the 1520 description by Alvares, aside from occasional brief mentions in Ethiopian and foreign documentation which do little more than confirm the existence of a church there. The hints from c. 1400 are that it was richly decorated, and important. True, something can be inferred from the excavations just noted, and from the remaining traces of Aksumite walling below the church. What do these tell us? Merely that there was a building, apparently of domestic use, close beside and probably running underneath the present podium of the church, in pre-Christian Aksumite times, followed by another structure

9. Sunset light falls on the west front of Maryam Seyon church, Aksum, and its two flanking towers on the west terrace. Photo Pamela Taor.

also Aksumite in date – far earlier than the epoch when Anbasa Wudem and Gudit are supposed to have ruled. We have no proof, even, that these buildings were religious in purpose. On top of these earlier remains rises the present podium, embodying at least two building phases, one certainly of Aksumite date. On top of that, embracing some fragments of the interior walls of an older church, we have the church built by Sarsa Dengel, restored by Fasiladas, Iyasu II and others. We can, therefore, observe at least six building periods, and we have records of some at least of the various subsequent restorations. The archaeological potential of this site is enormous – but detailed information that will reveal the true story of the church's history and development can only be obtained when permission to excavate on and around the podium itself is granted. The likelihood of such permission seems to me slight, given the attitude of the Aksumite clergy to modern research: but if granted it will be a major step forward.

DEDICATION TO MARY OF ZION

A point of exceptional interest in Heldman's analysis concerns the dedication of the church. If the church were named for the Zion church in Jerusalem in Kaleb's reign, that of course does not even remotely imply the existence of a legend that the Ark was in Ethiopia at that time. But if we discount this theory of the Zion church as a forerunner, but nevertheless find evidence for a church dedicated to Mary of Zion early in Ethiopian history, it should at least make us wonder if the Ark legend really did exist at a very early date.

In the paragraphs I have cited from Marilyn Heldman's work, the jump from a supposed dedication to 'Zion' after the Jerusalem church on Mount Zion, to the radically different 'Mary of Zion' dedication, also attributed to Kaleb, is unexplained. It is simply taken for granted. The church of Mount Sion or Zion was held to be the first church in the world, and its name 'Mother of all Churches' was extant even by the 4th century. It was connected with the Last Supper, Pentecost and Mary, as it came to be believed that she had lived and died there, in the house that was the property of St. John. The church was not dedicated to Zion. It was merely built on Mount Zion, 'in honour of the Lord and of his Holy Mother', as a *Guide* of c. 1100 reports. Another *Guide* of about the same time mentions that the Mother of God passed away here, 'which accounts for the name of the church', and a third actually states that the church 'is called Saint Mary of Mount Sion, where the Most Blessed Lady physically died'.[20] But these are documents from a later stage. Was the church on Mount Zion dedicated at this very early stage to Mary? More important, even if it were, what reliable evidence do we have to demonstrate that a dedication to Mary, with an allusion to Mount Zion, was followed in Ethiopia too, whether by Ezana or by Kaleb?

As it happens, we do not know the dedications of any churches of the Aksumite period. An inscription of King Kaleb in the 6th century records the construction of a *maqdas* (sanctuary, holy place, church) in Himyar, and continues with the phrase: 'I built his *gabaz* and consecrated it by the power of the Lord'. Mary of Zion church is often called *gabaza Aksum*, the 'cathedral', literally, the guardian, of Aksum. It is certainly tempting to wonder if Kaleb might have built or restored the main church of his capital at this time, perhaps employing some of the plunder from his victory in Himyar in this pious work. But the mutilated inscription may refer to another *gabaz*, even one in Himyar where the churches had been destroyed by the Jewish monarch Yusuf.[21] In any case, this inscription supplies no evidence for either of the two components of the later dedication: Maryam or Seyon.

In Ethiopia, in due course, as elsewhere, Christian theologians identified the Ark of the Covenant containing the Law, with Mary, the symbolic 'Ark' that contained the new Law, Christ. In Ethiopia the Ark itself came to be designated Seyon, or Zion. Yet it has never been established that this link between Mary and the Ark, Seyon, was part of early Ethiopian Christian belief, nor is Seyon named in any early Ethiopian source worthy of confidence.

Strangely, perhaps, the earliest alleged citation of the name Mary associated with Aksum church is in a Muslim *hadith* attributed to the 9th century. This is one of the innumerable traditional tales concerning the life of the prophet Muhammad, some of which have become accepted on the strength of their *isnad*, or chain of transmission: X heard from X, who heard from X, back to someone more or less plausibly connected with the events in question. *Hadith* are notoriously unreliable, sometimes no more than legend or unfounded hearsay. Thousands have been rejected and weeded out by Muslim scholars themselves when faults in the *isnad* have been detected: al-Bukhari (c. 810–70) reduced 600,000 of them to just over 7000 that he thought acceptable. In this *hadith*, Muhammad listens to some of his wives' reports about Abyssinia, where they had once lived in exile.

The *hadith* is recorded by Ahmad bin Hajar al-Asqlani (d. 852 AH, 1448–49 AD) in his discussions about the *hadith* attributed to al-Bukhari. The *hadith* states that the prophet's wife Aisha said that another wife, Umm Salama, had told the Prophet that in the land of the Habasha (*fi ard al-habasha*), in a church called Maria, she saw pictures (*suwwar*) and statues (*tamathil*). The prophet told her: 'These people when one of their righteous ones dies they build a house of prayers on his grave and draw pictures in it. They are the bad people among the slaves of God.' The next *hadith* contains the prophet's saying: 'Allah cursed the Jews and the Christians who turned the graves of their righteous ones into mosques.'

What does the evidence of this report amount to? European writers have offered different versions of the *hadith*, themselves transforming it into something very much more definite than it really is.[22] It does not prove that the name 'Mary' was actually used of Aksum's main church in Muhammad's lifetime (he died, according to official Muslim history, in 632). It does not mention Aksum. It indicates only that the 9th century recorder of the *hadith*, two centuries after the event, attributed such a dedication to a church somewhere in Abyssinia. If the story is true, it *may* have been at Aksum, but not necessarily. The land was doubtless full of churches, and we have no proof that Umm Salama was living in Aksum, nor even, in fact, any proof that Aksum was still Ethiopia's capital at the time of the exile of the early Muslims to Ethiopia (the so-called 'first *hijra*'). The exiles may have been living in the port city of Adulis, or at some other spot in Ethiopia selected for their residence by the king or his officials. They may not been at the king's court, wherever it might have been. Aksumite churches certainly existed at this time in Adulis, at Matara, as well as at Aksum, and there is evidence for many more churches as yet unexcavated both in Eritrea and the Aksumite area of Ethiopia. Even at Aksum, several ancient church ruins are known to date, and we cannot guarantee that only the largest must have been the one dedicated to Mary.

The land grant in the *Book of Aksum* that refers to the church as 'our mother Seyon, guardian of Aksum' [*emmena Seyon, gabaza Aksum*] is valueless for dating purposes, being attributed to the legendary King Anbasa Wudem. The '*tabot* of Seyon', and the church of Dabra Seyon, attributed to Zagwé times by the 15th century *Gadla Na'akuto-La'ab*, offer more encouraging evidence. The word Seyon does appear, if rarely, in Zagwé settings that may be genuine enough. The title *qaysa gabaz Seyon*, in copies of Lalibela's land grants,[23] confirms the authentic use of 'Seyon' in Ethiopian records from Zagwé times. We can therefore give other attributions of this period the benefit of the doubt. But there is no indication, up to this time, of any 'Seyon' church at Aksum.

Contemporary with the Zagwé kings, in the Holy Land the name St. Mary of Zion denoted the ensemble of the Latin community possessions on Mount Zion. The Cenaculum included the chapel of the Ascension of Mary, and from this chapel of Mary on Mount Zion the whole sanctuary took its name of St. Mary of Zion. Johannes Phocas, in the 12th century, refers to the church on Mount Zion as 'the holy Zion, the mother of churches'. It has been suggested that it was this formula that came to be adopted in Ethiopia to designate the church of Maryam Seyon in Aksum.[24]

The earliest actual records of the dedication to 'Seyon' of a church that *might* be the one at Aksum appear only in 'Solomonic' dynasty times, specifically in the reign of Amda Seyon. 'Seyon' may by then have been a term used to denote the Habash kingdom, and the phrase 'church of Seyon' is included among the king's titles by Mamluk officials in Egypt. The term is ambiguous. 'Seyon' might signify Aksum church, which historical records of Amda Seyon's time mention on other occasions as well, using the unambiguous term *gabaza Aksum*, the 'cathedral' of Aksum, but unfortunately without supplying any further detail about its dedication. Or it could designate the Habash kingdom. It was just at this time that the *KN*, the great exponent of the glory of Zion in Ethiopia, is supposed to have been 'translated' by *nebura'ed* Yeshaq of Aksum. But the book describing the Ark's arrival and installation in Ethiopia is exceptionally unhelpful here. It alludes neither to Aksum nor to its church, only to Queen Makeda's mythical city of Dabra Makeda.

Could the element 'Seyon' included in the royal name of King Yigba Seyon, who ruled over Ethiopia from 1285, indicate that the dedication to Mary of Seyon church was extant right at the beginning of the Solomonic dynasty? The name is recorded in a 16th century copy of a grant in the *Golden Gospel* of Dabra Libanos, which supposedly dates from the reign of Yekuno Amlak. Yigba Seyon is entitled *ma'ekala bahr*, a vice-regal title of the highest rank, appearing next in position to the king himself. This person was very probably identical with Yekuno Amlak's son Yigba Seyon, who assumed the regnal name Solomon.[25] Perhaps the church of Maryam Seyon in Aksum, ancient imperial capital and original Christian centre of Ethiopia, aroused a certain interest among the first rulers of the new dynasty, those capable of exercising power over the northern region. Such interest might have led to the city's reinstatement as a national sacred centre after the fall of the Zagwé of Lasta, and Yigba Seyon could have adopted the name out of respect for the church. On the other hand, the name Seyon could reflect no more than the monarchy's well-attested Jerusalem interests. A letter of Yigba Seyon's to the Ethiopian monks at Jerusalem is preserved in Arabic records.[26]

A land grant of King Sayfa Arad mentions the name *gabaza Aksum* together with a commemoration of Mary, and another in the *Book of Aksum*, c.1352, bestows lands on the monastery of Madhanina Egzi. This grant records the gift of a place called Beta Seyon, 'House of Zion', in Sarawe. If it is not a later insertion – sometimes when two copies of such grants exist, one is augmented with a few more fiefs – the name 'House of Zion' confirms the existence of a church named for Seyon not far north of Aksum by the mid-14th century. A text of the 19th century listing various monkish genealogies confirms this, including, among the successors of St. Takla Haymanot, not only Madhanina Egzi of Bankol, but a certain Yemselanna Egzi of Sarawe Beta Seyon.[27]

King Zara Yaqob, Sayfa Arad's grandson, imposed over thirty new feasts for Mary on the Ethiopian church, and greatly encouraged her worship. He also granted land to 'our mother Seyon the cathedral of Aksum' for 'the commemoration of my Lady Mary'. This mid-15th century grant of the lands of Na'eder and Dagna – though still deriving from a later copy of the original grant – may be the first credible document to mention the two names Mary and Aksum Seyon together in Ethiopian records: eleven hundred years after the church's alleged foundation in 340 AD.

Allusions to Zion seem to increase in Zara Yaqob's reign. It was 'for the greatness of Zion' that the king scattered gold at his Aksum coronation. Zara Yaqob encouraged the wearing of icons with portraits of Mary, and one survivor shows an image of Mary with, written beside her, the words: 'By the power of Zion'.[28] In Zara Yaqob's time, too, it is claimed in one of the miracles of Mary that the king received a letter from the Coptic patriarch, John XI (1428–52), concerning the burning of the convent of Dabra Metmaq in Egypt by Sultan Barsbay: 'Weep for us, O faithful people of Ethiopia, for our perished glory! Weep for us for Our Mother Syon who nourished it at her breast, who perfumed it with the sweetness of her perfume.'[29] The allusion is, of course, to Mary.

To sum up, we find nothing to confirm an ancient foundation already dedicated to Mary of Zion in Aksumite times by King Ezana ('Abreha and Asbeha') or King Kaleb. *A priori*, there is no reason to be suspicious of a dedication to Mary instituted at the very foundation of the church, nor that it was the choice of Ezana and Bishop Frumentius. But, unfortunately, the early record of a church of Mary in Ethiopia from the 9th century *hadith* cannot with certainty be applied to Aksum. It is only much later – under King Sayfa Arad (1344–72) perhaps, provided the copies of the land grants in the *Book of Aksum* are accurately rendered from the originals – that the dedication to Mary is actually confirmed. As for the dedication to Seyon, it could have appeared by the reign of Amda Seyon, but we can only be absolutely sure for the time of Zara Yaqob. The pairing of names in the final dedication of the church was logical enough, considering the identity between the Ark of Zion and the Virgin Mary as expressed in the *KN*. It could have been implemented at any time after the development of that theology in Ethiopia.

The first European mention of the dedication to Mary occurs after 1450, in an itinerary that evidently derives directly from the c. 1400 *Iter de Venetiis ad Indiam*. The Dominican friar Pietro Ranzano, perhaps informed on this point by Pietro Rombulo, ambassador of the Ethiopian emperor in Italy, whom he met in 1450, adds to the rest of the details about the church at 'Chaxum', the dedication to the Virgin Mary.[30]

MARIOLATRY AND THE KEBRA NAGAST

What else can we deduce from the importance given to Mary from Sayfa Arad's time onwards? The *KN*, apart from several times naming 'our Lady Mary, the likeness of the heavenly Zion' (*KN* 95; see also 11, 17), constantly keeps Mary in view.[31] Is this strong Marian emphasis really the work of a group of Aksumite clerics under the aegis of their *nebura'ed* Yeshaq, in the time of Amda Seyon?

Similar identifications throng works of piety like the *Mashafa Berhan*, attributed to King Zara Yaqob himself. One section informs us that 'the Ark is the image of the womb of Mary…the tables of stone are the image of her breast, the Ark of the Law the image of her womb, the tabernacle of testimony the image of all within her body'. Another passage declares that 'the tables, on which were written the ten commandments, are the symbol of

Mary, virgin in thought and virgin of body and pure of soul'. Further writings attributed to the emperor or to his court ecclesiastics cite Hebrews 9:

> Furthermore, he [Moses] received from the hand of God the tables of the Law (*sellata hegg*) on which the Ten Commandments were written. He gave him an order to make a golden *tabot* so that he might place the slab in it. The golden *tabot* is indeed the likeness of Mary, and the tablet the likeness of her womb, and the Ten Commandments are the likeness of her Son, who is the Word of the Father. Paul saw Mary in reality with his bodily eyes. He likened her to the tabernacle (*dabtara*) of Moses, making his words agree with his. He said about her, 'And after the second veil there is the tabernacle which is called the holy of holies, having the golden censer and the *tabot* on which was the *Orit* (Law)'. [32]

Considering these texts of Zara Yaqob's time, together with the first certain connection of the dedications to Mary and to Zion at Aksum, the 'revived' Aksumite coronation instituted by Zara Yaqob, his three year residence at Aksum and his recorded legislation there, intriguing possibilities emerge. Might certain parts of the *KN* – those that emphasise the cult of Mary – owe their composition and insertion in the book to the time of the great Marian reform of Zara Yaqob, or perhaps even to the time of his father King Dawit I, who also propagated the worship of Mary? Dawit I was 'responsible for the giant step forward that the worship of Mary took in Ethiopia'. [33] The sections of the *KN* that I have cited, filled with allusions to Mary, might more satisfactorily be regarded as succeeding this newly emphasised Mariolatry in Ethiopia, than as its precursor by well over half a century. The addition of a new Marian emphasis would constitute a part of that continuous development that the book was subject to over the centuries.

THE ARK AT DABRA MAKEDA

The *KN* is extremely vague when it has to suggest an itinerary for the coming of the Ark to Ethiopia with Ebna Hakim. Indeed, the itineraries for the journeys of the merchant Tamrin, and of the queen of Sheba to Jerusalem and back to Ethiopia, are also very vague. Fuller accounts appear in certain later elaborations of the story, such as *Gadla Marqorewos*. [34] The route from Ethiopia to Jerusalem was well known to pilgrims in much later times.

Tamrin merely 'went' on his journey, without any further details, although we are told that he possessed both camels and ships. He could, then, have journeyed by land or by sea. He was charged to bring 'whatsoever he wished from the country of Arabia' (*KN* 17), a journey which would have of necessity involved shipping across the Red Sea. When, encouraged by Tamrin's extravagant praise of King Solomon, his queen herself decided to set out, camels, mules and asses were loaded, 'and she set out on her journey and followed her road without pause…' (*KN* 24). On her return, the queen's train included examples of every possible mode of transport, and one impossible at the time: 'camels and wagons, six thousand in number…and wagons wherein loads were carried over the desert, and a vessel wherein one could travel over the sea, and a vessel wherein one could traverse the air (or winds)…' (*KN* 30). Travelling south, the queen was overtaken by the pains of childbirth in the country of Bala Zadisareya (*KN* 32) – identified with Azhit Bela, near the Mai Bela river, in one of the later tales on this theme (see Chapter 5: Exotic Embroideries). After the birth of Bayna Lehkem (Ebna Hakim) the queen continued homewards.

When, as a young man, Ebna Hakim departed for Jerusalem to meet his father, the only travel details supplied concern his visit to Gaza, 'his mother's country' (*KN* 33–34). On his return with his company and the stolen Ark of the Covenant they set out with wagons, horses and mules. By the agency of the Archangel Michael everything was raised above the ground. They progressed 'like a ship on the sea when the wind bloweth, and like a bat through the air when the desire of his belly urgeth him to devour his companions, and like an eagle his body glideth above the wind' (*KN* 54). Ebna Hakim, who did not know the Ark was with them, appears to have noticed nothing remarkable in this unusual method of transport. The party halted by Gaza, and the next day (normally 13 days' march) reached the border of Gebes or Mesrin (Egypt). They next reached 'the water of Ethiopia…the Takkazi which floweth down from Ethiopia, and watereth the Valley of Egypt': the river Nile. Here the Israelite conspirators who had plotted to take the Ark finally revealed to Ebna Hakim that Zion was with them, and they celebrated there so that 'the Brook of Egypt was moved and astonished'. The wagons then rose up again, and passed before the people of Egypt 'like shadows' until they came to the Red Sea, which – bettering the passage of Moses – actually rose up and worshipped Zion as it passed over. It has been remarked that this passage of the Ark from Jerusalem to Ethiopia is represented by the *KN* as a 'new exodus', though in the opposite direction.[35] The party arrived at a place opposite Mount Sinai, and stayed in Qades. This was Kadesh in the wilderness of Paran near the borders of Edom (Numbers 13. 25; 20. 1, 14–16) the place (according to Numbers 20. 8–10 and *KN* 98) where Moses struck the rock for water, and where the Jews received the refusal of the king of Edom to pass through his territory.

According to the itinerary offered by the *KN*, the wagons were next loaded for the journey on to Medyam (Medyan or Midian, the northern Hejaz, to the east of the Gulf of Aqaba) and to 'Belontos, which is a country of Ethiopia' (*KN* 55). Conti Rossini – though he commented: 'inventato il personaggio, inventato il viaggio' – suggested that this might mean Ptolemais. *The Periplus of the Erythraean Sea* records a town called Ptolemais of the Huntings on the western Red Sea coast, but it seems unlikely that the compilers of the *KN*, or of whatever original they used for this part of the story, could have known this ancient name.[36]

Unlike Graham Hancock, who supposes that the Ark was destined to spend some time in the Jewish temple on Elephantine Island near Aswan in Egypt, Conti Rossini assumed that the compilers of the *KN* envisaged the journey mainly by sea. The *KN* certainly seems to confirm this as the author's intention, though without describing the actual stages very clearly. It has been remarked, in reference to possible routes by which the supposedly Jewish Falasha people might have come to Ethiopia, that 'the hypothesis of a Nile route…completely ignores the fact that the Nile, from Egypt to Ethiopia, has never been navigable'.[37] This might be true in the strict sense of travelling by ship along the Nile, but nevertheless visitors to Ethiopia did come using by a combination of the river and the land route from Egypt. The Egyptian bishop Mikael, for example, in 1648, and later Charles-Jacques Poncet and his companion Father de Brevedent, reached Ethiopia this way. They left the Nile at Asyut, crossed the Libyan desert, rejoined the Nile at Moscho, then travelled on to Dongola, Korti, Gerri and Sinnar, and turned east to Gondar. The armies of Sinnar and Ethiopia, too, raided each other's lands using the southern part of this route, while journeys between Egypt and Sinnar, though perhaps disagreeable, were certainly not impossible. Bruce took the Sinnar route on his return. It tended to be unpleasant, but it was practicable.

While the Ark was on its way south, the *KN* indicates that King Solomon was meanwhile desperately trying to trace the route the Ethiopians had taken with Zion. He sent people to Egypt, some of whom went on to the Eritrean Sea (Red Sea). He himself went to Gaza, then to a place where he met and questioned an emissary of Pharaoh, who had seen the travellers passing. The

Egyptian nobleman had journeyed from Alexandria to Cairo, where he had met the Ethiopians. He confirmed that the fugitives with the Ark had reached Cairo after 'a passage of three days on the Takkazi, the river of Egypt' (*KN* 59). After this, the *KN* turns to other themes until *KN* 84–85, when the story is resumed – forgetting all the previous details of the itinerary – with the news that the wagons had journeyed in a single day from Jerusalem to the city of Waqerom. In Conti Rossini's account, this is identified with Uachiro, which is spelled Wik'ro on modern maps and lies c. 30km northwest of Massawa by the coast. From there, messengers were sent by ship to Ethiopia to alert the queen about the imminent arrival of the Ark. The queen came to the 'city of the Government, which is the chief city of the kingdom of Ethiopia':

> now in later times this [city] became the chief city of the Christians of Ethiopia…and her son came by the 'Azyaba road to Wakerom, and he came forth to Masas and ascended to Bur, and arrived at the city of the Government, the capital [city] of Ethiopia, which the Queen herself had built and called 'Dabra Makeda', after her own name…And pavilions and tents were placed at the foot of Dabra Makeda on the flat plain by the side of good water…and they set Zion upon the fortress of Dabra Makeda…

It is difficult to divine exactly what Yeshaq and his collaborators intended to say here. Masas seems likely to be the port of Massawa on the Red Sea, from

10. A *tankwa* or papyrus boat like this may have brought the Ark in flight to a safe haven on Lake Tana, if Ethiopian legends relate the truth. Photo Pamela Taor.

which one does pass through part of Bur on the way to the highlands. Bur, recorded under King Zara Yaqob and later as a province of the *bahrnagash*, ruler of the coastal area and northern Tigray, is now part of Akele Guzay in Eritrea. Bur is, in fact, associated with the Ark in another way, being the region where the Ark sought shelter from the Catholics during the reign of Emperor Susneyos (see Chapter 5: The Flight of the Ark).

The 'chief city of the Christians of Ethiopia' can hardly be anywhere else but Aksum. If so, Aksum is firmly identified here as Dabra Makeda. Or could this phrase signify Yeha? Here, supposedly – or so Alvares was told – was a city of the queen of Sheba and of Queen Candace, the conversion of whose eunuch treasurer is held by the Ethiopians to herald the conversion of their country. It is not difficult to imagine how the oldest, largest and best-preserved ancient structure in Ethiopia, the temple at Yeha, might have been attributed to Queen Makeda by the 'translator'-compiler of the *KN*. Interestingly, Henry Salt recorded a legend related to him by priests and local people that the Ark was once installed at Yeha for a period before moving on to Aksum.[38]

Makeda and the queen of the South are at times specifically associated with Aksum. In the *Book of Aksum*, Queen Makeda is said to have founded the city (of Aksum) 'a second time', building it in the territory of 'Aseba. One of the Bruce manuscripts of the *KN*, Bodleian MS 93 even provides a note that identifies the queen of Sheba directly with Aksum; 'the patrimony and country of birth of the Queen of the South is Aksum, for she originates from there'.[39] But apart from this explanatory gloss in one copy of the work, it is astonishing that the *KN* never otherwise mentions Aksum, even though the 'translator' of the book into Ge'ez was Yeshaq, *nebura'ed* of Aksum.

Could this imply that Aksum was *not* the place originally implied by the name 'Dabra Makeda'? Both Yeha and Aksum can be said to possess a 'fortress', or fortifiable hill, and a plain with good water nearby, and both towns were capital cities of ancient Ethiopian polities – D'amat and Saba, and the kingdom of Aksum and Habashat respectively. Jean Doresse thought that the *KN* was perhaps written at Dabra Libanos of Ham in Shimezana, Eritrea, and that Dabra Makeda was the place called Makeda in that region. Ancient ruins are still visible there.[40] This is Gulo Makeda, a name that Conti Rossini associates with the Mocadà and the Golò; the name was known in the 14th century, appearing in the *Gadla Basalota Mikael*. Conti Rossini speculated about a possible connection between this name and the name given to the queen of the South in the *KN*, as well as to her capital Dabra Makeda, which was, he considered, 'not identifiable with Aksum'. He thought Dabra Makeda should be sought in eastern Ethiopia, citing the *Book of Aksum*, which affirms that Makeda moved the capital, and built at 'Aseba (presumably Hasebo, the plain east of Aksum).[41]

The writers or recorders of the different Ge'ez legends were evidently themselves thoroughly confused about what was meant, and citing one legend as a gloss to another is not likely to prove very fruitful in 'identifying' what is anyway a mythical city. Today the story of Dabra Makeda has taken another turn, and recently 'oral tradition' has been found to identify the hill called Beta Giyorgis at Aksum with Dabra Makeda. Conti Rossini did not know this. Littmann did not report it either, and none of the Aksumites I have asked recall the name in association with Beta Giyorgis. It is, however, found in Girma Elyas' book on Aksum, and now is appearing in other reports as a 'traditional' name…another example of the way the old legends can be easily accommodated in the Aksumite ambiance.[42]

In the accounts of the wars waged by Menelik I other details occur, not too helpful either in trying to fix the whereabouts of the 'city of the Government'. During the Zawa and Hadeya campaign, the army camped first at Maya 'Abaw after leaving the city, reaching Zawa and Hadeya the next morning. If Hadeya is indeed the province of Hadya, well south of Addis Ababa and west of Lake Zway, the journey was as miraculous as that which the Ark had previously experienced on its way to Ethiopia via Egypt. They then returned to the 'city of Zion', remaining three months before going with their wagons to the 'city of the Government' (*KN* 94). From there they went on in one day to the city of Saba (Meroë?), which, with Noba, they laid waste. Returning again to the 'city of the Government' they emerged to encamp in 'Abat and wage war on the king of India. This section of the *KN*, in contrast to that cited above, seems to suggest that the 'city of Zion', was actually different from 'the city of the Government'. Again, the 'city of Zion' (presumably the place where Zion resided) can hardly be envisaged to mean anywhere else but Aksum, dwelling place of the Ark of the Covenant, which the earlier text tells us was installed 'upon the fortress of Dabra Makeda' – the city of the Government!

The 'old wrinkled priest' Gabra Wahed, from whom Littmann obtained some of his 'history of Aksum', stated that when the Ark reached Aksum it remained for forty years outside the city in the open. Later, in the time of

Abreha and Asbeha, a sanctuary was built in the city, and the Ark was brought into it, 'where it is now'.[43]

WANDERINGS OF THE ARK

The *KN* restricts the Ark to Dabra Makeda, and perhaps by inference to 'the city of Zion'. It never mentions that the Ark may have at times gone elsewhere. In later times Ethiopian tradition has always directly associated it with Aksum and the church of Maryam Seyon, even if, as we have seen, evidence for its residence there is lacking.

Did the Ark occasionally wander in Ethiopia? Tradition reports that it did, several times. There are several places where the Ark is supposed to have dwelt when the stresses of the times made Aksum, the holy city and its supposed selected dwelling place, a dangerous haven. Some of these peregrinations have been briefly noted above, on three occasions when the Ark – the sacred relic at Aksum church – had to flee from its sanctuary. The first of these is the legendary flight of the Ark to Dabra Seyon on an island in Lake Zway, to escape the *razzia* of Queen Gudit. Later, more authoritative records recall that the 'Ark' (in two different guises) had to flee twice more, once to Tabr in Lebna Dengel's time, and once to Digsa in Bur when the priests feared troubles for it from Emperor Susneyos' Catholicism (see Chapter 5: The Flight of the Ark). In addition, the British envoy Henry Salt, at Yeha in 1810, related that the priests and local people told him various tales about the local saint, Abba Afse, and about the buildings at Yeha. One story claimed that the Ark of the Covenant had been kept there for a period before it was taken to Aksum.

The flight to Zway is mentioned in the recent composite chronicle assembled by *qese gabaz* Takla Haymanot. It occurred, if we believe the tale, when Queen Gudit came to Aksum, destroyed the palace and church, banned Christian worship, and exiled the Levite priests:

> And Zion, the tabernacle of Law (*tabota hegg*), was exiled with them, and came into a region towards the east which is called Zway and was deposited there with all due respect and in a clean abode under a vigilant watch for forty years. After forty years Gudit died and Anbessa Wedem came to the throne and then peace and order were restored. The Levite priests returned to their country, Aksum, with Zion, the tabernacle of Law, with great honour and much joy, in the year of Mercy, 910.[44]

The date is about half a century out according to the Arabic evidence about the life of the late 10th century queen who conquered Abyssinia. Sergew Hable Selassie adds that 'according to tradition, the tabernacle was placed on the biggest island in this lake, Debre Sen (i.e. Däbrä Seyon). On the basis of this legend, the Aksum church has been granted land near the lake' – land presumably by now confiscated.

Another story relates that the Ark journeyed to an island on Lake Tana, remaining there for a certain period. Graham Hancock, ignoring the contemporary evidence of the *Futuh al-Habasha*, states that at the time of Ahmad Grañ's attack in 1535 the Ark went to Lake Tana, instead of to Tabr, and that it was reinstated in its previous place 'with due ceremony', by Emperor Fasiladas (1632–67).[45] In fact, although one assumes that the stone taken to Tabr did come back, there is no account of this reinstallation anywhere in the records, and it is unlikely to have been due to Fasiladas. Fasiladas is known from Barradas' report to have brought the '*Tabot* or Sion of Accum' back not from Tabr (or Tana) but from Bur, in 1633, and to have restored the church. When in 1655 it was consecrated, his daughter Yodit, 'carried on clouds of love for Our Lady Maryam Seyon *gabaza Aksum*', was present at the reception of the *tabot* (the object returned from Bur in 1633, or another *tabot* dedicated to Mary of Zion?) and its entry into the sanctuary.

An earlier emperor must have brought the holy relic back before Susneyos' reign. The most likely candidate is Sarsa Dengel, who was crowned at Aksum in 1579 in the presence of 'Zion the *tabot* of the Lord of Israel', and had a smaller church constructed in the ruins of the ancient one. Hancock's theory takes no note of the Ethiopian records, supported by Manoel Barradas and Balthasar Telles, telling how the sacred object had to flee a second time, around 1620, to Digsa in Bur. This clearly indicates that it had returned to the church in the interim (see Chapter 5: The Flight of the Ark) – unless one imagines that it was somehow lost, and that some new 'casket'-like version had replaced it.

The story of the Lake Tana connection, a version sometimes heard in Ethiopia in opposition to the Tabr version of the *Futuh al-Habasha* or the Bur/Digsa version of Barradas, Telles and the *Book of Aksum*, was apparently taken from archpriest Solomon Gabra Selassie, the London-based Ethiopian cleric. He informed Hancock that the Ark had been taken to Daga Estifanos, one of the island monasteries in the lake. This claim seems to have originated from fact: there was indeed a *tabot* of Seyon on Daga. One of the Daga

Estifanos manuscripts contains a note indicating that in the time of Abreha and Asbeha the *tabota Maryam Seyon* stayed (?) in Daga church for twenty years. More factually, two other manuscripts containing parts of a *Senkessar synazarium* that once belonged to Dabra Daga confirm the presence there of a *tabot* of Seyon. The manuscripts were bought by a certain Ma'qaba Egzi, and offered to the *tabota Seyon* at Daga.[46]

In this context of legends about the Ark and Lake Tana, it is possible that one of the 'maps' found occasionally in Ethiopian manuscripts, including copies of the *KN*, might allude to this purported residence of the Ark in the Tana region. Alula Pankhurst has published some of these curious maps.[47] One, for example, is in the manuscript containing the *KN* and the *Mashafa Aksum* (*Book of Aksum*) which was returned by the British Museum to Emperor Yohannes IV and was later given to the Raguel church at Entotto (Addis Ababa). It is interleaved between these two books, after the *KN* and before the *Mashafa Aksum*.

The oldest of these maps – which are circular in design and represent Aksum at the centre of concentric rings with divisions in which the names of other districts of Tigray and Eritrea are written – came from the monastery of St. Gabriel, on Kebran Island in Lake Tana. It dates to the late 18th century. Unlike any of the other examples found until now, it includes, within the central circle where Aksum's name appears, and written around the name, a cryptic sentence: 'In the seventh month after she went out from Ethiopia, she entered an island of Tana by reason of the conflict of the seven men who were in Tigray.' Because of its position, right in the centre of the map and directly associated with Aksum, and because the manuscript was found on an island in Tana, it seems that this text might allude to the Ark of the Covenant, and to the legend of its sojourn in the Tana region.

An otherwise unknown tale is tantalisingly alluded to in the reference to the 'seven men who were in Tigray'– unless, by some remote chance, this episode could refer to the time of the fall of the Zagwé, when 'six strong men' and *negus* Delanda seem to have ruled in the northeastern sector of Tigray in 1268.[48] It has been suggested that Delanda was a last scion of the Zagwé, clinging on to power, but since he is only attested here in the north, perhaps he was really a northern princeling trying for independence?[49] Could the story have emerged from the unrest of this period, when Zagwé power collapsed, with regional rulers like Delanda in the north and Yekuno Amlak in the south seizing territory? Is the Tana story pure myth to try to claim the

Ark to the credit of the Tana monasteries, or did something concrete gave rise to the story, such as the taking of a venerated *tabot* (of Seyon?) from 'Ethiopia' (i.e. Tigray?) to a place of refuge in Tana? In other times of difficulty, this was certainly done, and manuscripts and other treasures found a place of safety on the islands.

Graham Hancock, in the course of an expedition to Lake Tana with Richard Pankhurst, also heard another version of the Tana story, this time claiming that the Ark had remained for 800 years on Tana Qirqos island, until removed by King Ezana.[50] It had been brought there by Menelik I 800 years before by way of the Nile and the (un-navigable) Takkaze river. The story seems to be an amalgam of information from the *KN* and more modern accounts (Ezana's name was not known to older Ge'ez sources), and its chronology is evidently very confused. It was this tale – which, bizarrely, he considered 'by far the purest and most convincing' of the traditions he had come across in Ethiopia – that led Hancock to reject the *KN* story. He proposed instead, like Guidi long before, that Jews of Elephantine Island in Egypt could have been involved. Guidi had suggested that these Jews might have been the originators of the Jewish traits in Ethiopia. Hancock enlarged on this now-rejected theory, suggesting that fleeing Jews from Elephantine had brought the Ark, which had formerly been housed in their temple on the island, around BC 470, and installed it at Tana Qirqos. Hancock was even shown stones, supposed to be those where the blood sacrifices were made, at the tabernacle on Tana Qirqos in which the Ark was installed.

7

The 'Ark' at Aksum Seyon? Conclusions

The Ark at Aksum retains its impenetrable seclusion, as empires, dictatorships, civil wars and ever increasing misery under inadequate government come and go in Ethiopia. My quest to discover its past history, both in the real world and in the paranormal world of the imagination, in religion or in myth, has come to an end. All the obvious avenues of approach to the true story of the Ark at Aksum have been explored.

What was the Ark in Ethiopia, and what is it today? Can this question now be resolved? I believe that it can, without wild guesswork or straining ordinary credibility. The final picture, despite the intricacy and complexity of the evidence, is clearer than might be expected – though with the caveat that at any moment a new document might emerge from some little-known church treasury, or mountain or island monastery, to amend or augment it. I outline here some hypotheses – some notions about how and why the claim arose that the Ark of the Covenant is at Aksum, and what is in the chapel of the Tablet of Moses in Maryam Seyon church compound today. Perhaps only the guardian of the Ark can offer more.

ROYAL PROPAGANDA

The regal propaganda machine of Solomonic Ethiopia was startlingly effective in its long-term results. As in so many places where education is not universal, the written word has enormous power. It can be produced with a flourish as material evidence when necessary. The older it grows, the more venerable, even if modern textual criticism can often result in an entirely different story. An old book, claiming even older origins via exotic places and languages, and written, allegedly, by authors of revered status, gains ever more respect. By these means the final version of the royal myth of Ethiopia, written in the *KN* or 'Glory of Kings', assumed a quasi-biblical status among Christians in that country. It was not just read and copied, but believed and venerated. The last word added is credited on equal terms with the first, and the whole is envisaged as an unchanged original document despite constant updatings.

This book that took several centuries to complete is the living proof of how, in combination with the church, the Solomonic dynasty created a politico-religious manifesto for its rule that remained enshrined in the very heart of the state until 1974. Its basic premises were actually written into the mid-20th century Constitution of the Ethiopian empire. But this age-old polity needed more than myth to prolong its existence. It collapsed into complete ruin with the 1974 Revolution.

Although the political structure went, bloodily, the religious constituent still remains more or less intact. This is not to say that the Ethiopian Orthodox Church did not suffer badly after 1974. It did, and it still suffers in the sense that it has lost its established status, and its huge land holdings. Yet otherwise it maintains its strong grip on the minds and hearts of the Ethiopian people, particularly in the non-urban areas of the country. In revolutionary times many Ethiopians abandoned the church. It seemed fossilised, hand in glove with a decaying empire, its hierarchy and barely educated priesthood incapable of reflecting newer aspirations. Yet the horrors of the Mengistu régime offered little of ideological value to compete with it, particularly as the revolution progressed from bloodbaths to forcible deportations and famine on an even greater scale than before. Manifestly, the Ethiopian revolution was controlled by no inspired or even more-or-less competent leader. For the poor of Ethiopia, to whom perhaps a socialist government might once have represented hope, the path from bad to worse must have swiftly obliterated any such anticipation. Under the circumstances, for many Ethiopians the ancient religion remained the true repository of hope, and the preserver of many elements of the national (in the restricted sense of Christian Ethiopian) culture.

Respect for the church was deeply ingrained, and hard to shake off. During that revolutionary time, I remember seeing, in the streets of Addis Ababa, armed soldiers wearing the Red Star on their caps sweeping these off to bow profoundly when a *tabot* was carried by on great festival days. The Revolution could go only so far. Women robed in white prostrated themselves in the dust before the Communist Party headquarters, bowing through the ephemeral towards the eternal, represented by the Trinity church behind. Perhaps there is now an increasing urban indifference to the traditional church (though scarcely in Aksum). Protestant and evangelical churches, with different values, are rapidly increasing their influence –incredibly rapidly, tapping a vein of profound faith that the traditional church cannot satisfy. But among the people of the villages and the countryside, the old church is still a vital element in their lives. If one asks in Aksum, 'Why didn't Mengistu or his people come and take the Ark, or investigate what it was?', the answer is: 'They would not dare. All Tigray would have risen.' In the end, of course, Tigray did rise, but this was out of pure hatred for the régime, which the Tigray fighters, together with their Eritrean allies, finally destroyed.

Step by step, the so-called Solomonic kings and their priestly helpers constructed an ideological edifice which the vast majority of Christian Ethiopians still believe with complete faith has been in place for thousands of years. They have now adjusted to a land without an emperor, and one part of the old myth has been, if not quite discarded (Ras Tafarianism is a new manifestation of the power of the old story), at least shelved. Yet originally, and for some time, the two aspects ran perfectly in tandem: God and the king of kings, the Church and the State, Ethiopia-Israel and the rest of the world.

The Ethiopian regal-religious myth did not spring up fully formed. Like any other such manifestation it developed over time, adjusting its concepts as events moved on and new requirements were perceived. Ignoring the Christian Aksumite era, about which we know little beyond the fact that the Christian faith settled deeply into the land and its regal institutions, the earliest individualising aspect to develop seems to have been an inclination to Old Testament customs. By the 1080s, this aspect was sufficiently evident to worry the Egyptian metropolitan, Severus, and elicit a letter of admonishment from the Alexandrian patriarch to the king. Just over a century later, the association of the Zagwé kings with a dynastic ancestry from Israelite sources is recorded. Abu Salih wrote that they claimed descent from the family of Moses and Aaron. This theory (if we can trust Abu Salih's statement – no reliable evidence from Ethiopia beyond the reported devotion to the Old Testament supports it) drew Israel and Zagwé-ruled Ethiopia closer together, and bestowed upon the Zagwé monarch an extremely illustrious biblical pedigree. The New Jerusalem of Lasta at Roha or Adefa may or may not have originated with Lalibela, but if the 15th century *Zena Lalibela,* the king's own life story, reports the truth, it could have been employed by him to symbolise a powerful new element in the official view of the state – the Israel connection.

There may have been innovations in church ritual as well. The Ethiopians by Lalibela's time apparently employed a type of box-like portable altar called a *tabot* ('ark', chest). They perhaps also used the altar/tablet (*sellat,* later universally called *tabot*). The object that Abu Salih called the 'Ark of the Covenant' (*tabutu al-'ahdi*), which was carried, veiled, in processions in the Zagwé royal city, was one of these portable box-altars. A clerical title including the word Seyon recorded during Lalibela's reign might, just possibly, hint at some official recognition of this *tabot* as a symbol of the 'Ark', the *tabota Seyon,* but this seems unlikely – there is no recorded sequel to such a notion for hundreds of years. We have seen that King Na'akuto-La'ab completed a church named for Mount Zion begun by Lalibela – this is the claim, at least, by a semi-legendary hagiography – furnishing a possible alternative explanation for the Zagwé period title *qaysa gabaz Seyon.* At any rate, the allusions to Zion in Zagwé records incline to confirm the Jerusalem/Israel connection so much vaunted by Abu Salih and in the *Zena Lalibela.*

After a shaky start in the time of the first Zagwé ruler, who tried illegally to replace the aged Metropolitan Michael because he protested against his usurpation of the crown, it seems that church and state functioned together well under the Zagwé. Three Zagwé kings are remembered as saints in the Ethiopian church. Contemporary accounts record that in Lalibela's reign an erring metropolitan was punished by the Alexandrian patriarch after due investigation and correspondence between prelate and king. Lalibela may well have had contact with Jerusalem. We know that in 1200 he sent messengers to the ruler of Egypt, Saladin's brother al-'Adil, who also controlled Jerusalem, and again sent gifts in 1210. We cannot be sure, however, that the Ethiopian convent at Jerusalem, or the chapels of the Ethiopians in the church of the Holy Sepulchre, existed at this time.

The next phase of myth creation was obliged to take into account a major alteration in circumstances. The dynasty of saints credited with creating the

New Jerusalem in Lasta fell. Newcomers seized power. There are hints that monastic support helped promote this new order. Powerful encouragement for the new aspirant to the throne, Yekuno Amlak, is attributed to the great abbot of Hayq, Iyasus Mo'a (supposedly son-in-law of a Zagwé king, and raised to the abbacy also by the Zagwé), and later to St. Takla Haymanot. It was alleged that the cohesion of interest between these two elements was to free Ethiopia from 'those who were not Israelite', but what the reality actually was is too well buried by the later literature – or in the lack of it on the Zagwé side – for us to disinter. Zagwé hagiographies like those of Lalibela and Na'akuto-La'ab were written when the Solomonic dynasty was well in the ascendant, and were tailored to cater for that fact. They advance the unlikely claim that certain Zagwé kings, including Lalibela himself, actually wanted to hand power back to the 'legal' or 'Israelite' dynasty after their deaths.

That there was a power struggle, perhaps regional and racial, Lasta Agaw against semiticised Amhara, perhaps supported by the Egyptian church on one side and the Ethiopian monasteries on the other, is evident from its results. Tigray may have stood to one side, ready to seize independence if possible, during this conflict. Legend claims (in the *Be'ela Nagast* and *Gadla Iyasus Mo'a*, for example) that this alliance of monastic leader and aspirant to the throne concluded with the gift of one third of the country to the church, a sort of Donation of Constantine in an Ethiopian context. If there were such an alliance, it seems to have been with certain local ecclesiastics only. The patriarchate in Alexandria was not apparently in sympathy with these new kings, very probably regarding them as usurpers from the Zagwé, with whom they had dealt amicably for generations. To such an extent was this dispute pursued that even into the second reign of the new dynasty the emperors still retained Syrian metropolitans, in breach of canon law as it was accepted both by Alexandria and Ethiopia.

With the change of power, the mythmakers set to work to serve the new masters. We cannot be sure, so meagre is the evidence, what were the first elements they shaped. The new dynasty evidently valued the Israelite, Jerusalem connection, and it was not allowed to drop. Indeed, it was to develop into a cornerstone of the edifice they were to construct. This is suggested clearly enough right at the beginning of the rule of the Amhara princes, by the name assigned to Yekuno Amlak's son, Yigba Seyon, by the latter's adoption of the name Solomon as his regnal title and by his correspondence with the Ethiopian monks already installed in Jerusalem. Yet the successors of the Zagwé needed to reject the Zagwé claims (as Abu Salih states them) to descent from Moses and Aaron. A new myth had to be contrived embodying the best of the old, and if possible surpassing it.

Claims to descent from 'the former kings' were evidently not hard to construct. Whatever antecedents Yekuno Amlak had, it cannot have been difficult – when the dynasty had consolidated its power – to slot his father and ancestors into an older dynastic connection. Possibly there really was some claim to a line of descent through a former king. We know from the *History of the Patriarchs* that a usurper ruled in Ethiopia in 1152, not long after the traditional date for the advent of the Zagwé, 1137. Yekuno Amlak's claim might have derived genuinely from a pre-Zagwé royal house that reigned over 130 years before. Whatever the case, legitimacy was conferred by a genealogy asserting Aksumite ancestral claims either genuine or spurious, or perhaps even a part of both, something tenuous being strengthened into something firmer.

More mystical elements in the royal mythology were developed. The mythmakers may have turned their minds to Ethiopia's place in the biblical world. Exploiting the claim by the state that was the successor of Aksum and Habasha to all mentions of 'Ethiopia' (Kush) in the Bible – in reality referring to the Meroitic Ethiopia of the *kandake* (queen of Meroe in Sudan) – there was already a rich harvest of attributions. Psalm 68.31, 'Princes shall come out of Egypt; Ethiopia shall stretch forth her hands to God' became a particular favourite, indicative of Ethiopia's special place in the divine plan. It even became true, in a certain sense, since Christian Ethiopia has over the ages 'stretched out her hands to God' under pious kings like Kaleb of Aksum, some of the Solomonic rulers (the phrase occurs in Amda Seyon's chronicle) and Yohannes IV. Verses of this sort, evoking the biblical Ethiopia, throng the *KN* and other Ge'ez writings. Most Ethiopian Christians today would apply them unquestioningly to modern highland Ethiopia, not to a defunct state worshipping its own and some of the ancient Egyptian gods that once held sway in what is now Muslim Sudan.

A brilliant association was to improve even on this. From the time of Michael of Tinnis, writing in the *History of the Patriarchs of Alexandria* in the 11th century, and possibly even before, the queen of Sheba has been connected with Habasha/Abyssinia. Undoubtedly tales of the queen and her meeting with Solomon circulated widely, and some of them included speculation that there had been offspring of their union. The idea that the queen was from Ethiopia had been noted in Zagwé times by Abu Salih, but was not included in his account of the dynasty's royal mythology (though subsequently, perhaps during a period of anti-Solomonic protest, the queen of Sheba's maidservant was employed to give the Zagwé, too, a Solomonic claim). Now the queen's supposed origin offered a golden opportunity.

Some ingenious scholar – possibly Yeshaq, *nebura'ed* of Aksum – knew well how to exploit the material at hand. Staggering claims were made. They may not have been made at first on behalf of the Amhara dynasty that eventually came to enshrine them, but for another ambitious line, the 'dynasty' of Intarta, under whose aegis the *nebura'ed* Yeshaq of Aksum worked, and – we may guess – with whose political aims he was closely connected. The Amhara monarchy at this time was already associated with Jerusalem, and a monastery was maintained there. Next, with the falling into their hands of the possessions of the Intarta dynasty 'as far as the cathedral of Aksum' around 1322, together with the book that *nebura'ed* Yeshaq had written or developed, the dynasty could turn Yeshaq's work to its own benefit. The Amhara monarchy had found the myth it needed, and became 'Solomonic' and 'Israelite'. With the incorporation of the story of Ebna Hakim into its mythology Yekuno Amlak's dynasty came to physically embody the descent of the Jerusalem dynasty of David and Solomon, and the legacy of Israel itself. There may already have existed a tendency in Ethiopia to regard royalty and divinity as closely associated, perhaps even harking back to the old days of Aksum when King Ezana called himself 'son of [the god] Mahrem'.[1]

Mystery shadows the process by which possession of the tablet(s) of Moses came to be added to the fabulous connection between King Solomon and the queen of Sheba. By whom this was first asserted, and when, we do not know. Characteristically, developments in the *KN* story were added little by little as time went on – each new 'update version' advanced the thesis, becoming the accepted edition as books wore out and new copies were made. Different versions will have existed at the same time, and in different milieux. In the 1420s European legend, surely based on tales emanating from Ethiopia, already asserted that King Yeshaq possessed the tablets of Sinai. In the 1540s, the tablets travelled with a tent-church of the royal chapel, if we believe the note added from Ethiopian informants in Archbishop Beccadelli's version of Francisco Alvares' book. Contemporary with this, illogically enough, the tablets rather than the Ark are included in early versions of the *KN* story that have come down to us from Saga Za-Ab and João de Barros. This implies that they ought to have been the holy object at Maryam Seyon church, where it is claimed that the sacred talisman is none other than what came with Ebna Hakim from Jerusalem.

We are dealing here with developing strands of legend, intertwining or diversifying as time passed. It may have been in the interval between the reigns of Yeshaq and Lebna Dengel that the tablets first entered the *KN* story, while remaining outside it on another plane. With the identification between *tabot* and tablet of the Ten Commandments, the holy objects could easily reduplicate themselves. So it is that in mid-16th century Ethiopia we find the sacred relic taken from Jerusalem – the tablets of the Law, according to Saga Za-Ab – and supposed by Ethiopian tradition to have been kept for long ages in Aksum church, functioning also among the *tabotat* of the royal camp.

Abu Salih's claim that Ethiopia possessed the Ark of the Covenant in Zagwé times resulted from a mistaken translation of the word *tabot*. At most, this 'Ark' may have been a portable altar consecrated in the name of Seyon, which, with its servants alleged to be descendants of David, was part of the Judaising of local tradition. At any rate, it was forgotten – though of course it remained in the Arab Christian setting of Abu Salih's book, perhaps occasionally to be wondered at and mulled over; and perhaps one day to bear a new offshoot in another Arabic tale.

Unlike the tablets, the Ark was not part of the cycle of Ethiopian Solomon and Sheba stories related by Saga Za-Ab and João de Barros; Alvares' short account mentions neither tablets nor Ark. The story that seems to have been accepted for several centuries was that kings of the House of David, descendants of Solomon and the queen of Sheba, kin to the family of Jesus Christ himself, sat upon the throne of David in Ethiopia, and in their possession was a great talisman: the tablet(s) of Moses. They ruled their people, the Children of Israel, the true Israel, in the new Zion, Ethiopia. Their authority was shadowed and hedged about by a quasi-divinity.

Further accretions augmented the legend. In the official literature, apparently by Zara Yaqob's time at the latest, Ethiopia had become Zion: Seyon, the kingdom of the descendants of Solomon. The country's most ancient church, the church of the formerly glorious capital of Aksum, regained its decayed prestige as it came to be accepted that its altar tablet was a gift of the apostles, deriving from Mount Zion itself. Possibly it was this very stone – which from about 1520, following Alvares' description, we can properly call the *tabota Seyon*, or altar stone of Zion – that was to be identified as the tablet of Moses, brought in Ebna Hakim's company to Ethiopia. The church in Aksum, and the entire land, adopted the name of Zion. The church was also dedicated to Mary, possibly an early dedication, or possibly in tandem with the newly intensified worship of Mary that began perhaps as early as the reign of Sayfa Arad, increased under King Dawit I, and culminated in a tremendous upsurge of compulsory devotion under the most famous of the mediaeval emperors, Zara Yaqob.

Although there must certainly have been a conscious adoption of the splendid claims outlined above, it was not necessarily always mere cynical exploitation of popular credulity to maintain power. At some time in the early Solomonic period, the dynastic legend seems to have become accepted as genuine, both by those who claimed Solomonic descent, and by those whom they ruled. In their remote highlands, far from the rest of the Christian world, these kings who fought constantly against the Muslims and the local 'Jews' seemed to have little doubt that they were the Lord's Anointed, the kings of Zion, descendants of David and Solomon of Israel. Christianity, as 'fanatical' as the Islam of the 16th century invader Ahmad Grañ, completely governed the lives of some of these Ethiopian emperors, Zara Yaqob being perhaps the most remarkable of them all. A similar ruler of our time might be regarded as a cruel and bigoted dictator, meting out savage punishments to his subjects and his family alike for every minor step out of the path he designated. But for many Ethiopians he was another Christian hero.

The regal-religious myth of Ethiopia was now established. There was only one vital addition to set in place: the keystone of later faith, the crown of the propaganda edifice. Impelled by the great need engendered by two disastrous happenings, an even more wonderful talisman was to be added – the Ark of the Covenant.

ETHIOPIA'S TRIBULATIONS

The calamities that Ethiopia suffered were both inflicted from outside. The first was physical. The *amir* of Adal, Ahmad Grañ, launched his terrible assault on the Ethiopia of Emperor Lebna Dengel, named the 'Incense of the Virgin'. It was this emperor who, buoyed up by victory in war, failed to seize the moment to establish a treaty relationship with the Portuguese, who had sent an embassy to him in 1520. It was not really his fault – war with Adal had been endemic for generations, and there was no hint that this time it would bring unmitigated disaster. Lebna Dengel's churches, plated with gold, set with jewels and filled with books and paintings, were stripped. Everything not of intrinsic value was smashed or burned. The tombs of his ancestors were desecrated. The corpse of the dead Metropolitan Marqos was burned with his church. The torch was set to the emperor's painted palaces. The *tabota Seyon*, the sacred altar stone of Zion, was snatched in panic from Aksum with the other treasures of the church, and borne away to wait out events in a more easily defensible spot. It was deposited at Tabr, one of the emperor's secure fortresses. The emperor himself fled from place to place before the enemy. In 1535, Aksum was burned. The church of Mary of Zion was laid in ruins – only the outer walls and some walls and pillars of the sanctuary area survived in part. The Christian kingdom of Zion became an unreal dream as Muslim governors were installed in province after province. Emperor Lebna Dengel died at Dabra Damo in 1540. He never saw the rescue that was soon to come.

Yet even the saving of the Christian kingdom had its reverse face. The new Emperor Galawdewos, coming to the throne at a time when it seemed that the throne itself was doomed, had the luck to find a God-sent ally – Vasco da Gama's son, Cristovão. He and his musket-bearing troops first rescued Empress Sabla Wangel, Lebna Dengel's wife, from her hopeless four-year retreat on top of the impenetrable mountain of Dabra Damo. Adorned in court dress, the Portuguese emissaries were hauled up the vertical face of the mountain fortress in baskets to wait upon the empress, one of the strangest diplomatic receptions on record. Empress-mother and saviours then marched south to join with the emperor and his troops. The result was the destruction of the Muslim enemy. The European-Ethiopian alliance also installed, close to the throne, the Portuguese Catholics, particularly in the person of Jesuit missionaries.

It was they who inflicted the second misfortune on Ethiopia, this time a moral one. From the time of the first Portuguese embassy in 1520, the Ethiopians must have been only too aware of the increasingly horrified eyes the 'Franks' turned on their religious practices. The Ethiopians might have been shocked to see these strangers walking into church with their shoes on, or spitting in church when they felt like it (which Alvares says was 'our custom'), but the high ground on more vital matters of religious practice and doctrine was held by the Portuguese. In the 1550s, both Gonzalo Rodrigues and André de Oviedo took it upon themselves to present Emperor

Galawdewos with treatises of their own composition concerning the errors in Ethiopian belief. Galawdewos, not to be outdone, responded to the first with his *Confessio Claudii*, detailing the main elements of his faith: 'the faith of my fathers the kings of the Israelites'. He also seems to have fully concerned himself in correcting errors. A document in the *Book of Aksum* preserves an imperial decree suppressing what Galawdewos regarded as incorrect practises, such as marrying a deceased brother's wife or taking more than one wife. At the same time he regulated other questions concerning fasts, marriage, monks, godfathers and superstitions about blacksmiths.

But Bishop Oviedo wanted far more than this – he stood for obedience to the pope. In 1559 he went so far as excommunicating Ethiopians who did not accept his church's decrees, a gesture which intensely annoyed the emperor. Galawdewos, a man who had cause to be grateful to the Portuguese, was killed a month later, to be replaced by a much more intolerant brother who had no such scruples. Emperor Minas reacted with a decree of exile for Oviedo, who spent much of the rest of his life at Fremona, the Jesuit residence in Tigray.

The Jesuits were one thing. The Egyptian *abuns* of the Ethiopian church, who really do seem to have descended into a moral decrepitude hard to excuse, aroused no respect whatsoever. Faced with those sharpened Jesuit minds, inured to debate and confident of their knowledge, how could men like these argue the finer points of the faith? Emperor Susneyos excoriated the four last *abuns* in extremely harsh terms. The same, more or less, seems to have applied to earlier metropolitans, though by no means all were quite so deeply sunk in depravity. They were certainly, in comparison to the Jesuits, abysmally ignorant in theological and ecclesiastical matters. The Ethiopian church, materially ruined by Grañ, was now to suffer the additional humiliation of the contempt of the adherents of another Christian sect, who were, for the first time in all the country's long Christian history, able to offer a viable alternative within Ethiopia itself. Even Ethiopians were aware of the bad show they had made for their faith. We may suppose that the chronicler of Galawdewos erred on the side of the dramatic when he stated that 'hardly one in ten kept the faith', but enough stories survive of ex-Christians serving Grañ to make it certain that here was another unpleasant truth to be faced in Ethiopian Christian society. So many had turned away that the book *Mashafa Qeder* was written to prescribe the purification rites necessary for the reception of apostates back into the church.

METAMORPHOSIS

As my research progressed, the evidence seemed to point to these difficult decades of the later 16th century, when a Catholic patriarch and his priests dwelt at Fremona in Tigray, as the moment when the Ark of the Covenant at last gained its foothold in the records about Ethiopia. I suspected that it was under the special conditions of the moment, in the desperate circumstances of physical and moral damage to Ethiopia's traditional church, that the Ark was now manoeuvred into position. The last stone of the great edifice of the *KN*, it was required to lend its overwhelming potency to support the monarchy and church.

How did this happen? Was the Catholic pressure, this polemic conducted by clerics so manifestly contemptuous of the Ethiopian Orthodox Church, its ill-educated priests and its Egyptian *abun*, with the repeated charges of Judaic, even Muslim, practices and similar disparagements, the catalyst for a new development? Emperor Galawdewos, appreciative though he was of the enormous value of the military arm of the Portuguese mission, had been sufficiently stung by the religious criticism to take the trouble to compose his 'Confession' to rectify some of these ideas. Was this imperial effort symptomatic of a new consciousness among certain devout Orthodox Ethiopians? Might not recent, and continuing, developments have induced them to search deeper for elements in their own faith that could counteract not only the withering scorn of the Jesuits but the massive physical blow which Christian Ethiopia had recently suffered? A large part of the ecclesiastical heritage of Ethiopia had vanished in flames during Grañ's reign of terror.

Did some latter-day *nebura'ed* Yeshaq, knowing, as doubtless every cleric did, the story of the *KN* as it was told to date, formulate a new theory? Did he inspire (or find in some Arabic source) the suggestion that the sacred object, the altar stone from Mount Zion – the *tabota Seyon* that we suppose to have been returned to the reconstructed church dedicated to Mary of Zion, and to have already been identified with the tablet of Moses – represented something even more than that? Or was it already slowly metamorphosing of itself, gliding smoothly into identity with the Ark of the Covenant, in the same way that a tablet of wood used as an altar tablet had become known as *tabot*, strictly meaning casket, container: 'Ark'? Possibly the altar tablet of Zion already had a wooden container made for its transport, a casket, perhaps even gilded or overlaid with gold, that could logically enough be viewed as the Ark itself. Very likely even that was not necessary for the change in its identity. The mysterious stone of Zion, during its concealment at Tabr while the church of Aksum lay desolate in ruins from 1535 to the 1570s, perhaps simply augmented in sanctity in the eyes of those so long deprived of its presence. It came to be viewed no longer merely as the *tabota Seyon*, a *tabot* or altar tablet dedicated in the name of Zion and identified with the tablet(s) of Moses that came with Ebna Hakim from Jerusalem. Instead it became popularly identified as the other *tabota Seyon* – the Ark of the Covenant itself, *Seyon tabota amlaka Esrael*. Neither object nor name need have altered to effect this change – only the concept or interpretation. Kept always veiled, in an inaccessible sanctuary forbidden to all but its chosen guards, few could ever see it and judge for themselves.

We know the names of a few *neburana'ed* of Aksum at this time – Tasfa Hawaryat (c. 1554–55), *azmach* (general) Yeshaq (c. 1560–61), 'Enqua Sellase and *azmach* Takla Selus in 1578–79. In 1579, Emperor Sarsa Dengel came to Aksum for his tonsuring and anointing in the presence of the Ark, *Seyon tabota amlaka Esrael*, and it was shortly afterwards, having defeated the Falasha prince Radai, that the emperor named himself *nebura'ed* of 'the cathedral of Aksum, the glory of Zion, tabernacle of the God of Israel', appointing a favourite, Asbe, to actually exercise the office. Was it one of these *neburana'ed* or some other Aksumite ecclesiastic of this time who adopted and encouraged the augmented formula that envisaged the Ark itself at Aksum? This at once bestowed even greater sanctity on Maryam Seyon church, provided the Ethiopian Orthodox Church with a relic greater than anything lost in the flames to Grañ, and offered a dazzling card for the church to play in its humiliating contest against the Catholics. Given Emperor Sarsa Dengel's special reverence for Aksum, and the efforts he made to augment its status, the formula may have even had deliberate imperial patronage – certainly the emperor's chronicler emphasises the presence there of 'Zion'.

For this suggestion there is no evidence beyond the sudden presence of the Ark in the documentation on several levels, and my reflection on the current situation of the Ethiopian church. I offer further conjectures below. Yet the Ark *did* become conspicuous in the records at just this juncture. It would have been an appropriate concept to seduce the head of Aksum's church and clergy, and the heir to Yeshaq's post, at a tremendously emotive time. Vital events, rich in promise for neglected Aksum, took place in these years. The first modest rebuilding of its church was ordered, after some forty years of it lying in ruin. The event is recorded, as we have seen, in the *Book of Aksum*. More than likely, the exiled talisman, *tabota Seyon*, was immediately reinstalled. At the same time, under Sarsa Dengel, fresh from his victories over Turks and rebels, the first imperial tonsuring ceremony for 143 years, and only the second in reported history, took place at 'the house of the heavenly Zion', Maryam Seyon church. All this, with the emperor's personal adoption of the title *nebura'ed* of Aksum, his eulogies of the city's special status, and the granting of exceptional privileges, were to bring a splendid new éclat to devastated Aksum.

Whoever first developed the idea that the Ark itself was at Aksum – and the important thing is that someone did – it caught on. By the late 1500s or so it was firmly in place among the 'traditions' of the Ethiopian church, and was so recorded as the books were rewritten. The Ark's presence in Ethiopia is mentioned at this time in Sarsa Dengel's chronicle, and by the Iberian Jesuits. Strangely, none of the Portuguese who comment on it seem to have noticed that the Ark was *not* part of the old Ethiopian ecclesiastical traditions as reported by Alvares and others earlier, most of whom mentioned, instead, the tablet(s) of Moses.

A powerful talisman was certainly needed in Ethiopia. From the point of view of the old order the danger was far from over even after the Ark appeared. After the hiatus of the reigns of Minas and Sarsa Dengel, Catholicism revived, strengthened by the exceptional wisdom and discretion of the Jesuit missionary Péro Pais. Two emperors – mainstays of the whole traditional system – deserted the Alexandrian church and went over to Catholicism under his influence. In the early 1600s Emperor Za Dengel flirted with the new religion of the foreigners, was excommunicated by *Abuna* Petros, and died in the ensuing revolt. A little later Emperor Susneyos overtly abandoned the traditional church and attempted to make Ethiopia a Catholic country. The Ark fled to Bur as a Catholic priest desecrated its altar at Maryam Seyon church. Only in 1633 was the religious victory finally assured for Orthodoxy with the accession of Emperor Fasiladas, the return of the Ark from Digsa in Bur and the arrival of an Alexandrian metropolitan.

THE WHITE STONE

Can the intricate tale preserved in the documents over nearly seven hundred years be coherently unravelled? To me, despite all appearances to the contrary, the evidence testifies to a certain consistency, veiled, admittedly, by terminological chaos. The records indicate that the 'Ark' of Aksum is not a wooden chest, but a sacred stone.

Is it the same white stone rumoured to come from Mount Zion that some chroniclers mention from the 16th century? Perhaps the object at Aksum today, in the *enda sellat*, the chapel of the Tablet of Moses, is a more recent, smaller (recut?) version of it, unless Shihab al-Din's 16th century description of a stone so large that it could not pass through the church doors was mistaken or grossly exaggerated. Or it could simply be a replacement. The inextricable interweaving and overlaying of nomenclature and symbolism between Ark, tablets of the Law, and *tabot* or altar tablet permit such a transition, allowing the stone to actually 'become' the Ark of the Covenant. In modern times the presentation has turned full circle, and the original claim for the tablet(s) of Moses, which became the Ark in the later 16th century, has once again, among some Aksumite clerics at least, reverted to the tablet – even if it is still called the Ark!

Shifts are perceptible in the way Aksumite clerics refer to the mysterious relic in the chapel. They tend to speak of the *enda sellat*, the chapel of the tablet, and the *sellata Muse*, the tablet of Moses (the term used in the 19th century, for example, in a note in the Lady Meux 4 manuscript of the *History of Hanna*, and in Menelik II's chronicle), not the *tabota Seyon*, the 'Ark' of Zion, even though Patriarch Pawlos and *qesis* Kefyalew Merahi determinedly maintain the formal claim that the Ark itself is at Aksum. With the Ark of Aksum, we leave the scientific world of strict classification and method, and find ourselves in the shifting mysterious realm of symbolism and faith.

A 1998 newspaper report offers some tantalising information about the object at Aksum through interviews with previous guardians, and with the *nebura'ed*:[2]

> ...There is some confusion about what precisely the monks are hiding behind the faded red-velvet curtain over the doorway of the temple's domed sanctuary. Most people envision the ark as the large gold-covered chest with two cherubim on top described in the Bible and depicted by Hollywood in the Steven Spielberg movie 'Raiders of the Lost Ark'.

But in interviews in recent days, priests and monks who say they have seen the relic denied that they have the heavy chest Moses is said to have built, which they refer to as 'the chair of the ark'.

Instead, they say their ark is a white stone tablet inscribed with the Ten Commandments and kept in a shallow solid-gold case. They say that this tablet was inscribed by God and carried down from Mount Sinai by Moses.

'Yes, it is here, it is the original Ark of the Covenant, the one given to Moses,' the chief priest of St. Mary of Zion Church, Nebura-ed Belai, said. 'The chair of the ark is not there.'

…In separate interviews, a monk who briefly guarded the ark in 1983 and a retired head priest who said he had seen the relic twice described it as a single tablet of white polished stone inscribed with the Ten Commandments in Hebrew. They said the tablet is about 2 1/2 feet long and 1 1/2 inches thick and is housed in a gold box three inches thick, with a hinged lid and no designs

'The man who stole the ark hid it in the small box only, not the big one,' said the Rev. Gebreab Maru, who was head priest at St. Mary of Zion for nearly 20 years before retiring in 1985. 'It is true the larger box never came to Ethiopia.'

The monks said the relic seemed to have paranormal powers. They said that at night it sometimes appeared to give off light. They also said it was hard to look at the tablet in daylight because it was so smooth and mirrorlike.

'When I looked at it, it was completely difficult to understand it,' the former head priest said. 'It makes me very afraid and my eyes filled with tears.'

A former guardian of the ark, Wolde Giorgis Wolde Gebrial, said: 'It is like a mirror, very smooth, not quite white. Sometimes it looks like water.'

This is intriguing. An Aksumite friend with intimate church connections whom I asked about the nature of local belief replied that 'with regard to the conception of the people about the Ark, they believe that the sellat are exactly the tablets mentioned in the Bible which were made by Moses and brought to God for inscription at Mt. Sinai. A stone that glows and shines.' The identification ark = tablet(s) is automatic. I have also been told by a *dabtara* of Aksum the same story about a tablet that emits light. If the reports from the witnesses are accurate – when I spoke to the guardian and the *nebura'ed* Belai Marasa in October 1997, the last thing they wanted was to go into detail about the nature of the Ark, though we discussed many aspects of *tabotat* and ritual – the story confirms that a sort of 'super-*tabot*' of white stone, much larger than a normal *tabot*, but by no means as immense as Shihab al-Din implied, is kept at Aksum. From the earlier reports, this is exactly what we might expect.

Naturally, the article raises many questions. It seems that some among the Aksumite priesthood are anxious now to disclaim possession of the great box or chest that everybody outside Ethiopia imagines when they hear the term 'Ark of the Covenant' – despite the fact that the *KN*, the book that gives them the right to suppose the Ark is with them, firmly declares that the carpenter chosen by Azarias was to prepare planks of the 'height, and breadth, and length and size of our Lady' (*KN* 45), and despite what the patriarch asserts. The 'chair of the Ark' must have been translated from the Ge'ez words *manbara tabot* – the 'throne of the *tabot*'. If we credit this story, the clerics now seem to reject the claim to possess what represents the 'real' Ark to the rest of the world: the 'chair'. They say that this large box-like 'chair' was left behind. Instead, the contents of the Ark, one holy thing merging effortlessly into another, constitute another Ark – the fluid meaning of the word *tabot* assisting this process. This is the object now in Aksum.

When the journalist writes that the *nebura'ed* said 'it is the original Ark of the Covenant, the one given to Moses', we may be sure that what he actually said was: 'it is the original *tabot* (or *tabota Seyon*, *tabota hegg*, or even *sellata Muse*), the one given to Moses'. One of these terms, with its interchangeable significance, was translated to the journalist as 'Ark of the Covenant'. In Ethiopia uncertainty is intrinsic in the very words. According to this report, the most eminent of Aksum's clergy are able solemnly to declare that the Ark of the Covenant was left behind, while the Ark of the Covenant inside it was put into a new box and brought to Ethiopia. Bizarre as it seems, the concept *nebura'ed* Belai was expressing is exactly in tune with the facts, based on what is in every church: there was a *tabot* inside a *manbara tabot*, and only the *tabot* was taken. The problem of interpretation lies in the fact that *tabot* can mean two things: Ark of the Covenant; or altar tablet, tablet of Moses or tablet of the Law. True, *manbara tabot*, 'throne of the *tabot*', does not usually mean Ark of the Covenant, but the *nebura'ed* simply used the appropriate expression for the altar in which any *tabot* is enclosed. Dealing in concepts based on Christianity rather than on Jewish cult, he may also have subtly implied that what was taken was the thing of most value: the *tabot* within the *manbara tabot* is the sole consecrated item in the church. The Ark shrinks to insignificance, a mere 'large box', while its contents, the white (single) stone, takes on all the numinous power of the ancient palladium of the Israelites, and becomes itself the Ark.

If one believes one of the many Ark web pages on the internet, a golden Ark like that portrayed in the Bible was described by a hundred-year-old ex-guardian at Aksum. This version too is not surprising. What the Ark of the Bible was like is known to everyone, and if intrusive questioners ask about it there is only one answer for the guardian, or for that matter any other Aksumite ecclesiastic, to give. At the end of his book, Graham Hancock relates how the guardian of that time, Gabra Mikael, responded by implication in the same way, in the equivocal language of one who had no intention of answering leading questions:

> 'Can you at least tell me what the Ark looks like? I think I could go away content if you would tell me that.'
> 'I believe that the Ark is well described in the Bible. You can read there.'
> 'But I want you to tell me in your own words what it looks like. I mean the Ark that rests here in the sanctuary. Is it a box made of wood and gold? Does it have two winged figures on its lid?'
> 'I will not speak about such matters…'
> 'And how is it carried?…Is it carried on poles? Or in some other way? Is it heavy or light?'
> 'I have said that I will not speak of such matters, and therefore I will not speak…'

However, despite this sort of refuge in obscurity or silence, the reports of the past, and the conversation of priests, *dabtarat* and others of today make it clear that whatever other things might be kept in the chapel the principal object of reverence is a largish white stone. As I have explained above, it may or may not be the same as the altar tablet of Zion mentioned by Alvares, or the same stone that was removed by Lebna Dengel to Tabr. With the facility of replacement by symbolical transference, a new stone would have been acceptable if necessary. Among the priests of Aksum are certainly some who have seen the sacred object, and described it to others, friends or family. In that narrow society, the matter is not even a secret – why should it be? The mystery that has recently come more and more to preoccupy others from the outside world is no mystery there. The greater part of the clergy of Aksum must know perfectly well that their 'Ark' is not a large wooden chest on carrying poles, more than three thousand years old, covered with gold and surmounted by a massive solid gold top ornamented with two cherubim. But Aksum's Christian hierarchy do not operate according to the thought patterns of the modern scientific age, nor should we expect them to. Through the magic of symbolism and a mystifying vocabulary, and the capacity of more than one numinous object to merge into a single concept, the stone that they protect with such vigilance has become, for them, the 'real' Ark of the Covenant.

The claim is still sensational. The clergy of Aksum have not abandoned the contention that a supremely sacred object was taken from the Holy of Holies in the temple of Jerusalem in King Solomon's time. If what they say is true and correctly reported, they still assert that the stone plaque should be one of the two unbroken replacement copies of the tablets of Moses, now kept enclosed in a golden box that in no way attempts to be a replica of the Ark. The statement by one observer that it has the Ten Commandments written on it in Hebrew might evoke the stone that Dimotheos saw in 1869 with the commandments 'written obliquely in Turkish fashion', except for the matter of size. Dimotheos' 24cm is very far from 2 1/2 feet (90+cm) – let alone the huge stone described by Shihab al-Din – though the estimated thickness is in both cases about the same. However, verbal descriptions of this sort, over several centuries, hedged with mystification and uncertainty, may mean very little.

Stone objects inscribed in incomprehensible languages of the past are not uncommon at Aksum. Perhaps the stone is part of an old Aksumite inscription, written in Greek or in the strange false epigraphic South Arabian script used by some of old Aksumite kings. Von Heuglin in 1861 saw a mysterious tablet that contained 'many horizontal and vertical lines, in which stand single signs, I conjecture that it represents a calendar or astronomical table'. The stone was first reported, with several others, in the garden of the *qese gabaz* Qalamsis, provost of Aksum. The other ancient inscriptions found at this time at Aksum I inspected in 1997 in a storeroom next to the *nebura'ed*'s office in Aksum, but this particular calendar stone, it seems, no one has ever seen since… Could it repose, perhaps, in the chapel of the Tablet of Moses?

JESUIT OR CHRISTIAN ARAB?

Since the 17th century the sacred stone of Aksum has perhaps been housed in a box or casket, if we believe Manoel de Almeida's report. This casket, by virtue of being the container of the stone identified as the tablet of Moses, might have earned the designation 'Ark of the Covenant' because the original tablets of the Law had been placed within the original Ark in exactly the same way. But the presence of a true *tabot*, in the sense of box, container or casket ('Ark'), is not necessary to explain the term 'Ark of the Covenant', because the word *tabot* applies also to any wooden, stone or even metal altar tablet. The use of such a container fits, however, with Manoel de Almeida's description (and, in fact, with the modern ones I have cited, where a hinged gold box is mentioned).

A little earlier, I tentatively suggested certain factors that might have resulted in a change in the perceived identity of the altar stone of Zion, or tablet of Moses, raising it to a new level as the Ark of the Covenant. These factors could have been accidental, resulting from the modification of concepts about *tabota Seyon* during the several decades that it was concealed far from the ruined church of Aksum. The equivocal nature of the descriptive vocabulary could have allowed – indeed, almost asked for – subtle changes of perception to creep in almost unregarded over time. We cannot discount a possible element of calculation, too, in the response of Aksumite clergy to the difficult situation of the church in the decades after Grañ and the arrival of the Jesuits. The euphoria during the period of dramatic events at Aksum around 1579–80 – the restoration of the church, the return of the holy object from Tabr, the coronation of an emperor who so respected Aksum that he named himself its *nebura'ed* – would also have confirmed the enhanced glory of the holy talisman.

As my investigation continued, a further possibility presented itself, in which strangers, not Ethiopians, appeared to be the catalyst for change. I wondered if the elevation of the altar stone of Zion into the Ark of the Covenant might have come about in a completely different way, by a truly bizarre twist of circumstance – the consequence of a Jesuit's blunder. Might one of the Portuguese Jesuits living in Ethiopia during the second half of the 16th century have made that perennial error of understanding *tabota Seyon* (*tabot* by this date meaning altar tablet – the stone from Zion mentioned by Alvares) to refer to the other *tabota Seyon* (the Ark of Zion, or Ark of the Covenant, as it was later described by Manoel de Almeida)? Did this Jesuit become, by simple transference of meaning, the first to interpret that it was not a slab of stone from Mount Zion, or the tablet of the Law, that was supposed to be at Maryam Seyon church, but the Ark itself?

I am not suggesting something remote or improbable. João Bermudes claims that he spoke to Emperor Galawdewos about Ethiopian errors of belief. Both Gonzalo Rodrigues and the bishop and later patriarch André de Oviedo assumed the duty of writing treatises against the errors of the Ethiopian faith in this emperor's time, and almost every other Jesuit writer after them included pages and pages of the same kind of thing. Letters and reports between clerics, and to the pope, contained similar material. Cardinal Dom Afonso in 1539 was already writing about Ethiopia's religious errors to Emperor Lebna Dengel, and even in 1634 after the expulsion of the Catholics, Manoel Barradas expatiated on the same theme, in two chapters written during his captivity at Aden. Though not often mentioned in the surviving texts, *tabotat* and *manbara tabotat* – including the *manbar* from Aksum – figured high among these 'errors'. They headed the list of ecclesiastical impedimenta that were removed or destroyed the moment the Catholics had the power to do so. Manoel de Almeida and Barradas, and Emperor Fasiladas himself, all confirm this specifically, while Thomé Barneto's attack on the sanctuary at Aksum is related in his own report.

Could it have been Rodrigues, or Oviedo, or one of their companions, who in his eagerness to denounce the Ethiopians' faults, by misinterpretation added another facet to their general disapproval of the Ethiopian altar tablets: the assertion that the Ethiopians at Aksum claimed possession of the *tabot* of Zion, the Ark of the Covenant? Rodrigues presented his treatise on Ethiopian errors in August 1555. Oviedo was already writing to the emperor about religious differences in 1557, and on 2 February 1559 he issued his letter remitting Ethiopians to the judgement of the church because of their errors. By 1579, Emperor Sarsa Dengel could go to his new church of Mary of Zion at Aksum, meet the challenge of the 'daughters of Zion', and be acclaimed 'king of Zion' before the most holy thing on earth: 'my mother Seyon, the Ark of the Covenant of the Lord of Israel'.

Jesuits arriving in Ethiopia a little later, Péro Pais and Manoel de Almeida for example, found this claim presented as fact. Pais, the first to mention it, even confirmed that it was inscribed in the copy of the *KN* which he saw at Aksum around 1620, a version of the tale doubtless recopied – and augmented with this new concept – when the priests at Sarsa Dengel's restored church at Aksum were in the process of restocking their library, destroyed or dispersed many decades before in 1535. Replacement of texts was an ongoing and important element at the time, part of the programme for recovery set by the emperor. In Emperor Galawdewos' chronicle, we read how his concern with literature not only led him to purchase over 10,000 gold ounces' worth of books, but to encourage the resumption of translation from Arabic.

Up to this point all texts refer either to an altar stone of Zion, or to tablet(s) of the Law, the latter sometimes implied as being the object at Aksum, but sometimes appearing in the royal possession, travelling with the king. The claim to possession of the Ark – outside one single hazily dated manuscript, which I will deal with in a moment – exists in no Ethiopian book earlier than one version of the chronicle of Sarsa Dengel, attributed to 1579 but actually written down in or after 1591. Did the Ethiopians, learning that the Jesuits believed there was a claim that the Ark itself was at Aksum, simply adopt this claim as stated? It is important to reiterate that neither vocabulary nor material object need have changed in reality, only the concept or spiritual interpretation of what was kept hidden away at Tabr or in the rebuilt church at Aksum. It would be an extraordinary irony if it had been a Jesuit's misinterpretation of what *tabota Seyon* meant that bestowed upon the Ethiopian church its greatest religious relic.

Plausible though this tentative reconstruction of events appeared as my study neared its conclusion, there remained impediments hard to set aside. Two manuscripts seem to push back the story of the Ark in Ethiopia to the 15th century, rather than the 16th. Even if concern about an interval like this seems comical in the perspective of a claim that does not hesitate to think in terms of almost three thousand years, getting to the bottom of the matter of the dating was essential if I wanted to arrive at the truth about the Ethiopian Ark. Luckily, both manuscripts were in Paris, both were accessible to study, and the curators responsible were both informed and helpful.

The first of these manuscripts is a foreign work that may well claim precedence over even the Jesuits: the Arabic document that describes the story of the transfer of power from Solomon's Israel to Abyssinia. Is it true that the undated sections of the Paris ms. 264, including this tale involving the Ark, really belong to an earlier period than the section dated to 1594? Authoritative opinion seems to say that it does, suggesting the second half of the 15th century; and the copies we know of may record a story already somewhat older. If so, in this version we find the Ark story already current in Egypt some time before Francisco Alvares had come to Ethiopia in 1520. The story was, however, radically different, representing David, son of Solomon and the queen of Sheba, as a murderer and deceiver. Though patently of the same genre, with its *rukh* bird, goat-foot, water-covered temple court, wood from Paradise and other details, it was quite unlike the *KN* version.

The Ark element had not yet entered current belief in Ethiopia at that time – if the outline proposed above is valid – but evidently the potential for it to do so already existed. There were intimate ecclesiastical connections between the two countries. Was it from Egyptian Christian imagination of the 15th century – imagination perhaps even inspired by knowledge of what Abu Salih had written so long before – that the Ark eventually emerged in Ethiopia, rather than from a Jesuit error? The influence of the Arabic tale, emerging from the land that gave them their bishop and where their patriarch dwelt, could have been the catalyst that led to the acceptance by Ethiopian clerics of the sacred object as the 'real' Ark of the Covenant. It could, too, have been the influence behind certain statements in the *KN* colophon that differ radically from the information Alvares recorded in his version. Nevertheless, neither Alvares nor de Barros, nor Saga Za-Ab on the Ethiopian side, include the Ark in their versions of the story. As we have seen it only appears in Ethiopian records in the second half of the 16th century – one single manuscript, allegedly, aside.

We must now consider this last, vital, but equivocal piece of evidence, the single manuscript that might push the Ethiopian story of the Ark back a century or more in time. The Ethiopian manuscript no. 5 (94) in the Bibliothèque Nationale, Paris, was the gift of Sahela Sellasie, king of Shewa, to another king far away in France, Louis Philippe. The massive parchment manuscript, 45 x 35cm, includes several works, commencing the *KN* only on folio 108r., under a large and complex red *harag*, the typical decorative frame often found at the beginning of Ethiopic texts. The writing is elegant and attractive, in two columns with wide exterior margins. The problem is that the manuscript grows continually younger as savants study it.

Zotenberg in 1877 dated it to the 13th century – a date earlier even than Yeshaq and his colleagues, the people who are supposed to have been working on the *KN* under the Tigray ruler Ya'ibika Egzi in the early 14th century. He did, however, add that it could perhaps date to the 14th century. Very few of the early dates suggested by Zotenberg for Ethiopian manuscripts have survived the examination of more recent specialists. But what actually is its date? Budge doubted Zotenberg's estimate, but offered no concrete alternative. Guidi suggested the 14th century, as did Bezold, who used it, as 'die älteste und wichtigste…' version extant, for his translation. The latest palaeographic study, by Siegbert Uhlig, includes it in his phase II, embracing the end of the 14th century and the first half of the 15th century. At that time, under Zara Yaqob and even his predecessors, innovations were entering the Ethiopian church that are intimately associated with matters closely related to the Ark, such as the status of Mary, and the rank of Aksum and its church in the empire. But if the Ark entered into official religious theory during, perhaps, the reign of Zara Yaqob, why do later stories by both Ethiopians and foreigners still exclude it, and why does no material object appear to support its appearance? Indeed, given the nature of the emperor of the time, Zara Yaqob, why does it not figure high in the several still extant religious treatises he wrote or inspired? Until c. 1579 we hear in other documents only of the altar stone of Zion, not of the Ark.

The manuscript may, quite simply, be wrongly dated. There are many difficulties about the chronology of Ethiopian manuscripts. Styles of writing can be more conservative in some places than in others. Certain scribes have been specifically noted as employing antiquated forms in their writing. In this case, we might ask: which has the more authority, the history of the Ark as we have it from all other records, or the conjectures of the palaeographers – based, nevertheless, on a variety of elements growing slowly more and more precise as more dated manuscripts are studied? Is this single estimate of a still developing science – offering, even in the latest study, a period over something like seventy-five years during which the book might have been produced – sufficient to annihilate all the other evidence? Could this book be of later date, written in a region where an older style still prevailed, or imitating an older style? The dates according to style can only offer a very approximate guideline – a style does not cease at a given moment, particularly when it may be shared by several widely separated scriptoria, some very isolated. A young monk learning his orthography in, say, 1430, in some secluded monastery, might be writing in similar style, and teaching it to his own pupils, as an old man in 1480.

The way books changed in Ethiopia may also be an important factor here. A new version of the *KN* written for court or important ecclesiastical circles in the 15th century – and the size and elegance of the Paris manuscript seem to preclude its writing for some minor provincial church – might have told a tale that differed from the version current at the church at Aksum even in the early 16th century. Somewhere there had to be a first copy of each new version. One might argue that the edition with the Ark did exist at Aksum even in Alvares' time, but that he was only shown the other version. Yet Saga Za-Ab also supplies only the version with the tablets, and as we have seen, there is no other trace of the Ark in Ethiopia at this time. Clearly, when editing was undertaken of any of the documents of Ethiopian ecclesiastical history, whether *Miracles of Mary*, *Synaxarium*, *Book of Aksum*, *gadlat* of the saints, *KN* or any others, the new version, coined in one place for one reason or another, would take some time to prevail over existing older versions, if it ever did. For a while at least, different versions would have remained current. One can still find, for example, an old version of the *Life* of Takla Haymanot, or of Garima, or Libanos, lacking the developments of later times. Should palaeographic theory prevail, however, in the instance of King Sahela Sellasie's *KN*, we can envisage an Ethiopian version that had already, like the Arab version, adopted the Ark story in the 15th century. Did the Ge'ez work owe this innovation to the Arabic version, whose original date of composition we do not know? If so, it was carefully edited to reject other elements from that story.

To clarify this complex point, we possess today three different surviving versions of the *KN* story (excluding the several oral variants, natural consequences of localising a much loved theme, that I have described in Chapter 5: Exotic Embroideries above). The first is the Arabic version, known from a manuscript dated c.1450–1500 but almost certainly older in origin – we are unlikely to have, by chance, the original copy. It includes the Ark and the wood of the Cross. The second is a 16th century story, which must also be somewhat older than the period for which we have written evidence, c. 1520–50. This version mentions only the tablets of Moses, but also brings in the wood of the Cross. The third, whose dating before 1450 depends on imprecise stylistic considerations relating to the single Sahela Sellasie manuscript, is the story that eventually prevailed in Ethiopia. It includes the Ark but not the wood of the Cross, and differs quite substantially from the Arabic tale in other details as well. All other copies of this final 'official' version that survive date to the 17th century or later.

Whatever the precise mechanism or date, the claim to possession of the Ark was made, and in the end gained ground everywhere in Ethiopia. From the late 16th to early 17th century onwards – very recent, in terms of the claimed perspective of 2600 years or so – we hear no more of the simple acquisition of the tablets. Now all Christian Ethiopia paid lip service to the Ark legend enshrined in the final version of the *KN* – in theory at least. It is unlikely that everyone believed it. We can be sure that then, as now, there were doubters and cynics. The Portuguese, who were there, and knew the local ecclesiastics well, particularly in the first three decades of the 17th century, did not for a moment believe that either the Ark or the tablets of Moses were in Ethiopia. On the contrary, regardless of whether the claim for the Ark's presence was an Arab import, already quite old in Ethiopia, or whether it had come about by a European priest's inaccuracy, the Catholics viewed it as both bizarre and ridiculous, not to say fraudulent. Similarly, as far as we can tell, the Ethiopians who were converted to Catholicism, like Susneyos and his brother *ras* Sela Krestos, placed little importance upon the Ethiopian 'Ark' – though the emperor was apparently intrigued enough at one time to try to discover exactly what it was that lay concealed at Aksum.

The legend of the dynasty descended from King Solomon and the queen of Sheba, of the 'Israelite' nature of the kingdom, was to become enshrined in Ethiopian tradition together with the belief that the Ark of the Covenant dwelt by the desire of God in the church of Maryam Seyon at Aksum. One manifestation of this was the claim in the Ethiopian Constitution of the mid-20th century that asserted a 2900-year-old dynastic descent for the last emperor, Haile Sellassie. Much more recently (early 2002), enthroned between the flags of Ethiopia in his palace at Addis Ababa in quasi-imperial state, His Holiness *Abuna* Pawlos, 'Head of the Congregation of Archbishops, and Patriarch of Ethiopia, Successor to the See of Takla Haymanot and Archbishop of Aksum', as he officially entitles himself,[3] once again confirmed the claim to the Ark. Before the cameras for a documentary shown, and repeated, by Arte, the Franco-German television chain, he stated unequivocally that the Ark of the Covenant itself was at Aksum.

The pedigree of the Ark legend was pushed back by the final Ethiopian redaction of the *KN* – here tentatively dated to the later 16th or early 17th century, or at the very earliest, in restricted circles only, to the 15th century – to the time of Amda Seyon, and from then by the book's colophon into a still remoter period. Today, for some 25 million (or more) faithful of the Ethiopian Orthodox Tewahado Church, led by their patriarch, the presence of the Ark at Aksum Seyon church is an indisputable fact.

SURVIVAL

What are the chances that the Ark of the Covenant – the 'original' Mosaic-Solomonic one that the Ethiopian Christians still believe to reside at Aksum – might have survived until today? The object from the ancient world that most resembles the Ark of the Covenant as the Bible describes it, a beautifully decorated wooden chest on carrying poles from the tomb of Tutankhamun, has survived in almost perfect condition. It can be seen today in Cairo Museum. Its life history was probably one of almost total tranquillity. Carefully made of selected precious woods in the royal workshops, by skilled carpenters, for funerary purposes only, it was conveyed with the rest of the pharaoh's funerary furniture to his tomb and sealed in, supposedly for eternity. Shortly afterwards, with the tomb itself, it was opened and plundered. Then it was replaced – repacked with the wrong contents, as its written docket confirms – for over three thousand years of darkness and silence in the most perfect of preservation chambers, an Egyptian tomb. In that austere climate, no damp penetrated, and scarcely anything moved. Delicate cloth shrouds, their tissues slowly torn over the centuries by the weight of decorative gilded rosettes sewn onto the material, might every so often dissolve into dust, the rosettes sliding down to the floor. Everything else in that 'House of Eternity' remained utterly immobile - until the coming of Howard Carter.

In contrast, the Ark of the Covenant of Israel – if we follow the biblical story – led a vigorous, active life. Created in the desert from acacia wood, by artisans who, however skilled they might have been at their work, could scarcely have had much choice in the selection of fine woods, it travelled extensively in makeshift wagons, suffering the extremes of hot and cold. It swelled and shrank. It went on campaign, resting in tents. Its journeys were not smooth, and it was at times badly shaken in transit (killing those who tried to lend a hand to support it). It was conveyed on ox-carts or on the shoulders of priests. It was captured by the Philistines (whom, perversely, it did not strike down as they installed it in the temple of Dagon). It saved itself, to Dagon's detriment, and was sent away again in a cart. It was enshrined at Shiloh and finally in Jerusalem. If we imagine that it then had to go by wagon to Egypt, and onwards all the way to Ethiopia, it would have undergone yet more vibration and exposure to variations of temperature and humidity.

Aksum does not have the dry climate of Egypt, and there existed no preservatives against insects, white ants and the like. Very little of any age survives there, particularly artefacts made of wood. Wooden fragments, almost completely dissolved, are all that survive in the Aksumite tombs, themselves now ancient, although built more than 1500 years later than Tutankhamun's tomb. Wooden objects of even more recent date than these are extremely scarce in Ethiopia. Acacia wood panels from the time of the pyramids, long before the Ark was created, have survived in the sands of ancient Egypt, but the *manbara tabotat* at Lalibela might be almost the oldest surviving intact examples of wooden artefacts in Ethiopia: one quarter the age of the Ark. There are also some ceiling panels known from Ethiopian churches that might conceivably be of similar age.

If we credit the supposed history of the object kept at Aksum, we must envisage several more hasty flights to hide from enemies, and concealments on a number of occasions in out-of-the-way places, in islands, mountains and forests, at a time when its fabric must already have been extremely feeble. It seems that, however coddled the wooden chest – with or without its massive gold covering – might have been, it could scarcely be expected to have survived intact. If it were supposed to have still borne the immensely heavy solid gold mercy-seat, and to enclose the two stone tablets of the Law – relatively small though these must have been for Moses to carry them down the mountain – its chances of survival would have been even more remote.

The conclusion is inevitable. The second pair of stone tablets supposedly made by Moses at Sinai to replace the broken originals could certainly have survived, if they ever existed, but there is not the remotest evidence for their presence in Ethiopia or anywhere else. An object created, like so many 'arks' before, as the spiritual successor of the Ark of Moses, exists at Maryam Seyon church at Aksum, in the form of a stone tablet or slab of some sort. In a recent book on the queen of Sheba, Nicholas Clapp suggested that 'hidden in the Chapel of the Tablet was either a great mystery or a great hoax. It was difficult to imagine anything in between.'[4] But that is just what we do need to imagine. Imbued through a complex and esoteric symbolism with the holy aura of the Ark in which the tablets once rested, and bearing the same name, it is the substitute that receives the reverence and adoration of the Ethiopian Christians – not for a 'real', scientific, reason, but through its *mystical* identity with Zion, the Ark of the Lord. In terms of faith, this concept is entirely acceptable. The *KN* itself explains how the Ark is actually a heavenly thing, and that even the Ark of Moses was nothing more than an authorised likeness made by the hand of man.

Moses' Ark of the Covenant – if such an object were ever created in the form portrayed in the biblical narrative – would today be well over three thousand years old. Given certain particular physical conditions, the decayed remains of a casket from the temple of Solomon could, perhaps, still lie concealed, as Jewish legends assert, under the site of the temple at Jerusalem – but it is far more probable that anything that once functioned as the Ark of Israel long since perished. Of one thing we may be quite sure, perfectly in accord with the Ethiopian reports cited above – the 'chair of the Ark', the 'larger box' or golden Ark of the Covenant of Moses, David and Solomon, was never at Aksum.

Appendix: Selected Documentation

The Story of Menelik from Pêro Pais, *História da Etiópia*, I: 31–41, trans. by W.G.L. Randles. I have noted Budge's chapter numbers, and any significant textual differences:

Cap. III. In which is described how Menilehêc the son of the Queen of Sheba went to Jerusalem to see his father Solomon.

> Before describing the story of the son of the Queen of Sheba, it should be noted that the books which are kept in the Church of Aksum give him different names such as Bainalehequêm, Ebna Elchaquêm, Ebnehaquêm, Menilehec (and not Menilec, as writes Friar Luiz de Urreta, page 46). But the people of Ethiopia commonly use this latter Menilehêc, and in the ancient language it means that he resembled him, because he greatly resembled Solomon. But when Solomon raised him [Menilehêc] as King, they gave him the name of David like his father. And thus it has come to be that the Emperors of Ethiopia change their baptismal name when the Empire is handed over to them. The other names mean son of a wise man. Having said this so that the reader see nothing odd, in these names, let us continue with the history of Menilehêc which we started in the preceding chapter, in the same manner as the book records it. And it goes as follows:
>
> (Budge, *KN*, Ch. 32) The child grew and they gave him the name of Bainalehequêm, and when he was 12 years old, he asked those who had brought him up who his father was, and they told him that it was King Solomon. He also asked the Queen and she answered with ill humour. Why

do you ask me about your father and not about your mother? He went off without saying anything and returning three days later (Budge, 'and a second time, and a third time, he asked her') he repeated the question and she answered him that his [father's] country was a long way away and the road very arduous. Do not seek to go there. At this he waited till was 22, during [which time] he learnt everything about riding and hunting and then he asked the Queen with much insistence that she allow him to go and see his father. (BKN, Ch. 33) Seeing the great desire that he had, she sent for her merchant Tamarîn and told him to take [David] to his father, because he was continually importuning [her] night and day. But that he should endeavour to return quickly and safely if the God of Israel allowed. And preparing the necessary for the road, according to his honour [=according to what his station required] and the gifts he was to present to his father, she sent him off with a considerable escort enjoining them all that they should not leave him there, but that they should bring him back and that they ask King Solomon that he make him King of Ethiopia with a command that all his successors be engendered by him [David]. Because [previously] it was [had been] a custom for virgins to reign without ever marrying, and that he [Solomon] send her a piece of the covering [vestment] of the Ark before which she might pray. And in sending off her son, she only gave him the ring which Solomon had given her off his finger so that he [Solomon] might know that this was his son and that he remember the oath that she had made to him to only worship the God of Israel, as did all her vassals, and with this she sent him [David] on his way in peace.

Proceeding on his way, he reached the land of Gaza, which Solomon had given to his mother, (BKN, Ch. 34) and there he was received with great honour, it appearing to them [the local inhabitants] that he was Solomon himself, for in nothing was he different from him [Solomon] and in that which concerned their rank both seemed to be their king. But afterwards some of them said that he could not be Solomon, who was in Jerusalem. Others said that he was the same Solomon, the son of David. And in this doubt, they sent men on horseback to Jerusalem, where they found Solomon and they told him that their whole land was upset because a merchant had arrived there, who seemed to be just like him [Solomon] without any difference whatever. The King asked where he was going and they answered that they had never dared to ask him, on account of the great majesty he had, but that his people said that he was coming to him [Solomon]. Hearing this, Solomon felt a pang in his heart, though he remained joyful in mind, realising whom it might be, for until then he had only one son whose name was Jeroboâm. (Long section omitted, including mention of 'those who reigned, who were not [if] Israel'); (BKN, Ch. 35) And he sent one of his servants, on whom he relied, to go and meet him [David] carrying many gifts and a great number of carts, that he might be brought to him as fast as possible.

Solomon's servant went off in great style and arriving at where Bainalehequêm was, he gave him the gifts and told him to go with him because the king's heart was burning with love and he wanted to see him. As far as I am concerned [he said] I do not know if you be son or brother, but I do not mind if you are one or the other, for you look just like him. To which he [David] answered: I give great praise to the God of Israel, for I have found honour [sent] ahead from my Lord the King, and without actually seeing his face, he has given me joy with his words. Now I also have the hope that this same God will make me get there to see [Solomon] and return in peace to the Queen, my mother and my land of Ethiopia. Solomon's servant (named as 'Joas son of Yodahe' in Budge's version, with a note that this name is in error for Joab, Solomon's captain, and that other mss. have Benyas) answered: You will find much more than what you desire in my lord [Solomon] and in our land. (Long section omitted about the comparative qualities of Ethiopia and Israel.)Then Bainalehequêm gave rich vestments to Solomon's servants and set off with them to Jerusalem, and reaching that City, when they [the people?] saw him, they thought it was Solomon himself upon which they greatly marvelled. (*BKN*, Ch. 36) And when the King [David?] entered, he [Solomon] rose from his throne and embraced him saying: This is my David resurrected from the dead and renewed in his youth. You say that he looks like me. It is no more than the face of my father David when he was a youth. And taking him to his chamber he gave him rich vestments and put rings on his hands [=fingers] and a crown on his head and made him sit on a throne beside him. And the Princes and Great ones of Israel made him reverence and blessed him saying: Blessed be your mother who gave birth to you for you have come forth for us from the root of Jesse an eminent man, which is [the same line] as that of our King and our sons. And all, according to their station, brought him gifts. And he secretly gave Solomon his mother's ring, telling him [Solomon] to remember what he had told him. Solomon answered: Why do you give me this ring? as a sign? Verily I see in your face that you are my son.

After Solomon had spoken in secret with his son, Tamerîn came in and said to him: I have heard, my lord, what your maidservant the Queen has commanded to be told to you. She asks you that you anoint this your son as King of our land and that you command that henceforth no woman shall reign and that you send him back again in peace so that his heart be joyful. The King answered: What greater worth has a woman over a son than giving birth to him in pain and raising him? A daughter is for becoming a mother; a son for becoming a father. Hence I do not have to ask the Queen's [permission], I just make him King of Israel, since he is the first born of my line, which God gave me. And sending him [David] each day rich victuals and precious vestments: gold and silver, he [Solomon] said that it would be best that he [David] stay where were the house of God and the Ark and the Tables of the Law and where God himself dwelt. But he [David] answered: As for the gold, silver and rich vestments, these are not lacking in our country. I came only to see your face and listen to your wisdom and subject myself to your Empire and afterwards return to my country and my mother, for all are happy with the country where they were born. And thus however much joy you give me, I shall never be happy here, because my flesh draws me to where I was born and where I was brought up and if on account of my flesh [i.e. that half of his flesh that was descended from Solomon] I worship the Ark of the God of Israel, it will honour me. It will be enough that you give me something of the covering of the Ark so that I and my mother and those of our kingdom may revere it. My Lady [i.e. the Queen] has already destroyed all the idols and has converted our people to the God of Zion. For she has listened to you and learnt from you and as you have commanded her so she has done. (Reduced from B*KN*, Ch. 37) Solomon tried with many arguments and promises to persuade him to stay and that he would be King of Israel and that he would own the land which God had given to his people and the Ark of the Testament as well. (B*KN*, Ch. 38) And not being able to get him to agree, he called together all his counsellors and the Princes and the great ones of the Kingdom and said to them that as he had not been able to persuade him [David] to stay and that in any event he wanted to return, they should all prepare to anoint him as King of the land of Ethiopia. And just as they were there on his right hand and on his left hand, so their first born would be there with him [David] and that they should send priests to teach the law so that they [the people of Ethiopia] be subject to the God of Israel. They all answered: As the King orders, so it shall be done. Who should contradict the command of God and the King? (Section about Baltasor king of Rôm, and the three kingdoms ruled by the seed of David omitted.)

(B*KN*, Ch. 39) They forthwith prepared the most sweet smelling scents and oil and playing many sorts of musical instruments with shouts of joy, they led him [David] into the Holy of Holies and he was declared [king] by the mouth of the priests Sadôc and Ioas and he was anointed by the hand of the Prince of Solomon and they gave him David as a name. For in the law they found this as the name of a king. And coming out, he mounted Solomon's mule and they led him through the whole city crying: Long live the King. May the God of Israel be your guide together with the Ark of the Law of God and wherever you go, may all be subject to you and may your enemies fall down before you. After that his father gave him a blessing saying: The blessing of Heaven and Earth be in your heart. And they all answered: Amen. Solomon then said to Sadôc: Expound to him the justice and punishment of God so that he be guided by them. (B*KN*, Ch. 40) The priest Sadôc answered: Listen carefully to what I tell you, because if you follow it you will live with God and if not He will punish you with rigour and you will be less than those of your own people and vanquished by the multitude of your enemies. Listen to the word of God and follow it and do not stray from his law, neither to the right nor to the left. And he gave him a long talk, describing the punishments which God would give him if he did not follow the law and the rewards he would receive if he obeyed (i.e. the contents of B*KN*, Chs. 41–42).

(B*KN*, Ch. 43) The whole country was filled with joy that Solomon had made his son king, though they were sad at his having ordered that they give their first born, even if he [David] was to accord them the honours that Solomon accorded to they themselves. And Solomon told his son that just as he arranged his house and shared out the [different] duties, so he should do in his house and for this he gave him the first born sons, and their names were Azarias son of Sadôc the priest, and he designated as head of the priests Jeremias (Elmiyas in Budge), the nephew of Natan the prophet; Maquir, Airam, Finquinâ, Acmihêl, Somnias, Facarôs, Leoandôs, Carmi, Zarâneos, Adarêz, Leguîm, Adeireôs, Aztarân, Macarî, Abiz, Licandeôs, Carmi, Zeraneos. (This list contains 18 names – 20 if the repetition of Carmi and Zeraneos is counted in – to 21 in Budge's version. There are slight variations in the order as well.) All these were given to David, King of Ethiopia, son of King Solomon and to them were shared out all the duties and orderings of the house. (This last phrase is not in B*KN* 43.) He also gave him horses, carts and gold, silver, precious coins and people to accompany him with many other things necessary for the road.

The Princes of Ethiopia prepared to set off with much joy and contentment. But those of Israel were very sad, for they had their first born taken from them and there was much weeping, in which they were joined by their parents, relations and friends at the moment of departure. (Omission of speeches in B*KN*, Ch. 43, and Ch. 44, 'How it is not seemly to revile a king' is omitted completely.) (B*KN*, Ch. 45) But while they were preparing, the first born gathered together and said among themselves: Now that we are leaving our country and our relations, we shall swear to always keep our love [for one another] and [our] togetherness in the land where we are going. Azarias and Jeremias, the sons of the priests answered: We are not worried at leaving our relations, rather that we are being made to leave Zion our lady (*senhora*) and our hope. How can we leave our lady (*senhora*) Zion?. If we say that we do not want to go, the King will have us killed. We cannot avoid fulfilling his command and the word of our parents. What would we not do for the love of Zion our lady (*senhora*)? I shall give you counsel, said Azarias the son of Sadôc, if you swear to me that you do not speak to anyone. If we all die, we shall die together and if we live, we shall also be together. Swear now all in the name of the God of Israel and of the Ark of God. And after this he said. Let us take our lady of Zion for we can indeed take her, if God so wills. If they find us and we die, let us not worry for it is for the love of her that we die. They all rose and kissed his head for the satisfaction and great consolation that they had and they told him that they would do all that he said. Zacharias, the son of Joab (Yo'as in Budge) said: I cannot contain myself with joy. Tell me truly that you will do this? I indeed know that you can do it, for you are in the place of your father and you have in your keeping the keys of the house of God. Watch well what we have to do and keep awake so that we can take her and go with her for her to be a joy to us, albeit a sorrow to our country. He forthwith had a box made out of wood left over from the construction of the temple, of the length and breadth and height of the Ark of God, so that they could take it and he said that they must not reveal this, not even to the King, until after they had left and were a long way away.

(B*KN*, Ch. 46) At night while Azarias was asleep, the Angel of God appeared to him and told him to take four yearling goats, for his sins and those of Elmias, Abizô and Maquir and four unblemished yearling sheep and a cow which had never been put under the yoke and he told him to sacrifice them to the East, half of the sheep on the cow's right hand, the other half on the right left hand (Budge translates this passage as 'on the east side of her (i.e. Zion), and the sheep and the goats to the right and left thereof'). And our Lord King David shall say to Solomon that he desires to sacrifice in Jerusalem and the Holy Ark of God and that for him [David] the son of the priest also should sacrifice according to the way he knows [in the customary manner]. King Solomon will command you [Azarias] to sacrifice and you will take the Ark of God and I shall tell you how to take it away, for God is angry with Israel and wants to have His Ark taken away from them. When Azarias awoke he was very happy with the dream that he had had and with the words of the Angel, and gathering his companions he told them all and he said that they should go with him to King David their lord to recount it all to him. And so they went and told him [David] at which he rejoiced greatly and he sent for Joab (Yo'as) the son of Jodahe and sent him with a message to Solomon saying: Lord, let me go to my country with your permission (at your will) and may your prayer follow me wherever I go. One thing I implore of you, and, on account of it, may the love you show me not diminish. For my sins, I also wish to sacrifice sacrifices to Zion, the Ark of God in this holy land of Jerusalem. (B*KN*, Ch. 47) Joab (Yo'as) went to Solomon with this message and he [Solomon] was much filled with joy and sent to have great sacrifices prepared so that his son might sacrifice. And they gave him 10.000 oxen and cows [Budge, 'one hundred bulls, one hundred oxen'], 10.000 sheep, 10.000 goats and other comestible wild animals and among the clean birds, ten of each kind and one *zal* of wheat flour, 12 *siclos* of silver and 40 *memesrehâ abaioâ* [Budge, 'twenty silver *sâhal* of fine white flour, each weighing twelve shekels, and forty baskets of bread']. King Solomon gave all this to his son and afterwards he sent to tell Azarias, the son of the priest that he might sacrifice for himself at which he was greatly filled with joy and he brought a cow from his house on which a yoke had never been placed and four yearling sheep and also four yearling goats and he joined his sacrifice to that of the King [David], just as the Angel had told him to do.

(B*KN*, Ch. 48) The Angel appeared again to Azarias and said to him: Rouse your brothers Elmias and Abizô and Maguir, and as he roused them, the Angel said: I shall open the door of the temple for you and you shall take the Ark of God and without damaging it in any way, you shall carry it. For God has ordered me to always be with it. They then went to the temple and found the doors open all the way until they reached where Zion the Ark of God lay and it lifted itself up at once because the Angel of God controlled it. And they took it and carried it to the house of Azarias and laid it on sheets of silk, and they lighted candles and sacrificed an unblemished sheep and they offered incense and they stayed there 7 days.

(B*KN*, Ch. 49) At this King David, very pleased because he was going to his country, went to his father Solomon and in paying him his respects (making him reverence) asked him to give him his blessing. The King made him rise and taking him by the head said: May God who blessed my father David be always with you and may he bless your seed as he blessed Jacob and he gave him many blessings. (B*KN*, Ch. 50) With this he departed and they placed the Ark in a cart and they loaded into a hundred carts many rich things and garments which they received from King Solomon and golds [sic] (*ouros*). (Budge: 'And first of all they set Zion by night upon a wagon together with a mass of worthless stuff, and dirty clothes, and stores of every kind'; the last phrase in the Pais version does not occur in Budge.) And the priests ('masters of the caravan' in Budge) standing up, played many instruments and the whole land rejoiced with their voices. The eldest who were there wept with their parents and the whole people wept as if their hearts told them that the Ark had been taken away. So great was the sorrow and lamentation that even the animals seemed to weep and all threw ashes upon their heads. Until Solomon hearing the voices and seeing the weeping of the people and the honour of those who were going, wept and said: As from henceforth the happiness of our kingdom passes to an alien people who do not know God (B*KN*, Ch. 51) and calling Sadôc, he told him to bring one of the vestments of the Ark and to take it to his son David because the Queen had asked him through Tamerin his servant, to make a prayer in front of the Ark with all his people and to tell him that Zion the Ark of God must be his guide and that he must always keep that vestment in his encampment; and that whenever he or his people swore an oath, it must by the Ark, so that they no longer think of other gods.

(B*KN*, Ch. 52) Sadôc went and did all that Solomon told him to do, at which David rejoiced much and he said: Let this [vestment] be my mistress. Sadôc answered: Now swear to me that this vestment will always be in the hands of my son Azarias and his sons and that you will always give tithes to him from your kingdom. And he will always teach the Law of God to you and to your kingdom and he will anoint your sons as kings. And he swore thus and Azarias received from the hand of his father Sadôc that vestment of the Ark and they took it in a cart and went straight ahead on the way, Saint Michael being their guide who made them go so fast as if they were flying, so that the carts were lifted up off the ground as much as an ell [=3 spans] and the animals as much as a span (=0.228m) and they were protected from the sun by a cloud which followed them and it carried them across the sea as the sons of Israel had been carried across the Red Sea. (This last sentence is not in Budge's version.) The first day on which they travelled 'lifted up' (sentence not in Budge's version) (B*KN*, Ch. 53) they reached Gaza, the land which King Solomon gave to the Queen of Sheba and they passed over to Mazrîn, a land of Egypt. And they travelled all this distance in one day. And the

Princes ('sons of the warriors' in Budge) of Israel seeing that they travelled a distance of thirteen days in one, without fatigue, thirst or hunger either for men or animals, considered it to be a doing of God's. And as they saw that they had reached the land of the Egyptians, they said, let us rest here for we have reached the land of Ethiopia and the water of the Tagaçê even reaches as far as this, and putting up their tents they rested. Azarias then said to King David: 'Behold my lord, the wonders of God which have been fulfilled in you. Here you have the Ark of God, only through its will, not through yours. And thus it will always be wherever you wish and no one can take it away from you. Now if you obey the commandments of God, it will be with you and it will defend you.' Then King David amazed by so many wonders gave thanks to God, he and all his encampment. And such was the joy of all, that in wonder they raised their arms to the heavens, giving thanks to God. (This section, like many others, is much abbreviated in comparison to the Budge version; the last two sentences are not in Budge.) And the King leaped for joy, like a lamb and like a kid when it is sated with milk, just as David rejoiced before the Ark of the Testament; and going into the tent where the Ark was, he made reverence to it and kissed it, saying Holy God of Israel, glory be to you, since you do your will and not that of men. And he made a very long prayer (this is the contents of B*KN*, Ch. 54) giving thanks for the favours which had been granted him. And they played many instruments and all made very great festivities. And all the idols of the pagans fell, which they had made with their hands. And the following day they put the Ark on a cart covered with rich cloths and they set off with much music. And the carts went along lifted off the ground as much as an ell and they came to the sea of seas, the sea of Erterâ, which was opened by the hand of Moses and the sons of Israel travelled through it and because God had not yet given Moses the tables of the Law (Tabernacle of the Law of God in Budge), for this reason the water remained as a wall on both sides and they passed through the [sea's] bottom with their wives and children and animals. But when they arrived with the Ark, playing many instruments, the sea received them as if with joy, making festivity with its waves and though they were as high as mountains, the carts passed 'lifted up' over the waves almost as much as three ells. And the fish and the sea monsters worshipped the Ark. And emerging from the sea, they rejoiced much, just as had the sons of Israel when they came out of Egypt and came before Mount Sinai. And they halted there with much music.

(Abbreviation of B*KN*, Ch. 56) While they were on this journey, Sadôc the priest entered the temple and not finding the Ark, except for a few planks which Azarias had made to look like it and which he had placed there, (B*KN*, Ch. 57) he fell on his face as if dead from pain and surprise and as he tarried in coming out, Josias (Iyoas in Budge) went in and found him stretched out and making him get up, he also saw that the Ark was missing, and he threw ashes on his head and began to scream so hard from the door of temple that it was heard in the House of King Solomon. And when he [Solomon] learnt what was going on, he rose with great astonishment and ordered that a proclamation be made that all should gather to go and find the Ethiopians and that his son be brought to him and that they put all the rest to the sword for they deserved death. (B*KN*, Ch. 58) And as the princes and the high persons (*grandes*) and the important (*fortes*) figures of Israel gathered, Solomon came out in great anger that they go and fetch them. And the rest of the elderly men, the widows and the young girls gathered at the temple and wept much because the Ark of the Law of God had been taken from them. Solomon set off on the road to Ethiopia and sent people to left and to right in case they were travelling at a distance from the road in fear because they were carrying something stolen. And [Solomon] told his men to go ahead with horses as fast as they could and that those who found them should return to tell him where they were. And then discovering reliably from some of those on horseback who returned, as he did from the people of Gaza which was as far as he got, that he could not reach them, because they were travelling with their carts 'lifted up' in the air with the speed of birds (B*KN*, Ch. 59, about the servant of Pharaoh, omitted), (B*KN*, Ch. 60) he fell into great lamentation. And he said: Lord, while I live, have You taken the Ark? It would have been better to have taken my life. And he spoke many other words, which showed the great sorrow and anguish of his heart (long lament omitted). (B*KN*, Ch. 61) Afterwards he returned to Jerusalem and together with the elderly men he proceeded to make lamentation anew. And the great men seeing that he shed such tears, consoled him saying that he should not be so upset, since he knew that Zion could not be anywhere else than where it wanted to be, nor do anything other than God's will. He [God] was served [=It had been God's will] in that first the Philistines took it and then returned it. (Long section about the history of the Ark omitted.) Now through His will it had been taken to Ethiopia and [God] would make it return if he wished and if not, you [Solomon] have here the house which you built for God with which you can be consoled. (B*KN*, Ch. 62) Solomon replied: If He had taken me and you others or if He had decided that they possess our land, which is something that God would never do. There is nothing in heaven or earth which resists His will, or disobeys His command. He is King, whose kingdom will last for ever and ever. Let us go to his house and give thanks for everything and as they all entered the Temple, they wept much until Solomon told them to stop, that the pagans might not get satisfaction and enjoyment out of the loss. (B*KN*, Ch. 63) They all answered: May God's will be done and yours too. (A long section, largely a digression from the story, Chs. 63–83, is omitted by Pais. The text resumes with a line from Ch. 55.)

Continuing on his way, King David reached Balentos, at the border of the lands of Ethiopia (B*KN*, Ch. 84) and he entered [the country] with much joy and satisfaction and with many kinds of music and festivities, driving his carts and he sent people in great haste to bring [the] news to Maquêda the Queen of Ethiopia, that her son was on the way, and that he would reign and that he brought the celestial Zion. When the message reached the Queen she was filled with joy and she ordered it proclaimed throughout the kingdom that her son be welcomed and especially the celestial Zion, the Ark of the God of Israel. And they played many instruments before her, making great festivity and both the important people as well as the ordinary ones showed much joy and they went to the land of their power (*terra do seu poder*) (their power base?) which is the head of the Kingdom of Ethiopia where in later times the Ethiopians were made Christians and they spread sweet scents without number at Baltê as far as Galtêt and Alçafâ. And her son came along the road from Azêb and Vaquirôn and he came out through Mocêz and reached Bûr and the power base which is the head of Ethiopia, which she herself had built in her name and it was called Debrâ Maquêda. (B*KN*, Ch. 85) And King David arrived with much festivity and joy in the land of his mother. And when the Queen saw the Ark from afar that it shone in the sun, she gave thanks to the God of Israel with such great joy and satisfaction that she could not contain herself with pleasure and dressing herself richly, she made a great festivity and all the important people and the less important ones were overjoyed. And they placed the Ark in the temple of the land of Maquêda and they placed a guard of 300 men with their swords. And the Princes and the Great ones of Zion and the strong men of Israel placed 300 with swords in their hands. And her son also gave 300 men (700 in Budge) as a guard and his [David's] kingdom held sway from the Alibâ sea as far as Acefâ and he had more honour and wealth than anyone before him or anyone after him. For at that time there was no one such as King Solomon in Jerusalem and such as Queen Maquêda in Ethiopia. To both were given wisdom, honour, wealth and great heartedness.

(B*KN*, Ch. 86) The third day the Queen gave her son seven hundred and seven thousand (707,000, 17,700 in Budge) choice camels ('horses' in Budge) and seven thousand six hundred (7600, 7700 in Budge) mares that were pregnant and three hundred (1000 in Budge) female mules and as many male ones and many of them covered with rich vestments, as well as a large sum of gold and silver. (B*KN*, Ch. 87, beginning omitted) and she granted him the throne of her Kingdom and said to him: I have given you your kingdom and I have made King he whom God made King. I have chosen he whom God has chosen. King David then rose and made reverence to the Queen and said to her: You are the Queen and you are my mistress; all the things that you command I shall do, whether for life or for death. And wherever you send me I shall go, because you are the head and I am the feet, you the mistress and I the slave. And with many other words of humility (large part of B*KN*, Ch. 87, omitted), he offered himself. And when he ended, they played many instruments and made great festivity. (This sentence is out of context, appearing in Budge's version as part of a long speech of King David.) (B*KN*, Ch. 88, beginning omitted) And after that Elmias and Azarias took up the book that was written before God and King Solomon and they read it before Maquêda and the great ones of Israel and when they heard the words, all those present, great and small, worshipped God and gave him many thanks. At last the Queen said to her son: May God give you truth, follow it and do not turn from it to the right or to the left. Love your God, because He is merciful and in his works his goodness is known. And turning to speak with the priests and the people of Israel, she made them many offerings and she promised to consider them always as parents and masters, because it was they who were the guardians of the law and who taught the commandments of the God of Israel. They too gave her many thanks and Azarias in particular much praise and he said that all that they had seen seemed to them good, except that they had black faces. Then Azarias said: Let us go before the Ark of Zion and renew the kingdom of our Lord David. And taking his horn full of oil, he anointed him and thus he renewed the Kingdom of King David, the son of King Solomon in the land under the power of Maquêda in the house of Zion. And the Queen, gathering the Great men of the Kingdom, made them swear by the heavenly Zion and they would not henceforth allow a woman as queen on the throne of the kingdom of Ethiopia except [only] sons descending from David. And Azarias and Elmias received the oath of all the Princes, the Great men and the Governors. And the sons of the force of Israel [*da força de Israel*] with their King David renewed the Kingdom and the people of Ethiopia abandoned their idols and worshipped the God who created them.

Up to here are the words of the book which is kept in the Church at Aksum and it does not continue the story further and the people are not able to explain the lands of Vaquirôm, Baltê, Galtêt and Alcafâ. Only Bur is known which is a province of the kingdom Tigrê, a day's journey from the port of Maçua. As for the name Debrâ Maquêda of the city which the Queen built, Dêber, means a mount…

2 FROM JOÃO DE BARROS

Terceira decada da Asia de Ioam de Barros, trans. by W.G.L. Randles Lisboa, 1563, Facsimile reprint Lisbon, 1992. Livro quarto da terceira decada, Capit.ij, ff. 88r°–93v°; *How the Queen of Sheba went to Jerusalem to see Solomon King of Judea, by whom she had a son called David, from whom, according to the Abyssinian peoples, their kings descend and the rest of what they say of this Queen of Sheba and also of the so called Candáçe and of some things of this prince's [King of Abyssinia's] state (estado) and of his religion and customs*:

> According to what these Abyssinian peoples have in their writings, of which they are proud, the Queen of Sheba of this Ethiopia, hearing of the reputation that Solomon, King of Judea had for his power and his wisdom, sent a certain Ambassador to Jerusalem to find out about the truth of it for herself. And having been satisfied by him on his return by what he had seen and heard,

she desired in person to share his [Solomon's] wisdom, in spite of being [herself] idolatrous, She set off for Jerusalem with great pomp and riches, embarking at a Red Sea port where since has been built a city, Sabath, named after her in memory of her passage...Having crossed the Red Sea to the land of Arabia on the other side, and having crossed that desert, before reaching Jerusalem, she reached a lake at the end of which were some beams lying crosswise to form a sort of bridge for people to cross. There, seized with prophetic spirit, she refused to cross over on them, declaring that she could not place her feet on something that had caused the Saviour of the world to suffer. Later when she was with Solomon, she asked him to have the [beams] taken way from there. Solomon, when she arrived, received her with honour, not only on account of her person, but also on account of the rich gifts of gold, perfumes and precious stones which she had brought for the temple of the Lord and for domestic use in Solomon's residence. She stayed with him until she had been instructed in the matters of the law and she conceived a son by him, to whom she gave birth on the way back to her kingdom. When he had grown up, she sent him to his father with great pomp and riches, asking him [Solomon] that he agree to anoint him as King of Ethiopia before the tabernacle of the sanctuary for him to be her successor. This was in spite of the fact that up to that time the succession in her kingdom was by the female line and not by the masculine one, according to custom of the pagans of the land. When Meilech, (for that was his name) reached Jerusalem he was received by his father with much tenderness and he obtained from the latter his wish. And when the time came for him to be anointed by the King he changed his name to David like his grandfather. And being now instructed in all the things of the law of God, Solomon decided to send him back to his mother and to this end, out of each of the twelve tribes he gave him officials similar to those of Solomon's household, and as head priest, Azaria the son of Sadoch who was also head priest of the temple of Jerusalem. The which Azaria, a few days before their departure, succeeded, at David's request, in being able to enter the Holy of Holies to pray and sacrifice for the success of the journey. In doing so, he stole the tablets of the law, placing others in their place, which he had made for the purpose without telling David anything about it, until after having departed and being at the borders of Ethiopia, he [then] told him of it. David, as one who wanted to imitate his grandfather in zeal for the honour of the law of God, went with great pleasure and joy to Azaria's tent and taking the tablets from the place where he kept them, began to dance and to sing praises to the Lord and to glorify him, to which all those who were with him joined, seeing the cause of his joy. Finally when David had returned to his mother, she entrusted the kingdom to him. And from this prince, [David], the Abyssinians say that all their kings descend by the masculine line up to present, and that among them no woman has ever reigned since. And furthermore all the officials who serve the kings at present are of the lineage of those whom their first king David brought with him.

3 THE BOOK OF AKSUM

The church of Maryam Seyon, from Conti Rossini, *Liber Axumae*: 7 (trans. by Beckingham and Huntingford)

> This is the state of the constitution of Our Mother Seyon, the Cathedral of Aksum. The foundations have not been found to [the depth of] 15 cubits. Its stone pavement is raised 9 cubits (ells) above the ground to the gate of Seyon. The walls are 7 cubits thick, and 125 cubits long from east to west, and 92 cubits from north to south. Its width is 53 cubits [this measurement is missing in the translation provided by Beckingham and Huntingford]; its height, from the ground to the top of the roof is 32 cubits. There are 30 columns in brick and 32 in stone: in all, 62. There are large shutters in wood, at the doors, four outside, to the west, and four inside; there is one at the *tserh* [chamber], one to the north, one to the south, one at Beta Giyorgis, one at Beta Yohannes, two at the treasury, two at Beta Gabre'el, one at the *beta makhbar* (community house), one at Beta Maryam Magdalawit: in all, 20 shutters [19 are enumerated]. There are 461 *ma'eso zaqedros* (doors of cedar). There are 168 windows. The *mankuarakuer* ('wheels') number 780. The qasta damana (rainbows = arches?) are 10 in number; the *re'esa hebay* ('monkey heads) 3815; the *masraba may* (gargoyles, water spouts) 91.

4 IYASU I

Part of Iyasu I's letter to 'Lerons', relating to the earthly and heavenly sanctuaries:

> La grace la plus signalée de Dieu envers nous, et l'unique Sanctuaire, ou nous puissions nous assembler, et lui estre presens, est la Mystère de la Trinité. C'est le comble de nostre elevation vers sa Majesté divine, et c'est sa bonté, qui nous a accordé cette faveur, qui est une grande gloire pour nous et un bienfait signalé de sa part. Ainsi nous devons le craindre tous tant que nous sommes, veu quil nous a choisis et quil nous a appelles a la foy de la Trinité, et il nous a fait entrer dans ce sanctuaire per l'Evangile, comme Paul nous l'apprend par ces paroles: Ceux quil a choisis il les a appelles, et ceux quil a appelles il les a aimes, et ceux quil a aimes, il les a glorifies, et ceux quil a glorifies, il les a justifies et predestines pour estre conformes a l'image de son fils. Et certes ce sanctuaire nous fais entrer en nostre foy et nous approche de Dieu, a fin que nous le louions.
>
> Pour avoir une idée de ce Sanctuaire plus que celeste, nous sommes obligér de nous servir des allegories et des similitudes, prises du sanctuaire legal.
>
> Nous disons donc que les Juifs ont eu un Tabernacle et un Temple dans lequel ils s'assemblaient pour y chanter les louanges de Dieu. C'est pourquoy ils l'appelloient le Sanctuaire du Dieu de l'Univers, parce qu'il ny

avoit point de temple dans aucun autre lieu de la terre, qui l'egalait en beauté et en magnificence. Et dieu leur avoit ordonné de le faire le plus grand et le plus superbe quils pourroient, parce quil connoissait leur attachment aux choses de la terre, et leur penchant pour les vanites du monde; jusque la quils avoient couvert d'or les parois du Temple. Et nous lisons dans le second livre des Rois, que le Roy Exechias depensa des sommes immenses pour le reparer.

(Beside this paragraph, in the copy in the Bibliothèque Nationale (MS Eth. 162) the translator has added: Nota. Quoique le 2 temple l'emportat pardessus le 1er par la magnificance de l'architecture les ornam(ents) et les dorurues neanmoins le 1er avoit des avantages infinim(ent) plus grands c'est (?) le feu du Ciel, l'arche avec le propitiatoire et les Cherubims, Urim et Thummim, la presence divine, le Ste Esprit & l'huile de l'onction.)

Mais le second Temple l'emporta de beaucoup encore sur le premier, tant par les ornamens, que par la magnificence de sa structure. Et ce n'estoit seulement pour cela, quils l'exaltoient, mais parce quil estoit le seul sur la terre qui eust l'avantage d'estre le temple du Dieu de l'Universe; de sorte quils venoient des extremites du monde pour le contempler et pour l'admirer, suivant que nous l'apprens le Bien hereux Luc dans les Actes des Apostres. Les Parthes y accouraient, dit il, les Medes, les Elamites, ceux qui habitent le Corassan, les isles, la Mesopotamie, le Pont, L'Asie, la Phrygie, la Pamphilie, l'Egypte, et la Libye qui est proche de Cyrene: tant la reputation de ce temple estoit repandue par toute la terre. Mais pour rebattre la vanité que les juifs tiroient de sa magnificence, comme les disciples de Nostre-Seigneur luy en relevoient la beauté et la superbe architecture, il leur respondit: vous voyez tous ces bastimens. Je vous dit, quil viendra des jours auxquels il ne sera pas laissé pierre sur pierre, qui ne sont detruite. Ce qui arriva bientost apres par les armées Romaines commandées par Titus comme nous l'apprenons de l'Histoire des Juifs, et des Ouvrages de Joseph fils de Gorion. Cet auteur escrit, que les Romaines estant venus a Jerusalem, ils s'emparent de la ville et qu'avant de se rendre maistres du temple, Titus leur deffendit empressement d y mettre le feu, quoy que les Grands luy representassent, que tant que ce superbe Edifice demeureront sur pieds, les Juifs ne se rendroient jamais, au lieu que sil estoit detruit, leur ardeur se rallentiront aussitost, n'ayant plus rien, qui les animast a combattre. Il y avoit un passage qui menoit au temple, dont la partie interieure, que lon appelloit le Saint des Saints estoit toute ornée d'or, et qui estoit fermée par une grande porte couverte de plaques d'argent. Les juifs occupaient ce passage: mais les Romaines les ayant forcés, ils entrerent dans le Temple, et commencerent a y placer les images de leurs Dieux, a y offrirent les presens de Titus, eslevent leurs voix en acclamations de ses louanges. Les juifs ne pouvant souffrir cette profanation du temple du Dieu vivant, se rallient et attaquent vigoreusement les Romaines: mais Titus y estant accouru, il fit main basse sur la montagne de Sion. Les soldats s'estant assembles le lendemain, ils mirent le feu a la porte qui fermait le Saint des Saints ou le sanctuaire, jettant de grands cris de joye. De quoy Titus estant averty, il y vint aussitost pour faire eteindre le feu: mais ses efforts furent inutiles, n'ayant peu estre entendu a cause du bruit, et du tumulte: car outre les Romaines, il y avoit d'autres nations qui haissoient mortellement les juifs, ce qui de plus voulaient en cela complaire aux Romaines. Ce que voyant Titus, et quil ne pouvoit rien obtenir par ses cris ny par ses menaces, il entra dans cette partie interieure, qui estoit le sanctuaire, et dit en l'admirant: Certes ce superbe edifice meritoit d'estre la maison de Dieu seigneur du ciel et de la terre et la demeure de sa Majesté et de sa splendeur; et les juifs avoient bien raison de combattre et de donner leurs vies pour sa defence. Je l'avois tousjours reveré, et j'avois jugé digne dy envoyer des offrandes et de riches presens, parce quil estoit plus grand et plus magnifique qu'aucun, qui fust a Rome, et dont nous ayons entendu parler. Je voulois l'epargner, et le garentit du feu, mais je rien ay pas esté le maistre, et la malice et l'entestement des Romaines la emporté sur ma volonté. Depuis ce temps la les Juifs n'ont eu ny temple ny Sanctuaire.

Quant a nostre Sanctuaire, qui est la tres sainte Trinité, il subsistera tousjours malgré les reveries de l'heresiarque Sabellius ou de ses sectateurs disciples des juifs; ayant esté avant le monde, et devant demeurer eternellement apres que le monde sera finy. Et ce nous doit estre un perpetuel sujet de gloire, quand nous pensons au bonheur, que nous aurons un jour d'entrer dans ce sanctuaire, pour y chanter incessamment avec les anges, Saint, Saint, Saint, dieu unique en trois personnes, Pere, Fils et St. Esprit.

5 THE TESTAMENT OF SOLOMON

From *The Testament of Solomon*, F.C. Conybeare, *Jewish Quarterly Review*, October 1898: cited from the HTML ed., J.H. Peterson.

> TS108. And I Solomon had much quiet in all the earth, and spent my life in profound peace, honoured by all men and by all under heaven. And I built the entire Temple of the Lord God. And my kingdom was prosperous, and my army was with me. And for the rest the city of Jerusalem had repose, rejoicing and delighted. And all the kings of the earth came to me from the ends of the earth to behold the Temple which I builded to the Lord God. And having heard of the wisdom given to me, they did homage to me in the Temple, bringing gold and silver and precious stones, many and divers, and bronze, and iron, and lead, and cedar logs. And woods that decay not they brought me, for the equipment of the Temple of God.

> TS109. And among them also the queen of the South, being a witch, came in great concern and bowed low before me to the earth. And having heard my wisdom, she glorified the God of Israel, and she made formal trial of all my wisdom, of all love in which I instructed her, according to the wisdom imparted to me. And all the sons of Israel glorified God...

TS116. And the queen of the South saw all this, and marvelled, glorifying the God of Israel; and she beheld the Temple of the Lord being builded. And she gave a siklos of gold and one hundred myriads of silver and choice bronze, and she went into the Temple. And (she beheld) the altar of incense and the brazen supports of this altar, and the gems of the lamps flashing forth of different colours, and of the lamp-stand of stone, and of emerald, and hyacinth, and sapphire; and she beheld the vessels of gold, and silver, and bronze, and wood, and the folds of skins dyed red with madder. And she saw the bases of the pillars of the Temple of the Lord…

TS118. And I Solomon read this epistle; and I folded it up and gave it to my people, and said to them: 'After seven days shalt thou remind me of this epistle'. And Jerusalem was built, and the Temple was being completed. And there was a stone, the end stone of the corner lying there, great, chosen out, one which I desired lay in the head of the corner of the completion of the Temple. And all the workmen, and all the demons helping them came to the same place to bring up the stone and lay it on the pinnacle of the holy Temple, and were not strong enough to stir it, and lay it upon the corner allotted to it. For that stone was exceedingly great and useful for the corner of the Temple.

TS122.…And I said to him: 'What canst thou do?' And he answered: 'I am able to remove mountains, to overthrow the oaths of kings. I wither trees and make their leaves to fall off.' And I said to him: 'Canst thou raise this stone, and lay it for the beginning of this corner which exists in the fair plan of the Temple?' And he said: 'Not only raise this, O king; but also, with the help of the demon who presides over the Red Sea, I will bring up the pillar of air, and will stand it where thou wilt in Jerusalem.'

TS123. Saying this, I laid stress on him, and the flask became as if depleted of air. And I placed it under the stone, and (the spirit) girded himself up, and lifted it up top of the flask. And the flask went up the steps, carrying the stone, and laid it down at the end of the entrance of the Temple. And I Solomon, beholding the stone raised aloft and placed on a foundation, said: 'Truly the Scripture is fulfilled, which says: "The stone which the builders rejected on trial, that same is become the head of the corner." For this it is not mine to grant, but God's, that the demon should be strong enough to lift up so great a stone and deposit it in the place I wished.'

TS124. And Ephippas led the demon of the Red Sea with the column. And they both took the column and raised it aloft from the earth. And I outwitted these two spirits, so that they could not shake the entire earth in a moment of time. And then I sealed round with my ring on this side and that, and said: 'Watch.' And the spirits have remained upholding it until this day, for proof of the wisdom vouchsafed to me. And there the pillar was hanging of enormous size, in mid air, supported by the winds. And thus the spirits appeared underneath, like air, supporting it. And if one looks fixedly, the pillar is a little oblique, being supported by the spirits; and it is so today.

TS127...I, therefore, Solomon, having heard this, glorified God and adjured the demons not to disobey me, but to remain supporting the pillar. And they both sware, saying: "The Lord thy God liveth, we will not let go this pillar until the world's end. But on whatever day this stone fall, then shall be the end of the world."

6 M BARRADAS

M. Barradas' (trans. by E. Filleul) comments in final rebuttal of Urreta's story of the relic of Mount Amara:

> As to what he adds about Dom Balthazar showing him a petition signed by Cardinal Baronio to note down the details of what was inscribed on the piece of the broken stone tablet, which were the same details as those noticed by the author in his book...if he ever showed him such a document it was false and fabricated...the Fathers of the Company have been in Ethiopia for over one hundred years, and during that time Cardinal Baronio lived and flourished and he could have given him the petition of which he speaks and he could have gone to Ethiopia and returned with the answer, and yet in all this time the priests who were in Ethiopia never once heard any mention of such a relic. Nor have the present ones, who have gone to the kingdom of Amarâ and been very close to the famous Mount, never ever have they heard any mention of any such relic, which had it existed, they would have learned of it, or at least have heard it spoken of as being there or at some time in the past having been there...And herewith I add that, were there such a relic, which in fact there is not, and were it to be found on Mount Amarâ, as he says, this Mount could not be seen from the Monastery of Alleluia...

Notes

1   C. Chaillot, *The Ethiopian Orthodox Tewahedo Church Tradition*, Paris, 2002: 23, 39. This includes neither the 2 million plus Eritrean church members, not the diaspora. B. Hirsch and F.-X. Fauvelle-Aymar, 'Aksum après Aksum. Royauté, archéologie et herméneutique chrétienne de Ménélik II (r. 1865–1913) à Zär'a Ya'qob (r. 1434–68)', *Annales d'Ethiopie*, XVII, 2001: 59–109, see p. 102.
2   G. Hancock, *The Sign and the Seal*, Mandarin, London, 1993: 515.
3   Hirsch and Fauvelle-Aymar, *op. cit.*: 65. In a book I have not seen, reviewed in *Branna* magazine (2002: 1, 2), Messay Kebede's *Survival and Modernisation: Ethiopia's Enigmatic Present, A Philiosophical Discourse*, the author apparently assigns to the *KN* a central role in the forming of Ethiopia's concept of nationhood, but the review does not note when this element was installed.
4   Ibid.: 65.
5   R. Grierson and S. Munro-Hay, *The Ark of the Covenant*, London, 1999.

CHAPTER 2

1   C. Conti Rossini, *Liber Axumae*, Corpus Scriptorum Christianorum Orientalium, Scriptores aethiopici, series altera, T. VIII, 1909: 81.
2   For a fuller summary of the story, see Grierson and Munro-Hay, *Ark*...: Ch. 13. 'Makeda' is of uncertain derivation, sometimes regarded as a corruption of Candace – Hendake – or of Macedon, alluding to Ethiopian legends of Alexander the Great. D. A. Hubbard, *The Literary Sources of the KN*..., thesis presented to the University of St. Andrews, 1956: 303. See also I. Guidi, *Storia della letteratura etiopica*, 1932: 47 for other derivations; one of Iyasu II's horses

was called Makeda. B. Lourié, 'From Jerusalem to Aksum through the Temple of Solomon: Archaic traditions related to the Ark of the Covenant and Sion in the *KN* and their translation through Constantinople', *Khristianskii Vostock*, 2 (VIII), Novaya Seriya, 2001: 137–207 (brief English summary 206–7), suggests that it derives from Hebrew, 'in the sense of the Holy of Holies'.

3   Ebna Lahakim (Bayna Lehkem), 'son of the Wise Man', i.e. Solomon. This Arabic name, derived from *ibn al-hakim*, indicated to René Basset that 'the legend of the queen of Sheba is a foreign importation into Ethiopia'. R. Basset, 'Etudes sur l'Histoire d'Ethiopie', première partie, *Journal Asiatique*, ser. 7, 17, 1881: 414.

4   It may derive from a distortion of the word *melek*, 'king', or perhaps of Bayna Lehkem. Hubbard, *op. cit.*: 331.

5   Queen Hendake (Candace – a title and not a personal name) ruled Meroë, in modern Sudan, often called Kush or Ethiopia. Her eunuch treasurer, some thousand years after Solomon, was converted to Christianity by the apostle Philip. Ethiopian Christians claim that this makes their country the earliest Christian state, even though Candace belonged to a different Ethiopia.

6   'Zion' sometimes functioned as a magical word of power. The phrase *girma Seyon*, majesty of Zion, occurs in Ethiopian magical recipes, and *ebna Seyon*, stone of Zion: 'stone of Zion, stone of help...make me like the bear and the lion...' This seems to allude to the power that Zion, in the sense of the Ark or the tablet(s), was supposed to possess. Marcel Griaule, *Le livre de recettes d'un dabtara abyssin*, Paris, 1930: 38–39, 44–45.

7   The book nicely fulfils the required constants of myth systems – binary opposition and an extra-worldly mediator – as observed and classified by E. Leach, *Genesis as Myth and Other Essays*, London, 1969: 9, 11.

8   Greek is missing in the Ramusio version. Chaldean usually indictaes Ge'ez, or sometimes the vernacular. The editors of Alvares suggest Syriac (*The Prester John of the Indies; a true relation of the lands of the Prester John*, revised and edited with additional material from Narrative of the Portuguese Embassy to Abyssinia, translated and edited by Lord Stanley of Alderley (London, 1881), and by C.F. Beckingham and G.W.B. Huntingford, Cambridge, 1961: 147, n. 1).

9   Josephus, *Antiquities of the Jews*, VIII, 6, 5–6.

10   Aziz S. Atiya, *et al.*, eds., Sawirus ibn al-Mukaffa, *History of the Patriarchs of the Egyptian Church*, II, II: 118–20.

11   Abu Salih, *The Churches and Monasteries of Egypt and some neighbouring countries*, ed. and trans. B.T.A. Evetts with notes by A. J. Butler, Oxford, 1895.

12   Alvares, *The Prester John...*:145.

13   For some notes on D'amat and Saba, see S.C. Munro-Hay, *Aksum. An African Civilisation of Late Antiquity*, Edinburgh, 1991: 61ff, 196ff. For new information from recent excavations: C.J. Robin and A. de Maigret, 'Le grand temple de Yéha (Tigray, Éthiopie), après la première campagne de fouilles de la mission Française (1998)', *Comptes Rendus de l'Académie des Inscriptions et Belles-Lettres*, juillet-octobre 1998: 737–98.

14   Hubbard, *op. cit.*: loc. var. The citation is from p. 93.

15 E. Cerulli, *Storia della letteratura etiopica*, Rome, 1956: 38.

16 G. Hancock, *Keeper of Genesis: A Quest for the Hidden Legacy of Mankind*, London, 1996. P. Marshall, *The Philosopher's Stone. A Quest for the Secrets of Alchemy*, London, 2001.

17 F. Praetorius, *Fabula de Regina Sabaea apud Aethiopes*. Dissertatio inauguralis, Halle, n.d. (= 1870). Chs. 19–32 are relevant to the story of the queen. H. Le Roux, *Chez la Reine de Saba*, Paris, 1914.

18 C. Bezold, *Kebra Nagast. Die Herrlichkeit der Könige*, Abhandlungen der Königlich Bayerischen Akademie, Band XXIII, Abth. I, Munich, 1909; *The Queen of Sheba and her only Son Menyelek (I)*, translated by E.A.W. Budge, London, 1st edition, 1922; 2nd edition, 1932.

19 W. Wright, *Catalogue of the Ethiopian Manuscripts in the British Museum acquired since the year 1847*, London, 1877: 297–314 (CCCXCI = Oriental 818). He dates this copy to the first half of the 18th century. Wright adds that the *KN* had been described in detail by Dillmann (XXVI) and Chaîne (ms. d'Abbadie 97), and that Chs. 19–32 are those edited by Praetorius. Wright attributes the mention of Gabra Masqal in the *KN* colophon to Amda Seyon, 'when George was patriarch of Alexandria', though the name Lalibela appears in the Ge'ez text of the colophon in his catalogue (p. 74), and George was not patriarch of Alexandria at this time. Ms. Oriental 818 contains numerous other works as well.

20 Wright, pp. 297–98, notes that BM Orient. 819, which contained a copy of the *KN* written in the reign of Iyasu I, was restored to Prince Kasa, later King John, in December 1872. There is a short description of it in W. Wright, 'List of the Magdala Collection of Ethiopic manuscripts in the British Museum', *Zeitschrift der Deutschen Morgenländischen Gesellschaft*, 24, 1870: 614–15. It was dated to 'between A. D. 1682–1706' (the reign of Iyasu I). Getatchew Haile (pers. comm.) revises this dating, noting a sentence stating: 'And the number of metropolitans who came to Ethiopia from Abba Selama, Kesate Birhan, to Abba Kristodolus is 92.' Getatchew Haile adds: 'Kristodolus reigned from 1720–43, indicating that the author of the note (and possibly the copyist of the entire EMML 50/BM Or 819) could be talking about Iyasu II (1730–55), not Iyasu I.' In the EMML catalogue, no. 50 (which contains the *KN*, the *Book of Aksum*, some lists of kings, patriarchs and metropolitans, and two diagrams of the provinces) is therefore dated to the late 18th or early 19th century.

21 The *KN* also appears (with the colophon as Budge translates it) in the 17th century copy, ms. 146, in H. Zotenberg, *Catalogue des mss éthiopiens dans la Bibliothèque Nationale*, Paris, 1877: 222ff (see below). Zotenberg (p. 223) also noted an Arabic version of the story of the queen of Ethiopia's visit to Solomon, the birth of her son, and the stealing of the *tabot*, mixed with Muslim legends about the *rukh* and the queen's goat-foot, in ms. Supplément, no. 92, fol. 70v – 81v – the text translated by Budge. Like Or 819, the MS. Bruce 93, Dillmann XXVI contains the *KN*, an *Appendix de rebus Axumiticis*, which is the *Liber Axumae* with some extra additions like the description of the coronation ceremony ('Hic est liber, quem Salomo Rex Ibn-Hakimo dedit...'; it was also translated by Paez, Bk. I, ch. XII), and other texts.

22   Almost exactly the same contents appear in MS d'Abbadie 97, copied by
      Arnauld d'Abbadie from a ms. belonging to the son of King Tekla Giyorgis:
      Antoine d'Abbadie, *Catalogue raisonné de manuscrits éthiopiens appartenant à
      Antoine d'Abbadie*, Paris, 1859: 108–10. M. Chaîne, *Catalogue des manuscrits
      éthiopiens de la Collection Antoine d'Abbadie*, Paris, 1912: 64, ms. 203.

CHAPTER 3

1   Grierson and Munro-Hay, *The Ark...*: 3–4. I. Guidi, *Annales Iohannis I, Iyasu I,
      Bakaffa*, Corpus Scriptorum Christianorum Orientalium, T. 24, 27, Scriptores
      aethiopici, series altera, 5; text, Louvain, 1903, translation, Leipzig, 1903: 14–15,
      176–77, 253. 'Gimja Bet' was the 'House of Silk', one of the palace buildings in
      Gondar, and there was a church called Gimja Bet Maryam there; but an older
      'Gimja Bet' church was one of the camp churches. I. Guidi, 'Due nuovi
      manoscritti della "Cronaca Abbreviata" di Abissinia', *Rendiconti della R. Accademia
      Nazionale dei Lincei*, serie 6, II, 1926: 391. R. Basset, 'Etudes sur l'histoire
      d'Ethiopie', *Journal Asiatique*, ser. 7, 18, octobre-novembre-décembre 1881: 305.
2   *Coptic Encyclopedia*, 'Eucharistic vessels and instruments', (see Ark and
      Chalice), 1996, 4: 1064–65.
3   They are known from Lalibela, Yimrehana Krestos church near Lalibela, Zoz
      Amba, a church in Balasa, and Maryam Aba'o church near Dera, Tigray,
      though surely there must be others elsewhere as well. *Rock-Hewn Churches of
      Eastern Tigray, An Account of the Oxford University Expedition to Ethiopia*, eds.
      B. Juel-Jensen and G. Rowell, Oxford, 1974: pl. 59. The *manbar* from Maryam
      Aba, Asbi Dera, is illustrated in *Les Dossiers de l'Archéologie*, Découverte de
      l'archéologie chrétienne, 1975–78: 128; '"mambar" en bois sculpté du
      XIV–XVe siècle dans une église de la région de Dera (Tigré orientale). Le
      mambar est un meuble liturgique d'attribution incertaine, autel portatif ou
      réliquaire.' A.A. Monti della Corte, *Lalibelà...*, Rome, 1949, Tav. XXXIX also
      illustrated some. C. Lepage and J. Mercier, 'Une église Lalibelienne: Zoz
      Amba', *Annales d'Ethiopie*, 18: 149–54.
4   C.H. Walker, *The Abyssinian at Home*, London, 1933: vii. It is not just the
      Ethiopian terminology that causes confusion. Budge, in his translation of the
      KN (e.g. *KN* 17) offers 'tabernacle' for both *tabot* and *dabtara*. *Dabtara* is a
      word that means, in different contexts, tent (e.g. *dabtara* za-martul, or *dabtara*
      sem', the 'tabernacle of witness', or *dabtara* orit, 'tabernacle of the Old Testament'),
      or lay canon or cantor.
5   M.M. Moreno, 'La cronaca di re Teodoro attribuita al dabara 'Zaneb",
      Rassegna di Studi Etiopici, 2, 1942: 169.
6   D. Kessler, *The Falashas*, London and Portland, Oregon, 1996: 72. E.
      Ullendorff, *Ethiopia and the Bible*, London: Oxford University Press for the
      British Academy, 1968: 82.
7   Kefyalew Merahi, *The Covenant of Holy Mary Zion with Ethiopia*, Addis Ababa,
      1997: 14.

8   Aymro Wondmagegnehu and Joachim Motovu, *The Ethiopian Orthodox Church*, Addis Ababa, 1970: 46, 48, 152.

9   E. Ullendorff, 'Hebraic-Jewish Elements in Abyssinian (Monophysite) Christianity', *Journal of Semitic Studies*, 1, 1956: 234; repeated almost verbatim in *Ethiopia and the Bible* (p. 84 for the citation in question), with some responses to Rodinson's criticisms.

10   Ullendorff, *Ethiopia and the Bible*: 85.

11   Maxime Rodinson's review of E. Ullendorff, *The Ethiopians*...in *Bibliotheca Orientalis*, XXI, 1964: 243.

12   R. Grierson, pers. comm.

13   Ullendorff, *Ethiopia and the Bible*: 82.

14   M. Heldman, 'Architectural symbolism, sacred geography and the Ethiopian church', *Journal of Religion in Africa*, XXII, 3, 1992: 237.

15   Alvares, *The Prester John*...: 151.

16   R. Lefevre. 'Documenti e notizie su Tasfa Seyon', *Rassegna di Studi Etiopici*, 24, 1960–70: 74–133. See p. 78.

17   Getatchew Haile, 'A History of the *Tabot* of Atronesa Maryam in Amhara (Ethiopia)', *Paideuma*, 34, 1988: 13, citing BL Or 481, f. 209a, and Wright's 1877 *Catalogue*...: 83. In this ms., fols 20a and 208b, there is a 'list of books left after the persecution?' (in Susneyos' time) that includes a *KN*, and an 'inventory of the goods of the church of the blessed Virgin Mary at Aksum, in the time of Zara Yaqob and *nebura'ed* Gabra Mikael'. Wright, *Catalogue*...: 6.

18   J. Perruchon (trans.), *Les chroniques de Zar'a Yâ'eqôb et de Ba'eda Mâryâm, rois d'Éthiopie de 1434 à 1478*, (Bibliothèque de l'École Pratique des Hautes Études, Sciences philologiques et historiques, fasc. 93), Paris, 1893: 81.

19   *The Teaching of the Abyssinian Church as set forth by the Doctors of the Same*, translated by the Rev. A.F. Matthew with an Introduction by Canon J. A. Douglas, London, 1936. For foreigners' preoccupation with stories like the *KN*, see p. viii.

20   C. Conti Rossini, *Storia d'Etiopia*, Bergamo, 1928: 256–57.

21   There were other *tabotat* of Zion elsewhere – or at least there were later – and the designation Zion is not uniquely applied to the place where the Ark is supposed to be. See the references to Gimja Bet Maryam as Zion above. In the 19th century Sabagadis of Tigray granted tribute to the church of Seyon at Adwa (Carlo Conti Rossini, *Liber Axumae*, Corpus Scriptorum Christianorum Orientalium, Scriptores aethiopici, series altera, T. VII, 1910: 71). The church of Mary of Zion at Gondar (D. Mathew, *Ethiopia. The Study of a Polity*, 1540–1935, London, 1947: 56) seems to mean Gimja Bet Maryam. Dabra Seyon, Mount Zion, is a Lake Zway island monastery, where the Ark is said to have been concealed from Queen Gudit. Lalibela and Na'akuto–La'ab are said to have built a church called Dabra Seyon (Conti Rossini, 'Gli Atti di Re Na'akueto La-'Ab': 223). There is a monastery of Dabra Seyon in Geralta, Tigray. When Menelik II had the church at Addis Alem consecrated as a sanctuary, it was given the name Dabra Seyon.

H. Rassam, *Narrative of the British Mission to Theodore, king of Abyssinia*, London, 1869: 226, illustrates a *tabot* of Seyon. Which church it came from, and where it is now, is unknown. Rassam supplies no details.

22   There appears to be an ambiguity in the biblical texts concerning the second
      set of the Ten Commandments, based on different strands of traditions. When
      Moses descended the mountain with the original tablets (Exodus 32.15),
      written on by the finger of God on both sides, he broke them in fury at the sight
      of the Golden Calf (Exodus 32.19). Moses hewed out two more to replace them
      (Exodus 34.1), but this time – seemingly – he himself wrote on them following
      God's dictation (Exodus 34.28): 'And he was there with the Lord forty days and
      forty nights…And he wrote upon the tables the words of the covenant, the ten
      commandments.' Should the text rather be translated 'And [the Lord] wrote…'?
      Deuteronomy 10.2–4 is specific: God himself also wrote the second set. Even
      if not divinely inscribed as were the first tablets, the second set would also be
      of extreme holiness, the record of the instructions of God taken at first hand.
      The Ethiopians – as we learn from the *KN* – believe with Deuteronomy that
      the second set was also written by the 'finger of God'. *KN* 11 mentions that the
      tablets were written by God's hands, and *KN* 17 adds that God had the Ark
      made to contain the Law or Covenant had written 'with Mine own fingers, that
      they might keep My Law, the Two Tables of the Covenant'. This is confirmed
      (*KN* 95) by Gregory the Illuminator.
          Elsewhere, this is reiterated. E.A.W. Budge, ed. and trans., *The History of
      Hanna, The Mother of the Blessed Virgin Mary*, from the Lady Meux MS. No.
      4, Section I in *Legends of Our Lady Mary the Perpetual Virgin and Her Mother
      Hanna…*, London, 1922: fols 13a-b):
          'Now the Tabernacle (*dabtar*) of Testimony which abode with our fathers in
      the desert God commanded Moses to make…And the Temple (*bet*) that was
      builded and the Tabernacle (*dabtar*) that was made in the days of Moses and
      Solomon, were intended for the abiding place of the Tables of the Law (*sellata
      hegg*), on the sides of which the law and the Covenant, that is to say, the Ten
      Words, had been written by the Fingers of God.'

23   Kefyalew Merahi, *op. cit.*: 13–14. The date perhaps refers to the years of the
      Creation of the World in 5500 BC? However, in for example S.P. Pétridès, *Le
      Livre d'Or de la Dynastie Salomonienne d'Ethiopie*, Paris, 1964: 48, Menelik I's
      reign is dated from 982–957 BC, years 4518–4543 of Creation. 4570, or 930 BC,
      is the estimated date of the death of Solomon (c. 970–930 BC).

24   Pétridès, *Le Livre d'Or…*: 207, n. 2. For the list of 'firstborn' children who were
      sent to Ethiopia and their offices under Ebna Hakim or Menelik I, see the *KN*.
      Budge, *The Queen of Sheba…*: 62. C. Conti Rossini, 'Note per la storia
      letteraria abissina', RRAL, Classe di Scienze morali, storiche e filiologiche,
      Serie V, vol. VIII, 1899: 199, notes the tradition of the existence of the office of
      ''*aqabe heg wasahfe aksum*', custodian of the law and scribe of Aksum, in the 4th
      century AD. This title is given to Frumentius in the *Synaxarium* by the
      imagination of later Ethiopians, based on the office Rufinus says that he
      received from the king.

25   J. Bruce, *Travels to Discover the Source of the Nile…*, 2nd ed., Edinburgh, 1805:
      II: 399. See also below (Notes to The Dwelling Place of the Ark, 14) for a
      'Protector of the *Tabot*' (*tabota tabaqi*) mentioned in the time of *ras* Walda
      Sellassie.

26 D. Mathew, *Ethiopia. The Study of a Polity, 1540–1935*, London, 1947:12.

27 Kefyalew Merahi, *op. cit.*: 12.

28 *DAE* (Deutsche Aksum-Expedition) II: 84.

29 J. Doresse, *L'Ethiopie*, Paris, 1956; and *Ethiopia*, London, 1967: Fig. 2, the paintings in the entrance, and Fig. 49, a modern painting of St. George and the Dragon.

30 H. de Contenson, 'Les fouilles à Aksoum en 1958. Rapport préliminaire', *Annales d'Ethiopie*, 5, 1963: Pls. 1–II.

31 *The Glorious Victories of Amda Seyon...*91.

32 Exhibition catalogue, Musée nationale des arts d'Afrique et d'Océanie, 20 Oct. 1992–25 Jan. 1993; *Le roi Salomon et les maîtres du regard. Art et médicine en Ethiopie*, Paris, 1992: 113, Pl. 33.

33 Kefyalew Merahi, *op. cit.*: 10–11.

34 Guébré Sellassié, *Chronique du règne de Ménélik II, roi des rois d'Ethiopie*, translated from Amharic by Tèsfa Sellassié, published and annotated by Maurice de Coppet, Paris, 1930: 170, n. 5.

    Selected texts figure in the Hedar Seyon service. On the evening of Hedar Seyon, Psalm 137:1, 'By the rivers of Babylon, there we sat down and wept as we remembered Zion' is sung, and Matthew 23: 34–36, 'Therefore take notice: I will send you prophets and sages and scribes...', is read. Acts 7: 44–47, 'In the wilderness our fathers had the tent of testimony...', is also read. Early next day Psalm 132: 13–14, 'For the Lord chose Zion and cherished it for His dwelling place', is sung, Matthew 5: 17–20, 'Do not suppose that I came to annul the Law or the Prophets...', is read and during the mass Psalm 139: 19–21, 'If thou, O God, wouldst slay the ungodly...', is sung and Matthew 12: 27–28, 'Besides, if I cast out the demons...', is read. The mass is the *Kedase Maryam*, the mass of Mary. The key verse of the day is Psalms 87: 5–6, 'Yes, of Zion it will be said, "This one and that one were born in her", and the Most High himself establishes her. The Lord will count as He registers the peoples: This one was born there.'

35 The Ark does not figure in the Ethiopian *Synaxarium*'s entry for 21 Hedar, nor elsewhere in the compilation except where we might readily expect it: the commemoration of King Solomon on 23 Sane. References to Zion are set firmly in a Jerusalem context except for the story of Yared (11 Genbot), when Yared sings a song called 'Zion' in the 'first church in Aksum', or goes to pray before the Tabernacle of Zion and is raised a cubit above the ground.

36 M. Heldman, 'The Zagwe Dynasty', in *African Zion. The Sacred Art of Ethiopia*, ed. R. Grierson, New Haven and London, 1993: 71. M. Heldman and Getatchew Haile, 'Who is who in Ethiopia's past, Part III', *NEAS* (*North East African Studies*), 9, 1, 1987: 2, note 2.

37 H. Erlich, *Ras Alula...*, Lawrenceville NJ, Asmara, 1995: 181.

38 H. Adolf, 'New light on Oriental sources for Wolfram's *Parzifal* and other grail romances', *Publications of the Modern Language Association of America*, ed. P.L. Waldron, XLII, Menasha, Wisconsin, 1947: 306–24. She is mistaken in naming the Aksum church 'Sellaté-Moussié', an error taken from G. Lejean, *Voyage en Abyssinie exécuté de 1862 à 1864*, Paris, 1873.

39   Other Ark matters are touched upon in Adolf's work. She finds evidence, when
      the *KN* describes a dispute between Kaleb's sons, to suggest the existence of a
      rival version of the story of the coming of the Ark to Ethiopia. In this case, the
      prophet Jeremiah would have brought it. In a Jewish legend (2 Maccabees 2.4ff),
      Jeremiah is said to have secreted the Ark and other temple objects in a cave in
      the mountain whence Moses surveyed the Promised Land for the first time.
      The prophet was 'carried off with his followers from Jerusalem to lead a blessed
      life in a distant country'...Ethiopia? Adolf also finds a possible allusion to the
      Ark in Robert de Borron's early 13th century *Roman de l'Estorie dou Graal*.
      Joseph of Arimathea is told to build a wooden ark for the grail; and this ark, 'an
      object of great religious significance...must refer to the unique Ark of the
      Covenant at Aksum'.

CHAPTER 4

1   A. Mallinson, *The Leaning Tower, or Out of the Perpendicular*, Oxford, 1982: 18.
2   The volumes containing the *KN* are known as mss. Oriental 818 and 819. The
      latter had a dramatic history. Taken from Maqdala after Emperor Tewodros'
      defeat and suicide, it was given by the Secretary of State for India to the British
      Museum in August 1868. There Franz Praetorius translated part of it. The
      manuscript was returned to Ethiopia by the Trustees of the British Museum
      in 1872 at the request of *Dejazmach* Kassa of Tigray, the future Emperor
      Yohannes IV. He had been of service to the British during the Maqdala campaign.
      His letter emphasised the importance of the book in no uncertain terms: '...there
      is a book called *Kivera Negust*, which contains the Law of the whole of Ethiopia,
      and the names of the Shums (local chiefs), Churches, and Provinces are in this
      book. I pray you will find out who has got this book, and send it to me, for in
      my Country my people will not obey my orders without it.' (Budge, *The Queen
      of Sheba...*; xxxiv–xxxv. The second sentence, included in the official
      translation, does not appear in the original Amharic version.)
            Long after the emperor's death, in 1904 Hughes Le Roux was informed
      by a Tigrayan, Haile Maryam, that the book was in Addis Ababa. Emperor
      Menelik commanded that it be used for making a French translation. Le Roux
      described the seals and note at the end of the book that confirmed that it had
      been returned to Yohannes, 'the King of Ethiopia' on 14 December 1872.
            We may doubt that Yohannes needed simply a copy of the *KN*, which does
      not include the names of *shums*, churches and provinces. Although libraries
      were not common in Ethiopia, the emperor could surely have had access to a
      copy if he needed to refer to the *KN* tale. Doubtless, besides the 'law' of
      Ethiopia – which, in the *KN*, outside the theme of the Solomonic monarchy,
      consists of little more than repetitions of biblical law – what the emperor
      needed were the administrative documents of the *Book of Aksum* – lists of
      church rosters, festivals, offerings and servitudes, and dues and taxes from
      hundreds of individuals and villages, copies of land grants and other

documents, and the two rudimentary maps showing the provinces around Aksum – bound in with this copy of the *KN*.

3   See S. Munro-Hay and R. Pankhurst, *Ethiopia*, World Bibliographical Series, Oxford, 1995: 185–89, for a list of catalogues.

4   R. Schneider, 'Les Actes d'Abba Afsé de Yeha', *Annales d'Ethiopie*, 13, 1985: 105–18. Getatchew Haile notes that an older *gadl* of Abba Salama exists, a homily based on a Greek version of the foreign text (by Rufinus) about the saint's life: EMML 1763, fols 84v–86r, copied between 1336 and 1340, published in: 'The homily in honour of St. Frumentius, bishop of Axum…', *Analecta Bollandiana*, 97, 1979: 309–18. Evidently, it does not include the anachronisms, and the Ark does not appear. It renders the Latin original's titles for Frumentius, 'treasurer and secretary', as '*aqabe hegg*, which is sahafe Aksum' (guardian of the law, which is secretary of Aksum), which the Synaxarium makes into two titles, 'guardian of the law, and secretary of Aksum'. *Aqabe hegg* is not a very faithful translation of treasurer. Is there any concept at this early stage that the law involved is the tablets of Moses? If so, this homily might indicate that the first version of the *KN*, completed not long before, and perhaps read by the writer of the homily, already contained the story of the theft of the tablets, and that this influenced the change of the title. The compiler of the pre-1336/40 homily must have lived in much the same intellectual milieu as Yeshaq of Aksum and his companions. He may well have known them. He may even have been the metropolitan bishop of the time, Yohannes.

5   I. Guidi, 'Il "*Gadla* 'Aragâwi", *Atti della R. Accademia dei Lincei*, Ser. 5, Vol. 2, 1874, Rome 1876: 92.

6   Conti Rossini, *Storia*…: 160, 250; from C. Conti Rossini, 'L'Omilia di Yohannes, vescovo d'Aksum, in onore di Garima', *Actes du XIe Congrès Int. des Orient.*, Paris, 1897: 154–55, lines 163–64.

7   C. Conti Rossini, ed., *Acta Yared et Pantalewon*, Corpus Scriptorum Christianorum Orientalium, Scriptores aethiopici, Series altera, T. XVII, Vitae Sanctorum Antiquorum, I, Rome, Paris, Leipzig, 1904: 4–5, 7.

8   I. Guidi, *Storia della letteratura etiopica*, 1932: 61. Conti Rossini, *op. cit.*: 1; Yared acta in uno nobis cognito manuscripto servantur: nempe ms. aeth. D'Abbadie no. 227, quod, Antoine d'Abbadie iubente, exscriptum fuit. See also M. Chaîne, *Catalogue des manuscrits éthiopiens de la collection Antoine d'Abbadie*, Paris, 1912: 227; 'xixe siècle; papier…'

9   S. Strelcyn, *Catalogue of Ethiopian Manuscripts in the British Library acquired since the Year 1877*, London, 1978: 87–88, ms. 55, from the 'Archives de la Maison Impériale Angelo Comneno de Thessalie', given to Prince Marcus Bernardus Angelus Comnenus in Ethiopia by a priest.

10   The Ge'ez text reads 'before the *tabot* of the Lord of Zion in which is the *orit*'. Both '*tabot*' and 'Lord' are in construct state. 'Orit' can be translated in several ways: Law, Torah, Ten Commandments, Pentateuch, Octateuch (R. Grierson).

11   Conti Rossini, *Acta Yared*…: 40.

12   See S.C. Munro-Hay, *Ethiopia and Alexandria*, Warsaw-Wiesbaden, 1997: 78, n. 207, for bibliography. For a new translation of Theophanes, see also

C. Mango and R. Scott, *The Chronicle of Theophanes Confessor*, Byzantine and Near Eastern History, AD 284–813, Oxford, 1997: 257 for AM 6015, AD 522/3, mentioning Elasbaas, emperor of the Ethiopians, and p. 323 for AM 6035, AD 542/3, naming Adad of the Aksumites and Damianos of the Homerites. There has been doubling of one story deriving from two traditions. I. Shahid, *The Martyrs of Najran, New Documents*, Subsidia Hagiographica 49, Brussels, 1971: 45, 50. G.L. Huxley, 'On the Greek Martyrium of the Negranites', *Proceedings of the Royal Irish Academy*, 80c, 1980: 41–55. Axel Moberg, *The Book of the Himyarites, fragments of a hitherto unknown Syriac work*, Lund, 1924.

13   See the *Gadla Abba Pantalewon*; Conti Rossini, *Acta Yared…*, and Moberg, *op. cit.*

14   Dated in the text itself to 835 of Alexander, 523 AD, a date sometimes preferred since it agrees with other sources.

15   W. Wolska-Conus, *Cosmas Indicopleustès, topographie chrétienne*, Paris, 1968. J.W. McCrindle, *The Christian Topography of Cosmas*, London, 1897. D.J. Boorstin, *The Discoverers*, New York, 1985: 109.

16   I. Shahid, in *Byzantium and the Semitic Orient before the Rise of Islam*, Variorum Reprints, London, 1988 (from '"The Kebra Nagast" in the light of Recent Research', *Le Muséon* 89, 1976: 133–78). Budge, *The Queen of Sheba…*: xvi. See S.C. Munro-Hay, 'A sixth-century *Kebra Nagast?*' *Annales d'Ethiopie*, XVII, 2001: 43–58.

17   Twelve 532-year cycles, 6384 years, minus 5500 from the supposed year of creation, comes to 884 EC, or 891/2 AD: well past the time any son of Kaleb, reigning c. 520, could still be alive. If the text meant 'this cycle' plus twelve already passed, the date would be 1423/4, the end of the 13th cycle, in the middle of the reign of Yeshaq, Gabra Masqal. This event in Yeshaq's tenth year is emphasised in the chronicles. Could this 'prophetic' chapter have been inserted then, at the height of the literary revival of the time, in symbolic allusion to the reigning king? The 13th *qamar* is called the *qamar* of Gabra Masqal: Getatchew Haile, 'A new look at some dates of early Ethiopian history', *Le Muséon*, 95, 1982, fasc. 3–4: 315, and n. 12.

18   Since the text mentions the 'throne of Peter in Rome', the archbishop might be Pope Leo I (440–61), whose *Tomus* was so important in defining the accepted religious formulae constituting 'orthodoxy'. He became a favourite target for vilification by later Ethiopian ecclesiastical writers. However, Hubbard identifies the king and archbishop as Emperor Theodosius II (408–450) and Patriarch Nestorius, 'who so held the king in his sway that he would not heed the letters of Cyril', patriarch of Alexandria. From 428, Nestorius – who is named with Arius and 'Yasabo' (Eusebius of Caesarea, a reputed Arian and partly responsible for the expulsion of Athanasius of Alexandria?) in *KN* 93 – was patriarch of Constantinople. Constantinople, often called 'Rome' by Ethiopians, is not usually identified with the 'throne of Peter'. Hubbard, *op. cit.*: 257.

The nails forming the bit in Constantine's bridle when he went into battle was a favourite tale. 'Sir John Mandeville' mentions it about thirty years after the original *KN. The Travels of Sir John Mandeville*, translated with an introduction by W.R.D. Moseley, Penguin Books, Harmondsworth etc., 1983.

19   A. Caquot, 'La royauté sacrale en Ethiopie', *Annales d'Ethiopie*, 2, 1957: 209.

20   Unless this whole interpretation is wrong, and the emphasis in the text of the *KN* (*KN* 117) on the legitimacy of Gabra Masqal, Kaleb's supposed son, divinely inspired to select Zion when his elder brother Israel selected the chariot, alludes indirectly to Amda Seyon Gabra Masqal himself. The elder son Israel in this prophecy could symbolise the concept of the installation of *verus Israel* in Ethiopia. This explanation seems unlikely.

21   It has been suggested that Lalibela Gabra Masqal was the original of the Israel-Gabra Masqal tale in the *KN*. The *Zena Lalibela* relates that Lalibela suffered persecution, indeed a threat against his life, from his elder brother, though a peaceful solution was worked out by divine intervention. The *KN* version would have been modelled on the *Zena Lalibela* story, available to Yeshaq and his companions from the *Senkessar* (*Synaxarium*), for the date 12 Sane. However, the early 14th century is rather soon for the insertion of the story into the *Synaxarium*. The main text was translated from Arabic then, but the addition of local Ethiopian saints' lives was a later feature in an expanded version. Hubbard, *op. cit.*: 261.

22   The discoverer of these coins was R. Paribeni (1907). Since then other coins of Israel, including rare bronzes, have come to light. S.C. Munro-Hay, *Coinage of Aksum*, Butleigh and New Delhi, 1984; S.C. Munro-Hay and B. Juel-Jensen, *Aksumite Coinage*, London, 1995.

23   S. Kaplan, *The Beta Israel (Falasha) in Ethiopia*, New York and London, 1992: 39. Was there a relationship between King Israel and the 'Ethiopian Jews'? Might the name of the brother who opposed Gabra Masqal's path to the throne, Beta Israel, have significance with reference to the Beta Israel or Falasha, Ethiopia's 'black Jews'? Could the appearance of the name in this directly post-Kaleb period, when Aksumite Jews might have fled to exile in the Semien area, be more than a coincidence – was Beta Israel perhaps the head of a defeated Jewish party in the state? The evidence does not point this way. There was a post-Kaleb king called Israel – his coinage puts this beyond question – but any relationship with Judaism or Jews beyond the mere adoption of the name Israel remains unproven. The name was not exclusive to Aksum. We find Israel as the name of an official in an Old Nubian letter from Qasr Ibrim, in the neighbouring Christian kingdom of Nubia (pers. comm. Prof. W. Adams). The letter shows the name written exactly as it appears on Ethiopian coins. See *IN* II 25.11 and 26.10 for a domesticus of Faras called Israel. In Nubia, because there is no obligation to account for a 'Solomonic' tradition, such names are accepted merely as a Christian phenomenon. The name of the legendary Israel, son of Kaleb and brother of Gabra Masqal, is unlikely to represent the genuine Aksumite king. It is merely attributed to that period by the 14th century documentation, though the name might derive from the knowledge of coins of *negus* Israel. Only even later than that is the royal name Israel first rendered as Beta Israel, probably by analogy with the Falasha group then known under that name.

24   In Ethiopian folk belief, another element adds to Israel's part of the inheritance, though it is attributed to three unnamed sons of Kaleb rather than to Israel.

When Gabra Masqal became ruler of the kingdom of the day, they became kings of the demons or spirits (*zar*). They obtained from Kaleb the kingdom of the night. They created illnesses, or drove men to madness. J. Mercier, *Le roi Salomon et les maîtres du regard. Art et médicine en Ethiopie*, Paris, 1992: 88, 96–97.

25   In *Gadla Iyasus Mo'a* there is an allusion that might evoke the *KN* story, when Yekuno Amlak and Iyasus Mo'a refer to the 'kingdom of my/your father David'. The late 14th or early 15th century compiler of the *gadl* evidently knew of the reputed Solomonic origins of the dynasty, but did not associate the Ark with the restoration of the 'Israelite' dynasty. *Actes de Iyasus Mo'a, abbé du couvent de St-Etienne de Hayq*, trad. par S. Kur, avec une introduction par E. Cerulli, Corpus Scriptorum Christianorum Orientalium, vol. 260, Scriptores Aethiopici, T. 50, Louvain, 1965: 23.

26   Several writers mistakenly attribute Michael of Tinnis' note to the period of Patriarch Kosmas himself, or even earlier. They have failed to notice that Michael, author of Kosmas' biography and continuator responsible for the biographies of several patriarchs in the compendium, lived well over a century later. We have no reason to suppose that this remark is not Michael's own, rather than something copied from an earlier text. D. Levine, *Greater Ethiopia, The Evolution of a Multiethnic Society*, Chicago and London, 1974: 100: 'A passage in the history of the Coptic patriarch Philotheus shows that the Ethiopian legend ascribing the origin of Menelik I to the union of Solomon and the Queen of Sheba was known in Cairo as early as the tenth century.' In fact, the patriarch concerned was Kosmas III, and there is no mention of either Menelik, or of any union between king and queen. R. Grierson, 'Dreaming of Jerusalem', in *African Zion; the Sacred Art of Ethiopia*: 12, where the citation is dated 'three centuries later' than Kaleb's expedition of c. 520. S. Tedeschi, 'La Reine de Saba et le Roi Tabtahdj', *Annales d'Ethiopie*, XIV, 1987: 167-73; p. 168, 'C'est l'attribution à l'état abyssin, dès le début du Xe siècle, de la légende nationale...'; p. 170, 'tout en appartenant au début du Xe siècle, soit avant même la domination des Zagwé, ce texte attribue la Reine de Saba à l'Ethiopie chrétienne et cette attribution prouve l'ancienneté de cette adoption'.

27   M. Rodinson, 'Sur la questions des "influences juives" en Ethiopie', *Journal of Semitic Studies*, IX, 1, 1964: 19.

28   Dating to the late 7th or early 8th century, or according to others around 1200. C. Gilliot, 'La reine de Saba', légende ou réalité', in *Yémen, au pays de la reine de Saba'*, Paris, 1997: 64. Hubbard, *op. cit.*: 290, 293.

29   Ibid.: 292. See p. 296, n. 36 for the date.

30   Belai Giday, *Ethiopian Civilization*, Addis Ababa, 1992: 134.

31   A. Caquot, 'Les "Chroniques abrégées" d'Ethiopie', *Annales d'Ethiopie*, 2, 1957: 191. The text with a French translation was published by C. Mondon-Vidailhet, 'Notes et mélanges. Une tradition éthiopienne', *Revue Semitique*, 12, 1904: 259–68. This curious compilation has a preamble stating that it was found at Zway in the third year of Menelik II, 1892. It describes the assignment of the regional government of Ethiopia to the different companions who came with Ebna Hakim to Ethiopia, and details the costly materials of their thrones. There

is an allusion to this in the *Mashafa Tefut*: 'Au commencement régna la reine de Saba, puis Menelik, en compagnie de 12 rois et de 2 princes qui lui étaient subordonnés. Ceci ce trouve dans le *KN* d'Axoum, dans une île du lac Zway et dans l'ile de Daga.' A. Caquot, 'Aperçu préliminaire sur le *Mashafa Tefut* de Gechen Amba', *Annales d'Ethiopie*, I, 1955: 97. Sergew Hable Selassie, 'The problem of Gudit', *Journal of Ethiopian Studies*, X, no. 1, 1972: 117, see also n. 19.

32   Taddesse Tamrat, *Church and State*: 189. Alvares, *The Prester John...*: 435, 453.

33   Hubbard, *op. cit.*: 347.

34   A. Erman, 'Bruchstücke koptischer Volkslitteratur', *Abhandlungen der Königliche Preuss. Akademie der Wissenschaften zu Berlin*, 1897: 3–64; (Ein Mährchen von Salomo, 23–26). Hubbard, *op. cit.*: 307–8.

35   In the polyglot psalter (*Psalterium in Quatuor Linguis Hebraea Graeca Chaldea Latina impressum*, Cologne, 1518) Chaldea indicates Ethiopic, but in the polyglot psalter published in Geneva in 1516, *Psalterium Hebraeum, Graecum, Arabicum & Chaldeum cum tribus latinis interpretationibus & glossis*, Chaldeum stands for Aramaic. The 'alphabetum seu potius syllabarum literarum Chaldearum' in the 1548 *Testamentum novem* is the Ge'ez syllabary.

36   F.C. Conybeare, *Jewish Quarterly Review*, October, 1898. See the HTML edition by J.H. Peterson.

37   This derives from a note in the internet site quoted above.

38   Hubbard, *op. cit.*: 201.

39   In the 15th century *gadl* of Yimrehana Krestos there is an inconclusive statement that when the king erected a church at Zazya, he 'made there a similitude of the tabernacle of Moses', until the church was ready for the administration of communion. This simply alludes to a temporary chapel erected to house the *tabot* until a new church was completed. P. Marrassini, *Il Gadla Yemrehanna Krestos*, Supplemento n. 85 agli *Annali* (Istituto Universitario Orientale, Napoli), vol. 55, fasc. 4, Naples, 1995: 81.

40   Most writers assume that Aksum is meant, doubtless because Aksum was the old imperial and religious capital, and the Ark is said to be there now. E. Haberland, *Untersuchungen zum Äthiopischen Königtum*, Wiesbaden, 1965: 31.

41   Grierson and Munro-Hay, *Ark...*: 250ff.

42   Hancock, *op. cit.*: 128–29, 158.

43   Munro-Hay, *Ethiopia and Alexandria*, Ch. 52: 179.

44   Abu Salih, *The Churches and Monasteries of Egypt...*: fols 105a–107a.

45   Budge, *The Queen of Sheba...*: 228–29. In his preface to the *KN*, Budge identifies the ruler named in the colophon as Lalibela Gabra Masqal, with Amda Seyon, adding 'when George was patriarch of Alexandria'; in this he follows Wright (see Chapter 2, note 19). Yet the king concerned, as the date – and the name – indicates, was Lalibela Gabra Masqal, and the bishop was the Ethiopian metropolitan, not the patriarch of Alexandria.

46   C. Conti Rossini, 'L'Evangelo d'Oro di Dabra Libanos', *Rendiconti della Reale Accademia dei Lincei*, Classe di Scienze Morali, Storiche e Filologiche, ser. 5, vol. 10, 1901: 190, Document 7.

47   Conti Rossini, 'Gli Atti di Re Na'akueto La-'Ab': 230, 233. Taddesse Tamrat, *Church and State:* 64.

48   *A propos*, a *tabot* in the Vatican collection (dated, without explanation, by its publishers, to the first half of the 18th century) bears the inscription: 'This *tabot* of Na'akuto-La'ab and *tabot* of Seyon'. The authors cite the church of Maryam Seyon at Aksum, as typically whenever 'Seyon' is mentioned. But the association of King Na'akuto-La'ab with a *tabot* of Zion and a church of Dabra Seyon in his *gadl* encourages reconsideration of this attribution. The *tabot* also bears dedications to the Holy Trinity, and to the Cross. J.M. Hanssens and A. Raes, 'Une collection de tâbots au Musée Chrétien de la Bibliothèque Vaticane', *Orientalia Cristiana Periodica*, XVII, 1951: 448–9.

49   *The Chronography of Gregory abû'l Faraj, the son of Aaron, the Hebrew Physician, commonly known as Bar Hebraeus, being the First Part of his Political History of the World*, translated from the Syriac by E.A.W. Budge, London, 1932, Vol. I: 26.

50   C. Conti Rossini, '*Aethiopica* (II Serie)', *Rivista degli Studi Orientali*, X, 1923–25: 506–8, and after him many others; see for example *The Glorious Victories of 'Amda Seyon*…: 13. Shahid, The *KN*…: 141. Ullendorff, *Ethiopia and the Bible*: 75, 141.

51   C. Conti Rossini, 'L'Evangelo d'Oro…': 200, Document 17.

52   Hubbard, *op. cit.*: 360.

53   D. Levine, *Greater Ethiopia*…: 111.

54   S. Chernetsov, unpublished paper 'Riches and honor of Ethiopian Kings': 10. Partially cited by M. Kropp, 'Zur Deutung des Titels "Kebrä nägäst"', *Oriens Christianus*, 80, 1996: 112.

   If we evaluate the legitimate rights to the throne in the way they are set forth in the 'Glory of the Kings' the rights of Ya'ibika Igzi seem to be preferable to those of Yikuno Amlak's children. The descendants of the Aksumite *aqabe-sensen* ('keeper of the large fan') could probably trace their line directly from the Aksumite kings with more ease and likelihood than the Amhara southerners. Besides, the tabernacle of Zion, this most important relic of the Christian kingdom, was absolutely in Ya'ibika's possession, i.e. in the Aksum cathedral, whose dean Yishaq was among the courtiers of the governor of Intarta. Therefore the actions of Ya'ibika Igzi was not at all a rebellion of an unruly vassal or a revolt of a regional separatist; his pretensions seem to have aimed as high as the supreme throne of the Christian kingdom itself. And here both Ya'ibika Igzi and Yishaq went hand in hand: while the former was planning his rebellion and was looking for allies, the latter was compiling the ideological and moral justification for the actions of his sovereign, i.e. 'The Honor of Kings' [the *KN*].

55   J. Sorenson, *Imagining Ethiopia, Struggles for History and Identity in the Horn of Africa*, New Brunswick, New Jersey, 1993: 23. R.K.P. Pankhurst, ' "Fear God, Honor the King": The use of biblical allusion in Ethiopian historical literature, Part II', in *NEAS*, 9, 1, 1987: 26, discusses Amhara attitudes to an Aksum-based palladium: 'The Ark's supposed location in Aksum, over which the empire enjoyed only tenuous control, may not have been fully to the liking of most rulers based far away in Säwa. Interest in the Seyon story was perhaps for that reason far from constant.' Pankhurst suggests that though Zara Yaqob and Baeda Maryam went to Aksum for coronation (not quite true for Baeda

Maryam, though Aksumites came to Amhara for his coronation, and he planned to go to Aksum for a second coronation that was never realised), 'their chroniclers refrain from designating it as Seyon, let alone referring to their masters as kings thereof'. But Zara Yaqob does refer to Our Mother Seyon in (copies of) his land grants to Aksum; also, the chronicle was not written until Lebna Dengel's time.

Shewan politics are noted again when Pankhurst (citing Guébré Sellassié's *Chronique*: 544) contrasts the Seyon-filled chronicle of Yohannes IV with the terminology of that of Menelik II: 'Although his [Menelik's] chronicle repeated the *Kebra Nagast* story that the Ark of the Covenant had been taken by the Ethiopians from Jerusalem, it avoided calling it Seyon or stating that it was carried to Aksum. Toward the end of his reign, moreover, he founded a church of his own at Gannat, within easy access of his capital, Addis Ababa, and he named this place of worship Dabra Seyon ("Place of Seyon"), proclaiming that its status should be "equal to that of Aksum". Menelik, it may be added, made no use of the title "King of Seyon", which was never reintroduced.'

56   A. Cameron, *Continuity and Change in Sixth-Century Byzantium*, London, 1981: 21. J. Pirenne and Gigar Tesfaye, 'Les deux inscriptions du *Negus* Kaleb en Arabie du Sud', *Journal of Ethiopian Studies*, XV, 1982: 105ff.

57   *The Glorious Victories of 'Amda Seyon…*: 59.

58   D. Levine, *Greater Ethiopia…*:111.

59   S.P. Pétridès, *Le Livre d'Or…*: 103, states that the king's letter began with these titles. In fact, the reply from Alfonso of Aragon begins in this form. C. de la Roncière, 'La Découverte de l'Afrique au Moyen Age', *Mémoires de la Société Géographique d'Egypte*, VI, 1925: 115–16. The letter addressed '…Domino Ysach, filio David…' is register 2680, fol. 165, in the archives of Aragon at Barcelona. It actually reads '…Yeshaq son of David by the Grace of God Prester John of the Indies master of the tablets of Mount Sinai…'

60   A. Caquot, 'La royauté sacrale en Ethiopie', *Annales d'Ethiopie*, 2, 1957: 211, citing E. Littmann, *Die altamharischen Kaiserlieder*, Strassburg, 1914: 22. The song, no. V, mentioned on pp. 20–22 does use the phrase 'Lion of David' three times, but it is not certainly referring to King Yeshaq; Huntingford, in *The Glorious Victories of 'Amda Seyon…*, attributes it 'possibly' to Amda Seyon. However, song no. IV, pp. 17–19, does name Yeshaq, and does compare him to 'Der Löwe Davids, der Beharrliche'. For the dating, see G.W.B. Huntingford, *The Historical Geography of Ethiopia*, Oxford etc., 1989: 9.

61   For a general description of the coronation, see Munro-Hay, *Aksum…*: Ch. VII, 6, The Coronation.

62   Abu Salih, *The Churches and Monasteries of Egypt…*: 286–87.

63   P. Marrassini, *Il Gadla Yemrehanna Krestos*, Supplemento n. 85 agli *Annali* (Istituto Universitario Orientale, Napoli), vol. 55, fasc. 4, Naples, 1995: 69.

64   C. Conti Rossini, 'Gli Atti di Re Na'akueto La-'Ab'.

65   J. Perruchon, *Vie de Lalibela, roi d'Ethiopie*, Paris, 1892: 107–8.

66   In a note in the *Four Gospels of Iyasus Mo'a* at Dabra Hayq. Taddesse Tamrat, 'The Abbots of Däbrä-Hayq, 1248–1535', *Journal of Ethiopian Studies*, 1, 1970: 92–93.

67   S. Chernetsov, unpublished *History of Ethiopia*, cited by M. Kropp, 'Zur Deutung des Titels "Kebrä nägäst"', Or Chr 80, 1996: 112.

68   Conti Rossini, *Liber Axumae*: 81.

69   J. Perruchon (trans.), *Les chroniques de Zar'a Yâ'eqôb et de Ba'eda Mâryâm, rois d'Éthiopie de 1434 à 1478*, (Bibliothèque de l'École Pratique des Hautes Études, Sciences philologiques et historiques, fasc. 93), Paris, 1893: 49–50, 83.

70   J. Doresse, *L'Empire du Pretre-Jean*, Paris, 1957: 128.

71   Hirsch and Fauvelle-Aymar, *op. cit.*: 100–101.

72   J. Varenbergh, 'Studien zur abessinischen Reichsordnung (*Ser'ata Mangest*)', *Zeitschrift für Assyriologie*, 30, 1915–16: 1–45. I. Guidi, 'Contribuiti alla Storia Letteraria di Abissinia', I. Il "Ser'ata Mangest"', *Rendiconti della R. Accademia dei Lincei*, Ser. V, XXXI, 1922: 65–89.

73   Alvares, *The Prester John...*: 462, n. 2, cites the Bodleian Bruce ms. 92, fol. 7r.

74   C. Conti Rossini, *Historia regis Sarsa Dengel (Malak Sagad)*, Corpus Scriptorum Christianorum Orientalium, Scriptores aethiopici, series altera, T. III, Paris, 1907: 89–91.

75   P. Pais, *Historia da Ethiopia*, 3 vols, Porto, 1945–46: 115–21. Susneyos' chronicle also has a brief description of the ceremony; F.M. Esteves Pereira, *Chronica de Susneyos, rei de Ethiopia*, Lisbon 1892–1900 (2 vols, I, Ge'ez text, II, Portuguese translation). II, 1900: 95–96.

76   I. Guidi, *Annales Iohannis I, Iyasu I, Bakaffa*, text, p. 110; trans., p. 113–14.

77   Ibid.: text, p. 162–63; trans., p. 170.

78   Pankhurst, '"Fear God, Honor the King"...': 30. Bairu Tafla, *A Chronicle of Emperor Yohannes IV (1872–89)*, Wiesbaden, 1977: Chart III, Genealogy of Emperor Yohannes IV (1872–89). Bairu Tafla, *A Chronicle of Emperor Yohannes IV...*: 45–47. For the coronation ceremonies, see pp. 131–43. Sven Rubenson, 'The Lion of the Tribe of Judah. Christian symbol and/or imperial title', *Journal of Ethiopian Studies*, 3, 2, July 1965: 82, notes how the emperor called himself 'king of Seyon of Ethiopia', asserting his claim 'to be the heir of all that the Kibre Negest stood for'.

79   Pankhurst, '"Fear God, Honor the King"...': 30. One of these variations, Pankhurst writes, is that 'the chronicle differs again from the earlier work in stating that Menelik was not privy to the young Israelites' plan to seize the Ark'; but this is precisely how the *KN* presents the story as well.

80   P. Marrassini, ed. and trans., *Gadla Yohannes Mesraqawi, Vita di Yohannes l'Orientale*, Florence, 1981: 15.

81   See for example the *Ascension of Mary*: V. Arras, trans., *De transitu Mariae. Apocrypha Aethiopice*, II, Corpus Scriptorum Christianorum Orientalium, Scriptores aethiopiae, T. 69, Louvain, 1974: 1–2, 48. I thank R. Grierson for calling my attention to this and subsequent passages.

82   E.A.W. Budge, *The Contendings of the Apostles*, London, 1935: 425–33. I thank R. Grierson for calling my attention to this passage. For the date see I. Guidi, *Storia della letteratura etiopica*, Rome, 1932: 32.

83   Ullendorff: *Ethiopia and the Bible*: 75.

84   'Le Voyage d'Andre Corsal', in F. Alvarez, *Historiale description de l'Ethiopie*, Antwerp, 1558: 18–26.

85 *Ethiopian Itineraries circa 1400–1524*, including those collected by Alessandro Zorzi at Venice in the years 1519–24, edited by O.G.S. Crawford, Cambridge, 1958: 139, 167, 189–91.

86 Conti Rossini, *Liber Axumae*. Pais, Bruce (and Dillmann after him) referred to the whole of the *KN* as *Liber Axumae*, or *Book of Aksum*, but Conti Rossini, whose translation is cited here, employed this term only for three separate sections distinct from the narrative of the *KN*. Alvares, *The Prester John...*: II. There is an English translation of part of the *Liber Axumae*: 521–25. Huntingford, G.W.B., *The Land Charters of Northern Ethiopia*, Addis Ababa, 1965.

87 S. C. Munro-Hay, *Excavations at Aksum*, London, 1989.

88 These officials are probably the equivalent of the *tabota tabaqi*, guardian of the *tabot*, noted at Aksum from an unpublished early 19th century note in a manuscript of the *History of Hanna* in the Juel-Jensen collection: MS. Lady Meux 4, see below, Chapter 6, note 8.

89 See also C. Conti Rossini, 'Donazioni reali alla cattedrale di Aksum', *Rivista degli Studi Orientali*, X, 1923–25: 35–45.

90 A. d'Abbadie, *Catalogue raisonné de manuscrits éthiopiens appartenant à Antoine d'Abbadie*, Paris, 1859: 109, n. 1, discusses the phrase *emenna Seyon gabaza Aksum*:

'Zyon est vulgairement employé comme synonym de MARIE par une métaphore dont j'ai en vain demandé l'explication en Ethiopie. Dans les langues vulgaires, Gabaz est parmi les douze officiers de l'église celui qui relève du alaqa, ou curé, et qui est le guardien de la partie matérielle de l'église. Le chef d'Aksum est un laïque qui porte le titre de (*nebura'ed*) 'l'imposé des mains', et sous lui est un pretre dont le titre est gabaz. Celui qui remplissait ces fonctions lors de mon voyage m'a assuré que dans le passage du Kibra nagast [i.e. in the part now generally known as the *Liber Axumae*], (gabaz) signifie gardienne, protectrice.'

C. Conti Rossini, '*Aethiopica*', *Rivista degli Studi Orientali*, IX, 1921-23: 375; '*gabaz*...talvolta come semplice nome della cattedrale della città santa abissini, talvolta come epiteto di Maria'.

91 Hirsch and Fauvelle-Aymar, *op. cit.*: 102–3.

92 B. Lourié, 'From Jerusalem to Aksum...': 137–207 (brief English summary 206–7). I have not read this article, but the summary notes the *berota eben* as 'a stony chalice'. The reading from the *Book of Aksum* is 'corrected', and Conti Rossini's translation 'improved'.

93 The veneration accorded to a 'church of Seyon' in the chronicle of Baeda Maryam (1468–78) refers to another church, the church of Dabra Seyon in Shewa. A judge, Yakle, was ordered to 'swear by the church of Seyon (*ba seyon beta kristyan...*)' that an accusation was true. Seyon was to become a common dedication for churches. There was a Dabra Seyon at Waldebba to which Lebna Dengel made a grant, another in the Geralta in Tigray, yet another in Lasta, and a Beta Seyon in Sarawe. J. Perruchon, *Les chroniques de Zar'a Ya'eqôb...*: 163. Seyon, or Dabra Seyon, in Shewa, is often mentioned in Solomonic times. In Zara Yaqob's chronicle we are told that the emperor wanted to bring King Dawit's body to Dabra Nagwadgwad in Amhara: 'he had the remains of his

father Dawit brought from Seyon, despite the opposition of the inhabitants of Muwâ'âl...' pp. 83–86. Although Seyon can refer to Aksum in this chronicle, here it seems to refer to Dabra Seyon. There seems also to be a difference between 'Aksum' and 'Seyon' when the chronicle describes the disposal of the remains of Sultan Badlay. One section went to to Aksum, while some of Badlay's robes went to Seyon, pp. 65–66. In Ifat, Baeda Maryam visited Falaga Gasaye, a land of Dabra Berhan, where he addressed the *sahafe lam* of Dabra Seyon, also called the *sahafe lam* (title of a few very high provincial governors, literally meaning the counter of the cattle) of Shewa, p. 153. Syon Salam and Dabra Syon are also mentioned in a land grant of Lebna Dengel confirming the possessions of some northern monasteries: Conti Rossini, *Liber Axumae*: 47.

94   Alvares, *The Prester John*...: 115, 148–51.

95   Ibid.: 323, n. 2. The note is no. 14 in the Codex Ottobonianus Lat. 2789 in the Vatican Library. It is remarkable that Marin Sanudo the Elder, in his *Liber secretorum fidelium Crucis super Terrae Sanctae recuperatione et conservatione*, written around 1306, also mentions 13 altar tables carried in the train of Prester John and destined for tent-churches.

96   *Futûh el-Hábacha*, des conquêtes faites en Abyssinie au XVIe siècle par l'Imam Muhammad Ahmad dit Gragne, version française de la chronique Arabe du Chahâb ad-Din Ahmad; publication begun by Antoine d'Abbadie, completed by Phillipe Paulitschke, Paris, 1898: 354–55. Also, Shihab al-Din Ahmad bin Abd al-Qadr, nicknamed Arab-Faqih, *Histoire de la conquête de l'Abyssinie (XVIe siècle), par Chihab ed-Din Ahmed Abd el-Qader surnommé Arab-Faqih*, ed. and trans. R. Basset, 2 vols (Publications de l'Ecole des Lettres d'Alger, Bulletin de Correspondance Africaine nos. 19–20), Paris, 1897, 1909.

97   See for example R. Basset, 'Etudes sur l'histoire d'Ethiopie', *Journal Asiatique*, ser. 7, 18, août–septembre 1881: 98–99; In the 26th year of Lebna Dengel, 1534, the king celebrated the feast of the Epiphany (*Timqat*) at Aksum, the last such celebration centred on the old church there. In the next year, 1535, 'Aksum was burned, as well as Hallélo, Bankol, Lagâso, Dabra-Karbé (the convent of tears) and many other places'.

98   Aksum is described as follows: '...an ancient city and no one now knows who built it. It is said that it was Dhu al-Qarnayn (Alexander the Great) who founded it but God only knows the truth. There is a building there of stone the length of whose columns is 80 cubits (*dira'*, c. 50cm., pl. *adru'*), and the width of the colonnade is ten cubits; it is still standing.' This rather odd description can only, given the proportions, refer to one of the stelae, probably the still standing Stele no. 3.

99   Shihab al-Din, *op. cit.* '(The king of Abyssinia) brought forth the great idol from the church of Aksum; this was a white stone encrusted with gold, so large that it could not go out of the door; a hole had to be pierced in the church because of its size; they took it away and it was carried by four hundred men in the fortress of the country of Shire called Tabr, where it was left.'

100   R. Basset, 'Etudes sur l'histoire d'Ethiopie', *Journal Asiatique*, ser. 7, 18, août–septembre 1881: Conti Rossini, *Liber Axumae*: 49, for a grant issued by Lebna Dengel 'when I was staying on Tabor'.

101 Conti Rossini, *Liber Axumae*: 85–86.

102 Alvares, *The Prester John...*: 508–18.

103 Ibid.: 147–48. See also Barros, cited below (note 114). A version of the story of the queen and the wood of the Cross is told by Prutky around 1752, from a written sermon by Vincent Ferrer, but it forms part of his excursus on the queen of Sheba, and is not connected with Ethiopia; J. H. Arrowsmith-Brown, *Prutky's travels to Ethiopia and other countries*, London, 1991: 223.

104 Alvares, *The Prester John...*: 462–63, describes them as twelve officers, one from each tribe of Israel. 'They say' that some families still held positions transmitted hereditarily from the original. He adds that 'all the canons whom they call *debetereas* are also said to come from the families of those that came from Jerusalem with the son of Solomon, and on this account they are more honoured than all the rest of the clergy'.

105 Ibid.: 145, n. 3.

106 P. Butler, *Legenda Aurea – Légende Dorée – Golden Legend*, Baltimore, 1899: 130-1. The Caxton abbreviated version occurs in the book published by 'Wyllyam Caxton, Westmestre' in 1483, at the request of William earl of Arundel, with the colophon 'Thus ended the legende named in latyn legenda aurea, that is to saye in englysse *The Golden Legend*'. Fol. CLXVII is entitled 'Of Thynvencyon of tholy crosse', with a note that 'invencion' meant 'that this day the holy crosse was founden', two hundred years after the Resurrection. A woodcut was provided to illustrate the tale. From 'the gospel of Nychodemus' and other works an elaborate history of the Cross from the time of Adam onwards was set forth, including the story of the queen of Sheba:

'And it endured there unto the tyme of Salamon/and by cause he sawe that it was fayre he did doo hewe it doun/and sette it in his hows saltus/and whan the queen of saba came to vysyte Salamon/she worshypped this tree by cause she sayd the savyour of alle the world shold be hanged thereon/by whom the royaume of the jewes shal be defaced and sease...'

107 Joannes Belethus, *Rationale Divinorum Officiorum*, in J-P Migne, *Patrologia Latinus*, 202, col. 153:

'Ferunt sub Adamo Seth filium ejus missum fuisse in paradisum, qui ramem inde sibi datum ab angelo retulit ad patrem, qui statim illius arbores mysterium cognoscens, eam terrae inscruit, in magnam arborem procrevit. Postea vero cum in templi aedificatione ex diversis mundi partibus arbores afferunter, allata est illa et relicta tanquam inutilis. Unde deinceps ad foveas quasdam civitatis posita est, per quam commode transire possit. Hanc cum vidisset regina Saba, noluit transire, sed adoravit.'

108 For the *Hemamata Krestos* see the Amharic mss. EMML 1495, 2458, 3186. The text from which this story is taken is an anonymous publication, *13tu Hemmamata Masqal*, Addis Ababa, 1972, cited by J. Mercier in *Art That Heals, The Image as Medicine in Ethiopia*, The Museum for African Art, New York, 1997: 71, and n. 7. See also A. Caquot, 'La reine de Saba et le bois de la Croix', *Annales d'Ethiopie*, I, 1955: 137–47.

109 Damiano de Goes (Damião de Góis), *Legatio magni Indorum Imperatoris Presyteri Iohannis, ad Emanuelem Lusitaniae Regem, Anno Domini MDXIII,*

Dordrecht 1618). Góis also produced a treatise entitled *Of the Embassy of the Great Emperor of the Indians*, including notes about Abyssinian religion compiled by the first Ethiopian ambassador to Portugal, Matthew the Armenian (in which nothing remotely referred to the *KN*, or the Solomonic descent of the emperor). H edited the letters sent to the Pope and the king of Portugal by Empress Eleni, and Emperor Lebna Dengel. In addition, Góis published a treatise on religion. This document included Ambassador Saga Za-Ab's own treatise – *What we, the Ethiopians, believe and practice in matters of faith and religion*. Damiano a Goes, *Fides, Religio, Moresque Aethiopum sub Imperio preciosi Ioannis (quem vulgo Presbyterum Ioannem vocant)*...Louvain, 1540: Iii–Iiv; The section on the birth of 'Meilech' to Queen 'Maqueda' reads as follows: '...Habemus quoque a temporibus Reginae Saba circumcisionem...Erat aut huic Reginae Saba nomen proprium Maqueda, quae more maiorum colebat Idola. Ad cuius aures fama sapientiae Salomonis cum pervenisset, quendam virum prudentem Hierosolymam misit, ut re omni explorata, certior de regis prudentia redderetur. Quo reverso, & re explanata, subito se ad iter, Hierusalem versus componit. Atque cum eo pervenisset, praeter multa alia, quibus a Salomone erudita est, legem ac prophetas didicit, eaque in patriam (facultate impetrata abeundi) proficiscens, in itinere filium, quem ex Salomone conceperat, peperit, qui vocatus est Meilech...'

After the coronation of King David (Menelik), when he prays in the temple for a favourable journey, Azarias steals the tablets from the Ark and replaces them with others. In Egypt, he reveals that the tablets are with them. The translation relates to tablets taken out from the Ark: de Góis translates the important passage as 'veras foederis domini tabulas ex arca surripuit'; he removed the true tablets of the covenant of the Lord from the Ark. In the next section, too, Azarias reveals that the tablets are with the travellers in Egypt, and David runs to the tent 'where Azarias kept the tablets of the covenant of the Lord', and dances 'like his ancestor David, before the Ark, in which the tablets were'. Here again the difference between David (Menelik) and the tablets, and David of Israel and the Ark and the tablets, is specified: 'Quod cum Azarias intellexisset, Davidem hortatus est, ut ei a patre impetraret potestatem sacrificandi, pro successu itineris, ante arcam foederis domini. Qua re a Salomone impetrata, Azarias subito tabulas, que secretissime potiut, ad imitatione tabularum foederis domini dedolare curat. Quibus perfectis, ad sacrificandum se componit, in ipsoque sacrificio clanculum, atque mira arte, veras foederis domini tabulas ex arca surripuit, pro eisque adulterinas, quas secum portauerat, reposuit, se solo, ac Deo conicio. Haec narratio apud nos Aethiopes sanctissima & probatissima habetur, ut ex historia ipsius Regis Davidis (quae incundissima lectu est) apparet. Cuius historiae liber tantae crassitudinis est, quantae omnes Pauli epistolae.'

'Caeterum cum iam David ad fines Aethiopiae pervenisset, Azarias eius tentrium ingressus, id quod semper apud se occultum tenuerat, ei revelat, nempe tabulas foederis domini penes se esse. Qua re audita, subito David ad tentorium ubi Azarias tabulas foederis domini habebat accurrit ibique prae nimio gaudio ad exemplum avi sui Davidis, ante arcam, in qua tabulae erant, incepit saltare...' See also D. de Góis 1945: 127–86, especially 163ff. The Portuguese version was called A fé, a religião e os Costumes da Etiopia, and Saga Za-Ab's contribution bears the title Eis o que nós, etiopes, se crê e pratica (em materia de fé e religião).

M. Geddes, *The Church History of Ethiopia*, London, 1696: 94, later translated Saga Za-Ab's work into English in his church history, and Ludolf, too, commented on it: Job Ludolf (Hiob Ludolphus), *A New History of Ethiopia*, translated from the Latin by J(ohn) P(hillips), London, 1682, Bk. III, Ch. I, note c. This was reprinted, with an introduction and bibliography by R. K. P. Pankhurst, London, 1988. The original Latin version was the *Historia Aethiopica*, Frankfurt, 1681, with another volume of commentaries, *Commentarius ad suam Historiam Aethiopicam*, following in 1691. Ludolf cites the 'Damianus a Goez' publication in *'the 2. Tom. of Spain illustrated, p. 1302'*.

110 R. Basset, 'Deux lettres éthiopiennes du XVIe siècle. Mémoire traduit sur le texte portugais de M. Esteves Pereira', *Giornale della Società Asiatica italiana*, 3, 1889: 65–66.

111 A 1548 text written by an Ethiopian, Tesfa Seyon, fails to mention the Ark in a tempting spot. While adding nothing to the evidence, it helps confirm that the Ark was far from a central object in the Ethiopian mind of the time. See B. Juel-Jensen, 'Potken's Psalter and Tesfa Sion's New Testament, Modus Baptizandi and Missal', *Bodleian Library Record*, XV, Number 5/6, 1986: 487. Tasfa Seyon, after mourning the destruction wrought by Ahman Grañ, apostrophises Jeremiah:

'Thy sorrow, Jeremiah, was not as Ethiopia's sorrow. Its people is greater [more numerous] than yours, and their country bigger than yours. You had one kingdom, in Ethiopia there are sixty-two. You had a king who worshipped heathen gods, in this [Ethiopia] there is [a king who is] guardian of the Law and the Prophets and who worships the Trinity. You had to deal with hypocritical priests and pharisees, [in Ethiopia] there are priests and monks who fight [for their faith]. You had a single Temple with gold and precious stones, property which belonged to Egyptians, Moabites, and all heathens, property [obtained] by force and plunder gathered in campaigns until the time of Solomon. [In Ethiopia] is the Temple of the Holy Spirit, which is adorned with God's ornaments, namely faith, Hope, and Charity, and with legitimate property which has been acquired through sweat, as the Lord commanded [Gen. 3.19], and the books and the sacrifice which let us inherit Heaven.' Trans. by B. Juel-Jensen from Löfgren's Swedish.

112 In the Latin version: Job Ludolf, *op. cit.*, Book III, Chapter I. In the English version, the text inserts 'Tellezius' for Gregory.

113 In 1533 the *Legatio David Aethiopiae regis*...was published at Bologna. This work cites the royal titles of King David (Lebna Dengel) in Latin, including his Solomonic descent: *David, dilectus à Deo, columna fidei, cognatus stirpis Iuda, filius David, filius Salamonis, filius columnae Syon*...etc. – David, beloved of God, pillar of the faith, descendant of the line of Judah, son of David, son of Solomon, son of Amda Seyon etc. *Legatio David Aethiopiae Regis, ad Sanctissimum D.N. Clementem Papã VII...Euisdem Dauid Aethiopiae Regis Legatio, ad*

Emanuelem Portugalliae Regem. Item alia legation euisdem Dauid Aethiopiae Regis, ad Ioannem Portugalliae Regem...Bononiae (Bologna), 1533: Biv, D3. De Góis published the letters of the Ethiopian rulers in Latin. The original Ge'ez letters were translated by P. de Covilhão and Alvares into Portuguese, and written down by João Escolar, the embassy clerk. Later Paolo Iovius (Giovio) translated them into Latin. Damião de Góis published them as well, as did Ramusio in Italian, and they appeared in *Purchas His Pilgrims* (see for example the London edition of 1625: Vol. 2, 1118). Letters from Lebna Dengel with a similar titulary are cited in Alvares, *The Prester John*...: 476, 495.

114 João de Barros, *Ásia de João de Barros*, Dos feitos que os portugueses fizeram no descobrimento e conquista dos mares e terras do Oriente, Terceira Decada, ed. H. Cidade, Lisbon, 1946: 173.

The Ethiopian emperors themselves at this time continued to emphasise their lineage from 'King David' or Ebna Hakim in their contacts abroad. A 1543 letter from Galawdewos (1540–59) to João III of Portugal calls him son of Wanag Sagad (Lebna Dengel), son of Naod, son of Eskender, son of Baeda Maryam, son of Zara Yaqob, son of Dawit, 'descendants of Solomon, king of kings of Israel...' As with his father Lebna Dengel, the Solomonic descent of the kings was by now a normal ingredient in the official mythology. S.P. Pétridès, *Le Livre d'Or*...: 112, reproduces the beginning part of this letter, which was published by R. Basset, 'Deux lettres éthiopiennes du XVIe siècle. Mémoire traduit sur le texte portugais de M. Esteves Pereira', *Giornale della Società Asiatica italiana*, 3, 1889: 74ff.

115 Nicolao Godigno, *De Abassinorum rebus, deque Aethiopiae Patriarchis Ioanne Nonio Barreto & Andre Oviedo, Libri tres*, Lugduni (Lyon, not Leyden as in Budge), 1615: Liber I, Cap. VII, Unde Abassinorum Imperatorum feratur ductum genus: 32–37; Cap. VIII, Haereditate, an electione fiat Abassinus Imperator: 37–49.

Budge cites *De Abassinorum rebus*...as published 'in the first quarter of the sixteenth century' (in which error he is copied by Miguel Brooks...). *Prutky's travels*..., bibliography: 525, cites Book II of this work (correctly) as published at Lyon, 1615. Prutky, like Ludolf, occasionally quoted from Godinho. Prutky refers to an idea of Ludolf's, confirmed by Godinho and others, that the kings of Arabia Felix possessed colonies on the west coast of the Red Sea. He seems to believe that the Arabian kings of Saba ruled on both sides of the Red Sea, and that thus the 'Old Law was brought into her country by the Queen of Sheba, though not equally throughout all the provinces' (p. 106). Prutky firmly held that 'the Queen maintained her imperial throne in Ethiopian Saba' (p. 222). Prutky also cites Godinho among others as claiming that Queen Candace or Judith was baptised by the eunuch who had been himself baptised by the apostle Philip (p. 107). It seems assumed that the eunuch, serving Candace, queen of the Ethiopians, must have been a black Ethiopian himself. The Bible does not say this. He might have been a captive (if the story is historical in the first place) or a bought slave. He was, apparently, a Jew or Jewish convert, since he went to the Temple 'to worship'.

116 Vincent Le Blanc, *The World Surveyed, or, The Famous Voyages and Travels of Vincent le Blanc, or White, of Marseilles*, London, 1660: 252 trans., from *Les*

Voyages fameux du sieur Vincent le Blanc, Marseillois, qu'il a faits depuis l'aage de douze ans iusques à soixante, aux quatre parties du Monde; a scavois, aux Indes Orientales & Occidentales...par les terres de Monomotapa, du Preste Iean & de l'Egypte...Le tout recueilly de ses memoires par le sieur [Louys] Coulon, Paris, 1648. Le Blanc relates tales of the queen 'which savour of the Talmud fables, and the ragings of the Rabbins'...With her camels, elephants and mules, she traversed Nubia, Canfila, Dala, and Tamatas, then lower Egypt, passing the Red Sea to Ziden (Jidda) in Meca (Makka). She then travelled via Medina and Sinai to Palestine, and entered Jerusalem. Le Blanc also repeats the old story from *The Golden Legend* about the queen's refusal to pass over a bridge made from the wood destined for the Cross.

117 Ante Sabae Reginae tempora unum ex iis dicatum Soli, alterum Lunae fuisse. Sed a Reginae Candacis ad Christum conversione, quod Solis erat, Spiritu Sancto, quod erat Lunae, Sanctae Cruci fuisse consecratum.

118 Frey Luys de Urreta, *Historia eclesiastica, politivca, natural y moral de los grandes y remotos Reynos de la Etiopia, Monarchia del Emperador, llamado Preste Iuan de las Indias*, Valencia, 1610: 119: 'No se sabe quando los Emperadores de la Etiopia empeçaron a juntar piedras preciosas, porque las que tenia la Reyna Saba se guardan oy dia en la ciudad de Saba, en la Iglesia del Espiritu Santo, donde ella se enterrò.'

CHAPTER 5

1 Pêro Pais, *História da Etiópia* (Reprodução do Códice Coevo Inédito da Biblioteca Pública de Braga), Porto, Portugal: Livraria Civiliza, 1945–46, 3 vols. See vol. I: 25ff. C. Bezold, *op. cit.* Budge, *op. cit.*

2 M. de Almeida, *Some Records of Ethiopia, 1593–1646, Being extracts from 'The History of High Ethiopia or Abassia'*. Translated and edited by C.F. Beckingham and G.W.B. Huntingford, London, 1954. In Libro V, Cap. VI of Almeida's account published in Beccari, *Rerum*...VI, we read: 'tinhão muitas pedra d'ara feitas como huma arquinha quadrata em memoria da arca do testamento, e assi lhes chamão *Tabot*, que he o nome que dão aquella ara'.

3 Almeida, translation (by W.G.L. Randles) from U. Monneret de Villard, *Aksum*, Rome, 1938: 73. H. de Contenson, 'Les fouilles à Axoum en 1958 – Rapport préliminaire', *Annales d'Ethiopie*, V, 1963: pl. XIII. Budge, *The History of Hanna, Section I in Legends of Our Lady Mary the Perpetual Virgin and Her Mother Hanna*...

4 A. Raes, 'Antimension, Tablit, *Tabot*', *Proche-Orient chrétien*, I, 1951: 69, citing C. Beccari, *Rerum aethiopicarum scriptores occidentales inediti a saeculo XVI ad XIX*, Rome, 15 vols, 1903–17, Vol. IX, 1909: 31: 'et aras portatiles, si quae erant lineae, flammis comburentes, et lapideas, quasi sacrae non essent, iterum inungentes...'

5 M. Barradas, *Tractatus Tres Historico-Geographici* (1634), A Seventeenth Century Historical and Geographical Account of Tigray, Ethiopia, translated

from the Portuguese by E. Filleul, edited by R. Pankhurst, Wiesbaden, 1996: 122.

6   Barradas, *Tractatus*: 133. Barradas elsewhere alluded to 'places as remote as this monastery of Alleluia, where [Urreta] says merchants bowed down to the relic...'

7   A. Mendes, 'Carta di ill. et rev. D. Alfonso Mendes patriarcha de Ethiopia pera o padre Balthazar Telles'..., in B. Tellez, *Historia geral de Ethiopia a alta*, Coimbra, 1660, carte 1660, 2. Verso. Cited in H. Monneret de Villard, *Aksum*: 77, under 1655.

8   Translation (W.G.L. Randles) from de Villard, *Aksum*: 73.

9   C. Beccari, *Notizia e Saggi*, Rome, 1903: 136.

10   R. Pankhurst notes that this legend is not mentioned elsewhere, citing Hancock. It is in fact mentioned, naming Bur, in the *Liber Axumae* in two separate places, and by Balthasar Telles, and confirmed without mentioning the Ark by Barneto.

11   Balthasar Telles (Tellez), *Historia geral de Ethiopia a alta, Coimbra 1660, translated as The Travels of the Jesuits in Ethiopia*, London, 1710.

12   Conti Rossini, *Liber Axumae*: 92–94.

13   The abbreviated Ethiopian royal chronicle published by Basset states that in the first year of Fasiladas' reign (1632) 'the patriarch arrived, whose name was Rezeq, with the holy ark; he conferred the diaconate and the priesthood, and the intruding patriarch [Mendes] remained alone'. Rezeq's ordinations permitted the restoration of the orthodox faith in Ethiopia – though Rezeq turned out to be a false metropolitan, and was soon replaced. We might assume that he arrived with the returning 'Ark' from Digsa, or even accompanied it southwards as far as Aksum, but other versions of the same text confirm that Rezeq merely performed the usual activities of an *abun*: 'he consecrated the *tabot*, and conferred the deaconate and the priesthood'. Because he was a usurper, all this had to be repeated by the next legitimate metropolitan. R. Basset, 'Etudes sur l'histoire d'Ethiopie', *Journal Asiatique*, ser. 7, 18, octobre-novembre-décembre 1881: 285. J. Perruchon, 'Notes pour l'historie d'Ethiopie. Le règne de Fasiladas (Alam Sagad), de 1632 à 1667', *Revue Sémitique*, 1898: 84.

14   *Gadla Marqorewos seu Acta Sancti Mercurii*, ed. C. Conti Rossini, Corpus Scriptorum Christianorum Orientalium, Scriptores aethiopici, versio, Series altera, T. XXII, Leipzig, 1904. G. Lusini, *Studi sul monachesimo Eustaziano (secoli XIV–XV)*, Naples, 1993: 110.

15   I. Guidi, *Storia della letteratura etiopica*, 1932: 62. C. Bezold, *op. cit.*: v; 'den ältesten Zeugnisse über das Buch', which he dates to the first half of the 15th century. From this, he continued: 'Damit ist zugleich erwiesen, dass die Schrift, die selbst keinen Titel trägt, schon im 15. Jahr. unter dem Namen "Kebra Nagast" in Abessinien bekannt wurde'. Until we have a certifiably 15th century copy of the *Gadla Marqorewos*, this is simple conjecture.

16   In fact, the phrase *(la)Seyon tabota amlaka Esrael* is never exactly paralleled in the *KN* as we have it in the oldest extant versions. The closest parallels are: *KN* 26 *Egziatya tabota heggu la-amlaka Esrael seyon qeddista samayawit*, 'my Lady, the *tabot* of the Law of the God of Israel, the holy and heavenly Zion'; *KN* 28, 36, and 59 *tabota amlaka Esrael*, '*tabot* of the Lord of Israel', and in *KN* 84

seyon samayawit tabota amlaka Esrael 'the heavenly Zion, *tabot* of the Lord of Israel'. These locutions refer to the Ark in this late version of the book, and indicate that the Ark was included, as we would expect, in an Ethiopian source citing the *KN* in the 17th century.

17   Such a version presumably gave rise to the idea that 'Ethiopian history claims that the religious leaders brought the Ark of the Covenant to Ethiopia with the blessing of King Solomon...' (Kefyalew Merahi, *op. cit.*: 13). This is far from the situation outlined in the *KN*.

18   Budge, *The Queen of Sheba*...: xlvi ff. Bezold, *op. cit.*: xliv–li. H. Zotenberg, *Catalogue des mss éthiopiens dans la Bibliothèque Nationale*, Paris, 1877: 223. This manuscript, ms. Supplément, no. 92 (Saint-Germain 350), is the *opusculo* cited by E. Cerulli, *La letteratura etiopica*, 3rd ed., 1968: 38, from a Paris codex. He mentions the date 1594. I thank Mme. Marie-Geneviève Guesdon of the Bibliothèque Nationale, Paris, for information about MS Arabe Supplement 92, now 'Arabe 264': G. Troupeau, Bibliothèque Nationale, Département des Manuscrits, *Catalogue des manuscripts arabes*, première partie, Manuscrits chrétiens, T. I, Nos 1–323, Paris, 1972: 231–33. Ms. 264 contains eleven parts, of which the seventh is described as follows: 'F. 70v–81v. Récit du transfert de la royauté de David, de son fils Salomon au Négus d'Abyssinie...Une notice indique que ce texte se trouve dans l'histoire des anciens pères de l'église copte.'

    The ms., not particularly attractive, its different sections written in different hands, bears the printed label 'Bibliotheca MSS Coisliniana, olim Segueriana, quam Illust. Henricus du Cambout, Dux de COISLIN, Par Franciae, Episcopus Metensis &c Monasterio S. Germanis à Pratis legavit An. M.DCC.XXII'. A handwritten note of the contents includes : 'Transport de la Roiauté de la maison de Salomon fils de David, a la maison Roiale des Abissins'. The Arabic fols 70v–81v are headed by the Coptic word CYN_EW.

    The ms. was copied by three different hands. The date 1594 concerns only the first section, f. 1–69. The date of other sections (ff. 70–83 and 84–130) is unknown. This means that Arabic text concerning the Ark may be more or less contemporary with the dated part, or may not. Mme. Guesdon described the paper as of 'thick oriental' type, apparently from the XVth century. Such oriental paper was also used in the 16th century, but more rarely...Mme. Guesdon confirms the possibility of an early appearance of the Ark story in a note (September 2001): 'The other parts [aside from that dated 1594] are copied on an oriental paper which seems to be more ancient. The script also seems more ancient. Mr Gerard Troupeau proposes XVth century for the date, and I think he is right.' M. Troupeau, at my request, examined the ms. anew, and confirms (November 2001): 'la nature du papier et le type d'écriture de la partie de ce ms qui contient votre texte [the Solomon story], permettent de la dater de la seconde moitié du XVe siècle, sans pouvoir préciser davantage'.

    E. Amélineau translated the story from an almost exactly similar ms. bought in Cairo, in his *Contes et Romans de l'Égypte chrétienne*, Paris, 1886, I: 144–64 (see also Bezold: xliii). The story, no. VII, is entitled 'Comment le Royaume de David passa aux mains du roi d'Abyssinie'.

19   J. Kolmodin, *Traditions de Tsazzega et Hazzega, Textes Tigrigna*, Rome, 1912: 3–6, Tr. 3–5. See also C. Conti Rossini, 'Studi su popolazioni dell'Etiopia', *Rivista di Studi Orientali*, 4, 1911–12: translation: 611–16; E. Littmann, *The Legend of the Queen of Sheba in the Tradition of Axum*, Leyden, 1904; Budge, *The Queen of Sheba*...: lxvi–lxxi.

20   Conti Rossini, *Storia*...: 249ff.

21   Conti Rossini, *Storia*...: 249–52. Serpent tales are widespread in Ethiopia; see *Actes de Iyasus Mo'a*...: 14–15, 25. Taddesse Tamrat, 'A Short Note on the Traditions of Pagan Resistance to the Ethiopian Church (14th and 15th Centuries)', *Journal of Ethiopian Studies*, 10, 1972: 137–50. C. Conti Rossini, 'Note de agiografia Etiopica ('Abiya-Egzi, 'Arkaledes e Gabra-Iyasus)', *Rivista di Studi Orientali*, XVII, 1938: 415. S. Kaplan, *The Monastic Holy Man and the Christianization of Early Solomonic Ethiopia*, Wiesbaden, 1984: loc. var.

22   Taddesse Tamrat, *op. cit.*: 136–37. For other accounts of the birth of Zagua from the queen's companion Ya'bi Kebra, see Conti Rossini, 'Studi su popolazioni dell'Etiopia', *Rivista di Studi Orientali*, 4, 1911–12: 617, 623. Successors of the Zagwé, according to this tale, fled to Eritrea and have dwelt there ever since.

A note tending to 'rehabilitate' the Zagwé occurs in the copy of the *Mashafa Tefut*: A. Caquot, 'Aperçu préliminaire sur le *Mashafa Tefut* de Gechen Amba', *Annales d'Ethiopie*, I, 1955: 99. Commenting on the phrase 'strangers who did not belong to the house of David', the note adds that the book was in error, for 'it is false to suggest that the Zagwé did not belong to the people of Israel and the posterity of David. True, they did not descend from the queen of Sheba, but they nevertheless did belong to the posterity of David and Solomon. If one claims that they usurped royalty, it is because they did not descend from the queen of Azeb, queen of Ethiopia.'

Girma Fisseha, in *Athiopien in der Volkstumlichen Malerei*, Stuttgart, 1993: 32, states that one of the first pictures on the theme of Solomon and Sheba produced the one painted around 1907 to illustrate the translation of the *KN* for H. Le Roux. He illustrates the development of the story with five paintings of the comic-strip sort dating 1928–30, pp. 56–63. None show the subsequent history of Menelik, nor the theft of the Ark.

The development of the Solomon and Sheba paintings seems to run in two strands (R. Pankhurst, 'Some Notes for a History of Ethiopian Secular Art', *Ethiopia Observer*, X, no. 1, 1966: 5–80). First are paintings composed of several scenes. The earliest seem to be those of Blanchard, a member of the 1901–33 Duchesne-Fournet mission. His paintings are reproduced by Kammerer (*La Mer Rouge*, Cairo, 1947, III, pl. 88). Next comes H. Le Roux, who obtained paintings, not of the strip-cartoon style, from Mikael Ingida Work, an employee of the French trader Chefneux. The five of them appeared with Le Roux' translation of the *KN*. The Russian A. I. Kohanovski, residing in Addis Ababa 1907–13, also obtained paintings of the Solomon and Sheba cycle. There are two, by an artist called Mikael, one with three scenes, one with four, now in the Institute of Ethnology, St. Petersburg.

The comic-strip type of painting seems to derive not from the *KN* tale, but from the local tales which include Arwe the dragon in their prelude. At least two artists specialised in this for the tourist market in pre-war times, Belatchew Yimer and Tasso Habte Wold. One of Belatchew's was reproduced in W. Goldman, *Das ist Abessinien*, Leipzig, 1935: 48–49; another is in the Art Gallery of New South Wales in Australia. Norden in 1930 mentions such paintings of the Sheba story as common (*Abyssinia's Last Empire*: 10), and there seem to be many dating to around 1928–30 in different museums and art galleries.

23   Gigar Tesfaye, 'La généalogie des trois tribus Irob chrétiennes d'après des documents de Gunda Gundié', *Annales d'Ethiopie*, 13, 1985: 59.

24   G. Lusini, 'Philology and the reconstruction of the Ethiopian past', paper read at the First Littmann Conference, Munich, May 2002, also states that 'oral tradition transmitted ancient and important versions of the legend, different from the one exploited in the *KN*', giving no reason for the attribution 'ancient' beyond citing Littmann as the source.

25   C. Conti Rossini, 'Il libro delle leggende e tradizioni abissine dell'ecciaghié Filpòs', *Rendiconti dell R. Accademia dei Lincei*, ser. V, Vol. XXVI, 1917: 702–3. This text seems to be a conflation of legends. Atrayn and Sarayn probably represent Angabo; List F of Conti Rossini 1909 begins with 'Agabos, of Atray, of Sarawe: 300 years'.

26   A large part of the *KN* story, with additions such as that of the serpent which was killed by Makeda's father, Angabo (though he is not named in this source) is repeated in Guébré Sellassié's *Chronique*...I: 2–3, n. 11.

Zion or *tabota Seyon* is mentioned often, translated as Ark of the Covenant or tablets of the Law in the confusing manner common to this subject. Thus (p. 11), the sons of the Israelite priests took wood according to the measure of Zion, covering it with gold (and so presumably making a new Ark), but when they enter the *maqdas* the translation states that 'they removed the Tablets of the Law'. When Solomon sent Zadok to see what has happened, he found that the tablets of the Law were no longer there, but 'he found those which had been made to resemble them'; though the tablets of the Law were not gold-covered wooden objects. In the translation the tablets of the Law go to Ethiopia, and are installed by the queen of Azeb at Saba (p. 13). As in so many texts, there is complete inter-identity, regardless of logic, between tablets and Ark.

De Coppet remarks (*Le Tabot*: 549ff), that Azarias and his companions took not the Ark, but the tablets. In the passage on this subject, and in some others in the chronicle of Menelik II, the word *sellat* or even *sellata Muse* (tablet of Moses) were employed, but *tabot* remained the usual term. In the passage where the presence of the tablets of the Law are revealed to Menelik I (p. 12), he addresses them: 'You, Tablets of the Law, may you benefit the land to which you have come, and that to which you are going, for you are the Tablets (*sallat*) on which are written the law of God.' This locution, using the term tablet(s), seems to have been favoured in the 19th century, and again nowadays, when referring to the 'Ark'.

27   J. Kolmodin, *Traditions de Tsazzega et Hazzega*. See 5.3: A6–8.

28   E. Hammerschmidt and V. Six, *Äthiopische Handschriften 1: Die Handschriften der Staatsbibliothek Preussicher Kulturbesitz*, Weisbaden, 1983: 275, ms. 151,

Qerelos (c. 1808–30) and King Takla Giyorgis (six reigns between 1779–1800). V. Six, *Äthiopische Handschriften 3: Handschriften Deutscher Bibliotheken, Museen, und aus Privatbesitz*, ed. E. Hammerschmidt, Stuttgart, 1994: 316, No. 168 (ms. 1971. 3542), 'Die Erzählung von der Königin von Saba in Ge'ez und Amharisch'. The book has been described by A. Jankowski, *Eine amharische Version der Königin-Azeb-Erzählung*...Diss. Hamburg 1982.

Local Christian legend makes large claims, asserting that the Holy Family came to Ethiopia, remaining for three and a half years. They came via Najran, the desert of Senhit, Dabra Bizan, Dabra Damo, Aksum (where they heard the prophetic utterances of the high priest Achin before King Bazen), Dabra Abbai, and then over the Takkaze and on to the island of Tana. A Hamasen legend claims that Abba Salama was an Ethiopian too, son of a Hamasen woman. He was born, grew up, and learned the Old Testament in one day. Voyaging to Egypt, he studied with the patriarch, and on his return raised Abreha and Asbeha (about whom there are also numerous legendary tales) to the throne. They who brought the ten tables of the Law, previously kept for 42 generations in Hamasen, to Aksum. Conti Rossini, *Storia*...: 257–59.

29   I. Guidi, *Annales Iohannis I, Iyasu I, Bakaffa*, trans., pp. 57, 66.

30   Conti Rossini, *Liber Axumae*: 58: '...with the help of our Lady Mary of Seyon the Mother of God...in the 72nd year after the previous kings [Susneyos, in 1615] abrogated (the laws), we restored to our Mother Seyon the Cathedral of Aksum all her laws and ordinances, and all her charter lands, and the administration of her possessions by the *nebura'ed*.'

31   I. Guidi, *Annales Iohannis I, Iyasu I, Bakaffa*, text, p. 151–52; trans., p. 158–59. Later, Iyasu confirmed the fiefs of Seyon. In 1693 he returned for his coronation, entering the 'chamber of *tabota Seyon*'. The dignitaries rode in on horseback, unthinkable even in the area surrounding the church. Since the abbreviated chronicle describes them going to 'the palace', where the priests came with 'the Law', the 'chamber of the *tabot* of Seyon' in this case perhaps denotes a dwelling appointed for the king in or near the cathedral precincts. It is unlikely that it could refer to the sanctuary of the church.

32   R. Basset, 'Etudes sur l'histoire d'Ethiopie', *Journal Asiatique*, ser. 7, 18, octobre-november-décembre 1881: 297, 301.

33   S. Rubenson, 'The Lion of the Tribe of Judah...': 75–85. Ullendorff, *op. cit.*: 11. See also Pankhurst, ' "Fear God, Honor the King"...': 31–32.

34   *The glorious victories of Amda Seyon*...: 130–32. E. Littmann, *Die altamharischen Kaiserlieder*, Strassburg, 1914: 20–22, suggested that the first song cited here (his no. V, and Huntingford's no. II) referred to Yeshaq; both attribute the second song below (Littmann's no. VII, Huntingford's no. III) to Amda Seyon.

> Zan, fire in victory!
> The altar of the queen's church,
> When they set it on fire, Likewise they scorched him with fire,
> The Lion of David...

> Rubbing with onion,
> As the monk belches at the hour,

He showered upon them a plague of swords,
Lion of David.

Perhaps, in the royal context, another poem may be significant;

Zan, succeeder in victory,
His ancestor was Adal Mabraq.
As a hyaena eats poison, When he surprised Adal,
Their spirit declined –

Vulture of David, vulture...

In *Gadla Marqorewos*, Amda Seyon is called Mabraq Sagad instead of Gabra Masqal.

35 Frey Luys de Urreta, *Historia eclesiastica, politica, natural y moral de los grandes y remotos Reynos de la Etiopia, Monarchia del Emperador, llamado Preste Iuan de las Indias*, Valencia, 1610: 118.

36 N. Godinho, *De Abassinorum rebus..* I, VII: Unde Abassinorum Imperatorem fertur ductum genus: 34–35. For other notes on the title, see Pankhurst, 'Fear God, Honor the King...': 31–32.

37 S. Rubenson, 'The Lion of the Tribe of Judah...': 79–80. He cites a letter of Iyasu of 1687 in the Ministère des Affaires Etrangères (A.E.), Paris, Mémoires et documents, Asie 2, Indes Orientales 1635–1734.

38 W.E. Conzelman, *Chronique de Galâwdêwos (Claudius), Roi d'Ethiopie*, (Bibliothèque de l'Ecole pratique des Haut Etudes, fasc. 140), Paris, 1895: 130.

39 C.J. Poncet, *A Voyage to Ethiopia, 1698–1701, in The Red Sea and adjacent countries at the close of the seventeenth century'...*ed. Sir William Foster, London, 1949.

40 The letter is that cited by Rubenson above, but the year is 1701. It is listed under the name Adiam Saghed. I am grateful to M. François Limouzin-Lamothe, of the French Ministry of Foreign Affairs, for help in tracing a copy of a translation. A second, slightly variant, translation is in the Biblothèque Nationale. The letter itself is BN Mss Eth 162 (formerly Eth 88), published by Zotenberg, 1877: 264–65. Where the translator Claude Berault has written 'Your Majesty', the letter is in fact addressed to 'Lerons'. It is headed by a cross-crosslet with the letters I Ya Su S between the four arms – Iyasus, Jesus, followed by the address from *negusa nagast alam Adyam Sagad* to Lerons. An end note in French is doubtless by M. Berault: 'Cette letter d'Adjam Sagad Empereur d'Ethiopie a été traduite par feu N. Petis de la Croix en 1702, le 8 de fevrier. La traduction et de plus execrable, les contresenses, les ignorances...' M. Berault did not take it as addressed to Louis XIV. He continues: 'Par Lerons qu'on lit dans cette letter je ne crois pas qu'il faille entendre le Roy de Portugal mais le Duc de Lyria.'

41 Nothing in the *KN* itself helps on this theme. As when Yohannes IV of Ethiopia asked for the return of the *KN* to help him rule his country, the reference is to other documents often bound in with the *KN*.

42 Ludolf, *op. cit.*, Bk. II, Ch. III.

43 In this context, after describing the *manbara tabot*, and the 'table' or *tabot*, Ludolf launched into some conjectures about the origin of tables and altars,

arks and chests: '...it came to pass, that the Tables or Altars themselves were consecrated; and so the use of those Arks or Chests [the early Christian altars] ceas'd...But for the Ethiopians, they make use of their Chest and their Table both together; to the end the Service may be the more fully and absolutely perform'd, and nothing left undone...The little Chest which the Ethiopians use, is generally of wood, though they do not Prohibit those that are made of Stone, or cast Metal. However the Fathers of the Society [he refers to the Jesuits] would not permit them to make use of any but stone; the rest they either burnt or melted down.'

'Chest' in the English translation refers to the *tabot*. In his long disquisition on the *tabot* etc., Ludolf raises no questions about replicating the Ark or the tablets of Moses and records no comment of Gorgoreyos on the subject. It is left to Abbé Le Grand, in his *Fourteenth Dissertation*, published in 1728, to add, in reference to an engraving supplied by Ludolf: 'Il (Ludolf) a pris soin de faire graver cette espèce de Bière, tant cette pensée lui a paru belle, & il s'est imaginé que c'est de-là que les Abissins ont donné le nom d'Arche à ces Autels portatifs. Il étoit, ce semble, plus naturel de penser que ces peuples, persuadés qu'ils ont de tems immémorial l'Arche d'Alliance dans leur Eglise d'Axuma, & ayant pour ces autels portatifs un respect approchant de celui que les Juifs avoient pour l'Arche, ils les ont qualifiés du même nom, *Tabout* ou *Arche*.' Le Grand, *Voyage historique d'Abissinie du R. P. Jerome Lobo*...Paris, 1728.

44 *Prutky's Travels...*: 77, 81, 84, 102, 141, 177, 251–52. Among the 'Judaic superstitions' he cites are circumcision, dietary laws and Sabbath observation, pp. 254–55.

45 *Prutky's Travels...*: 94.

46 Ibid.: 99, 173.

47 V. Nersessian and R. Pankhurst, 'The visit to Ethiopia of Yohannes T'ovmacean, an Armenian jeweller, in 1764–66', *Journal of Ethiopian Studies*, 15, 1982: 79–104.

48 Athanasius Kircher, *Mundus subterraneus...*, Amsterdam, 1645, I: 73.

49 J. Bruce, *Journey...*, Edinburgh, 1790, Edinburgh and London, 1805.

50 See Hancock, *op. cit.*: 179 and Bruce, Edinburgh, 1805 ed., II: 398.

51 M. Bredin, *The Pale Abyssinian, A Life of James Bruce, African Explorer and Adventurer*, London, 2001: 2, 100, 180, 201.

52 Bruce, *Journey...*, Edinburgh, 1790, vol. III. Dr. Alexander Murray, in his biography of Bruce, supplied a 'List of the Ethiopic mss brought from Habbesh by Mr. Bruce'. Among them was no. 6, 'The Kebir Zaneguste, or Glory of the Kings; the celebrated book of Axum...' Under no. 45, a 'Particular account of the Ethiopic MSS from which Mr. Bruce composed the History of Abyssinia, inserted in his Travels' was supplied: 'Of this treatise [*Kebir Zaneguste*] Mr. Bruce brought two copies from Gondar, one [Bodleian MS Bruce 93, Dillmann XXVI] written in an older hand, divided into chapters...and another [Bodleian MS Bruce 87, Dillmann XXVII], beautifully, but more incorrectly, written, without sections, and probably a transcript, made for him while residing in that city...The oldest copy appears to have been a present to Mr. Bruce from Ras Michael, the celebrated governor of Tigré. It is ornamented at the beginning

with a beautiful drawing of an eagle in flight, holding in his beak and talons a scroll, which seems to have been executed by Mr. Bruce or his assistant...[the Italian artist Luigi Balugani].'

A. Murray, *Account of the Life and Writing of James Bruce, of Kinnaird, Esq. F.R.S., author of Travels to Discover the Source of the Nile...*, Edinburgh, 1808: 297, Appendix. No. XLIII; 334, 336. See also mss. Descriptive Catalogue, Division I, Ethiopic MS, Phillipps MS 20914 [1868], by Alexander Murray (see Hall's *Life of Salt*, 263). No. 5 = *KN*.

Dillmann's notes (August Dillmann, *Catalogus Codicum manuscriptorum Bibliothecae Bodleianae oxoniensis*, Pars VII, Codices Aethiopici, Oxford, 1848: 68–69) record the *KN* as follows:

XXVI. *Liber Axumae. Hic titulus in J. Brucii itinerario huic Codici jure inditus est.* The *KN* or *Gloria Regum* comprises fols 1–88 in 117 chapters without colophon. Section 2 is the *Appendix de rebus Axumiticis*, (i.e. the *Liber Axumae*), fols 89–96; 1.) Descriptio Ecclesiae Axumiticae, in qua Zion arca asservabatur. 2.) *Descriptio caeremoniarum, quae in coronatione Regis observantur*, (Description of the ceremonies which are observed in the coronation of the king), entitled in Ethiopic 'This is the book which King Solomon gave to Ebna Hakim'. Other chapters of the *Liber Axumae* follow, including a king-list etc. Fols 96–105 contain other works.

XXVII *KN*. This contains the same material as in XXVI fols 1–88, with a less correct text, and with a colophon similar to that published by Budge but without the name Lalibela, or the names of Yeshaq's five companions.

53 R. P. Dimothéos (Sapritchian), *Deux ans de séjour en Abyssinie*, Jerusalem, 1871: 136.

54 The 'sacristy' may be an older *enda sellat*. No separate chapel is mentioned a little later by Rohlfs. Approaching the church of Maryam Seyon, to the left from the vestibule is north, and the end of 'a row of other rooms' would take one to the position of the *enda sellat*, the small Zion church, which lay, according to the DAE 1906 plan, in front of the Treasury of Yohannes, at the end of a row of small buildings: the small church of Maryam Magdalawit, the small treasury, the mausoleum of Tewoflos, and the gate-house to the small Zion church. This small Zion church was not in the same position as the present chapel.

55 Dimothéos, *op. cit.*: 136–43.

56 Gerhard Rohlfs, *Meine Mission nach Abessinien*, Leipzig, 1883.

57 Recorded by the author during a conversation with Theodore Vestal at the 1997 XIIIth Conference of Ethiopian Studies in Kyoto.

58 1906; see DAE publication, 1913.

59 K. Stoffregen-Pedersen, *Les Ethiopiens*, eds. Brepols, Belgium, 1990: 10; 92, n. 77.

CHAPTER 6

1   Conti Rossini, *Liber Axumae*: 95.

2   Poncet, *A Voyage to Ethiopia*…: 148.

3   Bruce, *Journey*…, London, 1790. Edinburgh, 1805, IV: 322.

4   H. Salt, in Lord Valentia (George Annesley, Viscount Valentia), *Voyages and Travels to India, Ceylon, the Red Sea, Abyssinia and Egypt*, London, 1809, 3: 87–88.

5   E. Combes and M. Tamisier, *Voyage en Abyssinie, dans les pays des Galla, de Choa et d'Ifat*, Paris, 1838, I: 267.

6   Alvares, *The Prester John*…: II: 521–25 for an English translation of the relevant parts of the *Liber Axumae*. The text is translated also in Conti Rossini, *Liber Axumae*: 3.

7   Alvares, *The Prester John*…: 161.

8   Conti Rossini, *Liber Axumae*: 99. See 62–65 for other grants by Walda Sellassie. Walda Sellassie, as *ras*, is mentioned in another context with reference to the tablet of Moses at Aksum. Recently, inspecting the ms. Lady Meux 4, bought in 1897 from a British officer who had obtained it at Magdala, now in the library of Dr Bent Juel-Jensen, I noticed a preliminary page not published in Budge, *The History of Hanna*…. The note, fol. 10r, states in Amharic that the book was written in Shewa at Dabra Libanos:
'There is nothing greater and more honoured than Dabra Libanos except [inserted above, Jerusalem] the tomb of our Saviour…*Ras* Wolda Sellassie would (he see) that this (book) is taken to Aksum where it must be used by the protector (or guardian) of the *Tabot* (*tabota tabaqi*) for prayer and could *ras* Wolde Sellassie give a gold ring for the sake of the tablet of Moses (*sellata Muse*). (Trans. *Ras* Mengesha Seyum).'
    The Protector or Guardian of the *Tabot* mentioned here is equivalent to the *aqabet* of today. The office of *bet tabaqi*, a title similar to *aqabet* at Aksum and many other churches, probably included the guardianship of the *tabot* or tablet of Seyon (or Moses), with other church treasures. The present *aqabet* holds a similar office, and his jurisdiction is not limited to guarding one special relic.

9   Ullendorff, *Ethiopia and the Bible*: 87.

10   Hancock, *op. cit.*: 21.

11   M. Heldman, 'The heritage of Late Antiquity', in *African Zion. The Sacred Art of Ethiopia*: 118–19. Earlier in the same book, p. 71, Heldman also notes that 'It is dedicated to *Seyon* (Zion) or *Maryam* Seyon (Mary of Zion), and its altar tablet is inscribed *Emmena Seyon* (Our Mother Zion)'. See also Heldman, 'Architectural symbolism…': 222–41. J. Wilkinson, *Jerusalem Pilgrims before the Crusades*, Warminster, 1977: 83, quoting the account of the *Acta Sanctorum*, 24 October (X) 758, written before 597 AD, which says that Elisbaan (Kaleb) sent his crown to Jerusalem to be hung 'in front of the door of the lifegiving tomb'.

12   Bruce brought back the *Book of Aksum* with a copy of the *KN*, Bodleian MS Bruce 93, acquired in the 1770s, but of 17th century date. This, outside Pais' fragment, is the earliest example that we have. The version published by Conti Rossini was written in Year 7316 (of the World), 1816 EC/1824 AD. Monneret de Villard, and Hirsch and Fauvelle-Aymar, *op. cit.*: 59–109, plump for the time

of Zara Yaqob for the writing of the earliest, descriptive, part of the book, partly because they believe (p. 75) the description of the church to relate to a pre-Grañ edifice, making 1535 the *terminus ante quem*.

13   The letter of Emperor Constantius II and the notes of Athanasius refer to Frumentius, and to a bishop of Aksum at the court of King Ezana.

14   Heldman, 'Architectural symbolism...': 228.

15   Conti Rossini, *Liber Axumae*: 7. Alvares, *op. cit.*, Appendix I: 525. Pais, *História*...II: 126, in an early translation of this section of the *Liber Axumae*, cites the measurements in palms, doubling the figures as they are given in the Ge'ez and in later translations since two palms equal one of the Ethiopian 'coudees' or 'ells'. Pais supplies the measurements as follows; 184 palms wide, 250 long, 64 high, with walls 14 wide; the principal door was also 14 high (not mentioned in the surviving Ge'ez versions). The church was begun in Year 49 after the birth of Christ and completed in 92, according to this version. Monneret de Villard, *Aksum*, 1938: 52, gives these dates as 44 and 91. Littmann, DAE II: 139 read 39 for the first date, as did Beckingham and Huntingford, Alvares, *The Prester John*..., I: 525. A. d'Abbadie, *Catalogue raisonné de manuscrits éthiopiens appartenant à Antoine d'Abbadie*, Paris, 1859: 109, states that Aksum cathedral was built in 47, finished in 99 of our era.

16   D. Buxton and D. Mathews, 'The reconstruction of vanished Aksumite Buildings', *Rassegna di Studi Etiopici*, XXV, 1974.

17   Buxton and Mathews, who hazarded a 'restoration' of the church on paper, only mention the last of these measurements, which agreed satisfactorily with their estimated internal width for the structure based on the existing podium. Heldman assumes that 92 ells was the width at the east end only: making an odd T-shaped edifice. If one assumes instead that 53 ells refers to the interior width, and adds the 7 ells for thickness of the walls on both sides, the total exterior width still only comes to 67 ells, not 92.

    Relating the dimensions in 15th–16th century Ethiopian 'ells' – an uncertain measurement – and in 7th century Armenian cubits (in which measurements for the church of Sion in Jerusalem are available), the best that Heldman can say is that the proportions of length to greatest width more or less correspond in both cases – ignoring the T-shape. The simple proportions apply equally well to almost any oblong church. Evidently, no real reconstruction of plan or even overall size can be made from such guesswork.

    Almeida's information is detailed above, see n. 6.

18   M. Heldman, 'Maryam Seyon: Mary of Zion', in *African Zion. The Sacred Art of Ethiopia*: 71. Aksum 'Seyon' is supposed to derive from the Jerusalem Sion church; Heldman, 'Architectural symbolism...': 227, citing J. Wilkinson, *Jerusalem Pilgrims before the Crusades*, Warminster, 1977: 5, 66. A certain Theodosius, in his *Topography of the Holy Land*, a work dating perhaps to just after the reign of Anastasius (d. 518 AD), supplies the title 'Mother of All Churches' to Holy Sion, 'founded with the Apostles'.

19   C.J. Robin and A. de Maigret, 'Le grande temple de Yéha (Tigray, Éthiopie), aprés la première campagne de fouilles de la mission française (1998)', *Comptes rendus de l'Académie des Inscriptions et Belles-Lettres*, 1998: 737–98.

20   Wilkinson, *op. cit.*: loc. var.

21   For the Kaleb inscription, see Munro-Hay, *Aksum…*: 230.

22   Muir wrote: 'After this, the conversation turning upon Abyssinia, Um Selame and Um Habiba, who had both been exiles there, spoke of the beauty of the cathedral of *Maria* there, and of the wonderful pictures on its walls…' Lepage renders it as; 'les beautés de la cathedrale d'Axum et les merveilles peintes sur les murs'. Leroy includes both these attributions, Maria and Aksum, and adds Zion for good measure, describing 'the paintings…in the Cathedral of St. Mary of Zion at Aksum'. The *hadith* occurs – according to Lepage – in the *Tarikh al-rusul wa-al-muluk, the History of Prophets and Kings* of al-Tabari (839–923 AD). None of the authors cited provides a proper reference for this *hadith*. T.H. Muir, *The Life of Mohammad*, Edinburgh, 1923: 490; Sergew Hable Sellassie, *Ancient and Medieval Ethiopian History to 1270*, Addis Ababa, 1972: 186, n. 30; Claude Lepage, 'Bilan des recherches sur l'art médiéval d'Ethiopie; quelques résultats historiques', *Proceedings of the Eighth International Conference of Ethiopian Studies, 1984*, Addis Ababa, 1989, vol. 2: 52. Muir cites no original source, while Lepage mentions the *Chronique* of al-Tabari without details. J. Leroy, 'Ethiopian Painting in the Middle Ages', in Georg Gerster, *Churches in Rock*, London, 1970: 62, also provides no reference, nor does David Phillipson in *Ancient Ethiopia*: London, 1998: 83. I have not been able to trace the *hadith* in the new edition of Tabari's work. The earliest mention – but limited to noting 'la belleza e i dipinti delle chiese d'Abissinia', a far cry from a specific mention of Mary of Seyon and Aksum – that I can find is Carlo Conti Rossini, 'Un codice illustrato eritreo del secolo XV', *Africa Italiana*, I, 1927: 83, citing H. Lammens, 'L'attitude de l'islam primitif en face des arts figurés', *Journal Asiatique*, 1915, II: 246–47. Thanks to Haggai Erlich and Dr Lutfi Mansur, we find it in *Fath al-bari bi sharh sahih al-imam al-bukhari* by Ahmad ibn Hajr al-Asqalani, Beirut, 1, *Kitab al-Sallat*: 531–32, dealing with *hadith* 434 of al-Bukhari.

23   C. Conti Rossini, 'L'Evangelo d'Oro…': 186–91, Documents 6–7. See also *Dictionary of Ethiopian Biography*, Addis Ababa, 1975, I: entries for Abyekun and Yetbarak.

24   E. Cerulli, *Il Libro Etiopico dei Miracoli di Maria…*Rome, 1943: 137–38, and 138, n. 2 (h agia Siwn, h mhthr twn ekklhsiwn).

25   Taddesse Tamrat, *Church and State*: 69. Conti Rossini, *op. cit.*, 194–96.

26   Marilyn Heldman notes that the 'Marian feast of 21 Sane (June 28) celebrates the building of churches dedicated to Mary, and commemorates in particular the building of the first church, which was dedicated to Mary at the command of Christ'. The *Synaxarium* entry dates from the heyday of the Solomonic dynasty, when only legends survived about the founding of the original church. An allusion to Mary as 'Mary of Zion' in the homily of Theophilus comparing the mountain of Kuskam (Qwesqwam), where the Holy Family are said to have sojourned in Egypt, to Zion, and naming Mary as 'Mary of Zion', is similarly late. Marilyn Heldman, 'Maryam Seyon: Mary of Zion': 72, citing E.A.W. Budge, *The Book of the Saints of the Ethiopian Church*, 4: 1020–23, and R. Basset, *Le synaxaire arabe jacobite (redaction copte): Les mois de Baounah, Abib, Mesor*

et jours complémentaires, Patrologia Orientalis, 17, 1924: 583–88. Also, Heldman, *op. cit.*, 74 for Kuskam.

27   Getatchew Haile, 'A Fragment on the Monastic Fathers of the Ethiopian Church', *Studia in honorem Stanislaus Chojnacki...*, (Orbis Aethiopicus), Albstadt, 1992: 231–37. See p. 237.

28   Heldman, *African Zion. The Sacred Art of Ethiopia*: Cat. 1.

29   E. Cerulli, *Il Libro Etiopico dei Miracoli di Maria...*Rome, 1943: 124.

30   C. Trasselli, 'Un italiano in Etiopia nel XV secolo: Pietro Rombulo da Messina', *Rassegna di Studi Etiopici*, I, 1941: [173–202], 191; '...Caxum, città grandissima e popolosa dove è una chiesa dedicata alla Vergine Maria...'

31   In *KN* 71 she is called 'daughter of David' following the list of her ancestors in *KN* 70. In *KN* 68, 'Concerning Mary, our Lady of Salvation', a genealogy indicates that through her parents Joachim and Hanna the Pearl of Salvation which God had placed in Adam was to devolve on her. Mary is lauded in *KN* 96. She is identified with the burning bush, the fire being the 'Godhood of the Son of God'. She is the censer, Christ being the coals, and the odour of incense, the perfume of Christ; 'and upon the perfume of the incense the prayers of the pure go up to the throne of God' (*KN* 97). She is the rod of Aaron (*KN* 98), 'she liveth in Zion with the pot which is filled with manna, and with the two tables that were written with the Finger of God' (Hebrews 9. 4. These objects are said to be in the Ark in the tabernacle). Indeed, 'the *Gômôr* which is the pot of gold (*masoba warq*) inside the Tabernacle (*tabot*)' itself is Mary, the manna within being the Body of Christ. Mary is the Tabernacle (*tabot*), plated with the gold that symbolises the Godhead, the deity of Christ. The 'spiritual Pearl' contained in the Tabernacle is also Mary, 'the Mother of the Light' (*KN* 98). In *KN* 104 Mary is 'the similitude [of Zion, the Tabernacle of the Law of God – *seyon tabota heggu laEgziabeher*] and the fruit thereof': 'in her name is blessed the Tabernacle [*tabot*] of the Law of God'.

32   C. Conti Rossini with L. Ricci, trans., *Il Libro della Luce del Negus Zar'a Ya'qob (Matshafa Berhan)*, Corpus Scriptorum Christianorum Orientalium, Scriptores aethiopici, T. 48, Louvain, 1965, I: 38, 40, 42. Mary is identified absolutely with the Ark in Solomon's temple. See also the late 15th century psalter painting of the seated Virgin, the Child on her lap, flanked by the archangels Gabriel and Michael, whose wings form an arch over her, just as the cherubim 'overshadowed her with their wings'. Budge, *The History of Hanna...*, Section I in *Legends of Our Lady Mary the Perpetual Virgin and Her Mother Hanna...*: 4–5, 52–53; and E. Balicka-Witakowska, 'Un psautier éthiopien illustré inconnu', *Orientalia Suecana* XXXIII–XXXV (1984–86), fig. 32. Getatchew Haile, *The Mariology of Emperor Zär'a Ya'eqob of Ethiopia*, Rome, 1992: 99. Hirsch and Fauvelle-Aymar, *op. cit.*: 92. See Hebrews 9. 1–5: 'To be sure, the first covenant had its worship regulations and its earthly sanctuary; for the first tabernacle was furnished in this way: in what is called the Holy Place were the lampstand and the table and the presentation loaves. Behind the second curtain was the tabernacle called the Holy of Holies, containing the golden altar of incense and the ark of the covenant completely covered with gold; inside it the golden jar of manna, Aaron's rod that sprouted, and the tablets of the covenant.

Above it were the cherubim of glory overshadowing the mercy seat, about which we cannot now go into detail.'

The *History of Hanna* likens Mary (fol. 58b) to 'the Candlestick, the Mother of the Great Light, who was likened unto the Tabernacle of Moses and Aaron (*ba tabota Muse wa Aron*)', and (fol. 59b) 'the Tables of the Law of Moses (*sellata heggu la Muse*), and the almond rod of Aaron, and the inheritance of the priests of the Levites, and the breeches of fine linen, and the mitre and the tunic'. In this book a strange anachronistic claim was made. The text details the construction of the Tabernacle (fols 64b and 65a):

'Again God showed it unto Moses in the desert when he was telling him how to make the building of her Tabernacle (*dabtar*). And God commanded him to make a Tabernacle (*tabot*) of wood that could not be eaten by worms…In that holy Tabernacle (*tabot*) God commanded him to place the Two Tables (*sellat*) of stone…And above that tabernacle was the mercy-seat of gold, and above the mercy-seat were the Cherubim which were made of carved gold; and from the Tabernacle God was wont to appear unto Moses…And Solomon also built a Sanctuary (*maqdas*) in the form of this Tabernacle (*dabtar*)'. '…And inside the Holy of Holies, at the place where the holy Tabernacle rested, was a figure of Mary, the daughter of Joachim. And Solomon made two Cherubim of red gold which overshadowed her with their wings, and God was wont to appear there…' – incidentally, as in Budge's *KN* translation, 'tabernacle' is used for different Ge'ez words.

33   Getatchew Haile, 'Documents on the History of Ase Dawit (1382-1413)', *Journal of Ethiopian Studies*, XVI, 1983: 25.

34   *Gadla Marqorewos*…: 4–5. G.W.B. Huntingford, 'The Wealth of Kings' and 'The End of the Zagué Dynasty', *Bulletin of the School of Oriental and African Studies*, 28, 1965: 1; 'apparently of the late seventeenth century'.

35   Hubbard, *op. cit.*: 85.

36   C. Conti Rossini, *Storia*…: 253–54. For other itineraries see also pp. 255–56. *The Periplus of the Erythraean Sea, by an unknown author, with some extracts from Agatharkhides 'On the Erythraean Sea'*. Trans. and ed. G.W.B. Huntingford, London, 1980: 19–20.

37   S. Kaplan, *The Beta Israel (Falasha) in Ethiopia*, New York and London, 1992: 27. Poncet, *A Voyage to Ethiopia*…

38   H. Salt, *A voyage to Abyssinia and travel into the interior of that country, executed under the orders of the British government, in the years 1809 and 1810*, London, 1814: 433: 'the spot on which it [Yeha temple] stood had for ages been regarded as sacred, owing to the ark of the covenant, which had been brought into Abyssinia by Menelik, having been kept there for a considerable time previous to its removal to Axum'. See Bent, *Sacred City*…: 152–53: 'At first (says the legend) it was kept at Yeha (Ava), and then removed to Aksum. This is in conformity with existing proof. When Ava was destroyed the arcana of their religion and the capital of the kingdom was transferred to Aksum.'

39   E. Ullendorff, *Ethiopia and the Bible*, London, 1968: 10.

40   Southeast of Dabra Libanos on Doresse's map; Jean Doresse, *L'Empire du Prêtre-Jean*, Paris, 1957, I: 258–59.

41   C. Conti Rossini, 'Studi su popolazioni dell'Etiopia', *Rivista di Studi Orientali*, 3, 1910: 859.

42   R. Fattovich, K.A. Bard, L. Petrassi, V. Pisano, *The Aksum Archaeological Area: A Preliminary Assessment*, Naples, 2000: 84, referring to Yaqob Beyene's investigations into oral traditions: 'it was possible to ascertain that the ancient name of Beta Giyorgis was Dabra Makkeda, suggesting a traditional link with the Queen of Sheba'. Girma Elyas, *Aksumawit Fana Wezi (The Echo of Aksum)*, Aksum, 1991 (EC): 8–9.

43   Littmann *et al. Deutsche Aksum-Expedition*, 1913, I: 39.

44   Sergew Hable Selassie, 'The problem of Gudit', *Journal of Ethiopian Studies*, X, no. 1, 1972: 117.

45   Hancock, *op. cit.*: 175.

46   V. Six, *Äthiopische Handschriften vom Tanasee. Teil 3. Nebst einem Nachtrag zum Katalog der Äthiopischen Handschriften Deutscher Bibliotheken und Museen*, Stuttgart, 1999: 120, Tanasee 127, Daga Estifanos 16. C. Conti Rossini, 'Notice sur les manuscripts éthiopiens de la collection d'Abbadie', *Journal Asiatique*, juillet-août 1913: Part IV, pp. 5–64, see p. 30, ms. 157, fol. 180v. Ms. 158 was also presented to the *tabot* of Seyon.

47   A. Pankhurst, 'An early Ethiopian manuscript map of Tegré', *Proceedings of the Eighth International Conference of Ethiopian Studies*, 2, Addis Ababa, 1989: 73–88.

48   C. Conti Rossini, 'L'Evangelo d'Oro...': 187–91, Document 9.

49   Taddesse Tamrat, *Church and State*: 68. See 'Delanda', *Dictionary of Ethiopian Biography*, I, Addis Ababa, 1975. Conti Rossini, noting the non-Semitic name, suggested that he might have been an Agaw holding the office of *ma'ekala bahr*. See also the 'Lettre de M. Conti Rossini', in *Revue Sémitique*, 11, 1903: 326; 'un capo del Tigrè'.

50   Hancock, *op. cit.*: 212ff.

CHAPTER 7

1   C. Conti Rossini, 'Aethiopica (IIe Serie)', *Rivista degli Studi Orientali*, X, 1923–25: 483, citing Budge, *Queen of Scheba* (sic.) pp. xi–xiii.

2   *The New York Times*, 27 January 1998: 'What Ethiopians believe is the Ark of the Covenant Rests in Aksum', by James C. McKinley Jr.

3   In the Ethiopian version, 'His Beatitude and His Holiness *Abuna* Pawlos, Head of the Archbishops and Patriarch of Ethiopia, *echege* of Dabra Libanos, Archbishop of Aksum'.

4   N. Clapp, *Sheba. Through the Desert in Search of the Legendary Queen*, Boston, New York, 2002: 233.

c. 950 BC	Solomon of Israel receives a visit from the Queen of Sheba (Bible, Kings and Chronicles)
c. 930 BC	Ebna Hakim (David, Menelik) returns to Dabra Makeda with the Ark (*KN*)
1st century AD	Josephus calls the queen of Sheba Nikaula, queen of Egypt and Ethiopia
c. 340	Conversion of King Ezana of Aksum to Christianity
8th century	Qur'an story about queen of Sheba includes no reference to Ethiopia, a son by Solomon etc.
c. 960s–970s	A queen ('Gudit'/queen of the Bani al-Hamwiyya?) ravages Abyssinia. Late chronicles claim Ark taken to Lake Zway
10th–11th century	Coptic story about Solomon and the queen (of Sheba?)
1047–77	Michael of Tinnis, secretary of Patriarch Christodoulos; identifies Sheba with Ethiopia (Habasha)
1165	Letter from 'Prester John' circulated
1177	Pope Alexander III replies to letter of 'Prester John'
1187	Saladin takes Jerusalem; Ethiopian privileges (said to be) confirmed there

c. 1185–1225	Reign of Lalibela. First use of *tabotat* (i.e. *manbara tabotat*, box-like altar tables) attested
c. 1200	Abu Salih identifies Sheba with Habasha; claims that Ark and tablets of the Law are in the Ethiopian capital (Adefa/Roha/Lalibela); Ethiopians also possess the throne of David
c. 1210–25	*Qaysa gabaz Seyon* a court title under Lalibela (cited in land grants copied much later)
1225	*KN* colophon claims translation of *KN* from Coptic to Arabic
pre-1270	Na'akuto-La'ab and the (15th century) story of the *tabot* of Seyon
1270–85	Yekuno Amlak establishes Solomonic dynasty
1285–94	Solomon Yigba Seyon, writes, 1289/90, to the Ethiopian monks at Jerusalem
pre-1322	Yeshaq, *nebura'ed* of Aksum 'translates' *KN* from Arabic to Ge'ez for Ya'ibika Egzi, ruler of Intarta
1322	Amda Seyon seizes territory 'as far as the cathedral of Aksum'. Church of Seyon mentioned in royal title in Egyptian records. Amda Seyon's chronicle (written some time later?) claims Davidian descent for the king, refers to Ethiopia as the kingdom of Seyon
1344–72	Sayfa Arad; land grant (in late copy) mentions Mary

End 14th–1st half 15th	most recent dating of Paris MS with final version of *KN*
1414–29	King Yeshaq Letter from Alfonso of Aragon attributes possession of the tablets of the Law and the throne of David
1434-68	Zara Yaqob; land grant (in late copy) mentions Mary and Seyon together
1436	Zara Yaqob crowned at Aksum. No mention of Zion ritual
Second half of 15th century	Arabic version of Sheba story mentions Ark
1508–40	Reign of Lebna Dengel. Letters attribute to him descent from David and Solomon
1517	Andrea Corsali mentions the ring of Solomon, throne of David etc. but no Ark or tablets
c. 1520	Francisco Alvares describes old church at Aksum with altar stone from Mount Zion Alvares cites an early version of the *KN*, not mentioning either tablets or Ark
c. 1534	Ambassador Saga Za-Ab mentions the taking of the tablet of the Law to Ethiopia
c. 1535	*Futuh al-Habasha* records removal of white stone encrusted with gold from Aksum church to Tabr
1535	Maryam Seyon church burnt
c. 1539	João de Barros writes about the theft of the tablets

1540–55	Galawdewos; 1543 letter attributes to his family descent from Solomon
1542	Annotation by Ethiopians in Italy in Beccadelli's copy of Alvares' book mention the tablets of the Law in the king's possession
1563–97	Sarsa Dengel; first mention of 'Daughters of Seyon' at 1580 coronation in Aksum in the presence of '*Seyon tabota amlaka Esrael*'. Church of Maryam Seyon restored
1603–22	Péro Pais in Ethiopia. Records the *KN* story, for the first time with the Ark, from '*livro de Agçum*'. Earliest record of section from *Book of Aksum* describing the church of Aksum
c. 1620	*Book of Aksum* records flight of Ark to Bur. Confirmed by Barradas and Telles
1626	Thomé Barneto destroys altar at Maryam Seyon church
1626–7 Ark	M. de Almeida records casket, *tabot* of Sion, or of the Covenant, in Maryam Seyon church
1633	Ark returns from Digsa in Bur, according to *Book of Aksum* and Barradas
1633/4	Manoel Barradas discusses the broken tablets, the object at Aksum believed to be the Ark of the Covenant. The *dabtarat* say this is their *tabot*, an altar stone which they call Sion of Aksum, because it came from Zion
1660	Balthasar Telles' book published, also cites chest or *tabot* at Aksum, supposed to be the Ark

Late 17th century	*Gadla Marqorewos* mentions the name '*KN*' and cites from the book
1680s?	Abba Gorgoreyos tells Ludolf about '*KN*' (with the Ark), first recorded citation of the name of the book after the *Gadla Marqorewos*
1691–3	Iyasu I sees Ark in the sanctuary at Aksum
1764	Tovmacean sees tablet at 'Saba'
c. 1770	Bruce told by Tekla Haymanot II that Ark was destroyed by Grañ
1869	Dimotheos Sapritchian sees tablet kept in coffer in sacristy attic near Aksum Seyon church
1881	Nebura'ed of Aksum informs Rohlfs that Ark is concealed in church wall

Index